Post-Soviet Social

Daniela Nahmias

Post-Soviet Social

NEOLIBERALISM, SOCIAL MODERNITY, BIOPOLITICS

Stephen J. Collier

PRINCETON UNIVERSITY PRESS
PRINCETON AND OXFORD

Copyright © 2011 by Princeton University Press
Published by Princeton University Press, 41 William Street,
Princeton, New Jersey 08540
In the United Kingdom: Princeton University Press, 6 Oxford Street,
Woodstock, Oxfordshire OX20 1TW

press.princeton.edu

Library of Congress Cataloging-in-Publication Data

Collier, Stephen J.
Post-Soviet social : neoliberalism, social modernity, biopolitics / Stephen J. Collier.
p.   cm.
Includes bibliographical references and index.
ISBN 978-0-691-14830-4 (hardcover : alk. paper)—
ISBN 978-0-691-14831-1 (pbk. : alk. paper)
1. Russia (Federation)—Economic policy—1991– 2. Neoliberalism—
Russia (Federation) 3. Biopolitics—Russia (Federation)
4. Post-communism—Economic aspects—Russia (Federation) I. Title.
HC340.12.C647 2011
330.947—dc22   2010048983

British Library Cataloging-in-Publication Data is available

This book has been composed in Sabon

Printed on acid-free paper. ∞

Printed in the United States of America

10 9 8 7 6 5 4 3 2 1

For my family

Contents

Illustrations and Tables

ILLUSTRATIONS

TABLES

Preface: Formal and Substantive

> What would need to be studied now . . . is the way in which
> the specific problems of life and population were raised
> within a technology of government which, without always
> having been liberal . . . was always haunted since the end of
> the eighteenth century by liberalism's question.
> —Michel Foucault, *Birth of Biopolitics*[1]

IN 1994, JEFFERY SACHS DELIVERED an address on Russia to the World
Bank's annual conference on development economics. Sachs was, at the
time, an important voice in U.S. discussions about Russia; a commenter
on his paper called him the world's leading advisor to countries "seeking
to make the transition from socialism to markets" (Williamson 1994:
81). After a turbulent first few years—marked by progress in privatization and liberalization, but limited success in stabilization and persistent
economic decline—the project of "transition" seemed to be at a crossroads, having barely staggered through a series of crises that included
the shelling of the Russian Parliament in 1993. Characteristically, Sachs
did not waver in his advice or outlook; despite the difficulties, he saw an
opening. In conditions of state breakdown, with opposition disorganized
and the risk of social chaos acute, it remained "possible for a small group
of policymakers, backed by international support, to begin stabilization"
(Sachs 1994: 72). The road ahead required renewed focus on "structural
adjustment," which he defined in an article published two years later as
the "initial reallocation of resources in the economy following the introduction of market forces" (Sachs 1996: 128).

Sachs's vision of post-Soviet transformation was laid out in the language of what Karl Polanyi—in a discussion that is seminal in economic
anthropology—called "formal economics," which referred to problems
of efficiency in a "definite situation of choice," paradigmatically, a market
(Polanyi 1977). But this vision of structural adjustment also had profound implications for what Polanyi called the substantive economy that
evolved under socialism—the "instituted processes" involved in the material satisfaction of human wants. This substantive economy included
the mechanisms of planned production, controlled prices, and collective
property, all of which seemed easily dismantled (at least to some observers). But it also included the sedimented *products* of socialist institutions of industrial coordination, social welfare, and urban planning. The

"resources in the economy" to which Sachs alluded were, to paraphrase Polanyi, nothing other than the universe of human settlements, resource flows, and elements of production that comprised the fabric of collective life. Their "reallocation" suggested a tremendous upheaval.

The problem of structural adjustment dominated Russian politics from Soviet breakup in 1991 to the devaluation in 1998. As observers of post-Soviet affairs have long pointed out, developments in this period resonated profoundly with those described in Polanyi's classic study, *The Great Transformation*, which examined the tangled births of market society and what he called the "liberal creed" in the early nineteenth century.[2] This was true of economic developments—which pitted the creative destruction of markets against the existing organization of the Soviet substantive economy. It was also true of the political and intellectual battles over transition. As Polanyi noted, the last defense of the liberal was never that marketization had failed but that it had not been tried. So it was for supporters of transition like Sachs—the problem was always one of too little reform, too little marketization. And for critics of both the early nineteenth- and late twentieth-century versions of the liberal creed this starkly utopian project was bound to founder: on the intransigence of the "existing organization of society," and on the resistance of politicians, bureaucrats, and citizens to the stresses introduced by the market mechanism.[3]

More than a decade after the devaluation of 1998 it is striking that the figures of "transition" and the Washington Consensus now seem to be the barely discernable features of an already-distant horizon. In the ensuing decade, high politics in Russia were no longer dominated by the problems of stabilization and liberalization—wrapped up in the government's delicate dance with foreign creditors—but, rather, with the centralizing and state-building projects of a government that became defiantly independent of foreign influence. Reform, meanwhile, has apparently been decoupled from the global project of liberalization with which "transition" and the Washington Consensus were associated. To the extent that neoliberal reforms have continued to be pursued—and I will be at some pains in this book to show that they have been—they have not emphasized the austere vision of marketization that dominated the 1990s. Instead, they have addressed more complex questions relating to the mundane elements of the post-Soviet substantive economy: the material infrastructures, apartment blocks, urban utilities, social norms, and budgetary routines that were created under socialism and have had persistent significance after its demise.

One premise of this book is that the questions first posed in the fractious debates around "transition"—and that, in the 1990s, were so convincingly framed by Polanyi's analysis of an epochal battle of markets versus society—have not lost interest. The fate of the substantive economy produced by socialism; the tradition of thought that claims the mantle of classical liberalism; and the governmental adjustments among the population, production, and social welfare—all remained crucial problems in the second decade of post-Soviet change. But the Polanyian vocabulary for thinking about them—and this is a second premise—is no longer adequate. We require a different intellectual apparatus to ask how—in Russia, but not only in Russia—the problems of economy and society, health and welfare, are raised in (liberal) technologies of government.

A Note on Transliteration and Translation

I have used the ALA transliteration scheme in all cases except for commonly translated words and names, and for names referred to frequently in the text that are more easily grasped with alternative transliteration (e.g., Belaya Kalitva). All translations from Russian texts are my own.

Acknowledgments

A NATIONAL SCIENCE FOUNDATION Graduate Study Fellowship helped pay for my first research trips to Russia. Since then I have accumulated debts of varying magnitudes and types to people rather than organizations. Among these, I am particularly grateful to Jonathan Bach, Neil Brenner, Carlo Caduff, Michael Cohen, Ippolita Di Paola, Zamira Djarabova, Ashraf Ghani, David Gold, Vova Grishaev, Lisa Hoffman, Caroline Humphrey, Chris Kelty, Mansura Khanam, Oleg Kharkhordin, Andrew Lakoff, Martha Lampland, Adam Leeds, Turo-Kimo Lehtonen, Kirstin Mikalbrown, Aihwa Ong, Onur Ozgode, Tobias Rees, Antina von Schnitzler, Miriam Ticktin, and Lucan Way. Anton Ginzburg generously created the iconography for figures 1.2, 4.2, 7.1, 7.2, and 8.1, and Dimitri Karetnikov of Princeton University Press put all the figures in proper shape for publication.

Paul Rabinow has been an enduring source of intellectual orientation and friendship over the none-too-few years since I came to Berkeley to study with him after reading *French Modern*, which is the model, in many ways, for the present book. Finally, my gratitude to my family—Masha Berek, Sasha Berek Collier, David Collier, Ruth Berins Collier, and Jennifer Jennings—is big and deep, and eludes my capacity for expression. Since I don't seem to finish books very quickly, I thought it prudent to dedicate this one to all of you.

Introduction: Post-Soviet, Post-Social?

> So we cannot say that liberalism is an always unrealized
> utopia—unless one takes the kernel of liberalism to be the
> projections it has been led to formulate by its analyses and
> criticisms. It is not a dream that comes up against a reality
> and fails to insert itself within it. It constitutes—and this is
> the reason for both its polymorphism and its recurrences—a
> tool for the criticism of reality: criticism of a previous
> governmentality from which one is trying to get free; of a
> present governmentality that one is trying to reform and
> rationalize by scaling it down; or of a governmentality to
> which one is opposed and whose abuses one wants to limit.
>
> —Michel Foucault, *Birth of Biopolitics*[1]

WHAT IS THE RELATIONSHIP between neoliberalism and social modernity? How have neoliberal reforms critiqued and reworked projects of state planning and social welfare found in so many countries in the twentieth century? A generation of scholars has answered these questions in virtually one voice. Neoliberal doctrine, they argue, is opposed to social welfare and to the public ends of government; it is "congenitally blind," as Peter Evans has written, "to the need for social protection" (2008: 277). Neoliberal reforms, meanwhile, deconstitute institutions of social protection and economic regulation, either through a general retrenchment of government in favor of the market, or through programs that move the locus of governing outside the state. Most broadly, if the twentieth century was characterized by the rise of "social" government, then as Nikolas Rose has argued, neoliberal thinkers have "challenge[d] the rationale of any social state" (1999: 135).

The argument of this book begins from a dissatisfaction with this conventional wisdom about neoliberalism. Scholars have taken too much for granted about neoliberalism and social modernity, and taken too little care in examining the thought of actual neoliberals, the technical details of neoliberal reforms, or the prior institutions of planning and social welfare that these reforms critiqued and sought to reprogram. My aim is to redress some of these shortcomings through a study of urbanism, social welfare planning, and neoliberal reform in Soviet and post-Soviet Russia.

During the 1990s, the Russian case and the battles over "transition," the Washington Consensus, shock therapy, and structural adjustment, stood as emblems of the neoliberal project's grandiose transformative ambition—and catastrophic failure. But the dynamics of this period proved to be both contingent and temporally circumscribed, bracketed roughly by Soviet breakup in 1991 and the devaluation of 1998. My gambit is that ten years beyond the collapse of the Washington Consensus—and with the luxury of a broadened and perhaps historically deepened perspective—the Russian case provides a good site for revisiting the legacy of an important and distinctive form of social government, and for asking how neoliberal reforms propose to reshape it.

The first half of this book examines the Soviet urbanist paradigm of city-building or *gradostroitel'stvo*. City-building grew out of the thoroughly researched experiments of the urbanist and architectural avant-garde in the late 1920s. But here I am interested in city-building as a key element of the Soviet Union's more enduring project to constitute its population's health, welfare, and conditions of daily existence as objects of knowledge and targets of governmental intervention—that is, I examine city-building as a key figure of the Soviet project of social modernity. I show how planners of the 1920s and 1930s invented city-building as an alternative to a liberal framework for understanding and governing life in industrial cities. Then, shifting focus to the late Soviet period, I examine city-building as a window on the mundane elements such as pipes, wires, apartment blocks, bureaucratic routines, and social norms, through which a new form of collective life was assembled.

The book's second part examines how, after Soviet breakup, these elements have become targets of neoliberal reform. In this analysis I do not identify neoliberalism with a set of abstract principles, a rigid ideological project, or specific governmental techniques (of calculative choice, privatized risk, and so on). Rather, following Michel Foucault's methodological orientations, I examine neoliberalism as a form of critical reflection on governmental practice distinguished by an attempt to reanimate the principles of classical liberalism in light of new circumstances—most centrally, for my purposes, the rise of the social state. This investigation takes us far from the Russian scene, to key figures in the American neoliberal tradition who criticized and sought to reform the regulatory regimes, technical infrastructures, and welfare mechanisms that comprised the social state. By tracing the influence of these figures through "minor traditions" of neoliberal thought such as the new economics of regulation and fiscal federal theory, I will show how neoliberal reforms took hold of mundane instruments of the *Soviet* social state as key targets of intervention. Thus, surprisingly, pipes and valves, budgeting formulas and bureaucratic norms, emerge as privileged sites where the relationship between neoliberalism and social modernity can be reexamined.

The conclusions that emerge from this analysis suggest a critical revision of accepted understandings of neoliberalism. I did not find that neoliberal thinkers were blind to the need for social protection. I did not find in neoliberal reforms a total program of marketization or government through calculative choice that wiped away the existing forms of Soviet social welfare. In the domains I studied, neoliberal reforms propose to selectively reconfigure inherited material structures, demographic patterns, and social norms. They suggest new ways of programming government *through* the state that retain the social welfare norms established by Soviet socialism. An important implication of this analysis is that, following the recent comment of Jacques Donzelot, although neoliberal programming calls for "a completely different compromise with the idea of social justice than the one represented by the Welfare State" (2008: 117), we have to understand how it may involve, in some cases, a compromise nonetheless. In this sense, neoliberalism should be analyzed not *beyond* but *within* the history of what Foucault called biopolitics: the attempt to govern a population's health, welfare, and conditions of existence in the framework of political sovereignty.

ORIENTATION: THE CITY OF THE FUTURE, TODAY

These questions about social modernity, neoliberalism, and biopolitics took me over a broad empirical field, one that encompassed crucial dimensions of the genealogy of Soviet government—reaching back to Peter the Great—and selected thinkers in the development of post–World War II neoliberalism in the United States. I will say something in a moment about how these various sites came into focus, and about the difficulties of organizing inquiry into such a far-flung field. But my starting point—the scene that provided an initial orientation to these diverse sites—was for an anthropologist rather traditional: a small industrial city in the southern Russian province of Rostov, called Belaya Kalitva. Following Anna Tsing (1993), small industrial cities are "out of the way" places—neither the administrative capitals (sites of political dramas) nor the major industrial centers (those privileged loci of early socialist construction) that have been the focus of much work on cities and urbanism in Soviet and post-Soviet Russia.[2] Given my concerns, the reasons for starting in such places were straightforward. Small industrial cities were identified as ideals of the socialist urban future by the architects, urbanists, and social planners who invented the norms and forms of Soviet social modernity.

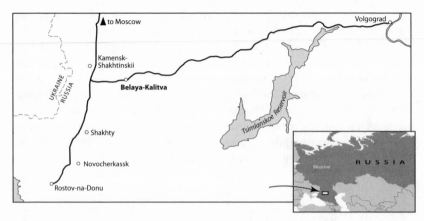

Figure 1.1. Belaya Kalitva, Rostov *oblast'*

Such cities seemed, therefore, like good places to study both the emergence of this project and its proposed reformation after Soviet breakup.

In the nineteenth century, Belaya Kalitva was a small *stanitsa*, the administrative center of an agricultural district. Industry in the area was restricted to mines that lay on the northeast extent of the Donbass, the coal basin that spans what is now the Ukrainian-Russian border. It was only in the mid-twentieth century that substantial industrial and thus urban development took place in Belaya Kalitva proper, triggered by the construction of what is still called, in one of those peculiar and telling Soviet terms, the city's "city-forming" (*gradoobrazuiushchee*) enterprise, an aluminum plant connected with defense aviation. Through the 1950s, a growing industrial workforce drove a modest expansion of the local population, as well as the construction of new schools, a hospital, a stadium, a "House of Culture," and some communal housing. But at the end of the decade the city was little more than a rural-industrial settlement, in which most locals lived in small huts.

Urban transformation quickened in the 1960s following an event that was to have great significance in my research: the approval in 1964 of Belaya Kalitva's first general plan. The plan was produced by the Leningrad State Institute for the Design of Cities (*Lengiprogor*), one important center of the distinctive Soviet urbanist practice of city-building (*gradostroitel'stvo*). In contrast to familiar forms of urbanism, city-building was not limited to questions of zoning, transport, or the use of public space. Rather, employing planning methodologies developed in the late 1920s and early 1930s, city-builders produced detailed blueprints for every possible element of a future city. They began from plans for "settlement" (*rasselenie*) that projected the correlative development of the local population and industrial production. On this basis, city-building plans proceeded to lay out a new substantive economy or, to borrow another key term from the vocabulary of Soviet urban modernity, a new city *khoziaistvo*—apartment blocks, schools, and clinics; doctors, teachers, and communal service workers; parks, clubs, and other recreational facilities; pipes, wires, roads, heating systems, electric substations, and other elements of urban infrastructure. The result was a vision of the future that totalized the field of collective life. Belaya Kalitva's future was simply the sum of those elements described in the general plan. And the path between the present and the future was, simply, planning.

Belaya Kalitva's development over the last twenty-five years of the Soviet period did not precisely follow the lines laid out in the general plan. City-builders complained constantly about the lack of planning control. There were perpetual imbalances in urban development—for example, industrial production was favored at the expense of housing, schools, and urban infrastructure. And Belaya Kalitva, like many small Soviet cities, grew less than city-builders had hoped (the Soviet Union's large cities, meanwhile, grew much more). Nonetheless, a visitor to Belaya Kalitva in the late 1970s or early 1980s would have found a city that closely resembled the one envisioned in 1964: central avenues lined with apartment blocks; parks; centralized urban infrastructures; nearly universal social and urban services; and increasingly balanced adjustments between the local population and available local industrial employment. Even works that were not completed—a second "city-forming enterprise" or a new residential settlement—pointed to the modest but stable future of city-building.

Belaya Kalitva was hardly atypical. The preponderance of small and medium industrial cities dispersed over Russia's vast and frigid territory was one key characteristic of an urban pattern that is, as a 2005 World Bank report put it, unique to Russia. By the end of the Soviet period just under sixty million people, or nearly 60 percent of the Russian urban population lived in cities of under 500,000 people; almost half that number—nearly 30 percent of the urban population—lived in cities under 100,000 (Goskomstat 1999). And as residents in these cities were linked to systems of urban need fulfillment that became nearly universal over the Soviet Union's last decades, the cities were themselves plugged in to national mechanisms of economic coordination and circuits of resource flow, embedding the substantive economy of cities in the staid certainties of Soviet planning.

With the breakup of the Soviet Union, these certainties were thrown into disarray in all Soviet cities. But the collapse of national planning and the introduction of markets for most industrial goods were particularly devastating in small industrial cities like Belaya Kalitva. By the late 1990s, Belaya Kalitva's aluminum enterprise, stripped of guaranteed orders, was running at a tiny fraction of its capacity. Industrial employment, correspondingly, dropped to a fraction of its former levels. Economic collapse affected every facet of local life. Belaya Kalitva had literally lived on its city-forming aluminum factory, both directly through industrial wages and services and, indirectly, through taxes that were the primary source of revenue for the city government. Thus, as a direct consequence of industrial collapse, wages for teachers and doctors fell into arrears, apartments were chilly, parks were dilapidated, and buildings in what once had been a tidy city center were in a state of increasing disrepair.

This, perhaps, was neoliberalism in the sense it is conventionally understood: as a totalizing and utopic project of deregulation, state retrenchment, and marketization that wreaked havoc on the existing organization of collective life. In cities like Belaya Kalitva the devastation was as much existential as material. The mundane elements that comprised urban life and that formed the stable horizon of a certain future were viewed by many, particularly of older generations, as the fruit of decades-long struggle and mind-numbing sacrifice. Belaya Kalitva literally arose from the rubble of World War II, from the ashes of burned buildings, from a dismantled prison camp that was constructed by Nazi occupiers on the foundation of the city's aluminum enterprise, started just before the onset of hostilities. The collapse of this urban reality offended everything that had given meaning to the lives of many Soviet citizens. Literally, the future was at stake, and not only in the obvious sense that it was bleak or uncertain. After Soviet breakup the landscape of half-built enterprises, crumbling apartments, and deteriorating parks stood as stark reminders of a vision of the future—a mode of relating the present to a possible future—that was now past. An entire way of life in hundreds of cities like Belaya Kalitva, spread across the vast territory of post-Soviet Russia, was thrust into question: Would people simply move away? If they stayed, how would they survive? What new forms for governing this peculiar human collectivity—for relating its grim present to a better future—would emerge?

POST-SOVIET SOCIAL?

These questions provided a starting point for my research—the beginnings of an orientation. The answers I found surprised me, and pushed me in unexpected directions. A first surprise was that despite obvious signs of decline during the difficult years of the 1990s, local life in Belaya Kalitva held together. Teachers and doctors were not paid regularly, but clinics and schools still functioned. Radiators were tepid, but in most cases they kept apartments livably warm as hot water continued to flow through central heating systems (something that was not true in all post-Soviet countries[3]). Pension payments were intermittent, but frequent enough that older residents could support younger members of their families—at least some of the time. Finally, and perhaps most strikingly, the 1990s did not witness a dramatic outflow of people from the city.[4] Many Belo-Kalitveans began to travel to Rostov (the regional capital), Moscow, or other cities for work. But these were often temporary migrations, and people generally returned. In sum, things were bad but, following the economic geographer Ann Markusen (1996), they were also "sticky." The substantive economy created by Soviet city-building proved stubbornly intransigent. The pipes, apartments blocks, radiators, and boilers; the flows of gas, hot water, heating oil, and rubles; and the existing routines of bureaucrats who had little to do but nowhere to go—all seemed to hold things together. The industrial heart of Belaya Kalitva was torn out. But the mundane systems built to support daily life—the elements of the substantive economy, the city *khoziaistvo*—somehow survived.

Here was a second surprising observation: the vital importance of these material structures, bureaucratic routines, and resource flows that had, during the Soviet period, plugged people into centralized systems of urban provisioning, and plugged cities into national mechanisms of economic coordination. Such sociotechnical infrastructures, which make modern life possible, generally escape our notice. But as Paul Edwards (2002) has observed, they become visible when they break down, or seem threatened with breakdown. In post-Soviet Belaya Kalitva they were the objects of urgent concern, perpetually discussed in local papers and among friends and acquaintances. They were also the constant preoccupation of the city government, which, paralyzed by fiscal crisis, could only "govern" local life through frantic attempts to squeeze transfers out of the regional government so that teachers' wages could be paid, or through in-kind transactions with local enterprises to exchange heat for tax debt so that the city government could keep apartments warm. Thus, following Oleg Kharkhordin (2010), in some improbable way these mundane sociotechnical systems were among those "common things" that made Belaya Kalitva a unit of collective fate.[5]

When I was in the field these common things were also coming to the attention of reformers, both foreign and domestic, in Moscow and in regional capitals, who were thinking about problems of government in post-Soviet Russia. For most of the 1990s, reforms focused on privatization, liberalization, and stabilization, those explosive themes of macroeconomic policy and enterprise governance that dominated the rancorous debates around "transition" and the Washington Consensus. But attention shifted by the early 2000s to "second-generation" reforms (Naim

1994). International consultants, development organizations, Moscow think tanks, federal functionaries, and regional policymakers turned a critical eye to those sociotechnical systems that in the difficult years of the 1990s had been crucial to the preservation of cities like Belaya Kalitva. By the early 2000s, they were among the most important targets of federal and regional reforms. All of this attention caught my attention. And the more time I spent in Russia, the more I became convinced that budgets, spending norms, pipes, and wires were key sites where the relationship between Soviet social modernity and neoliberal reform could be examined.

The character of these reforms was a third surprise, one that is central to the claims of this book. These reforms had many of the features that are often associated with neoliberalism. They proposed to transfer previously centralized powers of decision-making to citizens and local governments, and to replace, in some cases, state economic coordination with mechanisms of market allocation. They aimed to "responsibilize" citizens not just as subjects of need but as sovereign consumers making calculative choices based on individual preferences. But in other respects, these reforms did not map easily onto our conventional understandings of neoliberalism.

Take, for example, reforms of urban heating systems, centralized behemoths that could provision an entire small city. During the Soviet period, heating systems "bundled" Soviet social modernity, linking households to urban utilities and utilities to national circuits of resource flow in a system that was driven by a substantive rationality of need fulfillment. Reform programs formulated by both the Russian government and international organizations such as the World Bank and the United Nations proposed to "un-bundle" these systems through marketization (of gas provision and maintenance), commercialization (of heat production), and "responsibilization" (of "users"). But this un-bundling was blocked in significant ways. The material setup of heating systems—the absence of meters or control valves, the technical integration of the distribution network—meant that the flow of heat could not follow "effective demand." Consequently, reforms took shape as a selective intervention to reprogram key nodes in the system while leaving much of its structure—its hardware, if you will—intact. What is more, reforms did not abandon existing norms of social welfare. Thus, the Russian government's 2001 framework for sectoral reform affirmed that heat was a basic need whose provision should, at the end of the day, be guaranteed by the state.[6] Were these reforms simply not "neoliberal"? Were they examples of a neoliberalism that had been accommodated to the exigencies of local circumstances? Or was it necessary to revisit accepted understandings of what neoliberalism is?

Another example is found in reforms of the budgetary system. Like centralized heating systems, budgets were crucial to the articulation of Soviet social modernity. Through them, norms for social provisioning were translated into resource flows that made a range of social and urban services (from education to health care to gas, heat, electricity, and water) available to the Soviet urban population. Post-Soviet reforms proposed to "budgetize" the behaviors of local governments, in Nikolas Rose's (1999) sense, giving them the freedom to determine which public values should be pursued through state spending but simultaneously imposing hard constraints. But reforms *also* proposed new formulas for redistribution—transferring resources from rich to poor regions, and from rich to poor cities—that drew precisely on existing socialist norms for social provisioning. In this sense, these reforms re-inscribed the substantive *ends* of Soviet social welfare.

Once more, these observations suggested puzzlement about neoliberalism as a technical, political, and ethical project. This puzzlement, in turn, posed a methodological question about where to direct inquiry. Having begun my research with fieldwork in small industrial cities, the instinctive anthropological response might have been to analyze a distinctively Russian variant of neoliberalism, through which a marketizing project was reshaped, both through creative adjustments by policymakers and through resistances and blockages that constrained the utopian aspirations of neoliberal ideology when it "hit the ground." Material infrastructures like heating systems might, in this view, be analyzed as intransigent elements that made post-Soviet change path-dependent.[7] Concessions to existing norms of social welfare might be understood, following Jamie Peck and Adam Tickell (2002), as "ameliorative" measures that address contradictions in the neoliberal hegemonic project. The problem with such an approach, in my view, was that it would take for granted the "neoliberalism" that is supposedly at stake in post-Soviet developments. I was thus led to ask: How could "neoliberalism"—rather than its effects—be brought into the field of inquiry?

THE CRITICAL CONVENTIONAL WISDOM

If there is a particular difficulty in posing this question today it is due in part to the dominance of a "critical conventional wisdom" about neoliberalism, whose main effect, I contend, has been to obscure neoliberalism rather than make it visible as an object of inquiry.[8] To justify this claim, and to clarify its meaning, it may be helpful to briefly consider two recent studies that have played a significant role in shaping critical discourse: David Harvey's *Neoliberalism* (2005) and Naomi Klein's *Shock Doctrine*

(2007). Harvey and Klein cannot, of course, stand in for all critical scholarship on neoliberalism. Certainly there are strains of critical discourse—notably work by Nikolas Rose and others (Rose 1999; Rose et al. 2006) in the framework of "governmentality," and the work of Dieter Plehwe and others (Plehwe et al. 2006; Mirowski and Plehwe 2009) on the neoliberal "thought collective"—that have made neoliberalism a much more meaningful and effective object of inquiry than these authors have. But Harvey and Klein provide a useful orientation if only because they state explicitly what is often taken for granted in discussions of neoliberalism.

Harvey, working in a Marxian framework, understands neoliberalism as a "system of justification and legitimation" for a project to "re-establish the conditions for capital accumulation and to restore the power of economic elites," following the economic crises of the 1970s. He argues that

> In so far as neoliberalism values market exchange as "an ethic in itself, capable of acting as a guide to all human action, and substituting for all previously held ethical beliefs" it emphasizes the significance of contractual relations in the marketplace. It holds that the social good will be maximized by maximizing the reach and frequency of market transactions, and it seeks to bring all human action into the domain of the market.

Neoliberalism thus abandons the solidaristic and equalizing norms of the social state. Regressive "redistributive effects and increasing social inequality," Harvey concludes, have "been such a persistent feature of neoliberalization as to be regarded as structural to the whole project" (Harvey 2005: 3, 16, 19). Klein meanwhile, argues that:

> The movement that Milton Friedman launched in the 1950s is best understood as an attempt by multinational capital to recapture the highly profitable, lawless frontier that Adam Smith, the intellectual forefather of today's neoliberals, so admired—but with a twist. Rather than journeying through Smith's "savage and barbarous nations" . . . this movement set out to systematically dismantle existing laws and regulations to re-create that earlier lawlessness. And where Smith's colonists earned their record profits by seizing what he described as "waste lands" for "but a trifle," today's multinationals see government programs, public assets and everything that is not for sale as terrain to be conquered and seized—the post-office, national parks, schools, social security, disaster relief, and anything else that is publicly administered (2007: 241–42).

Many scholars would, no doubt, object to the epochal and totalizing terms in which these authors present neoliberalism as a ubiquitous force in post–World War II history. But few would question the basic claims Klein and Harvey advance concerning neoliberalism and the social state: neoliberalism is for the market and opposed to government provision of services; for an ethic of individual responsibility and opposed to "all previously held ethical beliefs"; for a private definition of value and against value created by government—except, in Klein's account, when public value can be plundered by corporate interests.

One major task of this book will be to ask whether, and in what sense, any of these claims about neoliberalism can be supported. To do so, it is necessary to address another question that is not *substantive*, concerning the "content" of neoliberalism, but *methodological*: What *kind of thing* is neoliberalism? And how should it be studied? Is neoliberalism the *kind of thing* to which one can attribute a coherent position on such diverse issues as redistribution, schools, security, disaster relief, and the post office? How is it connected to the vast range of historical experiences in which contemporary scholars purport to discover its workings?

Here, too, Harvey and Klein lay out a story that is implicit in most, though certainly not all, critical work. This story begins by identifying neoliberalism as an intellectual movement that is associated with a number of prominent economists, political philosophers, and motley fellow travelers, many of whom were associated with the Mt. Pelerin Society or the University of Chicago's department of economics. This intellectual movement took shape in the wake of a vast expansion in the role of governments in managing social and economic life. In response, "neoliberals" revived but modified the tenets of classical liberal thought, both as a critique of these developments and as a source of proposals for reform.

There is nothing wrong with this starting point. Indeed, in the discussion that follows I will insist on employing an "emic" definition of neoliberalism that refers to those figures Dieter Plehwe (2009a) has called the "self-conscious" neoliberals, who sought to revive the tradition of classical liberalism and modify it in response to new problems.[9] Troubles arise, however, when these thinkers are connected to all those other things—reform programs, techniques of governing, broad processes of transformation or, most generally, a sweeping hegemonic project—that are often analyzed under the rubric of neoliberalism. The standard narrative unfolds roughly as follows: First, a handful of thinkers (certainly Milton Friedman; perhaps Fredrik von Hayek) are taken to be the paradigmatic neoliberals while other self-consciously neoliberal thinkers are ignored. Second, a simplified account of their thought, generally based on selective reading of popular writings and neglect of the "serious speech acts" found in their scholarly work, is offered in some general formulae about support for the market, opposition to social welfare, and emphasis on individual choice and autonomy.[10] Third, links are then established

between these individuals and a range of experiences—from Ludwig Er-
hardt to Boris Yeltsin; from Augusto Pinochet to Bill Clinton; from Deng
Xiaoping's "Four Modernizations" to the Washington Consensus to the
post-Soviet project of "transition"—either by discovering some purportedly decisive interpersonal or institutional connections or, more crudely
but unfortunately more commonly, by simply registering every instance
of marketization, opposition to social welfare, and "government through
calculative choice" as a case of neoliberalism.[11] Thus, after beginning on
solid ground, we observe what Bruno Latour calls an "acceleration" in
the analysis, in which neoliberalism is understood as a dark and pervasive
force that can explain "vast arrays of life and history" (2005: 22).

My objection to such accounts is not that they attempt to link neoliberalism to programs of reform and processes of transformation that are
quite distant from the thinkers we would want to call "neoliberal." Quite
the contrary: the significance of neoliberalism must be sought, at least in
part, in the disparate experiences in which neoliberal styles of reasoning,
mechanisms of intervention, and techniques have played a significant role
in shaping the forms of government. The problem, rather, is that such
analyses fail, as Foucault once wrote, to "pay the full price" of making
the connections that they wish to establish (2008: 187).

Toward Reconstruction

The way forward, it seems to me, is a conceptual and methodological reconstruction of the field of inquiry. Reconstruction begins with unlearn-
ing much of what we think we know about neoliberalism. It then requires
reconstituting the field of investigation in a way that makes neoliberalism
appear as a topic and *problem* of inquiry rather than its premise.

To explain what I have in mind it will be helpful to return to the Russian case. In what sense can Russia's post-Soviet experience be linked
to neoliberalism? The answer to this question may seem self-evident; it
has certainly been taken for granted by observers of post-socialist transformation. As Bruce Kogut and Andrew Spicer have shown in a comprehensive review of relevant literature, post-Soviet transformation has
overwhelmingly been understood as the product of a "'Neo-liberal Economic Ideology' that. . .framed foreign aid strategy in post-communist
countries" (2004: 3).[12] And the Russian experience during the 1990s—
particularly policies of structural adjustment and shock therapy, un-
leashed in a final triumphant dismantling of Soviet socialism—marks
the neoliberal apotheosis.

But there are problems with this story. First, as Venelin Ganev points
out, the actual process of reform in all post-socialist countries was "incoherent, tentative, and contradictory." Thus, to portray post-socialist

developments as "emanations of an ideology that is both comprehensive and radical would amount to committing a grand simplification" (Ganev 2005: 350). Second, the claim that structural adjustment and shock therapy are distinctly and specifically "neoliberal" at least requires qualification. When it was initially proposed by pragmatists at the World Bank as a program of massive *intervention* in response to economic crisis, structural adjustment was an anathema for many self-consciously neoliberal thinkers. In any case, as I argue in chapter 6, structural adjustment was the product of contingent historical factors, not the distilled essence of the neoliberal project.

But even if we grant that, in some qualified way, policies like structural adjustment and shock therapy can be associated with neoliberalism and that they have had enormous implications for post-socialist change—and in some qualified way, both claims are indeed true—we encounter a third and for my purposes decisive problem. Namely, such an account limits the reference domain of neoliberalism in Russia to a specific set of problems—relating to macroeconomic reform and privatization—and to the specific historical conjuncture of the 1990s, whose dynamics were more temporally circumscribed than many observers assumed they would be at the time. We are thus left to ask whether there is continued meaning in speaking of neoliberalism "beyond" the Washington Consensus, whether the reforms that moved to the center of attention in the 2000s can, indeed, be called "neoliberal" in some meaningful sense. I want to insist that as my research turned to mundane systems like planning norms, budgets, and heating systems, these were, in fact, questions: Could the reforms of such systems be linked to something that could be called "neoliberalism"?

Ultimately, my answer was "yes"—although there was, indeed, a high price to be paid for arriving at it. After some digging through reform documents and technical studies and, from there, through relatively obscure traditions of economic and technocratic thought, I found that these reforms could be traced to key exponents of American neoliberalism. Of most immediate relevance was the work of George Stigler and James Buchanan, two thinkers who have been largely ignored in relevant scholarship, but who were major figures of post–World War II neoliberalism in the United States.[13] Buchanan and Stigler were explicitly concerned with how the precepts of classical liberalism could be accommodated to the norms of what they called the "social state." They made original contributions to a new liberal understanding of basic concepts such as the social contract, public interest, and equity. And they deployed this reworked conceptual toolkit to critique the budgetary mechanisms, infrastructures, and regulatory regimes through which the social state had been articulated, first of all in the United States. Their work was then taken up in traditions of technocratic practice. Buchanan, thus, made key contributions to fiscal federal theory, which, among other things, has become a central framework for a neoliberal programming of redistribution. Stigler, meanwhile, catalyzed a new economics of regulation that addressed, among other things, the government of infrastructures and utilities. By the 1970s the schemas of analysis and programs of reform they and others proposed had become central to a new liberal programming of the social state in rich countries; by the 1980s, 1990s, and 2000s their proposals were circulating around the world. In post-Soviet Russia, international consultants, aid agencies, federal, regional, and local officials, and Russian experts deployed these forms of critique and programming to reform institutions inherited from the Soviet social state.

Through these long detours, a set of disparate objects came into focus as essential to investigating the puzzles about neoliberalism and social modernity that had initially been framed by small cities like Belaya Kalitva: city-building and Soviet planning; Stigler, Buchanan, and a neoliberal critique of the social state; fiscal federal theory and the new economics of regulation; and the mundane sociotechnical systems—pipes and wires, bureaucracies and budgets—that tied the other elements together, both materially and conceptually (see figure 1.2). These elements comprise, certainly, a complex and unwieldy field of study. The questions that emerged were: How to shape the disparate elements of this field—and the genealogical lines that run through them—into some kind of coherent narrative form?; How to craft general claims about neoliberalism as an intellectual project with broad and diverse effects without losing hold of its specificity in the thought of actual neoliberals?; and How, finally, to place post-Soviet neoliberal reform in a broader history of governmental forms in tsarist and Soviet Russia?

REORIENTATION: NEOLIBERALISM, SOCIAL MODERNITY, BIOPOLITICS

My answers to these questions, which I outline in the remainder of this introduction, have been shaped by Foucault's reflections on liberalism and biopolitics. Substantial literatures have drawn on Foucault's work to analyze contemporary neoliberalism, and have debated the applicability of key concepts such as discipline to the Soviet Union and Russia.[14] Since I am pushing Foucault's analysis in a somewhat different direction, it bears outlining what I find distinctive in his reflections before explaining how they animated my own inquiry. This will require a brief comment on the historical and conceptual problems that Foucault tried to analyze in the frame of biopolitics. But this discussion will soon lead us back to the central themes of my argument.

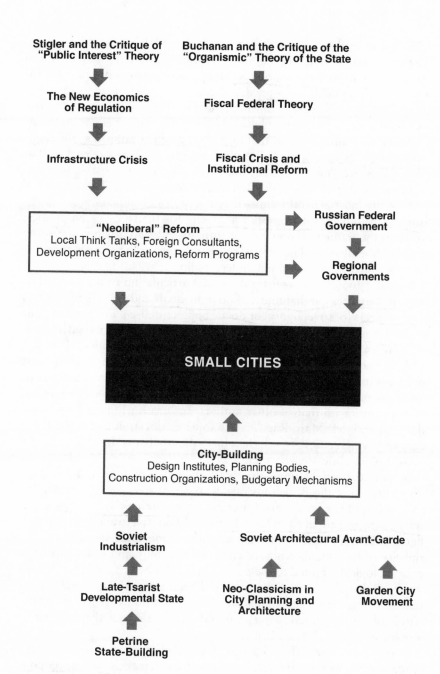

Figure 1.2. A Complex Field of Problematizations

The analysis that follows is rooted in Foucault's lectures at the Collège de France in 1978 and 1979. In these lectures Foucault initially set out to develop a genealogy of biopolitics. Many commentators have concluded that this initial plan was dropped, and that he turned instead to an analysis of liberalism and neoliberalism in the frame of "governmentality." But as I have argued elsewhere (Collier 2009b), this reading is not quite satisfactory. Foucault observed that liberalism could be studied as the "general framework of biopolitics" (Sellenart 2007: 383), and remarked that "only when we know what . . . liberalism was will we be able to grasp what biopolitics is" (Foucault 2008: 22). Indeed, I would like to show—if only in the most general terms—that Foucault's examination of liberalism and neoliberalism suggests a template for the study of biopolitics; and that the frame of biopolitics, in turn, provides an orientation for the study of liberalism and neoliberalism that diverges substantially from the one suggested by conventional understandings.

Foucault found in liberalism the initial articulation of a new kind of governmental reason that understood individuals and collectivities not as legal subjects (of sovereignty) or docile bodies (of disciplinary power) but as living beings. At the most general level, it is this feature of modern government that Foucault designates with the term "biopolitics." I cannot address here the important historical question of whether and in what precise sense the "government of living beings" is distinctive of modern government, although it bears noting that on this point Foucault's analysis converges with that of other authors, such as Karl Polanyi and, in a different fashion, Marc Raeff.[15] But some clarification about the reference of "living beings"—and, therefore, about what is designated by the "bio" in biopolitics—is in order.

In its initial articulation—that is to say, in the thought of the French Physiocrats and the British liberals, who are at the center of Foucault's story—biopolitics was shaped around the naturalistic conceptions that were characteristic of early liberal thought. Foucault argued that the key figure of liberal political reflection was *population*, understood as a "multiplicity of individuals who are and fundamentally and essentially only exist biologically bound to the materiality within which they live."[16] Following Polanyi's piquant observation, liberalism learned to understand human beings "from the animal side"; in liberal thought "the biological nature of man appeared as the . . . foundation of a society that was not of a political order" (2001: 119).

Though this connection has not been made by many of Foucault's readers, it seems uncontroversial to conclude that the "bio" in biopolitics refers precisely to this early liberal naturalism—the proposition that government had to be thought of as a relationship between the juridico-legal domain of the state and the quasi-natural order of "population," which was radically heterogeneous to the order of sovereignty. That said, it should be underlined that biopolitics, at least in these lectures, did not refer to the political management of questions that we would today call biological. Liberal and protoliberal thought could not have been concerned with the biological in the contemporary sense since it simply did not exist at the time[17]; and in current usage the problems with which Physiocracy and British liberalism *were* concerned, and that were the focus of Foucault's analysis in these lectures, such as trade, patterns of habitation, urban conditions, means of subsistence, and so on, would be called "economic" or "social." It is most accurate to say—and, in so many words, Foucault *did* say—that if a new figuration of "Man" or "anthropos," defined at the "finitudes" of life (biology), labor (economic activity), and language (sociocultural existence), emerged in the late eighteenth and early nineteenth centuries as the object of the human sciences, then biopolitics designates the entry of this figure into the workings of political sovereignty.[18] In this sense, the term "biopolitics" may serve (and has indeed served) as a source of confusion. Foucault might just as well have referred to an "econopolitics" or a "sociopolitics," or invented a more general term. But since he did not, since the obvious alternatives do not exactly roll off the tongue (*anthropos*-politics?), and since biopolitics is an accepted term of art, I will stick with it.

At one level, then, biopolitics refers to a taken-for-granted (though not necessarily very well conceptualized) fact: that all modern governments are concerned with managing the biological, social, and economic life of their subjects. But we should be careful. Like other diacritics of modernity (Max Weber's analysis of rationalization, for example), this is best seen not as the diagnosis of an age but as an analytical orientation. There is no underlying "logic" of biopolitics but different ways in which the government of living beings is made a problem of reflection and intervention. What is most interesting in Foucault's work—and what I try to develop for the Soviet and post-Soviet cases—is an analysis of the successive *formations* of biopolitical government, and of the different ways that biopolitics has been *problematized*.

Here it will be helpful to briefly consider Foucault's treatment of these topics in the first lectures of 1978, which focus on the "protoliberal" French Physiocrats.[19] His analysis revolves around a number of individuals who formulated proposals for understanding and managing nascent processes of urbanization and industrialization in the eighteenth century: Vigne de Vigny's plan for the city of Nantes that sought to manage the pressures of population growth and expanded trade; Emmanuel Etienne Duvillard's study that employed statistics to establish the distribution of smallpox risk over a population; and Louis-Paul Abeille's proposals for regulating the grain trade. Foucault found in these thinkers fundamentally novel propositions about the realities with which government had to grapple. The Physiocrats argued that to understand phenomena such as urbanization, famine, and pandemic disease, governmental knowledge and intervention had to concern itself with living beings in their patterns of habitation, production, and trade. They began, thus, to "carve out" new realities that would later be called "society" and "economy" as sites of veridiction—fields of objects about which truth claims could be advanced—and as the grounds for a new "political ontology" —that is, propositions about what government is, about the objects on which government works, and about the ends toward which it is directed (Gordon 1991).

We should not pass too quickly over this point. In contrast to most "Foucaultian" work on liberalism and neoliberalism, Foucault's analysis of the Physiocrats—like his subsequent analyses of the British liberals and of the German and American neoliberals—insistently focuses on *thinkers* and *thinking*. In his lectures of the late 1970s Foucault did not understand thinking as a static or closed system of reasoning—an *episteme*—or as an abstract practice of theorizing. Instead, as Paul Rabinow has argued, he analyzed thinking as a "temporally unfolding situated practice" (2003: 17) that constitutes new ways of understanding and intervening, new kinds of veridiction, and new political ontologies.[20] Here, then, is a first methodological orientation that we can draw from Foucault: to study liberalism and neoliberalism not as ideologies, hegemonic projects, or governmental rationalities but as forms of "critical reflection on governmental practice" (Foucault 2008: 321). In a nominalist spirit, and following the suggestion of Stephen Holmes (1995), we could identify some orientations that are shared by all or at least many liberal and neoliberal thinkers. But the real interest of Foucault's approach lies in its analysis of how these thinkers took up particular historical situations and recast them as problems of *thought*: the Physiocratic response to the economic difficulties of Absolute monarchy; the German ordo-liberal response to the legitimacy crisis of the post-Nazi state; and, most relevant for my purposes, the American neoliberal response to the rise of the social state.

Our next question is how Foucault links such analysis of governmental reflection to an analysis of the instituted forms of biopolitical government. Here, too, the Physiocratic example is instructive. Foucault argues that in their analyses of disease, urban conditions, and trade the Physiocrats provided the grounds for a practical assessment and critique of an existing governmentality. They showed that the disciplinary and juridico-legal mechanisms of classical power were too invasive, too disruptive of the self-regulating mechanisms of the social and economic milieu. The Physiocrats also invented new forms of intervention that worked within and sought to modulate the autonomous laws of the market, the dynamics of disease, and the vicissitudes of population. Foucault thus found in Physiocracy a new form of *critique* and a new kind of *programming*. This couplet of critique/programming or analysis/programming, which is repeated many times in these lectures, is crucial to understanding Foucault's project. Liberal and neoliberal thinkers are not understood to have presented a "system" of government that displaced prior forms. "There is not," Foucault argues, "a series of successive elements, the appearance of the new causing the earlier ones to disappear." Rather, Foucault is interested in political reasoning as a situated practice through which existing governmental forms are reflected upon, reworked, and redeployed. Foucault thus shows how liberal critique and programming shapes "complex edifices" of government in which disciplinary mechanisms, elements of sovereignty, and new liberal techniques of government are combined.[21] The Physiocrats inscribed the "liberal" doctrine of laissez faire within the aims of sovereignty; their purpose was not to overturn but to preserve sovereign power (Foucault 2008: 285). In a subsequent analysis Foucault shows how British liberals took up and redeployed existing governmental forms, as in the integration of disciplinary techniques in Bentham's workhouse, or the adaptation of the juridico-legal edifice of rights to the new questions of biopolitical government.

Ultimately, Foucault is telling a nuanced and very dynamic story about the relationship between critical reflection and successive forms of government, documenting their intimate relationship but also insisting that they be held apart analytically so that their actual interconnections can be studied. And this is the kind of analysis I pursue in what follows. I am not treating biopolitics as a theory that could be somehow "applied" to Russia, or a "logic" that could also be found in Soviet government. Nor is the story I want to tell about how an existing (Soviet) biopolitics is "neoliberalized," as though an abstract blueprint was imposed on a prior reality. Instead, I understand Soviet government as a distinctive formation of biopolitics, the result of a specific and original response to the most basic problems of modern government: How should the state govern living beings? How should it manage adjustments between population, production, and social welfare provisioning? And I examine neoliberalism—in its initial formulation and in the Russian reforms it made thinkable—as a form of reflection that arose precisely in response to the problems of the social state, and a source of proposals for criticizing and reprogramming the social state.

BIOPOLITICS AND SOCIAL MODERNITY—LIBERAL AND SOCIALIST

The first half of this book examines the emergence of Soviet biopolitics, focusing in particular on the project of Soviet social modernity: not the modernization of society, as though "society" was a pre-existing entity waiting to be modernized, but the forms of veridiction, the kinds of programming, and the apparatuses through which figures like society and economy were "carved out," as Foucault has put it (2007: 79), as objects of knowledge and targets of intervention in Soviet Russia.[22] My analysis centers on city-building, the distinctive Soviet form of urban planning. Conceptually, it revolves around a distinction between the liberal and Soviet variants of social modernity.

We have seen that the problem of social modernity was inaugurated in liberal (or protoliberal) reflection as a response to processes of urbanization and industrialization—and the problems to which they gave rise—first, as a *critique* of excessively rigid and invasive frameworks of sovereignty and discipline and, second, as a form of *programming* that worked within the autonomous laws of the economic and social milieu. But the forms of social modernity have not always been "liberal"—far from it. One can point to innumerable projects—from programs of social welfare, to frameworks of international development, to twentieth-century socialism—that, as Mariana Valverde (2008) has recently reminded us, rested on a rejection of liberalism's core tenets. Among these latter traditions the Soviet case is of fundamental importance, looming over the twentieth century as the great alternative and challenge, to which liberal thought—or, more precisely, *neo*liberal thought—had to provide answers. But surprisingly little attention has been paid to the distinct formation of socialist biopolitics. Analyses of totalitarianism in a Foucaultian frame have focused on "limit" experiences (the camps, for example), which are often treated—rather mysteriously—as a hidden *nomos* of liberalism rather than as distinctly illiberal formations of government that have to be analyzed on their own terms.[23] And although a number of excellent studies have drawn on Foucault's concepts to study tsarist and Soviet Russia, most focus on questions of subjectivity and power, or on problems of "cultural modernity."[24] No study, at any rate, has tried to construct for the case of Soviet biopolitics and social modernity what Foucault (and a massive subsequent scholarship) provided for the liberal cases: an account of the political ontology on which it rested and of the kind of critique and programming through which it reflected upon and reshaped existing governmental forms.[25]

An analysis of Soviet biopolitics and social modernity must begin from the fact that the problems confronted by Soviet planners were entirely different from those faced by the French Physiocrats or British liberals. The most important feature of the tsarist inheritance was understood as the *absence* of urbanization and industrialization; the key challenge was to create through state initiative what had arisen "spontaneously" (because these processes were thought to take place "outside" the state) in the liberal cases.[26] In response to these challenges, key figures in early debates about Soviet government explicitly rejected liberal political ontology. They cast aside its concern with the autonomous realities of economy and society and its strictures on governmental intervention, and they reconceptualized collective life as a space of total planning. Soviet city-building extended this biopolitical gambit into the domain of urban modernity and social welfare. Economic planners called for the state to reorganize populations around new sites of industrial production; city-building was a framework for building cities and mechanisms of need fulfillment around these new collections of people. If, in liberal thought, "economy" and "society" were discovered as autonomous realities not subject to the laws of the state, then for key theorists of Soviet city-building, such as Nikolai Miliutin and Mikhail Okhitovich, the problem of settlement (*rasselenie*) concerned the *planned* adjustments between populations and production. If, in liberal thought, the laws of the social milieu had to be respected, the Soviet city (*gorodskoe*) *khoziaistvo*—the key problem domain of city-building—was a substantive economy planned and programmed to its minutest detail.

These basic orientations of city-building and social modernity were established by the early 1930s, as the attention of architects and urbanists turned from a "revolution in daily life" to the problem of building cities around the new industrial works foreseen in the first five-year plan. But it was only after World War II that city-building consolidated as an apparatus of transformation. In the postwar decades the planning institutes expanded; resources were increasingly channeled to housing construction and social welfare provisioning; and the population, violently reorganized over national space in the first several decades of the Soviet period, slowly settled into a stable pattern. It is during this period that sociotechnical systems like urban utilities and budgetary systems emerged as key mechanisms through which a new pattern of substantive provisioning was established. And it is during this period that small industrial cities—the longstanding ideal for city-builders—emerged as the exemplars of a particular form of modern life comprising:

- *Forms of expertise* in domains such as architecture, urbanism, demography, geography, and social welfare planning;
- *Values and normative orientations* to equality and to universal social provisioning;
- *Institutional and material apparatuses* such as infrastructures and budgetary bureaucracies through which cities, people, and resource flows were stitched together;
- A *project of transformation* that oriented these different elements toward the *telos* of a planned future;

- *Patterns of adjustment* between populations, production, and social welfare provisioning defining the size structure of settlements and the relationship between social provisioning and industrial production.

These elements make up what I will call the "Soviet social": not Soviet "society," whose existence was such a contentious question of late Sovietological debate, and not the analytical field that provides the explanatory background for the social sciences, but instead a particular configuration of collective life in whose assembly city-building played a central role.

NEOLIBERALISM: REPROGRAMMING THE SOCIAL STATE

If the first half of this book is concerned with the project of Soviet social modernity and the assembly of the Soviet social, then the second half asks: How do neoliberal reforms critique and program the systems of social welfare and the urban forms created by socialism?; Can these reforms be considered "post-social"? If, on the one hand, we understand Soviet social modernity as a *project of transformation*, with corresponding knowledge forms and apparatuses, we would have to conclude that post-Soviet Russia *is* post-social in a rather straightforward sense. The mechanisms of Soviet industrial coordination and the framework of city-building were rapidly disarticulated with the collapse of Soviet socialism. On the other hand, years of scholarship on post-Soviet Russia has demonstrated the often surprising persistence of the material structures, demographic patterns, spatial forms, bureaucratic routines, and underlying values produced by Soviet socialism. My aim is not to sort out precisely what has been preserved and what transformed. Instead, following Foucault's emphases, I am interested in how the elements of the Soviet social are being reproblematized in new approaches to thinking about government in Russia.

For reasons I have already rehearsed, this orientation took me far from Soviet and post-Soviet Russia, to the post–World War II United States where James Buchanan and George Stigler enter our story as crucial figures in neoliberal reflection about the social state. Buchanan and Stigler were both "neo" and "liberal" in a specific and, it seems to me, meaningful sense. Writing after World War II, both understood that they lived in a different world from that of the classical liberals. They recognized that the existence of a large government whose expenditures were directed overwhelmingly to health, social security, and welfare posed a challenge to classical liberalism. They hoped, certainly, to limit the growth of the state, and both, at times, denounced government in strikingly categorical terms. But they had no illusions about returning to the *status quo ante*. A "social state" of some size was a reality. The question was how liberalism could be adapted to the problems of the social state, and how, in turn, the social state might be modified to conform to the political and economic principles of liberalism. Thus, most basically, Buchanan and Stigler's *neo-liberalism* was defined by their attempt to modify liberal critique and programming *in light of* the social state.[27]

Central to this effort was what might be called a critique of public value—a critical approach to analyzing the value produced by government for its constituents. Buchanan and Stigler argued that since the Progressive Era and the New Deal in the United States, economic critique focused on "market failure"—that is, the failure of unregulated markets to ensure competition or maximize welfare. On this basis, economists (and other experts and policymakers) justified a substantial expansion of state intervention across many areas of social and economic life. For Buchanan and Stigler (and many other neoliberals), the problem with the dominant forms of economic reasoning about the state began from the fact that "government" was treated as a benevolent actor, and the "public" as a homogeneous mass whose needs and values could be known. In response, they raised fundamental questions about the production of "public value" (a term of which both were suspicious) in a complex modern society. For whom, they asked, are public values valuable—a broad swath of the citizenry or powerful private groups such as corporations? Through what mechanisms are these values defined? How can public values such as health and welfare—values that, as Foucault once remarked, have no "internal principle of limitation" (2000: 373)—be reconciled with the reality of scarcity and the diverse desires of constituents?

The answers that Stigler and Buchanan formulated struck directly at the regulatory institutions, redistributive mechanisms, and infrastructures through which the American social state expanded; their effect, as one not particularly sympathetic commentator observed, was like a "shotgun blast" that challenged the assumptions and institutions of "the Progressive era, the New Deal, and the Great Society" (McCraw 1976: 297). On one level, their critique drew attention to the failure of many government interventions to produce the outcomes that policymakers and technocrats explicitly sought to achieve. But this new critical reflection was not only an economic "test" of government activity (Do policies achieve their goals?). It was, also, a "criticism of reality"—an intervention at the level of political ontology. Stigler and Buchanan articulated what I will call a "microeconomic" critique of government that comprised, following Foucault, an entirely new "method of analysis and . . . type of programming" (2008: 219) of the social state. In referring to a microeconomics of government, I do not mean to suggest that they worked on the microeconomy as a *pre-existing* field. Rather, I refer to a form of reflection and intervention that served to *constitute* the incentives of individuals as a register of reality that could be known and governed.[28] Buchanan and Stigler (and many other neoliberal thinkers) decomposed what they saw as unwieldy aggregate concepts like "the state," the "public interest," and "society" into calculating actors, whether firms, interest groups, or individual citizens. They defined a new *critical visibility* of government activity, uncovering previously ignored behavioral questions about how regulatory officials, corporations, policymakers, the beneficiaries of public programs, and citizens responded to the incentives that were created, often unwittingly, by government intervention. At the same time, this microeconomic perspective provided the conceptual grounds for a new *programming* that identified these actors' incentives as a key target of reform.

It is central to my story that the form of critique and programming that Stigler and Buchanan formulated did not arrive in Russia because the agents of "neoliberal hegemony" transported it there; there are no hidden connections between major neoliberal thinkers and the experts and policymakers who formulated heating or budgetary reform in Russia, and these latter individuals, no doubt, would never think of themselves as neoliberals. Instead, we will see that a crucial intermediary role was played by two "minor traditions" of neoliberal thought: fiscal federal theory and the new economics of regulation. Borrowing loosely from Gilles Deleuze and Felix Guattari's (1986) discussion of minor literature, I have in mind a tradition defined not by an overriding ideological or political agenda, or by great thinkers, but by a style of reasoning and an accumulation of exemplary experiences that contributes to shared understandings. Akin to Michel Callon's "hybrid knowledges" (1998a), these minor traditions were constituted between academic disciplines, domains of technical expertise, and policymaking, and produced an entire body of knowledge, and a toolkit of highly original practices. As Nikolas Rose (1999) has shown in his work on "advanced liberalism," these new governmental mechanisms that work through individual choice and calculation—we might call them "microeconomic devices"[29]—introduced a vast range of new possibilities into the programming of government: markets in social "bads" such as pollution; voucher programs for schools; the monetization of social welfare payments; decentralizing reforms of government; incentive pricing for regulated industries; formulas for budgetary redistribution; mechanisms of quasi-competition in contexts where competitive markets cannot function, and so on. These minor traditions, though not exclusively associated with neoliberalism, can be called "neoliberal" in, again, a specific and meaningful sense, and it is through them that neoliberalism can be meaningfully associated with the areas of reform that I studied in Russia.

POST-SOVIET SOCIAL

The question I want to pose explicitly—precisely because it is so often taken for granted—is how this microeconomic programming relates to the norms and forms of the social state. At first glance it might seem that the multifarious realms of *substantive* organization of economic and social life are reengineered through mechanisms of *formal* rationalization and calculative choice. Following Rose, O'Malley, and Valverde, to the extent that they are "autonomizing and responsibilizing" of individual citizens, these "advanced liberal" techniques of government enable the state to "divest itself of many of its obligations" for the population's health and welfare, and to devolve these to "quasi-autonomous entities" (2006: 91). To recall Harvey, the market ethic replaces all previous ethical systems. "Advanced liberal" government, on this account, would also seem to be "post-social" government.

But we should not move too quickly from the identification of neoliberalism with a microeconomic critique and programming to any assumptions about the formations of government that neoliberal reform shapes. What Buchanan proposed, what the theorists and practitioners of fiscal federalism elaborated, and what a collection of international consultants, local experts in fiscal reform, policymakers, and government officials articulated through proposals for budgetary reform in Russia, was not the abandonment of the social welfare goals of the Soviet state. Instead, by programming systems of transfers, reforms aimed to accommodate the reality of scarcity and a preference for decentralized government to the quite stringent redistributive standard of "fiscal equity." In doing so, neoliberal reforms did not reject Soviet social norms. Quite the contrary: we will see that the technical definition of "fiscal equity" requires meticulous calculation of citizens' norm-defined "needs" in order to determine appropriate budgetary distributions. This orientation to fiscal equity was not an exception to a neoliberal project that was *really*, in its dark and hidden moments, devoted to evacuating the public purposes of the state. Nor was this simply an "ameliorative" accommodation, meant to overcome contradictions in the "neoliberal hegemonic project."[30] Rather, fiscal equity was the central theme of Buchanan's classic essays of the late 1940s and early 1950s, which articulated a new liberal reflection on growing inequality in industrial societies and suggested a practical approach to organizing distributions of wealth that would be, as he put it, more "ethically acceptable" (1950: 590). If Buchanan took from classical liberalism a concern with limiting the state and fiercely defending individual autonomy, he also took from it a concern with justice.

What Stigler began to conceptualize, what was elaborated through a new economics of regulation, and what was articulated in federal reforms of heat provision formulated in the 2000s in Russia, was not the abandonment of the principle that the state should guarantee delivery of essential infrastructure services, or of the proposition that in certain sec-tors of a modern economy markets fail and government must intervene. Instead, it was a new critique and programming of heat provisioning that deployed microeconomic devices—meters, targeted (rather than blanket) subsidies, incentive pricing—to *partially* reprogram the delivery of heat while preserving a prior orientation to universal provisioning, and man-aging the natural monopoly characteristics of heat production imposed by the stubborn material structures and spatial forms of Soviet social-ism. This, again, was not an "exception" to a neoliberal project bent on marketizing public services. Rather, it was *precisely* an application of a tradition of neoliberal thought that acknowledged the failure of markets to produce desired efficiency or welfare outcomes in some sectors or sub-sectors, and that sought, in these cases, to deploy microeconomic devices in a way that could be accommodated to the *substantive* orientations of universal need fulfillment. This was less a "marketization" or "privatiza-tion" of a public service—the universal slogan of neoliberalism's critics—and more a new patterning of social welfare mechanisms with techniques of commercialization and calculative choice.

These observations suggest no definitive answers to the question of whether post-Soviet government is post-social government. If there is a global argument it is negative: the antinomies that have long been accepted as defining neoliberalism—public versus private value; social versus post-social; the state versus the market; solidarity versus individualism—do not perform the conceptual labor we require of them. My point is not precisely that existing formulations about neoliberalism are wrong; they are in some cases but not in others. Rather, it is that they are of the wrong *kind*. They are seeking in neoliberalism explanations for "vast arrays of life and history," to repeat Bruno Latour's phrase, when we should be trying to establish better tools for studying this significant form through which population, society, and economy are being reshaped as objects of governmental reflection and intervention.

OBJECTS AND METHOD

In concluding this chapter, a few comments about the objects of analysis that appear, and the methods of inquiry employed in this book are in or-der. A central strategy, motivated by the methodological concerns already discussed, is to cast a suspicious eye on terms like "Soviet society," "mar-ketization," or "neoliberalism" and to identify objects of analysis—and terms for describing them—that get closer to the actuality of how the social was assembled in the Soviet period, and how it is being reshaped today. Thus, I spend a good deal of time on detailed analyses of pipes and budgetary routines, norms and standards, calculative tools such as socialist "tabulations" of social welfare needs, and neoliberal redistribution formulas. I also devote considerable attention to the analysis of technical documents and the "styles of reasoning"[31] that can be discerned in them: articles written by neoliberal economists and Soviet planners; strategy statements issued by technocratic institutions such as the World Bank; and reform proposals propagated by the Russian government or Russian think tanks. This may make for rough (or dry) going at times. But I am convinced that only in this way can we make headway in addressing questions whose answers have too often been taken for granted.

In some respects this approach bears an affinity to the style of inquiry associated with Actor-Network Theory (ANT). It places great value on detailed and careful technical description. And my broader methodological orientations echo ANT's antisociological arguments: its insistence on taking figures such as "the market" or "society" or the "calculative actor" not as *pre-given categories* of social scientific analysis but as *assemblages*. Their construction has to be accounted for by making "the social" traceable, as in Latour's recent formulation (2005: 164), or, following Michel Callon, by showing how markets are made through the "framing" of calculative agencies (1998a).[32] Thus, my inquiry was very much concerned with understanding how, through "humble" infrastructures, the Soviet social was assembled, and with the way that calculative agencies were (or were not, thanks in part to the intransigence of the same infrastructures) framed through neoliberal reforms.

That said, as my fieldwork progressed, this mode of inquiry was complicated by a simple fact: other observers in the historical and contemporary fields I was studying were asking precisely the same questions. Tsarist ministers, planning theorists, and Soviet city-builders were all concerned with understanding how "the social" had been assembled in liberal countries, and with inventing alternative ways that, through infrastructures, standards and norms, and budgetary mechanisms, it could be assembled differently. Neoliberal reformers, from Buchanan and Stigler to the often anonymous authors of innumerable Russian and foreign technical reports, asked not whether it would be possible to "marketize" these assemblies—as though markets and calculative agencies would magically emerge when the state was withdrawn. Instead, they asked how calculative agencies could be constituted by disentangling actors and framing their choices through the details of material apparatuses and administrative arrangements. From this perspective, the questions of ANT did not have to be *introduced* into these fields as the special contribution of a detached observer. They were already there, posed through diverse forms

of critical questioning that were historically shaped through an entire accumulation of arguments, now obscure technical debates, and historical
experiences. The challenge, thus, was to analyze these actors as *thinkers*,
and to analyze *thinking* neither as abstract reflection nor as a fixed "system" or *episteme* but as a practico-critical activity through which, following Paul Rabinow, "historical conjunctures [are] turned into conceptual
and practical problems" (2003: 47).[33]

In this light, my approach diverges from ANT—and converges with
alternatives such as Foucault's history of the present and Rabinow's anthropology of the contemporary—in its explicit concern with what might
be called the historicity of the assemblages or "actor-networks" that ANT
has made its privileged object of analysis. By "historicity" I do not mean
just that the formation of these assemblages can be temporally traced—
that they can be situated historically (arising at a certain time, animated
by certain actors or actor networks). Instead, I refer to their relationship
to broader fields of significance and historical conditions of intelligibility
that are themselves temporally circumscribed, and whose identification is
a critical moment of inquiry.[34] Consequently, if a first step in the analysis is
"deconstructive" in the sense that Latour (2005) uses the term—a process
of breaking down the vague abstractions of the social sciences and of beginning to trace how collectivities are actually constituted—then a second
step might be called the conceptual reconstruction of historical conditions
of intelligibility or what Ian Hacking (2002) calls historical ontology.[35] It
is to this end that the technical analyses in this book are directed.

Thus, though city-building plans were never implemented in full, they
tell us something essential about the project of Soviet social modernity.
Their analysis suggests a set of terms—*khoziaistvo*, settlement, and so
on—that are not meaningless abstractions but valuable tools for grasp-
ing how the health, welfare, and conditions of existence of the Soviet
population was constituted as an object of knowledge and a field of intervention. And although the reforms I examine may not have worked out
as anticipated in plans—and indeed have not, in some cases, even been
implemented—they provide us with ways to think about the relationship
between neoliberalism and social modernity that are better in the sense
that they are closer to the actuality of neoliberalism as a form of critique
and programming in particular domains. Buchanan's concept of fiscal
equity tells us something about contemporary reformations of the state
that is entirely missed by the usual boilerplate about austerity and state
retrenchment. Stigler's economics of regulation allows us to understand
neoliberalism not as a "privatization" of social services that simply abandons central commitments of the social state but as a microeconomic
programming of social welfare that reworks but in some cases retains the
ends of social government. In this sense, conceptual reconstruction does

not mean abandoning middle range concepts like neoliberalism. Instead, it means investing in them by clarifying their meaning and significance.

Since I am an anthropologist, it bears closing these brief notes on method by commenting on what is usually taken to be the defining feature of anthropological work—ethnography. This book is not an ethnography, and it does not have the typical traits of an ethnography. I do not draw on extensive quotation from conversations in the field; I do not investigate "difference" or structures of experience; and I do not try to portray my fieldwork in Russia as an existential journey in which the experience of the ethnographer is foregrounded. In fact, my fieldwork did offer opportunities to pursue ethnography in these familiar forms: classic rites of ethnographic passage such as fluency and immersion, unhappiness and existential quandary; and candidates for thick description, such as the *nostal'giia* of those who built small cities after World War II and lived to see their collapse, or the struggle of younger residents to gain their ethical bearings in small cities whose horizons closed down with the "opening" that attended Soviet breakup. But I did not pursue these "ethnographic" concerns for the simple reason that ethnography, thus conceived, did not offer answers to the questions I cared about.

And why should it? As various commentators have observed, ethnography was invented in relation to a specific theory of anthropology's object—the culture or ethnos (Clifford 1988; Gupta and Ferguson 1992; Rabinow et al. 2008). Given the proliferation of other kinds of objects in contemporary anthropology, it seems reasonable to ask not whether a certain study is "an ethnography" but how certain practices associated with ethnography can fit into a toolkit for contemporary anthropological inquiry. For ultimately I did use a practice that is derived from traditions of ethnography in a fashion that seems to me typical of much anthropological work today: a technique of inquiry that begins from the specificity of a certain place, is oriented by the weight of its problems, by the density and polyvalence of the experiences that one finds in it, and that leads to other sites, where other techniques of inquiry must be used. This, at any rate, is what fieldwork in Belaya Kalitva and Rodniki—a second city in which I worked—provided: insight into critical nodes where fields of power come into contact and are made visible; into singular realities whose intelligibility has to be found in diverse experiences that lie beyond them. The detailed engagement of ethnography provided, thus, an orientation to a grouping of sites and a set of problems that I simply could not have stumbled upon otherwise. These cities also provided an ethical orientation to the fate of a curious and preponderant kind of human collectivity, to the apartment blocs, heating pipes, budgets, and people whose lives depend on these mundane systems—and whose modernity has been shattered.

A Note on Organization

The two parts of this book share a common structure. After a brief introduction, each begins by asking how the broad adjustments between population, production, and social welfare were made targets of expert reflection and intervention in the early Soviet period (chapter 2) and at the onset of the post-Soviet period (chapter 6). Subsequent chapters trace these biopolitical frameworks to the elements through which a form of social modernity is assembled, digging in to pipes, wires, and norms. My argument about neoliberalism comes late in the book—in chapter 7 (on the fisc) and chapter 8 (on heat systems). For this reason, although these chapters draw extensively on prior material, I have written them in a way that should allow them to be read on their own.

PART ONE

Soviet Social Modernity

Figure P.1. "Tomorrow—Sunny Cities!" A poster from the late Soviet Baikal-Amur Railroad (*BAM*) proclaims "Where today there is taiga, tomorrow—sunny cities!"

IN 1930 THE STATE PUBLISHING HOUSE issued Nikolai Aleksandrovich Miliutin's book, *The Problem of Building Socialist Cities, Basic Questions Regarding the Rational Planning and Construction of Settlements in the USSR*. The book—frequently referred to as *Sotsgorod*, or *Socialist City*—is among the celebrated documents of the Soviet architectural and urbanist avant-garde. Its best-known proposal was for a "lineal city," a planning concept that, as George Collins and Arthur Sprague (1974) have argued, can be located in a tradition that extends from Toni Garnier's *Cite Industrielle* to the precepts put forth by CIAM in the Athens Charter. As in these other schemes, Miliutin called for careful planning of the functional relationships among residential areas, recreational facilities, and industrial enterprises in cities. The lineal city was distinguished by the vision of total transformation that underlay it.[1] The premise was massive state-led industrialization, around which cities would have to be shaped, down to their most minute details. Even "the communes ... the dwellings, and ... the other similar parts of settlements," he wrote, should be planned as inputs to productive processes. This was a vision of human settlement as a "flowing functional-assembly line"—urban modernity as an adjunct to industrial enterprise (Miliutin 1974: 64–65).

Miliutin's *Sotsgorod* arrived at a critical juncture in the evolution of Soviet planning discussions. As the construction of major industrial works came into focus as the central task for building socialism in the late 1920s, architects' early utopian experiments with reconstructing daily life gave way to the problems of building cities around new sites of industrial production. This shift sparked the last great discussion of the urbanist avant-garde, concerning the design of socialist cities. But the space for utopian musings about new urban forms opened only briefly. It soon became apparent that industrial plans would dictate terms to Soviet cities, which were not loci of experimentation but rather, as a 1931 article in the journal *Soviet Architecture* put it, mere "details" in regional and national plans for industrial development. The "official" message to urbanists, observes the Russian historian Mark Meerovich (2007), was "Enough discussing! You will build and plan what the government orders! [*Khvatit diskutirovat'! Stroit' i proektirovat' budete to, chto prikazhet vlast'!*]."

In retrospect, one can see how Miliutin's *Sotsgorod* was delicately balanced in this quickly changing and ultimately dangerous terrain. His lineal city was located in a tradition of avant-garde thought that imagined a central creative role for architects and urbanists. At the same time, the lineal city was nothing other than a city designed as a "detail" in plans for industrial mass production, one whose elements—its inhabitants, its social welfare facilities, its housing—would be planned and organized as productive factors. And the concerns addressed in *Sotsgorod*, beyond the lineal city, conformed to new pragmatic mandates to support the work of the five-year plan.[2] The book discussed the mundane task of training specialists who could undertake the vast amount of work required for planning Soviet cities. It also outlined a technocratic framework that would allow urbanists to link industrial development, population growth, and social welfare in a common frame of total planning.

The ideas presented in *Sotsgorod* had a complex fate. Collins and Sprague point out that Miliutin recanted his earlier work in 1932, arguing that his writing from that time on "represents an about face that is incomprehensible in terms of *Sotsgorod*" (1974: 29). But the concerns of *Sotsgorod* were not simply abandoned. As scholars have recently recognized is true in so many domains, the dramatic shifts of the late 1920s and early 1930s are hard to characterize in terms of a simple rejection of prior ideas.[3] Key elements of a new urbanism laid out in *Sotsgorod*—not only the general orientation to functional planning but the pragmatic vision of design institutes, of cadres of architects and urbanists, of substantive norms that tied urban planning to total planning, and of a "socioeconomic theory of planning by which society could be totally transformed" (Collins and Sprague 1974: 1)—were assimilated into Soviet urbanism. In particular, they can be found in the theory and practice of *gradostroitel'stvo* or city-building, the paradigm of Soviet city planning.

Gradostroitel'stvo was not a neologism of the 1920s. But in Soviet practice it referred to something distinct from tsarist precedents. Soviet city-building was also distinct from modern urban planning as it had evolved elsewhere during the nineteenth century. It was not confined to questions of land use, zoning, urban infrastructure, and planning of public spaces; it was not a modulated and partial intervention into autonomous "social" processes. Rather, city-building was a form of total planning applied to urban life.

COMPARATIVE SOCIAL MODERNITIES

In the first part of this book I take the initial articulation of city-building in the early 1930s as a kind of pivot, whose *intelligibility* should be established in relation to the distinctive trajectory of tsarist and early Soviet biopolitics, and whose *effects* can be traced through the development of Soviet urban modernity. I begin, in chapter 2, by outlining the background of developments against which we can understand the emergence of Soviet city-building—painting, with a broad brush, a picture of successive formations of government from Petrine absolutism to Soviet total planning. Chapter 3 focuses on the urbanist discussions of the late 1920s and early 1930s in which city-building was articulated as a form of total planning applied to problems of social modernity. Chapters 4 and 5 turn to Soviet developments in the two small industrial cities where I worked—Rodniki and Belaya Kalitva—examining how the planning apparatus took hold of such cities as objects of knowledge and intervention; how these cities were transformed in the late Soviet period; and how the institutional bases of this distinctive form of collective life came unraveled after the Soviet Union broke up, leaving the spatial, demographic, and material inheritance of city-building as a problem for post-Soviet reform.

Although my analysis of city-building is not explicitly comparative, an implicit comparison lies behind it, and will be periodically invoked in the chapters that follow. This comparison follows a long and rich tradition of scholarship that has emphasized that potent force-field of *backwardness* that profoundly shaped political and economic institutions in Russia.[4] In pursuing this theme, I am guided by the work of Alexander Gerschenkron (1966, 1970), an economic historian who is most famous for his theses on the relationship between the timing of industrialization and the varying institutional forms of industrial modernity across Europe. For Gerschenkron, the relative "lateness" of industrialization—that is, the degree of "backwardness"—is intimately related to the institutional pattern of industrialism: its capital intensity, the relative importance of the state, and the amount of coercion employed. In this sense, backwardness referred in part to "objective" features of economic and social organization, such as the levels of urbanization and industrialization. But it is crucial to Gerschenkron's argument that these factors became significant because leaders of state, intellectuals, and aristocratic or military elites *saw* them as problems. These actors produced what Foucault called a "grid of historical and sociological decipherment" (2008: 291) that allowed them to diagnose contemporary problems as products of backwardness, and to develop plans for overcoming them. Backwardness, in short, was a problem-space—a challenge first of all on the level of thought.

This understanding of backwardness is connected to one of Gerschenkron's most trenchant and enduring insights: the response to backwardness is often not imitation. Gerschenkron famously rejected Karl Marx's dictum that "[t]he industrially more developed country presents to the less developed country a picture of the latter's future" (Gerschenkron 1966: 6). Instead, anticipating a key insight of postcolonial studies, he argued that backward countries take up, critique, and rework received elements from the most "advanced" countries. Backwardness was thus a site of critique, but also a site of innovation. In this sense, Gerschenkron's comparative analysis does not explain divergent developmental outcomes in different countries by reference to independent variables. In his view, Russian industrial development was utterly different from British industrialization, but it is unintelligible without reference to the British experience, in part because the British experience was an essential object of reflection for those engaged in organizing industrial development in Russia. Similarly, though Soviet social modernity diverged absolutely from the liberal cases, it can only be understood as a response to the institutional forms and the kind of problem making associated with the liberal experience.

In Foucault's account, liberal reflection on government was shaped by two interlinked developments. The first was the transformation of rural economic and social institutions, leading to the weakening of feudal bonds and overpopulation in the countryside. The second was the development of early market cities, initially as exceptions in systems of power "founded and developed on the basis of a territorial domination defined by feudalism" (2007: 64). The confluence of these two developments in the eighteenth and early nineteenth centuries, fueled by an expansion of trade, incipient industrialization, and ever broadening concessions to urban autonomy, led to a chaotic and uncontrolled reorganization—"tropismic," as Lewis Mumford (1934: 151) famously put it, like moths to light—of populations around new centers of economic activity. These new industrial centers were what Mumford famously labeled the "non-cities" of early capitalist urbanization: large and dense industrial settlements that lacked the utilities, services, and regulatory controls that make a city livable. Early industrial cities "posed new and specific economic and political problems of governmental technique" that, in turn, triggered novel governmental responses in areas such as sanitation, public health, and housing.[5] And these responses constituted one register—the national "market economy" was another—on which the figures of "society," "economy," and "population" were "discovered" as autonomous realities with their own regularities and laws. These new figures also imposed a new principle of limitation on governmental intervention. If classical monarchy worked on juridico-legal or disciplinary fields that were in principle subject to total governmental control, then liberal government worked through modulated intervention into the autonomous processes of a social and economic milieu.[6]

RODNIKI: A TSARIST NON-CITY

Two-hundred years of tsarist development presented very different problems for those who, in the late 1920s and early 1930s, fashioned Soviet government. Here, as an initial window on their contours—and an orientation to the themes that occupy the first part of this book—we can juxtapose the early industrial city in Western Europe to the very different scene of early industrialism in the last centuries of tsarist rule by introducing the second city in which I conducted fieldwork—Rodniki, in Ivanovo *oblast'*.

Rodniki was first identified in sixteenth-century monastery records that noted a small collection of peasant households engaged in home textile production based on local flax.[7] The local economy was not dynamic. In 1794, two centuries later, Rodniki consisted of 28 households containing 208 inhabitants. But by the first decades of the nineteenth century a distinctive—and, for Russia, entirely typical—pattern of economic transformation was taking shape. Members of a peasant family by the name Krasil'shchikov (dyer) emerged as leaders of the local textile industry. The first Krasil'shchikov workshops were constructed in 1820. By the middle of the century these workshops had acquired steam-powered looms, and were eventually consolidated into a single Krasil'shchikov enterprise that operated a network of trading houses throughout Russia. A watershed in industrial development came with the advent in the 1860s of railroad lines in what was then called the Ivanovo-Kineshma region, which plugged this rural center of textile production into the nineteenth century's expanding global capitalist economy.

Apparently we have, albeit with significant delay, a pattern of market-driven industrial development mirroring that of the early industrial city of Western European capitalism. But there was a crucial difference: industrial development in Rodniki did not spur urban growth. Most workers at the Krasil'shchikov manufactory were men from peasant households whose industrial wages supplemented a "householding" pattern of subsistence.[8] The majority of workers did not live in Rodniki or its immediate environs, but came from the surrounding countryside. Those from remote settlements were accommodated in factory-owned dormitories that, by the late nineteenth century, could temporarily house 2,500 workers. Despite an industrial workforce that swelled to almost 10,000 at the end of the tsarist period, in 1897 Rodniki's population stood at only 4,176. Since many of these residents must not have been employed at the Krasil'shchikov manufactory, it follows that a relatively small portion of the industrial workforce resided in Rodniki. It is no surprise, in this context, that urban development was limited. Rodniki was never classified as a city during the tsarist period, and had no institution of local government. Local conditions were left to the owners of the textile manufactory, who constructed only a handful of buildings in the city center, including dorms for workers, a theater, and two modest stone houses that served as the Krasil'shchikov residence when the family was in town. The balance of the housing stock was comprised of small wooden huts, constructed by the families of textile workers. In sum, Rodniki was a kind of "non-city," but one whose form differed totally from the urban forms of early capitalism in Europe. Rodniki was not, like a typical market town of Western Europe, an "exception" in a regime of territorial sovereignty. It was simply undifferentiated from the areas around it. And the onset of industrial development in Rodniki did not spur a tropismic accumulation of population. Even after large-scale industrial development, the Krasil'shchikov manufactory remained a relatively lonely industrial enterprise in a rural region.

I do not mean to make too much of this small, out-of-the-way place in what was a vast empire. As we will see, the "rural industrial" pattern found in Rodniki was not the only form of industrial development that emerged over the last 200 years of tsarist rule. And the cardinal fact of late tsarist development was that the Russian economy remained overwhelmingly agricultural to the end of the nineteenth century. But Rodniki serves nonetheless to illustrate two points that are crucial to the story that follows. First, during the tsarist period the nexus between industrialism and urbanization that spurred the development of social modernity in Western Europe was confined to a few major centers, and was blocked by the rigid framework of classical power. In most of Russia the problems of social modernity were never addressed because they were never posed. Second, when a project of social modernity *did* emerge in the early decades of the Soviet period, it took shape in relation to problems that differed fundamentally from those of Western Europe. If in Europe the problem was to manage *ongoing* processes of urbanization and industrialization, then in Soviet Russia planners were concerned with the *absence* of urban and industrial transformation. Backwardness and underdevelopment were the key problems to be overcome.

This is not to say that the urban-industrial nexus was not in the end the critical context in which a project of Soviet social modernity took shape. But the problem of backwardness—and the responses to backwardness—meant that it took an entirely different form. Soviet industrialization was not organized through "spontaneous" social and economic processes outside the state but through state initiative. And Soviet city-building, conforming to Miliutin's vision, was one part of an effort to coordinate urban planning and social welfare provisioning with state-led industrial transformation. Soviet planners implicitly accepted certain parts of liberal political ontology, such as the proposition that it was not legal subjects but living beings in their productive and reproductive lives that were the proper objects of government. But they explicitly weighed, debated, and ultimately rejected the liberal "principle of limitation" on governmental intervention into the social and economic milieu, and proposed that an alternative approach would allow them to circumvent the pathologies of early industrialization in other countries. Making virtue of necessity, Soviet planners tried to avoid the reckless tropism of capitalist urbanization through total planning, advancing the radical biopolitical proposition that the adjustments between processes of population, processes of production, and apparatuses of social welfare could be programmed by the state.

CHAPTER TWO

The Birth of Soviet Biopolitics

> We have seen [socialism] function ... within
> governmentalities that would no doubt fall more under ...
> a hyper-administrative state in which there is, so to speak, a
> fusion, a continuity, the constitution of a sort of massive bloc
> between governmentality and administration. At that point,
> in the governmentality of a police state, socialism functions
> as the internal logic of an administrative apparatus.
> —Michel Foucault, *The Birth of Biopolitics*[1]

THE PATTERN OF SOVIET BIOPOLITICS took shape during the 1920s, a decade that was as momentous for the history of modern government as were the years of early liberalism in Britain or France. By 1925, with growth based on the recovery of the pre–World War I economy nearing completion, the Soviet leadership resolved to pursue an intensified program of planned industrial development. The debates over how industrialization should be organized, in particular the disputes between the "genetic" and "teleological" approaches to planning, explored fundamental questions concerning the political ontology of Soviet government. *Genetic* planners developed techniques for constraining government investment budgets within limits imposed by factors such as market trade and agricultural production that were autonomous of the state. In this sense, although it imagined a vastly expanded role for government in promoting industrial development, genetic planning worked within the strictures of liberal political ontology. *Teleological* planners, by contrast, rejected those laws that, according to liberal political economy, limited government intervention and restricted the pace of growth.[2] They "discovered" population, economy, and society not as autonomous domains but as fields that could be reshaped by the state through total instrumental intervention. By the late 1920s, as Soviet political leadership settled on a course of forced industrialization, the dispute had been resolved in the teleological direction. Government was no longer approached as a problem of modulating the relationship between the state and society. Rather, it functioned as the "internal logic of an administrative apparatus" (Foucault 2008: 93).

In this chapter I situate this distinctive political ontology genealogically, by examining successive configurations of institutions, techniques, material elements, forms of reflection, and modalities of intervention, through which political government took shape in tsarist and early Soviet Russia. I focus in particular on three *formations* of government: first, an "absolutist-disciplinary" pattern that emerged during the eighteenth century, and can be traced to Peter the Great's importation and reconfiguration of institutions associated with European Absolutism; second, the "sovereigntist-developmental" pattern of the late nineteenth century, associated in particular with the railroad building program that intensified under the finance minister Sergei Witte; and third, the Soviet "disciplinary-biopolitical" pattern, in which the total intervention and teleological orientation of disciplinary power was deployed in a project whose aim was to transform collective life.

The episodes addressed in this chapter are among the most exhaustively researched in Russian history. I do not pretend to add historical facts to existing studies, nor, for the most part, do I take up the debates and controversies that animate them. What I hope to do, rather, is to paint in the very broadest strokes a picture of developments in tsarist Russia and the early Soviet Union that can serve as a kind of counterpoint to Foucault's schematic genealogy of liberal government in his work of the late 1970s. In doing so, I will emphasize two themes that are particularly significant for the broader arc of this book's narrative. First, we will see how the city—whether as a space of industrial production, as a site of administrative activity, or simply as a locus of relatively dense settlement—is constituted as an object of reflection and intervention in different formations of government. In the tsarist period cities were circumscribed within the strictures of sovereign power, which was fundamentally "conservative" when it came to large-scale readjustments of the population's distribution and way of life. In the Soviet period, by contrast, the city emerges precisely as that space in which such readjustments can be governmentally managed. Second, we will trace the articulation and subsequent redeployment of two critical instruments of government—budgets and infrastructures. Initially developed in the state-building and modernizing projects of the Russian absolutist state, these instruments were turned, first in the late tsarist period, then in the Soviet period, to various subsequent tasks of development and social welfare, and embedded in the mechanisms of Soviet planning. Their present significance lies, in part, in the fact that they were identified as critical targets of neoliberal reform after Soviet breakup, and will thus be crucial for assessing the postsocialist fate of Soviet social modernity in the second part of this book.

TABLE 2.1.
Formations of Tsarist and Soviet Government

Governmental Formation	Guiding Aims	Technologies of Power	Exemplary City Forms	Budgets and Infrastructures
Absolutist-disciplinary (18th century – Petrine "importation" of absolutist institutions)	Aggrandize sovereignty through military power, administrative control, territorial expansion	Sovereignty as a principle of territorial rule; disciplinary and feudal mechanisms deployed in circumscribed spaces of classical power (factory cities, military garrisons, etc.)	*City-Factory:* city inscribed in classical power; temporary populations of soldiers or *corvée* laborers *"Service" Cities:* garrisons or administrative centers comprised largely of bureaucrats and soldiers	Emerge as key elements of tsarist state building, related to the mobilization of resources and the extension of "infrastructural power" over the territory
Sovereigntist-developmental (Late 19th century – railroad construction and rural reform)	Aggrandize sovereignty through selective state interventions in the economic sphere (infrastructure, state budget)	Sovereignty combined with "developmental" orientation to intensifying autonomous activities of private entrepreneurs and traders (through infrastructure investment)	*Rural Industrial Non-city:* site of industrial development without significant urbanization, based on itinerant labor (19th Century *Rodniki*) *Growing Industrial City:* based on "freed" labor from countryside; typical problems of early industrial cities; nascent social modernity	Mobilization of resources for capital accumulation through trade regime and state budget; construction of railroads as the "flywheel" of economic development
Biopolitical-disciplinary (1920s – Soviet total planning)	State-led transformation of collective life based on general planning, initially driven by infrastructure (GOELRO) and heavy industry	Wholesale transformation of the spatial distribution and conditions of existence of national population; disciplinary power in a regime of totalitarian biopolitics	*Early Soviet Non-city:* permanent population around new or existing industrial sites; limited apparatus of need fulfillment (early Soviet *Rodniki*, cities of first five-year plans) *Soviet Small City:* a "city by an enterprise" planned to its minutest detail	Infrastructure (specifically electricity infrastructure) as the backbone of total planning; budgets reduced to a reflection of decisions taken elsewhere in the planning apparatus

PETRINE ABSOLUTISM: THE SOVEREIGNTIST-DISCIPLINARY FORMATION

The first great transformative wave of modernizing reform in Russia was undertaken by Peter the Great, who ruled from 1682 to 1725. Peter oversaw the importation and creative adaptation of institutions associated with the centralized states and territorial empires of European absolutism. In his classic study, Perry Anderson (1979) identifies two defining characteristics of absolutist government. First, absolutism consolidated the power of central states at the expense of nobles and the church. The bases of this power were juridico-legal; the revived theories of sovereignty and imperium of Roman law defined legitimate authority. Second, absolutist states introduced diverse forms of rationalization and bureaucratization into governmental practice. These included the expansion of what Michael Mann (1986) calls "infrastructural power": extending the scope of state administration through roads, military control, and, crucially, fiscal apparatuses. At the same time, within the "circumscribed spaces" of classical monarchy—the army, the workshop, and the prison—discipline functioned as a key mechanism of sovereign power (Foucault 2007).

As Gerschenkron has argued, the full range of absolutist institutions, with the possible exception of mercantilist trade policies, were either imported or greatly strengthened during Petrine rule (Gerschenkron 1970; Raeff 1975). But Russian absolutism differed from European variants in important respects, and these divergences are crucial to understanding why the problems faced by those who articulated a Soviet biopolitics two hundred years after the end of Peter's rule were distinct from those faced by the liberals of eighteenth-century France or Britain. According to Anderson, European absolutism was a contradictory affair. On the one hand, the reassertion of the absolute authority of the *imperium* of Roman law was the basis for a dramatic centralization of sovereign power. On the other hand, a revived Roman *civic* law, championed by increasingly assertive bourgeois and merchant classes, began to replace the tangled obligations of feudal relations with institutions of absolute property (Anderson 1979: 27). Civic law established bases for authority and social power outside the structures of monarchy. It also spurred the growth of trade and the expansion of cities, processes that, as we have seen, presented problems that could not readily be managed within the framework of sovereignty, thus introducing tensions into the heart of the absolutist order.[3]

The Russian absolutist pattern was different. Peter's reign established (or reinforced) absolute state dominance at the expense not only of nobility and church but also of urban merchant or industrial classes, which were never the source of threats to central authority. And it strengthened rather than weakened certain elements of feudal authority, most centrally serfdom. In the absence of those tensions that transformed European absolutisms, crucial elements of the absolutist pattern persisted in Russia well beyond their decline in Europe. This is not to say that Russian absolutism was unchanging where other countries were dynamic. Rather, beginning with Peter, absolutist institutions were creatively redeployed and intensified to address tasks they had not addressed elsewhere.

An example is the promotion of industrial development. Peter the Great transformed Russia into a world industrial power, largely (as was typical for absolutist states) in the name of military goals.[4] A key instrument of Petrine industrialism was the so-called "city-factories" (*gorodazavody*)—relatively isolated industrial settlements, generally connected to military needs, particularly for metallurgic production. The city-factory was, as Foucault (2007) observed in a discussion of similar "artificial cities" in France, an exemplary disciplinary space that was inscribed within the order of sovereignty. They were planned on a tabula rasa—not in an existing settlement—and organized as sites for inserting human bodies into processes of production, and for controlling labor through disciplinary mechanisms.[5] Industrial settlements of this type were not unique to Russia. But as Rena Lotareva (1993) has shown, the preponderance, institutional bases, and function of such settlements in Russia diverged from the pattern in other countries. In much of Europe, city-factories were limited in number, and for a variety of reasons they declined as industrial initiative shifted away from the state. In Russia, by contrast, city-factories were both pervasive and persistent. An estimated 500 settlements of this type developed from the late seventeenth century to the mid nineteenth century in metallurgy alone, and they remained important sites of industrial activity to the end of the tsarist period.

The preponderance and persistence of Russian city-factories is particularly significant when one considers the institutional bases upon which they rested. City-factories were founded, as Lotareva puts it, in the "soil of the feudal order" (1993: 11). Perhaps it would be more appropriate to say that they were founded in the soil of feudal institutions that had been redeployed and intensified in the structures of Russian absolutism. Workers in city-factories were not free laborers but serfs. The mobilization of serf labor for work in city-factories resembled the *corvée*, conducted in fulfillment of service debts to tsar or noble. Once these debts were extinguished, laborers returned to a rural life based on "traditional" institutions and techniques of land tenure. Meanwhile, the industrialists who organized city-factories were not members of an emergent capitalist class. Rather, those city-factories that were not directly managed by the state were given on lease to landowners whose social position rested on aristocratic rights and privileges.[6] They were not classified as cities and they lacked institutions of local government.

If eighteenth-century industrial development was focused in the circum-scribed space of the city-factory, urban development was largely indepen-dent of industrialism or trade. As Grigorii Lappo (1997) has pointed out, administrative centers and military garrisons accounted for most urban growth in tsarist Russia during the eighteenth century. Such cities were primarily tied not to commercial or industrial activity but to the state's drive for territorial expansion and strengthened administrative power.[7] Michael Hittle (1976), thus, referred to the eighteenth-century Russian city as a "service city," in which a large portion of residents were en-gaged in functions of state. Urban reforms, in this context, were oriented not to urban autonomy but to expanding the "infrastructural" power of the state.[8]

Petrine absolutism, in sum, initiated an eighteenth-century pattern in which significant industrial development and limited urban develop-ment were triggered by state initiative and were subordinated to the needs of the absolutist state. This fact was significant for political de-velopments, particularly when viewed in comparative perspective. In the leading industrial and military powers of Western Europe, autono-mous merchant or bourgeois classes challenged monarchical power, and the institutional bases of rural life were dramatically transformed. In contrast, during this period the tsarist state sought ways to promote industrial development and military power precisely *without* disrupting the matrix of classical power, particularly as tsarist governments felt increasingly threatened by peasant uprisings and other challenges to central authority. One implication was that, for all the substantial gains initially accomplished by the Petrine "intensification" of absolutist insti-tutions, broader-based processes of industrialization and urbanization were fundamentally blocked. The industrial sectors that had flourished under the impulse of state initiative in the eighteenth century weakened in the first half of the nineteenth. Precisely those governmental forms that had initially allowed Russia to "catch-up" with Europe's leading military powers contributed to subsequent "backwardness" (Gerschen-kron 1970; Crisp 1976).[9]

Late-Tsarist Industrialism:
The Sovereigntist-Developmental Pattern

The absolutist legacy shaped developments to the end of the tsarist pe-riod (and beyond). But the patterns of Russian industrialism and urban-ization were not static.[10] During the nineteenth century, particularly after Russia's ignominious defeat in the Crimean War (1854–1856) and the waves of reforms that followed it, a number of significant shifts occurred.

First, after the emancipation of the serfs in 1861, industrialism was increasingly based on institutions of free rather than bonded labor.[11] Second, although state consumption and production remained significant to the end of the tsarist period, a growing proportion of industrial activity was organized by autonomous entrepreneurs.[12] Third, even as the relative weight of state-sponsored industry diminished, the government began to play a novel role in industrialization—one that shaped a new "sovereigntist-developmental" formation of government in the second half of the nineteenth century. It involved redirecting key instruments of absolutist power to new ends. Crucial among these were the linked redeployments of the state budget and what I will call—anachronistically—"infrastructure."

As already noted, "communications" such as roads and canals were important mechanisms of absolutist state-building throughout Europe, serving both to expand and control trade and to augment the state's capacity to project coercive power and administrative control. During the nineteenth century, however, the initiative in building these works shifted in some countries. As canals, railroads, and other works became essential to industrial capitalism, private entrepreneurs played an increasingly important role in their construction. Seeds of a parallel development can be traced in Russia from the middle of the nineteenth century. A decree in 1857 passed Russian railroads into private hands. This transfer sparked a significant increase in railroad building that contributed to major industrial developments of late tsarism such as Baku oil, Donets coal and metallurgy, and textile production in the Ivanovo-Kineshma region where Rodniki was located (Von Laue 1963: 12). But the dominance of private initiative was short-lived. The Turkish War of 1877 convinced the tsarist government that poorly coordinated railroads presented a major strategic liability. In response, during the 1880s the Russian government took a more active role in regulating and building railroads.

The expanded state role in railroad construction presented a significant challenge to the tsarist government in raising the massive resources required for such works. The intimate link between railroad construction and capital accumulation was unexceptional. Railroad building everywhere in the world placed unique demands on the mobilization of financial resources, and sparked financial innovation, whether in international bond markets (as in the United States) or in industrial banks (as in some continental cases). In "backward" Russia, as Gerschenkron famously argued, the weakness of both capitalists and of banking meant that the fiscal mechanism of government provided the prop for railroad construction.[13] Thus, railroad construction was intimately linked to the state budget, another instrument of state-building under European absolutism that, in Russia, was redeployed to new ends.

The "modernization" of the Russian state budget was given an impetus during the Alexandrine reforms. A key development was the unification of the budget in 1963, which made the Ministry of Finance the single point through which all revenues and expenditures flowed, thus framing a series of problems—concerning budgetary balance, currency stability, and the balance of trade—that preoccupied Russian finance ministers until the end of the tsarist period (Von Laue 1963: 8). Unification also meant that the Ministry of Finance was given control over a range of state economic interests, most important among them the government's increasingly expansive role in railroad construction.

The first finance minister to deal extensively with railroad construction and management was Nikolai Bunge, who served from 1881 to 1886. Bunge extended regulatory control over private lines—creating, for the first time, a unified Russian network. His successor, Ivan Vyshnegradskii (1887 to 1892) pursued a conservative fiscal policy, emphasizing, in William Blackwell's phrase, the "austere disciplines of sacrifice and savings."[14] He forced exports, reduced imports through the highest tariff then in existence, and squeezed the peasantry while strictly limiting expenditures to available resources. Although Vyshnegradskii achieved balanced budgets for the first time since the Crimean War, his harsh taxation policy contributed to a disastrous famine in 1891 that ended his tenure.[15]

Vyshnegradskii's successor, Sergei Witte, was a major figure in shaping the pattern of the late tsarist governmentality. Witte had worked in the private railways of southern Russia before the resumption of state control, dealing with logistics and pricing problems for lines that were vital to Russia's grain exports. He then moved to the Department of Railways under Vyshnegradskii's Ministry of Finance, where he took further steps in consolidating the ministry's control over the railroads at the expense of the Ministry of Communications, which was reduced to addressing engineering problems.

As Theodore Von Laue has shown in a classic study, during his time in the railroad department Witte came to hold an expansive vision of the role that railroads could play in Russian economic development. But it was a vision that was still very much circumscribed by the imperatives of classical power. Witte evinced an "almost fanatical loyalty to autocracy" and, like many contemporaries, he saw the growing gaps between Russia and the leading industrial countries of the period as a threat to its survival. But his commitment to the strength and endurance of sovereign power was combined with a "deep interest in the theories of political economy," and a recognition of the autonomy of social and economic processes (Von Laue 1963: 49). Following the theories of Fredric List, Witte was convinced that the only way for monarchy to survive in Russia was through rapid industrial advance.[16] Rapid industrial advance, in turn, depended on a vastly expanded program of railroad construction, which, he imagined, would serve as the "flywheel" of economic development by spurring the activities of capitalists and workers.

The immediate challenge that presented itself was one of financing. In some respects, Witte's approach extended the policies of his predecessor. He continued to emphasize exports, and placed the fiscal burden on the "lower classes," in part because he was reluctant to impose business taxes that might curtail entrepreneurialism (Von Laue 1963: 34–35). But Witte did not share his predecessor's concern with fiscal balance. According to Von Laue, after being dissuaded from resorting to the printing press to fund his railroad program, Witte adopted the gold standard and then proceeded to develop a massive program of spending based on borrowing, both domestic and foreign. In doing so, he dramatically increased the volume of outlays on the railroads, launched the Trans-Siberian—a dream of successive tsarist governments—and vastly expanded the capacity of the network in European Russia.[17]

For Von Laue, Witte's program was the boldest initiative "[i]n the history of Russian economic policy since the Crimean War—or, in fact, since Peter the Great" (1963: 35). And it can, indeed, be situated in a genealogical line that extends from the Petrine effort to promote state-led industrialization. But it differed from earlier governmental forms in important ways. Previous efforts to spur economic development had been "conservative" in that they aimed to reconcile industrialization with the preservation of traditional institutions of land tenure and structures of authority. In other words, they tried to industrialize without disrupting the existing patterns of adjustment between population and production. Witte, by contrast, imagined that railroad construction would spur significant reorganization of the population, particularly of the still enormous peasantry. To this end, he introduced a "fourth" class in order to make the railroads more accessible to the poorest Russians. Even more crucially, in Witte's hands railroad construction was no longer a prop for state sanctioned or organized industry. Rather, it was intended to spur *private* economic activity.[18]

At one level Witte's program was spectacularly successful. The "big push" of capital accumulation was followed by a "big spurt" of industrial development, based in part on direct government consumption (particularly in railroad construction and military equipment), and in part on the activities of private entrepreneurs.[19] This spurt was interrupted by the revolution of 1905, but resumed afterwards. The question of whether it would have been enough to put Russia on a path to self-sustaining industrialization based on private capital has been a topic of intense dispute. Here we can just make two points about events as they actually unfolded. First, in the longer term, the late-tsarist redeployment of key instruments of absolutist state-building was crucial to the future formation of Soviet government, which began from the nexus of capital accumulation, infrastructure development, and industrialism.

The second point concerns the development of urban modernity in late-tsarist Russia. Notwithstanding the significant episodes of industrialization that followed the railroad construction boom, the reorganization of populations around cities was limited. The Emancipation Act of 1861, which freed large parts of the population from rural bondage, paradoxically created disincentives for rural communes to allow members to leave permanently (Gerschenkron 1968). These disincentives left their mark on Russia's urban-industrial pattern. In the late nineteenth century over 60 percent of manufacturing jobs were in rural areas (Rowland 1976: 124, n. 34). Even where industry was located in cities, urban growth was limited. A phenomenon of itinerant labor was prevalent in urban industry, due, in part, to continued barriers to permanent relocation from the countryside that were removed only with the Stolypin reforms following the 1905–1907 revolts. On the eve of World War I, only 20 percent of the total Russian population was urban. This level had been reached in the United States by 1850, at which time over 50 percent of the British population lived in cities.[20] In sum, industrial growth was only weakly linked to urbanization. To the end of the tsarist period, Russia lacked those critical conditions in response to which, in other countries, projects of social modernity took shape. We return to the theme of social modernity in the next chapter. The present discussion addresses the broad biopolitical pattern of Soviet government.

TOWARD TOTAL PLANNING:
THE DISCIPLINARY-BIOPOLITICAL PATTERN

The problem of government in Russia was fundamentally reconfigured by the emergence of national planning over the Soviet Union's first decade. The point may seem obvious, but it has not always been taken for granted. Scholars have long noted that Soviet planning had much in common with tsarist institutions of development driven by state initiative and by massive coercion. These continuities are significant, but it is equally crucial to keep in view what was new in the Soviet system.[21] As we have seen, successive tsarist governments were reluctant to disrupt patterns of life in a way that would lead to large-scale migration or urbanization. The mobilization of populations for industry or urban construction continued to be circumscribed by sovereign power. In this sense, and with the possible exception of its very last years, the tsarist regime had always been conservative with respect to transforming collective life, even when it was successfully promoting industrial development. By contrast, Soviet state-led industrialization was accompanied by explicit efforts to revolutionize the national population's conditions of existence, first of all by rearranging it over national space. These efforts encompassed the agrarian sector, from which the Soviet government ultimately resolved to derive a surplus not only by extracting resources through taxation or confiscation, as had been the absolutist pattern, but also through violent transformation of rural production. They also included a readjustment of population around new industrial enterprises and, by extension, the creation of new cities. It was the Soviet resolve to promote industrialization, *accompanied by* state-led transformation of collective life, that defined the distinctive formation of Soviet government. In the remainder of this chapter, I trace the emergence of this dynamic through three key episodes: first, the formulation of the state plan for electrification in the early 1920s; second, the planning debates in the middle of the decade; and third, in the late 1920s, the onset of total planning with the five-year plan.

GOELRO: Infrastructure and National Economy

It has long been recognized that Marxist theory provided the young Soviet state with little guidance in the practical management of a socialist society; and scholars agree that the Soviet leadership had no clear understanding of the institutions that would be appropriate to a socialist country after the Revolution (e.g., Treml 1969). The tight administrative controls over production and distribution established under War Communism (borrowed, in part, from tsarist wartime measures) were dispersed among different planning organs, and were ad hoc, unconnected to a central plan.[22] The first substantial efforts at national planning are generally traced back to GOELRO—the State Commission for the Electrification of Russia (*Gosudarstvennaia Komissiia po Elektrifikatsii Rossii*)—formed in the midst of the Civil War in early 1920.[23] In one sense, the Commission took up a familiar role of the tsarist government: investing in infrastructure to promote national development and military strength. But it introduced a novel *biopolitical* proposition that would prove to have shattering implications. Namely, that state-directed infrastructure development must be linked to a total plan for the industrial development of the country as a whole.

Russia was not the only country in which "infrastructure" emerged as a matter of state concern in a new way in the early twentieth century. In the nineteenth century government involvement in infrastructure and economic discussions of infrastructure focused on individual "public works," from which some general benefit would accrue. In the early decades of the twentieth century, by contrast, these works were linked to more systemic understandings of national economies—indeed, to the articulation of the national economy per se as an object of knowledge and as a space of regulation.[24] Taking the point one step further, the distinction between "public works" and what came, by the mid twentieth century, to be called "infrastructure," is that where the former focused on relatively local and specific benefits, the latter tended to be conceptualized in broader terms as an "underlying system"—or, as Soviet planners of the 1920s called it, a "network" (*set'*)—that was vital to the national economy as a whole.[25]

In most combatant countries, this problem of infrastructure and national economic coordination was posed with clarity and urgency during World War I, particularly in relation to railroads and, crucially for our story, electricity. The fragmented character of existing power production facilities and distribution grids, many of which had been developed piecemeal by private entrepreneurs, limited governments' ability to mobilize the totality of national resources for war. In various countries proposals emerged to invest in new production facilities and to integrate national grids. In these respects, the tsarist government's policy during World War I conformed to the broader pattern. It was after World War I that the Soviet path diverged. In most countries, conservative reaction to the expansion of state prerogative during World War I led to retrenchment after its conclusion. In the Soviet Union, however, institutions of planning and administrative control first developed during the war were adapted initially to the mobilizational requirements of the Civil War and, subsequently, to the demands of industrial development, as those who ultimately prevailed in the industrialization debates understood them.

According to E. H. Carr, whose multivolume work on the 1920s is drawn on extensively here, discussions during the early period of War Communism focused on individually planned "public works"—such as power stations and industries related to the extraction of raw materials—that were thought crucial to postwar reconstruction. Incipient plans for these projects, most of which had been inherited from pre-war or wartime initiatives of the tsarist government, receded during the Civil War, as resources and the attention of the Soviet leadership were focused on short-term crises (Carr 1950: 366–67). Among these were energy shortages, which intensified in 1919 with the interruption of deliveries from the coal basins of southern Russia. In this context Lenin sought advice from Gleb Krzhizhanovskii, an old Bolshevik with training, not coincidentally, in railroad engineering. Krzhizhanovskii had recently become the head of the Moscow power utility, Elektroperedacha, where he worked on the integration of the Moscow grid and on its supply through a regional power station. His initial response to Lenin's request for help focused on the use of locally available fuels—in particular peat—to power regional electric stations. But it was Krzhizhanovskii's suggestion that regional power stations might play a broader role in industrial reconstruction and development that, according to Alex Cummins' study, "The Road to NEP," caught Lenin's attention (1988: 69–70).

Lenin encouraged Krzhizhanovskii to elaborate this dimension of his thinking in a direction that, though not entirely novel in conception, was revolutionary as a practical proposition. Krzhizhanovskii was convinced that industrial advance in Russia depended on the development of electricity infrastructure. And he was convinced that developing this infrastructure was an appropriate role for state intervention. In one sense, the tsarist government had already been down this path in the state railroad construction drive. But Krzhizhanovskii, the former railroad engineer, saw the problems of electricity development as distinct. In a telling comment, he noted that where railroad planning had focused on individual lines, electricity had to be planned in terms of a network (*set'*), that is, an integrated complex of facilities. We can better understand this comment if we consider how late-tsarist ministers and Soviet planners, respectively, saw the problem of economic development.

According to Von Laue, by the early 1890s it was assumed that the basic geography of the Russian railroad system had already been established (the Trans-Siberian was one key exception).[26] The main task for tsarist railroad planners was to improve existing lines and to add capacity, thus, the focus on individual lines. This was not, however, the assumption of Soviet planners, who anticipated massive industrial construction in undeveloped regions of the country. In order to determine the "location, type, capacity, and number of regional power stations," it was necessary to know where industrial development would take place, and what requirements for power would be (Cummins 1988: 274). Krzhizhanovskii's "network" was precisely the complex of facilities—not just the electrical grid itself but the entire set of interrelated industrial enterprises, transport systems, and human settlements—for which electricity infrastructure had to be planned. The revolutionary implication, as Cummins observes, was that a "state plan for the entire economy had to be developed prior to the emergence of a detailed one for the electrification of Russia" (1988: 113). And this was precisely how Krzhizhanovskii defined the scope of GOELRO's work. In the introduction to GOELRO's final report he wrote that, "[d]rawing up a plan for the electrification of Russia means furnishing a guiding line to all constructive economic activity, the framework for the realization of a unified state plan of national economy" (Krzhizhanovsky Power Institute 1936: 11). We are a long way from public works as the "flywheel" of economic development.

GOELRO's work—which began in February 1920 and continued to the end of the year—focused on precisely this problem of relating electricity development to industrial development in the economy as a whole. The Commission was divided into working groups comprised of economists, engineers, agronomists, chemists, metallurgists, and hydrologists, each of which was given responsibility for planning in a region of the country. As Jonathan Coopersmith points out in *The Electrification of Russia, 1880–1926* (1992), the form of planning conducted by these groups was substantive, concerned with planning input-output relationships among diverse areas of a future industrial economy: relevant fuel sources for various means of electricity production, the probable future needs of industry for inputs and services and, crucially, the needs of future populations. Through such planning, industrialization, energy development, the distribution of populations, and the creation of cities were linked to production of the most mundane goods for satisfying a population's daily needs. Thus, in a 1921 article published in *Pravda*, Lenin wrote admiringly that thanks to GOELRO

> We have export calculations [*raschety spetsov*] for all basic questions. We have calculations for all sectors of industrial production. We have—one small example—a balance of the volume of production of leather, shoes for two pairs per person (300 million pairs) etc. In sum, we have the material and financial balance of electrification" (Lenin 1967 [1921]: 341)

We will see that precisely this kind of substantive, integrated planning that balanced the correlative needs of population and production became the basic model for the Soviet social welfare planning.

The timing of GOELRO's activities—which concluded at the end of 1920—proved felicitous. With the end of the Civil War in sight, and a war with Poland ended by treaty agreement, opinion consolidated around a revived program of industrial planning. In this context, GOELRO's work stood out from various plans created by other agencies engaged in administering the Soviet wartime economy. It was the only attempt to link developments in one sector to those in the economy as a whole. Consequently, at the time of its publication the GOELRO plan was, as Cummins notes, "the only significant compilation of data for the entire economy" (1988: 232), and, as Lenin wrote in 1921, "[t]he only serious work on the question of a unified economic plan" (Gosudarstvennaia Komissiia po Elektrifikatsii Rossii 1960: 68). It was ultimately accepted by the Eighth Congress of Soviets as the basis for a national economic plan (Cummins 1988: 261–62).

Scholars have located the longer-term significance of GOELRO's work at various levels. The "First Priority" projects it identified were quickly completed. Specific organizations and individuals (first of all, Krzhizhanovskii) who were central to GOELRO were also central to the first five-year plan. GOELRO itself was incorporated into Gosplan, the agency formed in early 1921 that, by the second half of the 1920s, became the preeminent planning body in the Soviet Union (Cummins 1988: 271). And GOELRO's planning process provided a rough template for the approach taken in the five-year plans, which also rested on material balances and a vision of transformation driven by large capital-intensive projects (Carr and Davies 1969: 837).

But most critically for our purposes, GOELRO was a decisive step in the changing ontology of government in the Soviet Union. As Cummins notes, Soviet leaders were beginning to believe that "reality was more malleable than had previously been thought possible" (1988: 230); that the "laws" of the social and economic milieu might not be as rigid as previously assumed. In this sense, the electrification plan pointed definitively to the future of total planning. The radicalization of the propositions put forth in GOELRO—that electricity development had to rest on a plan for the economy as a whole—was that electricity development had to rest on an actually planned (or at least centrally administered) economy. Indeed, subsequent Soviet authors treated GOELRO precisely as a decisive step in that direction. As one elegiac text put it a little over a decade later, "the trend of development of electrification in the U.S.S.R." could be "expressed in the following terms: *the creation of a unified electric power system covering the whole country, including the production, transmission and consumption of energy on a single technical and organizational foundation. The necessary conditions for this are real planned economy and planned electrification, organically interrelated.*"[27]

Dictatorship of Finance

Having a national economic plan, of course, does not mean that one has a "command economy," that is, an economy run by administrative decree.[28] And a "real planned economy," or even a conception of what that might mean in practice, was far from developed in GOELRO. Nor was it obvious that the Soviet road would lead in that direction. With the sudden loosening that ended War Communism and ushered in the New Economic Policy (NEP) the question of the appropriate state role in the economy was reopened, and hotly discussed. One scene for these debates in the 1920s was the struggle from the onset of NEP to define the character of the government budget. These debates deserve attention here as a key space in which the political ontology of Soviet socialism was worked out.[29]

In the second half of the nineteenth century, particularly with the unification of the budget mentioned earlier, tsarist ministers of finance increasingly had to manage the budget as a tricky balance between the expenditure needs of the state and a variety of external constraints on available resources, including the amount of taxes that could be collected from the peasantry, the limits to the government's willingness to tax entrepreneurs, and the whims of domestic and foreign creditors. Thus, the state budget of late tsarism increasingly bore the key characteristics of a liberal technology of government. It served as a mechanism of translation between the external domain of the economy and the activities of the state, and was specifically concerned with the *limitations* that the former imposed on the latter. This "liberal" function of the budget was significantly diminished during World War I. Administrative control was extended over much of the economy, meaning that state intervention increasingly took on a planning or administrative rather than a financial character, and budgetary institutions were substantially undermined, due to massive money emission and the transference of war financing to an "extraordinary" budget (Davies 1958).

This state of affairs persisted into the period of War Communism. As R. W. Davies observes in his comprehensive study of the Soviet budgetary system, in the period 1918 to 1921 a "wide range of activities and functions [were] included in the budget, and therefore, on paper at least, subject to budget control" (1958: 35). But "budget control" did not involve adjusting expenditures to match available revenues (this problem was obviated by printing money, effectively wiping out fiscal constraints—and the value of money[30]). Rather, the budget reflected material processes in an economy organized by administrative decree. And it did this, Davies points out, in a rather imprecise way.[31]

Various developments during War Communism found their way into Soviet budgetary practice. Among these was an initial experimentation with a norm-based—rather than money-based—system for allocating resources (Davies 1958: 43–44). But in the nearer term these tendencies were reversed with the onset of NEP. As administrative controls were withdrawn from significant areas of the economy, the state budget reflected a narrower range of activities. The practice of "budgeting" changed accordingly. Currency reforms in 1922 and 1923 imposed a requirement of monetary stability. Consequently, for the first time the Soviet government had to worry about a balanced budget—and, therefore, about limiting state activity to what could be paid for with current revenue—rather than depending on the printing press or outright coercion.

In this context, The People's Commissariat of Finance, or Narkomfin (Narodnyi Komissariat Finansov), emerged as a central figure in defining the activities of the state—or, at least, in defining the *limits* on those activities imposed by a logic of budgetary constraints. In 1923 and 1924, Narkomfin developed an increasingly systematic approach to compiling revenue estimates in relationship to which the size of expenditures could be constrained. These limits were expressed in what were called "control figures" (*kontrol'nye tsifry*)—quantitative limits imposed on the expenditures of each government department. The control figures were, as Davies notes, the only "economic plan" that existed during the early years of NEP, and their growing importance in regulating the activity of state agencies meant that "the extent to which the state sector could expand depended primarily on the resources which the financial system could accumulate 'from outside'" (1958: 98). "Outside," here, referred to activity in the market, small artisan production, and most importantly in the rural sector, which continued to dominate the Russian economy.[32] The crucial point is the general model of budgetary regulation. Based on expected economic activity and, thus, projected tax receipts, planners sought to project the financial constraints within which expenditure plans had to work. The economist Iurii Larin, who played an important role in importing lessons of the German wartime planning experience to the Soviet Union (Treml 1969), wrote of a "dictatorship" of finance (Carr 1958: 460). Many contemporaries referred, in a phrase with contemporary resonance, to financial discipline.

According to Davies, this shift from a "planning" budget to a "financial" budget (we might say, following Nikolas Rose (1999), to a *budgetized* budget) also corresponded to a significant professionalization in budgeting practice. "The ambitious, hasty, crude, and erroneous" budgets prepared during the period of War Communism, which largely reflected decisions in physical planning, "bore little resemblance to the realistic and carefully prepared, if still not very refined" budget of the mid-1920s (Davies 1958: 59). But the meaning of a "realistic" budget would soon be hotly disputed. What was the reality that mattered? As the 1920s progressed, and as emphasis shifted to rapid industrialization and, thus, to increased levels of capital investment, two positions emerged. One, associated with genetic planning, saw budgeting as a mechanism for modulating an expanded range of state activities in relation to the "autonomous" processes of the social and economic milieu. The other, associated with teleological planning, effectively adapted the budgetary practice of War Communism; it saw the budget not as a key (liberal) governmental technology but as a reflection of administrative decisions made in a system of total planning.[33]

Genetic and Teleological

Genetic (*geneticheskoe*) planning—whose main proponents included non-Party economists such as Vladimir Groman and Vladimir Bazarov in Gosplan and Nikolai Kondrat'ev, founder of the Conjuncture Institute— began by studying existing conditions and historical tendencies in

order to determine, by extrapolation, likely future trajectories of transformation. As Raimondo Cubeddu has written, the emphasis in genetic
planning was placed on understanding "the manner of, or the laws governing, the formation of present and future conditions."[34] The "genetic"
element is one part of what Foucault, in his analysis of liberalism, called
the *series*: that succession of events that extends from the past into an
uncertain future that can be known only probabilistically. This emphasis
on past tendencies and probable trajectories of future development corresponded to a vision of intervention that was constrained by external
processes, which, in the mid-1920s, meant peasant production and conditions in the market (such as demand for manufactured goods). The major
task of planning activity, in the genetic view, was to accurately predict the
dynamics of these autonomous processes, to identify resources available
to the state and, thereby, to estimate the possible scope of investment. In
sum, genetic planning distinguished between the sphere of government,
in which planners had instrumental control, and the milieu that they did
not control or, rather, that they could modulate but not totalize. In this
important sense genetic planning shared the political ontology of liberalism and the emphasis on limits found in Narkomfin, but adapted both to
an expanded state role in economic life.

Teleological planning—whose major exponents included the Gosplan
economist Stanislav Strumilin, as well as Krzhizhanovskii, who was by
the late 1920s serving a second tour as the head of Gosplan—focused
on the telos, or the endpoint, that planners wished to achieve. It did not
entirely ignore present circumstances, but as Carr and Davies note, when
seeking to understand the limits of planned transformation, teleological
planners tended "to talk in terms not so much of market limitations"—
that is, of constraints imposed by autonomous processes "outside" the
state—"as of physical limitations in general" (1969: 791). Teleological
planning did not recognize the distinction between the sphere of planning
activity and an external environment or milieu. It simply assumed that
the entire field of collective life could be subject to instrumental control
by the state. Planning was effectively an exercise in optimization that
was, as Strumilin argued, closer to the problems of engineering than to
those of liberal political economy.

For some subsequent observers, the genetic and teleological approaches
were two sides of the same coin. Thus, for Peter Rutland, the choice
between genetic and teleological approaches was simply a question concerning the "selection of means appropriate to a given end" (1985: 79).[35]
But in fact, these two positions implied utterly different views of government, of its instruments and possible activities, and of the objects on
which it worked. And these differences became increasingly apparent as
the political environment shifted. Genetic and teleological planners were

TABLE 2.2.
Genetic versus Teleological Planning

	Genetic	Teleological
Object of Knowledge	The regularities of the milieu	The end-point or *telos* of planning efforts
Knowledge Form	*Prognostication* of social and economic processes based on "laws" of development	Catalogue or *inventory* of physical elements available to be rearranged through instrumental intervention
Mode of Intervention	Modulated intervention in selected domains	Total intervention to physically re-order the elements of collective life
Constraints on Planning	Limited state resources; social and economic laws	Physical limits of elements that can be reordered
Political Ontology	The state works on external processes fundamentally heterogeneous to the state	The state as a total "system without environment" (Hughes 1987: 53)

initially aligned against the planning skeptics in Narkomfin. But by the mid- to late 1920s genetic and teleological defined the two major positions on the future development of the Soviet economy. The choice between them was of enormous consequence.

The point of inflection in this development was 1925, when Soviet economists began to anticipate the end of growth based on the recovery of the prewar economy.[36] General sentiment shifted toward greater planned intervention, particularly in industry, and Gosplan made a bold claim for relevance by issuing its own set of "control figures" for 1925–1926, formulated by the organization's leading economists (Dobb 1948: 324–26). These control figures contained elements of both genetic and teleological approaches. In contrast to the control figures of Narkomfin, they proposed a clear orientation to a telos—a planned future to be attained through the will of the state. Trotsky, thus, wrote that Gosplan's 1925–1926 control figures showed that state planners were not "in the position of astronomers who 'try to grasp the dynamics of processes completely outside their control.'" Each control figure presented "not merely a photograph"—that is, a reflection of external reality—"but a command."[37] At the same time, Gosplan's control figures evinced a strong genetic emphasis on the external factors that limited the scope of state intervention. Gosplan's introduction to the published control figures noted, thus, that "regularities" had become apparent in the postrevolutionary economy, and that the task for planners lay in "extrapolating the time series, in ascertaining trends of development and finding coefficients describing the dynamics of the present and the near future" (Gosplan 1964 [1925]: 393).

The Gosplan control figures' focus on regularities of the milieu and on the *series*, that extended from a known past to an uncertain future, corresponded to an emphasis on the limits imposed by outside forces. This concern with constraints was reflected in the process through which the control figures were formulated. Gosplan's economists consulted extensively with industry and economic ministries to arrive at realistic projections of aggregate production, profit, and export in various sectors of the Soviet economy (Carr 1958: 501). By basing the control figures on these projections, planners sought to ensure that, as Groman put it, the state "should expand only in proportion to the value of goods in circulation," thus fixing "the central quantities in our prognosis for the future."[38] Gosplan's control figures thus continued to function as a kind of regulatory mechanism that modulated planned intervention by the state in relationship to market dynamics.

But even as Gosplan's control figures gained in prominence and professionalism, a new split developed, this time within Gosplan itself. Between the 14th Party Congress in December 1925, when Stalin announced the path to industrialization, sealing the fate of the planning skeptics in Narkomfin, and the 15th Party Congress in 1927, when the discussion focused exclusively on the five-year plan, Bazarov and Groman continued to work on the control figures for 1926–1927 and for 1927–1928. Chastened by, among other things, the failure to anticipate a bad harvest in the first set of control figures, they prepared their plans with increasing circumspection and caution. Meanwhile Strumilin, the Party economist, shifted to work on the five-year plan—which meant a focus on major projects, and on the teleological problem of defining the endpoint of planned development.

Initially, it seemed to many observers that the genetic and teleological approaches were simply appropriate to different planning tasks. Since 1925 "perspective" planning had been recognized to contain a greater teleological element, since over the long term government decisions would have greater weight. Genetic planning, meanwhile, was seen to have greater relevance for year-to-year operational plans. In the mid 1920s, thus, genetic and teleological approaches were seen as complimentary. But the genetic planners' circumspection and restraint could not be reconciled with the pace of planned growth demanded by the first five-year plan, and by the late 1920s genetic planning was fatefully associated with a cluster of untenable positions: an insistence on conforming to the regularities and laws of development posited by liberal political economy; an emphasis on constraints and limits to growth; and, corresponding to these, submission to a historical legacy of backwardness bequeathed to the Soviet state by Russia's imperial past. As R. E. Vaisberg, a supporter of Strumilin's approach to five-year planning and the author of attacks on Bazarov and Groman, put it, "the genetic approach implied acceptance of the 'genetic inheritance' of 300 years of Tsarism."[39]

In this atmosphere, the teleological planners rejected the relevance of genetic planning to the conditions of Soviet socialism in categorical terms. In doing so, they also rejected the entire political ontology of liberalism upon which it rested: the very premise that government had to conform to laws of an "external" social or economic reality, that it should be bound by the extrapolatory line that connected the past to the future. Thus, Krzhizhanovskii wrote in 1927 that conditions of socialist economic transformation, in which the "economic organism will be torn asunder," are particularly difficult "for any prognosis, since the very nature of [the economy's] transitional structure largely *precludes extrapolation from the economic dynamics of the past*" (Krzhizhanovskii 1964 [1927]: 415; italics added). Strumilin wrote in similar terms:

> We ... deny that extrapolation methods are in any significant degree applicable in the realm of perspective planning, and do so not only because these methods are in general most unreliable for extending observed development curves several years into the future, but because of another factor that is far more important for us. We are entering a new phase of development, with the creative will of the revolutionary proletariat *irresistibly driving a wedge between our past and our future*" (Strumilin 1964 [1927]: 84).

The genetic planners defended themselves, arguing that in ignoring the genetic element—in driving a "wedge" between the past and the planned future—the realism of plans was eroded. Kondrat'ev, in a critique of the planning methods Strumilin outlined for the first five-year plan, wrote that in neglecting the regularities of the economy, teleological planners were "cutting the thread between ... projections and reality" and that from there it was "but a step, and a small one at that, to the framing of plans that are completely arbitrary" (Kondrat'ev 1964 [1927]: 442). Indeed, the practices that had lent "realism" to genetic planning were abandoned. As Carr and Davies write, "from 1928 onward, adherents of the teleological approach to planning were no longer limited by the need to show that their plans were compatible with the market situation" (1969: 801). What is more, "the lengthy procedure of consultation followed in preparing the control figures in 1926 and 1927"—a procedure that was necessary if these figures were to accurately reflect the reality of economic life in the country, and to achieve internal consistency—was deemphasized (Carr and Davies 1969: 818). Financial scarcity, that crucial reality principle of liberal government, was excluded from serious consideration in long-term planning; budgeting, Davies notes, was dealt with "in complete isolation from the economic plans in physical terms" (1958: 99).

That said, we should be attentive to what kind of "realism" was in question in each case; for precisely the question of reality—which is to say of ontology—was in question in these debates. If one means by realism the extent to which plans reflected an autonomous social or economic reality, then the genetic critics were right: planners ignored "objective" constraints. But teleological planners saw themselves as introducing a new kind of "realism" and a new kind of "objectivity." Our concern here is not with the *value* of this alternative "truth" (a question upon which subsequent events have rendered sufficient judgment) but with the conditions of its intelligibility.

For teleological planners, the question was no longer that of the historical series or of economic equilibrium or balance, achieved by modulating state activity in relation to external circumstances. Rather, emphasis was increasingly placed on establishing the *internal consistency* of planning assumptions. In this light, key terms of genetic planning practice—and, thus, the terms of liberal government that still persisted in it—were not so much rejected as redeployed and given new meaning. Krzhizhanovskii, thus, wrote in 1927 of the "series" as a key figure of teleological planning that referred not to a sequence of autonomous events that extended from the past to the unknown future, but a series "in the mathematical sense, i.e. a series coordinated by an internal law." This series did not reflect external dynamics, but was "the demonstration of a system of numbers" (1964 [1927]: 422, n.1). Similarly, a new conception of "balance" emerged. Strumilin wrote in the same year that planning targets must be "sufficiently realistic," by which he meant that they had to be "coordinated with each other, in all their parts—linked like a chain in their interdependence—and brought strictly into line with the country's available resources and the real potentials for its development" (Strumilin 1964 [1927]: 432).[40]

The new demand for "internal consistency"—entirely distinct from the prior emphasis on external constraints—certainly implied its own form of realism, and its own form of veridiction, a fact that need not be diminished by the crude practice of teleological planning in the early years. If teleological planning no longer required extensive consultation with industry or careful projection of historical "series" into an uncertain future, then it demanded an expanded and more meticulous concern with input-output planning of various sectors of the economy. It also demanded an increasingly complex process of "successive approximations" through which plans for individual projects and for industrial development in regions could be brought into balance.[41]

Once the logic of teleological planning took hold it gained a momentum of its own, whose direction was a universe away from the control figures of 1925–1926. The earlier control figures had retained a focus on limits, on the constraints placed on new investments and on the need for carefully targeting them to bottlenecks in the economy. "As for new construction," Gosplan had noted in the restrained atmosphere of 1925, "for the time being it is feasible only within very narrow limits: only where it is necessary for activating existing means of production or where low points that are beginning to appear in particular segments of the economy threaten to be a draw on the growth of the national production as a whole" (Gosplan 1964 [1925]: 397). But by the end of the decade, when planners encountered inevitable bottlenecks, shortfalls, and resistances, their response was no longer to moderate the scope of planned state investment or to carefully target investments in order to remain within budgetary constraints. Rather, as Moshe Lewin has put it, "[t]he more bottlenecks and crisis areas that appeared, the greater the urge to close loopholes by putting the hand on more levers" (1973: 276). "Putting the hand on more levers" meant that administrative and coercive apparatuses had to expand to cover ever more areas of economic and social life, and that planning apparatuses had to grow in step. "By 1928," according to Carr and Davies , "the constellation of experts in Gosplan reproduced in miniature the structure of economic administration in the country as a whole" (1969: 806). With all the absurdity of Borges's map—drawn on the same scale as the territory it described—the logical conclusion of teleological planning was that the planning apparatus had to replicate the complex substantive totality that it sought to control and transform.[42]

The Political Ontology of Total Planning

In the discussions of teleological planning, and in the practical steps taken by the Soviet government, a series of radical biopolitical propositions took shape that opposed, in every way, the political ontology of liberalism. The point should be emphasized: illiberal *but* biopolitical. The foundational assumption of liberalism was that "society" should be understood as an autonomous realm, whose natural law was the market. Liberalism was initially articulated as an injunction against state intervention, or at least as an argument against interventions that ignored the specific reality and laws of the economic and social milieu. Liberal government had to reconcile itself to an uncertain future that, as Foucault noted, "is not exactly controllable, not precisely measured or measurable" (2007: 31).

The teleological approach that took shape around the first five-year plan dismissed the strictures imposed by the putatively autonomous laws

of society. It insisted on the possibility of governing things in their immediate physical reality. Such physical planning was not unique to the
Soviet Union. It inherited, as we have seen, the institutions of War Communism, tsarist wartime measures and, for that matter, wartime planning
in capitalist countries during World War I.[43] All of these approaches, in
one fashion or another, at one scale or another, sought to know and manage the physical resources of national economies as a whole. But these
other approaches to total planning were responses to the exigency of exceptional situations—most centrally war. In the discussions of the 1920s,
teleological planning was, to be sure, justified in part by a war that was
feverishly anticipated by many in the Soviet leadership. Krzhizhanovskii
was referring to the battle between genetic and teleological planners
when he wrote in the summer of 1928 that "'planned discipline' rather
than finance would be the artery of war in the Soviet Union."[44] But the
schemas of planning evolved, over time, into the routinized and normal
operation of the state.

The name that has been given to a political *regime* based on such total
intervention—that is, a political system with relative stability and capacity for reproduction over time—is totalitarianism. In Sovietological discussions, the basic features of totalitarianism include a distinctive ideological formation, the indiscriminate and pervasive use of terror, and state
control in all areas of collective life. Certainly, there is a connection between terror and teleological planning, which, as its proponents insisted,
"freed" the present from constraints imposed by external circumstances,
from the "genetic" inheritance of the past, and subjected it to the pure
instrumental will of planners. Alexander Ehrlich, in his classic study of
the industrialization debates, cited one proponent of the teleological approach who captured this connection between planners' "freedom" and
teleological planning in an exemplary fashion: "[w]e deliberately depict
a model of industry to ourselves as we want it, so that it may be brought
into existence. ... [W]e free ourselves to a considerable extent in the
given circumstances from the clutches of what is given by history; we
break the old bounds and gain a considerably greater creative freedom."[45]
It takes no great imagination to understand that this "creative freedom"
was, as Erlich notes, intimately related to a "supreme readiness to eradi-
cate everything that cannot be effectively controlled" (1960: 180).

But what form of power is exercised in this regime of total control
and pure instrumentality? For totalitarian theory, the answer is rather
straightforward: it is a form of repressive power, power-over; and that
thing over which power is held and exercised, in this view, is "society."[46]
My objection to this formulation is not that of the "revision" to classic
Sovietology that took shape in the 1970s, which argued that the Soviet
system could be better understood in terms of interest groups and dis-

persed bases of power—in other words, that Soviet "society" was active, that it was not entirely subjugated. Rather, it is that the original Sovietological claim—that totalitarianism was defined precisely by the total domination of society by the state—takes *liberal* political ontology for granted. The principle of teleological planning was not exactly the domination of society. Rather it was that society, as such, was irrelevant to the considerations of total planning. Through which general technology of power, then, *did* total planning operate?

Here the Foucualtian interpretive analytic provides an essential guide, even if he never took up the totalitarian cases as objects of sustained analysis. Krzhizhanovskii's note that financial planning had to give way to "planned discipline"—a phrase frequently used during this period—was, at one level, precisely accurate. "Discipline" was, to be sure, a critical technology of power in the Soviet Union. The dimension of disciplinary power I have in mind is not that meticulous hold on the body, the carefully rationalized economy of movements that has attracted the attention of most observers who have taken up Foucault's concepts in studies of Russia.[47] Rather, I have in mind Foucault's concept of disciplinary space and the form of control exercised within it. Foucault wrote that disciplinary power "consists first of all in positing a model, an optimal model that is constructed in terms of a certain result" (2007: 84). The words could have come from a teleological planner. So too could Foucault's description of the "totalizing" assumptions of disciplinary power.[48] "By definition," he noted, "discipline regulates everything. Discipline allows nothing to escape. Not only does it not allow things to run their course, its principle is that things, the smallest things, must not be abandoned to themselves" (Foucault 2007: 45).

But what was the formation of government in which discipline was mobilized? At one level, Soviet teleological planning, with its deployment of disciplinary power to meet the aims of the state, was continuous with tsarist precedent. One only need compare the city-factories of the eighteenth century to small Soviet cities—or, for an even more precise analogy, to the "special settlements" recently analyzed by Lynn Viola (2003)—to find a certain affinity between the two. But this comparison has limits that are as revealing as the convergences. The city-factories evolved within, and were circumscribed by, feudal and absolutist institutions. Soviet "disciplinary" forms, by contrast, no longer operated in such circumscribed spaces. It might be simplest to say that discipline became a general technology of *biopolitical* government, through which the basic relationship between state and population was defined.

As such, Soviet total planning raised problems that were never raised in the context of classical monarchy. In tsarism disciplinary technology was attached to and circumscribed by a form of government that sought to avoid disrupting existing adjustments between population, production, and mechanisms of need fulfillment. Soviet discipline, by contrast, proposed to utterly transform these relationships. The five-year plan itself framed the problem: it proposed to begin from the needs of industry, to identify bottlenecks and seek to address them. This was planning as a logistical optimization problem from which everything else flowed. In order to plan for the development of industry, one needed to plan inputs to production, not only material inputs but also human labor. If human labor had to be planned, then the distribution of human beings across national space had to be planned. If the distribution of human beings had to be planned, then the means for satisfying their daily needs— health facilities, schools, and housing, which was itself conceived as an "essential instrument of production" (Carr and Davies 1969: 618)— also required planning. The implication was that another technology of power had to be introduced into the totalitarian "system of correlation," one that dealt with the health, welfare, and conditions of existence of human populations. In this sense Soviet industrial planning posed the questions to which city-building, the diagram of Soviet social modernity, provided answers.

CHAPTER THREE

City-building

> So we see how a technological norm gradually reflects an
> idea of society and its hierarchy of values, how a decision
> to normalize assumes the representation of a possible whole
> of correlative, complementary or compensatory decisions.
> ... The representation of this totality of reciprocally relative
> norms is planning.
> —Georges Canguilhem, "From the Social to the Vital"[1]

THE INDUSTRIALIZATION DEBATES, and their conclusion with the rise of a centrally administered economy, established the framework for a distinctive Soviet biopolitics based on teleological planning. Its logical implication was that the entirety of collective life must be part of a plan: not just industrial production, but the people who work in industrial enterprises along with the apparatus required to meet their daily needs. This chapter examines how Soviet planners worked out these latter questions, which relate to the Soviet effort to constitute the health, welfare, and conditions of existence of populations as objects of knowledge and targets of intervention.

One crucial scene in the development of this Soviet project of social modernity was the discussions among architects and urbanists in the late 1920s and early 1930s. The 1920s were a fertile period of experimentation with the reconstruction of daily life (*perestroika byta*), and leading figures of the architectural avant-garde explored the possibility that architecture could be an instrument for generating new forms of sociality and, ultimately, men and women of a new type. But by the late 1920s these discussions were being reoriented by the turn toward forced industrialization. The five-year plan presented architects and urbanists with a host of new enterprises across the Soviet Union, around which cities had to be built. This exigency raised two problems that became central to urbanist discussions of the period. The first, the problem of *rasselenie*, or settlement, referred to the adjustments, both spatial and institutional, between production and population. Thus, the urban theorist Mikhail Okhitovich identified "the settlement [*rasselenie*] of people and the geographical distribution [*razmeshchenie*] of productive power in their interrelationship" (1930: 7) as the key question for urban planners in the context of the first five-year plan. The second, the problem of the city (*gorodskoe*) *khoziaistvo*, referred to the *substantive* economy of the Soviet city—the nexus of material structures, administrative apparatuses, and resource flows through which, following Karl Polanyi (1977), the "material satisfaction of human wants" was planned and organized.

The figures of settlement and *khoziaistvo* are of interest here because they became the central concerns of city-building, the Soviet form of urban planning. During the Soviet period the term "city-building" was attached to various things: a certain class of planning problems, a group of experts, and a network of technical institutes. The aim of the present discussion is not to examine this technocratic apparatus or its historical development (a topic that has been understudied[2]). Nor do I focus on the practices of planners or the relationship between plans and the construction of cities (a topic I address in the next two chapters, which focus on developments in Belaya Kalitva and Rodniki). Rather, I examine city-building as a lens on the political ontology, the form of veridiction, and the modes of intervention through which the Soviet state shaped a new form of urban modernity.

Extending the analysis of the prior chapter, the present discussion compares the Soviet project of social modernity with the liberal variant of that project as it has been analyzed in Foucaultian scholarship. At one level, the Soviet and liberal projects of social modernity can be situated in a common problem-space. Liberalism was always concerned with the processes through which populations and production were spatially distributed and institutionally linked. And early liberalism, as Polanyi demonstrated in *The Great Transformation*, was preoccupied with the challenges of need fulfillment in the growing cities of the industrial age. But city-building took these problems up in an entirely distinctive way. Soviet city-builders did not recognize liberalism's constitutive distinction between the state and society. As the Russian sociologist O. Yanitskii puts it, Soviet city-building proposed to know and transform the city "not as a social organism, with its own laws of development, but as a construction or a 'machine,' that one could plan and bring into being [*voplotit' v zhizn'*] down to the smallest details of the organization of production and daily life" (1998).

I explore these distinctions by examining how Soviet city-builders took up and reworked two concepts that were central to liberal social modernity. In liberal thought *population* was "discovered" as one part of the general system of the economy, conceived as an autonomous domain. By contrast, Soviet discussions of settlement in the early 1930s began to treat population as a mass of human individuals whose labor could be instrumentally deployed in production. It was not part of an autonomous field, but one element in a system of total planning that had to be coordinated

TABLE 3.1
Population and Norm in Liberal and Soviet Social Modernity

	Liberal social modernity	Soviet social modernity
Population	Autonomous domain outside of the state that imposes new limits on state activity	Collection of individuals as labor power and subjects of need
Norm	Distribution of phenomena over populations	Quantitative ratio between elements in a system of total planning

with others. *Norms*, meanwhile, emerged in liberal thought as statistical reflections of regular, ongoing phenomena (disease and health, wealth and poverty) in a population. Soviet city-building, by contrast, worked through *prescriptive* norms that were not statistical reflections but teleological projections; to recall Trotsky's phrase, they were not pictures but commands.[3] These prescriptive norms defined quantitative relationships among the various elements—housing, urban utilities, and social services— that were required to meet the needs of a given population. Thus, following Georges Canguilhem, the *khoziaistvo*, the substantive economy of Soviet city-building, was planned as a complex of "reciprocally relative norms" (1989: 247).

URBAN MODERNITY—FROM LATE TSARISM TO EARLY SOCIALISM

Before proceeding to a discussion of the debates in architecture and urbanism in the late 1920s and 1930s, it bears taking up a thread that was left off in the prior chapter, concerning the development of urban modernity in the late tsarist period. Notwithstanding the significant industrial surge in the last decades of tsarist rule, Russia remained a predominantly rural country up to the Revolution, and industrialization continued to be only weakly related to urban growth. The "big" story of the Russian nineteenth century was that no project of urban modernization emerged that was equivalent to those that took shape in European countries. That said, significant urbanization did take place in the late tsarist period, and it generated many of the problems associated with the growth of cities in other countries: inadequate housing, increasing demands on urban services, and worsening health and sanitary conditions. Poor urban conditions, in turn, exerted some of the pressures that drew European thinkers to the problems raised by an urban and industrial form of collective life

(Hanchett 1976: 96). These pressures were reflected in the orientations of architecture and urbanism over the last decades of tsarist rule.

Since Catherine the Great (1762–1796), city plans had been required of all Russian cities. But these plans were largely restricted to classical questions of layout and design, and the scope of their application was limited to urban centers. Thus, on William Blackwell's account, in the growing Russian cities of the late nineteenth century, "the spacious and graceful stone carved inner city of the state and the wealthy" was starkly contrasted to "the ramshackle and haphazard wooden city of the factories and the poor" (1968: 100). Classical concerns persisted. According to S. Fredrick Starr, late tsarist urban planning was dominated by a classical revivalism oriented to preserving old aristocratic centers against the advance of industry and nonaristocratic populations. But other tendencies emerged in the last decades of the nineteenth century. Liberal reforms in the 1870s—which marked, according to Walter Hanchett, "the apex of statutory freedom for municipal self-rule in the history of the Russian empire" (1976: 98)—greatly expanded the leeway of urban governments in addressing social problems. The urban planning and architecture of the period reflected these concerns. The classical school began to turn its attention to the conditions of life in industrial cities. Meanwhile, a nascent Russian garden city movement based on the influential ideas of Ebenezer Howard was preoccupied by the problems of a new urban modernity. Thus, Starr notes, by 1917 "there existed two well developed programs for the further development of Russian cities: the application of modified classical principles to the larger industrial and administrative centers, and the garden city for satellite towns and smaller rural communities" (1976: 235).

Both tendencies proved significant for subsequent developments. Neoclassical motifs and an emphasis on ceremonial central districts were central to Soviet architecture from the early 1930s to Stalin's death. The influence of the garden city movement, meanwhile, is found in many enduring tenets of Soviet city planning: an emphasis on limited city size, planned interrelationships among functional areas of a city, and planned provision of urban services. And both schools experimented with planned settlements for workers, contributing to what Starr identifies as a longstanding orientation in Russian urbanism to "deliberately conceived urban settings" (1971: 173). But viewed in broader perspective, these developments were of limited scope and significance. Any tendencies toward an urban modernity were ultimately crushed by reactionary reforms that limited the autonomy of local governments and undermined their financial bases.[4] Urban modernization—like industrial development—was ultimately blocked by the rigid framework of classical power.

The Early Soviet Non-City: Rodniki after the Revolution

What Michael Hamm calls the "breakdown in urban modernization" in the late tsarist period was consequential. By the end of the nineteenth century, urban conditions were substantially worse than those in European cities, and they were among many factors that "accelerated the demise of the imperial order" (Hamm 1976a: 198).[5] It is consequently no surprise that they were on the agenda immediately after the Revolution. For a snapshot of developments before and just after the Revolution, we can return to Rodniki—the textile settlement described earlier—and to broader developments in Ivanovo-Kineshma, a major industrial region of the late-tsarist period, and an important locus of revolutionary activity.

As William Husband (1988; 1990) has shown in his research on the workers' movement in Ivanovo-Kineshma, union organization, which played a critical role in placing urban conditions on the political agendas, was initially limited in the area. The region was dominated by rural-industrial settlements like Rodniki, and mobilization was constrained by the isolation of enterprises and the absence of densely settled urban areas. But a workers' movement eventually did consolidate. Workers' demands focused primarily on wages, but also addressed conditions of life in the region's many industrial settlements. These demands were initially directed to specific factory owners, who were the only plausible addressee for protests given the absence of local governments. But over the course of 1917, in the interregnum between the February and October revolutions, particularistic claims were linked, and workers presented demands to an organization of factory owners. Mobilization culminated on October 21, 1917 with a general strike that demanded worker control of the region's textile enterprises (Husband 1990: 454).

These local developments were quickly superceded by broader events of the Revolution. The Soviet government created an organization called Centro-Cloth on November 16, 1917—the first step toward centralized, administrative control of the textile sector. In Rodniki, the Krasil'shchikov enterprise was nationalized and renamed—imaginatively—Bol'shevik. The Revolution and the events immediately following it had a number of important implications for Rodniki as a city. The first concerned the composition of the local population. A tendency toward feminization of textile labor, which had begun in the late nineteenth century across the region, eroded the peasant-industrial pattern, which, in turn, spurred growth of the population residing in Rodniki's immediate environs.[6] These trends were intensified by the Civil War, which initially caused a sharp population decline, as men were drawn away to fight and many families retreated to the countryside, but ultimately drew women into the industrial workforce.[7] Though patterns of itinerant labor persisted, the permanent population of industrial workers swelled in Rodniki, as it did in most other Soviet cities.[8]

A second significant change in the immediate aftermath of the Revolution concerned Rodniki's administrative status. In one of the sweeping waves of administrative reorganization that have played such a critical role in Russian urban developments over many centuries, Rodniki was declared a city.[9] City status meant the establishment of a local government—a local soviet—that was made formally responsible for local conditions. But in Rodniki, as in the vast majority of cities, improvements in the conditions of urban life were inevitably limited by resource constraints. A 1926 report of the Local Soviet's Executive Committee complained of these constraints and offered a picture of the city's condition at the time. Rodniki, the report noted, was "not equipped with basic infrastructure." There were "no sidewalks in the majority of the city," electrification was "primitive," and there was "no sewage system, no water system, no fire station, nor other basic elements of a city." The municipal housing stock, meanwhile, was found to total only 3.80 square meters per person, a number that, as the report noted, was "far from the norm." And the housing that existed was in a state of "total dilapidation."[10] Of the 75,000 square meters of housing in Rodniki, 80 percent was accounted for by small privately owned huts; the remainder belonged to the nationalized textile manufactory.

The picture painted in this report reflects, of course, the inheritance of the rural industrial pattern of late tsarist Russia. It also reflects local governments' limited capacity to improve urban conditions in the early years of the Soviet period. In important respects, Rodniki remained a large industrial enterprise surrounded by small huts; "city" was little more than an administrative designation. The patent irony was that urban conditions in Rodniki, and in most other cities during the Soviet Union's early decades, recalled precisely the conditions of the early capitalist non-city that urbanists of the 1920s were so keen to avoid.

Stirrings of Social Modernity: Urbanism and Architecture

If little improvement in the conditions of urban life could be reported in the 1920s—indeed, for most of the period before World War II—we do observe a substantial change in how urbanists, architects, planners, and Party functionaries constituted urban life as a field of governmental reflection and intervention. The report of Rodniki's local soviet indicates that even if conditions were not rapidly improving, their sorry state was examined from a new light. At the very least, the report's authors assumed that this collection of wooden huts clustered around an industrial enterprise in the midst of an agricultural region should be something more than that. Rodniki ought to be a city, not only in terms of its administrative designation, but in terms of those "elements of a city" that comprise it. Here, Rodniki was just one remote indicator of a new problematization of urban modernity that began to take shape in the 1920s.

With the end of War Communism and the onset of NEP, local governments experienced a period (fleeting, as always in Russia) of expanded autonomy, during which they were able to pursue various initiatives to raise resources and improve local conditions. And as Milka Bliznakov has shown, in the field of architecture, classical orientations inherited from the tsarist period were quickly superceded by a range of new concerns.[11] Among these were problems of social welfare, hygiene, and land use that had been central to modern urbanism in all countries. But architects and urbanists of the mid-1920s also began to pursue entirely new lines of experimentation with what was called a revolution in daily life. Architecture in particular came to be seen as a crucial instrument in providing "the specific environment that Marxists believed necessary to mold human beings into the desired proletarian form" (Bliznakov 1971: 124). Designs for factories, communal facilities, and apartment blocks were meant to create new models of social interaction, intimacy, and reproductive behavior. Institutions such as the family and the private apartment were subject to critical scrutiny as features of a bourgeois society that, in the view of the avant-garde's most radical exponents, had to be eliminated. This period of experimentation, the subject of a tremendous amount of scholarly attention, is among the great creative outpourings of the twentieth-century avant-garde.[12]

As David Hoffman has argued, there is a standard story about the fate of the 1920s avant-garde in many fields, architecture and urbanism among them. This story follows the narrative of "Great Retreat" that Nicholas Timasheff (1946) famously developed in a classic study by that name. On this account, the extraordinary experimentation and innovation of the 1920s was cut off by Stalinist intervention in many professional fields, from economics to the sciences to the arts. In urbanism and architecture, this intervention took familiar form: murder or professional destruction of leading figures; a return of neoclassical motifs; and an end to avant-garde experiments. These developments, in the story of great retreat, ended all that was interesting about Soviet urbanism and architecture. As Hugh Hudson put it in a characteristic statement, Stalinism "joined forces with technological backwardness to first cripple and then devour the revolutionary architectural movement and reduced modernist architecture in the Soviet Union to a history of bastardized projects, half-finished constructions, and undeserved reputations as one more experience in the vacuity of utopianism" (1994: 13).

Of course there is something to this. The decimation of the architectural avant-garde ended a great efflorescence of experimental thought and brought discussions about the reconstruction of daily life to an abrupt halt.[13] But as a growing range of scholars has recognized, the search for new norms and forms appropriate to urban life in the Soviet Union was not abandoned (Hoffman 2003; Lampland 2009, 2010). And the new directions in architecture in the early 1930s were not only capitulations to terror and political necessity. They should also be understood as coherent attempts to reposition architecture and urbanism in response to changing circumstances. We will see that transitional figures such as Mikhail Okhitovich and Nikolai Miliutin tried to adapt—unsuccessfully, if judged by their personal survival; more successfully, perhaps, if judged by the enduring relevance of their ideas—to new demands. In the process, key preoccupations of the avant-garde were not abandoned so much as they were reinflected and redeployed in the face of new problems. The occasion for this redeployment was the rise of an administered economy focused on large industrial works. This development provoked a shift in the register of modern urbanism and architecture: from a revolution in daily life to a new biopolitics of population.

SETTLEMENT—POPULATION AND PRODUCTION

The new questions posed by rapid industrialization were at one level straightforward. If socialist construction meant building a whole series of new industrial centers, what urban forms would be appropriate to them? And how should they be spatially distributed? These problems were central to the last great theoretical debate of the urbanist avant-garde, concerning the linked questions of settlement (*rasselenie*) and the proper form of the socialist city.[14]

According to Viacheslav Glazychev, the discussion about settlement was opened in the summer of 1929, and was soon taken up in the Communist Academy and in the major journals on urbanism in 1930, including *Construction of Moscow (Stroitel'stvo Moskvy)*, and *Contemporary Architecture (Sovremennaia Arkhitektura)*, the journal published by the Society of Contemporary Architects (OSA).[15] Initial discussions advanced familiar propositions of modernist city planning, first among them that large cities in an industrial society *would* be planned so as to avoid the "reckless tropism" of early capitalist industrialization and urbanization. An early specification of this basic orientation to planned urban development was articulated by Leonid Sabsovich, who favored the late nineteenth-century garden city model—which he saw as an ideal form for developing collective life in a "planned and organized way" (Glazychev

1989: 19)—and the house-commune as a primary form of residence. Some positions outlined in these initial discussions by Sabsovich and others persisted throughout the Soviet period, including the orientation to small city size and to planned and collectivized provision of urban services. But a debate soon broke out over the broader questions of settlement, concerning the form, size, and spatial distribution of cities.

These questions were debated over the course of 1930 in the pages of *Contemporary Architecture*, an important forum of the architectural avant-garde. In the year's first issue, the journal's editors announced that socialist settlement would be addressed in order to clarify misconceptions that had emerged in public commentary on the topic ("Ot Redaktsii" 1930).[16] This announcement was followed by an article entitled, "Notes on the Theory of Settlement," by Mikhail Okhitovich, a leading OSA theorist during this period. As Hugh Hudson (1992) documents in *Blueprints and Blood,* his study of the architectural and urbanist avant-garde and its demise, Okhitovich was a complicated figure who rejected the more utopic proposals of the late 1920s avant-garde, among them the house-commune and the destruction of the nuclear family. And he was responsive to the new demands placed on architecture and urbanism by the five-year plan. His "Notes" can thus be read as a point of inflection in the shift from the revolution in daily life to an emerging concern with planning cities in light of industrial development.

"The notes offered here," Okhitovich began, "aspire to indicate the path for a serious development of the Marxist theory for the settlement of people and the geographical distribution [*razmeshchenie*] of productive power in their interrelationship" (1930: 7). The basic framing was familiar. Since GOELRO, Soviet planners linked the spatial distribution of industry to energy. Okhitovich simply extended this concern to the distribution of people and, thus, to the distribution and form of cities, arguing that the spatial organization of energy and industry determined the spatial pattern of settlement. Okhitovich noted that previously—which is to say in capitalist countries—large, crowded cities grew at the junctions of roads and rivers, or around sources of energy that was expensive to transport. But with electrification this spatial pattern would change since "[t]here is no center of [electric] energy." Rather, Okhitovich argued— taking up a vocabulary that was already in circulation during discussions of GOELRO—"there is a single energy NETWORK [*SET'*]. There are no central sources, there are local, large and small, the smallest ubiquitous sources of energy [*povsiudnye istochniki energii*]. Every center is a periphery and every point on the periphery is a center" (Okhitovich 1930: 14). Based on this analysis of energy, Okhitovich proceeded to articulate a *dezurbanist* or "desurbanist" vision of development, in which ribbons of settlement would be arrayed along energy and transport corridors.

Underlying Okhitovich's argument was a crucial premise. The form of the socialist city and the pattern of settlement had to be conceived in a single indissoluble whole with industrial planning. An article in *Contemporary Architecture* at the end of 1931, written in support of Okhitovich's position, thus argued that socialist planning was to be "based on the planned distribution of productive forces in an economic region in a single national economy [*narodnoe khoziaistvo*]." Socialist planning was not concerned with "the separate management of distinct enterprises of the national economy." Rather, it was concerned with "the region as a whole, in its mutual relationship with other regions that influence its structure." City planning, by logical extension, would not focus on "a city or a village or a settlement of workers of this or that enterprise, or even a totality of these." Rather, the object of planning was "a unified network of settlement [*rasselenie*] of an economic region" ("Tezisy Doklada" 1930: 1).

This basic premise—that "the method [*sposob*] of settlement" was dependent on "the method [*sposob*] for the distribution of industry" ("Tezisy Doklada" 1930: 2)—was never called into question. As we will see in the next chapter, city-building plans were always based on the adjustments between industrial production and the population. In urbanist discussions of the early 1930s the *form* of this complex object of total planning was the topic of a hot dispute that pitted Okhitovich's desurbanism against a vision of large and densely settled urban centers promoted by the *urbanisty*. This debate has received a great deal of scholarly attention, but from the perspective of longer-term historical developments it was not of cardinal importance.[17] Ultimately both "urbanist" and "desurbanist" positions were rejected, due neither to the specifics of their proposals nor to their understanding of the link between industrial and urban development, but to their shared assumptions about what role urban planners could play in defining the proper form of settlement.

The City as a Detail of Regional Planning

The shifting position of urban planners and architects—particularly with respect to the problem of settlement—was evident in a session of the Communist Academy in May 1930, which presented a wide-ranging discussion of the various positions of architects and urbanists on the form of the socialist city ("K Probleme Planirovki Sotsgoroda" 1930).[18] The discussion was introduced and moderated by Nikolai Miliutin, another star-crossed urbanist who managed to work for a time in the changing climate of the early 1930s before, most scholars believe, perishing in the terror.[19] Miliutin is best known for his much misunderstood "lineal city" concept. But as a leading figure in the urbanist establishment of the time he weighed in on most of the period's obligatory themes. In 1930 the problem of settlement was foremost among these. In his presentations to the Academy, Miliutin did not so much take a strong position on the raging debate between *urbanisty* and *dezurbanisty* as put them in their proper place.

Miliutin began the discussion from a position that was virtually identical to Okhitovich's. "The direction of new construction under our conditions," he argued, "is unavoidably determined by the distribution of industry; the task of production [*proizvodstvennoe zadanie*] should define the construction of cities" ("K Probleme Planirovki Sotsgoroda" 1930: 110). But for Miliutin this connection between the distribution of industry and the construction of cities did not open a broad new domain for urban theory. Quite the contrary, it meant that the spatial distribution and structure of cities were determined by prior decisions about industrial development made elsewhere in the Soviet planning apparatus. Urban planners had no business discussing the proper form of future settlements; *urbanisty* and *dezurbanisty* alike were giving answers to questions that need not be posed, at least not by them. "The only correct conclusion that can be made," Miliutin noted in his closing remarks to the conference, "is that [urban planners] should proceed from the organization of production." There could be "no argument about urbanization or desurbanization." Questions of settlement were tightly connected with the general plan, "and should be determined simultaneously as it is realized" ("K Probleme Planirovki Sotsgoroda" 1930: 144). Another participant in the debate, a certain G. Puzis, argued along similar lines: the question of settlement, he reasoned, was simply a "translation of the economic plan, created by Gosplan, onto the territory" ("K Probleme Planirovki Sotsgoroda" 1930: 141).

Miliutin's position conformed to the emerging official doctrine. In the June Plenum of the Central Committee in 1931, Kaganovich famously defined the socialist city as any settlement on the territory of the Soviet Union. The claim has often been taken to be a mindless tautology: a socialist city was simply a city in a socialist country.[20] But the point, given the context, was in part to assert that urban planners had no role to play in the theoretical questions of socialist settlement. The "socialist city" was a city whose planning proceeded in light of plans for industrial development. The scope of urban planners' concerns was clearly delimited by a 1931 article in *Soviet Architecture*—a journal edited by Miliutin that displaced *Contemporary Architecture* as the leading forum for discussions of architecture and urbanism—whose authors asserted that "the planning of a settlement can be only a detail in the plan for an economic region" (*Sektor Arkhitektorov Sotsialisticheskogo Stroitel'stva* 1931: 98). At one level this position was in total accord with the problematization

of settlement found in Okhitovich's "Notes"; the difference was that urban planners were confined to that "detail" of a regional economic plan
that was, in fact, the city.

This new official line obviously reduced the role of architects and urbanists; indeed, many scholars have concluded that it reduced their role
to triviality. Bliznakov, thus, argued that architects and urban planners
were confined to conventional problems—"housing, the aesthetic unity
of the urban environment, and the appropriate form of the administrative
urban center." To ensure that this urban ensemble reflected a city's socialist character, there was no need to invent new urban elements. Rather,
urban planners could "reuse those of the preceding century" (Bliznakov
1971: 254).[21] The Soviet urban theorist, Tat'iana Govorenkova has noted
that after 1930 the socialist city was just "a city in a single system of
socialist economic planning" (1989: 79): it was simply, she quipped, a
"*gorod u predpriiatiia*"—a city by an enterprise.[22]

These assessments capture something important about developments
during the period but require qualification. First, as we will see, it is not
quite true that forms of the "prior century" were adequate for Soviet
urbanism. A number of distinctly "modernist" principles—limited city
size, planning and centralization of services, and strict divisions among
functional zones of a city—were always retained in Soviet city-building.
And if neoclassical motifs were revived, they were combined, as Vladimir
Paperny (2002) has argued, with a bewildering array of other styles and
theories about architecture and urban form.[23] Second, we will see that as
time passed, city-builders exerted more influence on broader questions
of settlement. By the late Soviet period the strict unidirectional relationship between industrial planning and urban planning had loosened, and
in some cases the "needs" of an existing population for labor drove the
distribution of industry. The third, and perhaps most important qualification to the claim that political intervention reduced Soviet urbanism to
triviality was that there was in fact a great deal left for architects to plan
and build after the *theory* of settlement was taken out of their hands.
After all, the "detail" of regional economic development to which they
were confined included all possible elements of a city outside the immediate organization of industrial production. The call of Party leaders was
not for urbanists to abandon the quest to develop new norms and forms
for the socialist city. Rather, as Meerovich has recently observed (2007),
it was to drop the theoretical and utopic discussions and get on with the
planning problems dictated by industrial developments.

It is from this twin perspective—the end of theoretical speculation
about the proper form of the socialist city, and the renewed emphasis
on the practical problems of planning new cities around industrial enterprises—that developments in the early 1930s are best understood. This

dual emphasis was reflected in the contributions to *Soviet Architecture* during this period. Its pages were dominated by those architects (Miliutin among them) who, through robotic incantations of the Party line, led the denunciation of the avant-garde with murderous fervor.[24] At the same time, these attacks were, at least in some cases, followed by much more pragmatic discussions that took up crucial propositions of the avant-garde and adapted them to the conceptual needs and the practical realities of the early 1930s. In this context the problem of settlement was not so much abandoned as reframed—no longer concerned with the *theory* of the distribution of populations and production but with the practical problem of planning urban development on the basis of industrial development (Bater 1980: 26). As such, the problem of settlement remained central to city-building theory and practice throughout the Soviet period, situating the problems of urban development in relation to broader processes of economic development. A postwar Soviet handbook thus identified settlement as the "connecting link [*sviazuiushchee zveno*]" that united "city-building practice with general economic planning [*s narodnokhoziaistvennym planirovaniem*]."[25]

Population

The key figure in establishing this "link" was the population (*naselenie*), which became an important topic of planning discussion in the early 1930s. The reasons for a renewed focus on population were in part related to the immediate exigencies of that period, as Soviet authorities struggled to attract and retain workers at new sites of industrial construction.[26] At the same time, population was a key consideration in creating long-term plans for the development of cities. In the third issue of *Soviet Architecture* in 1931, the editors introduced the theme of population, and in particular the problem of determining population targets for urban growth, as a "planning factor of enormous and decisive importance." Population targets, they argued, were crucial not only for planning the physical development of a city, but also for "the development of a correct social and economic plan [*khoziaistvennogo plana*] that would define the labor and material expenditures required for creating housing and service enterprises." Of concern were both the overall size of a future population—essential for defining the dimensions of a city's territory and the "general requirements for buildings and facilities [*sooruzheniia*]"—and its age and sex structure, upon which planning for "processes of production and consumption" would be based ("Ot Redaktsii" 1930: 4).

The question, then, was what methods were appropriate for projecting the size and structure of urban populations under socialist conditions. Predictably, the editors concluded that "the old practice"—referring to existing practice in advanced capitalist countries—"does not offer any help." Echoing the teleological planners' arguments against genetic assumptions (see previous chapter), they singled out "old statistical methods" for determining the size of cities that used a "method of abstraction" to determine future population growth from "concrete real conditions" ("Ot Redaktsii" 1930: 4). Puzis, in an article entitled "The Calculation of Population in the Planning of Population Points" that followed the editorial announcement, explained this initially obscure distinction. "The prior planning practice," he wrote, "defined the size of population based on the dynamic curve of natural and mechanical growth," that is, it was a "statistical" reflection of migratory processes and rates of birth and death. Such an approach was appropriate in capitalist conditions, but was "inappropriate in a socialist economy" (1931: 4).[27] As one illustration, Puzis referred to a theory of industrial location developed by Max Weber that, according to Glazychev (1989), Sabsovich introduced into the debates on the socialist city. Anticipating a standard (though disputed) hypothesis in the economics of industrial location, Weber had argued that industry would tend to accumulate in areas where labor was plentiful and cheap. For teleological planners like Puzis, the position was doubly unsatisfactory: it left these questions to the "spontaneous" dynamics of the market, and put "population" first and industry second, as the dependent variable. In a "socialist economy [khoziaistvo]," Puzis countered, just the opposite tendency would predominate: "Industrial development is itself the reason for massive migratory processes" and the abundance of labor would not in any way affect the wages of the workers (1931: 4–5). Population was a productive factor in industry; therefore, its size and structure in a given city would be first of all determined by the needs of industrial production.

This rejection of "statistical" methods resonated with teleological planners' refusal of the constraints on planned transformation imposed by current conditions of society or economy. It also upended an entire problematization of population that had emerged with classical liberalism. Population became the central problem of liberal government as an autonomous field that could be managed only by conforming to its laws and regularities: the distribution of poverty and welfare; of sickness and health; the dynamics of markets; patterns of migration; rates of birth and death. Population was thus a new site of veridiction; statistics—initially invented as a method for knowing the reality of the state—made it possible to base liberal government on the "truth" of population (Foucault 2007).

The figure of population that replaced this liberal-statistical understanding in Soviet city-building recalls the disciplinary-sovereigntist conception of population that Foucault associated with mercantilism and classical absolutism. Foucault argued that mercantilism was concerned with population as a "productive force, in the strict sense of the term" and required, therefore, "an apparatus that will ensure that the population, which is seen as the source and the root, as it were, of the state's power and wealth, will work properly, in the right place, and on the right objects" (2007: 69).[28] The Soviet socialist conception of population was similar, but it was inscribed in a different formation of government. In absolutism the "mobilization" of populations was circumscribed by sovereignty and by its basic reluctance to transform the "way of life" of massive parts of the population, first of all by redistributing it over national space. The Soviet project, by contrast, deployed disciplinary mechanisms in a biopolitical project whose aim was to utterly transform the spatial distribution and conditions of existence of the national population. In this context, something more than a "disciplinary" mobilization of labor was implied: the creation of an apparatus of social welfare, not only in exceptional spaces but for the national population as a whole. If settlement was the "hinge" that linked city-building to industrial planning, then the problem of population suggested a series of logical steps that linked industrial planning to urban planning to mechanisms of social welfare. Thus, where the problem of settlement initially *displaced* discussions of a revolution in daily life, the problem of population pointed *back* to daily life, but with a twist. The central problem was no longer to create new socialist men and women but to meet the daily needs of new populations in socialist cities.

THE MODERNIZATION OF *KHOZIAISTVO*— NEEDS AND NORMS IN SOVIET PLANNING

The discussions of daily life in architecture during the 1920s had proceeded along two intersecting axes. One was the preoccupation with "machines for living" intended to produce new forms of sociality and consciousness. The other dealt with the mundane problems of providing for daily needs in new socialist cities. If the former discussions were largely cut off, the latter were posed with greater urgency by the industrialization drive. In the early 1930s, the Soviet government identified the improvement of urban services as a central priority. The June Plenum of 1931, thus, issued a declaration on Moscow's urban services proclaiming that "the improvement of the material conditions of daily life for the working class should be at the center of attention for all Party organizations" ("Iiun'skii Plenum TsKVKP[b] Ob Organizatsii Gorodskogo Khoziaistvo" 1931). Housing, urban infrastructure, and social services were instruments of production, and their absence was recognized as a bottleneck in the push for industrialization. As Kaganovich wrote, the city was therefore "a weak point in the socialist transformation of our country, from the point of view both of satisfying the material and cultural expectations of the working class and of the growth of industry."[29]

The challenges of planning for an apparatus of social welfare were addressed in another article by Miliutin in *Soviet Architecture* in 1931. Its immediate purpose was to report on new norms for residential buildings and "complexes" formulated by the section of the Communist Academy charged with coordinating the work of technical institutes in the sphere of urbanism and architecture.[30] It is of interest here because, in introducing these norms, Miliutin carefully repositioned urbanists and architects in relation to the broader problem of socialist construction, distinguishing his position from that of the discredited avant-garde, and delimiting the proper domain of city-building activities.

Miliutin began by defining the scope of the discussion, marking out a division of labor between the work of industrial planners, the ideological labors of the Party, and the activities of urbanists, that could be mapped on to different functional zones of a city. What processes, he asked, were "underway in the residential areas of new cities" and, thus, within the scope of urbanist concerns? Miliutin's answer, significantly, began by noting what did *not* take place in these areas, carefully disavowing those issues that had been declared off-limits for urbanist reflection. "Labor, and also training [*ucheba*] and ideological work," he noted, take place "primarily in productive (industrial and agricultural) zones" and in the "green zones" of parks in which workers' clubs and houses of culture were located" (Miliutin 1931: 2).[31] What remained in residential zones, and thus, for consideration by city-builders, were "processes of daily life," by which Miliutin meant primarily the processes through which basic needs were satisfied.

Miliutin's next question concerned the form these "processes of daily life" were to take. Here he carefully distinguished his position from that of the avant-garde, particularly on the crucial question of the family. Avant-garde architects and urbanists of the late 1920s had criticized the family as a tool of bourgeois capitalism, whose function was to oppress women and to extract surplus value from their labor.[32] More utopic exponents of the avant-garde proposed that under socialism the family should be done away with.[33] Miliutin, by contrast, forcefully swept aside all speculation about the end of the family: "In the area of daily life at the present time," he insisted, "we find only the family form" (1931: 2). He then advanced what was essentially the obverse of the avant-garde argument against the nuclear family. With an obligatory nod to Marx, Miliutin noted that under the exploitative conditions of capitalism, a significant portion of workers were left *without* families; capitalism, thus, was now accused not of using the family as an instrument of oppression but of destroying it. Socialism, by contrast, would create conditions under which the family form could be retained, first of all through a "significant increase in standards of living of the workers and the development of collective forms for the satisfaction of daily needs of workers" (Miliutin 1931: 2). Thus, families would still exist under socialist conditions, and they had to be accommodated by city planners. But their character would change dramatically.[34] The family would continue to be the central "unit of daily life and consumption [*bytovoe, potrebitel'skoe soedinenie*]." But it would rapidly cease to be a "unit of production," or a unit of *"khoziaistvo* [*khoziaistvenno-proizvodstvennoe soedinenie*]" (Miliutin 1931: 2). Here Miliutin introduces a crucial term that requires some explication, for it will be essential to the discussion that follows.

The Russian word *khoziaistvo*—an essential term in many contexts[35]—shares some of the semantic constellation of the English word "economy" in its original usage. Comparison of the two terms is illuminating. "Economy," as is well known to economic anthropologists, for whom these distinctions were once crucial, originally referred to the *nemein*, or management, of the *oikos*—the household. But it could be used in other domains as well. As the *Oxford English Dictionary* defines this now basically obsolete range of uses, economy concerns "[t]he management or administration of the material resources of a community ... or other organized body; the art or science of managing such resources."[36] In Polanyi's sense, these prior usages referred to forms of *substantive* economy—instituted mechanisms of need fulfillment—not to the *formal* understanding of economic that emerged with the rise of liberal political economy. Similarly, the Russian root *khoz* originally referred to the household, and is closely linked to problems of management: a *khoziain* is the head of a household or of some other substantive economy; the verb *khoziaistvovat'* is the activity of managing and transforming a *khoziaistvo*. *Khoziaistvo*, as a noun, can refer to a farm, a household, or virtually any nexus of production and need fulfillment—that is, to almost any unit of substantive economy. But *khoziaistvo* can *not* imply the formal meaning of "economic." Thus, while there was a *narodnoe khoziaistvo SSSR*—in the standard translation, a "national economy of the Soviet Union"—it is somewhat discordant to call post-Soviet Russia's market economy a *"khoziaistvo."*

Thus, returning to our story in the 1930s, in claiming that the family would no longer be a unit of *khoziaistvo*, Miliutin meant that it would no longer be the primary unit for organizing the fulfillment of daily needs. Rather, these functions would be a problem for state administration and planning, and in particular for *urban* administration and planning. What was in question for Miliutin, then, was a transposition of *khoziaistvo* from the family to the city. And this new form of *gorodskoe*—or city—*khoziaistvo* was defined as the object-domain of Soviet city-building.

The use of the term *gorodskoe khoziaistvo* to designate a central object of urban administration was not new to the 1930s. It was widely used in the tsarist period, when it referred rather narrowly to services provided by local governments. As Tat'iana Govorenkova (1989: 75) has documented, a similar usage was found in early Soviet discussions, designating competencies of local governments such as land use, housing, roads and transport, general maintenance and sanitation, and so on. All of these problems continued to be included in discussions of city *khoziaistvo* in the 1930s. But as both a concept and a field of practical activity, city *khoziaistvo* was transformed in at least two important ways. On the one hand, the problem of city *khoziaistvo* no longer had an exclusive relationship to local governments, which, as we see in the next chapter, were only one among a tangle of organizations responsible for "daily life" in Soviet cities. On the other hand, the scope of activities included in the concept of city *khoziaistvo* vastly expanded to include the entirety of a socialist city's substantive economy, the integrated complex of elements that were required for the "material satisfaction of human wants." It was this expanded definition of city *khoziaistvo* that defined the proper concern of city-building: not a revolution in daily life or the ideological tasks of the state; not the planning of industry or the theory of the socialist city; not the proper spatial distribution of population; but that entire complex of material structures, urban utilities, social services, housing, and an expanding range of other amenities that were required to meet an urban population's daily needs.

This, at any rate, was the central concern of Miliutin's article, which, after its careful ideological positioning on the problems of the family, turned to its central task: announcing new norms for what were called "housing and residential complexes."[37] A "complex" was an integrated unit of planning—for example, a cluster of apartment blocks, education, health, and leisure facilities. The key mechanisms in designing these complexes were substantive or *prescriptive* norms. These norms were simply ratios that defined the proportions in which different elements of a complex would have to be built. The central function of such norm-articulated complexes was to allow planners to move from a projection of population—itself based on plans for industrial development—to the apparatus required for need fulfillment. In his article on housing and residential complexes, Miliutin illustrated this use of norms and complexes through the example of planning for a preschool. "One preschool," he reasoned, "serves 30–40 children, which means 160–240 adults. One kindergarten for 60 children serves 500–600 adults. One cafeteria for 150–500 people (that is, for 50–160 places) for a three shift work." Based on these assumptions, it could be recommended to "build housing for no less than 30 and for no more than 100 individuals. And on this basis houses can be united in complexes for 500–600 people" (Miliutin 1931: 4). Through such complexes, planners could translate human needs into a set of material requirements by encoding them in a general system of equivalencies.

Here, again, a contrast with liberalism will help us pin down what is distinctive about this Soviet approach to social welfare planning. In the liberal cases, as we have seen, the norm was primarily a statistical concept, a reflection of the regularities of an autonomous milieu. The norm in Soviet planning, by contrast, is much closer to the disciplinary norm that Foucault analyzed in *Security, Territory, Population*. Foucault wrote that the norm in discipline has an "originally prescriptive character," by which he meant that it reflects a conscious determination of the desired telos or endpoint that intervention is supposed to achieve (Foucault 2007: 57). Likewise, the Soviet planning norm precisely defined an *endpoint*, the desired relationship among elements that had to be produced. But again, the differences between Soviet and disciplinary norms are also illuminating. As noted in the prior chapter, Soviet planning norms were not applied in closed disciplinary spaces circumscribed by a regime of sovereignty. Rather, they were the very elements that—at least in the ideal world of planners—articulated the broad correlations between population, production, and an apparatus of need fulfillment. If Soviet planning norms were *prescriptive* they were also biopolitical oriented to problems of need fulfillment in a complex modern economy.

To summarize, in Miliutin's discussion, we see two constitutive movements of Soviet biopolitics. The first is the *displacement* of the *khoziaistvo*—the nexus of need fulfillment—from the family to city. The second is the articulation of the city *khoziaistvo* by prescriptive, substantive norms that coded human needs into "complexes" of elements that could be plugged into plans. These two movements shaped the basic contours of a *modernization* of the substantive economy of cities, through which need fulfillment was constituted as a problem of expert knowledge, a task of bureaucratic planning, and a target of state administration. If we add to this picture the place that the city *khoziaistvo* occupied in the overall conception of total planning—a "detail" in a plan for an economic region that was logically derived from prior assumptions about industrial planning and development—then we have some general grasp of the technology of power that defined the Soviet variant of social modernity.

CHAPTER FOUR

City-building in Belaya Kalitva

THE CONCEPTUAL DEVELOPMENTS in Soviet city-building in the early 1930s were matched by some initial steps in creating a technocratic apparatus to handle the massive amount of planning and technical work implied by rapid urbanization and industrialization. In the early 1930s, city planning and architectural activities were increasingly carried out not by independent organizations of architects and urbanists but in a growing range of "official" planning institutes. These included the "city-building institutes"—first among these Giprogor, the State Institute for the Design of Cities (*Gosudarstvennyi Institut Proektirovaniia Gorodov*), in Moscow—as well as a number of more specialized organizations dealing with housing, communal infrastructure, and other problems.

Given the circumstances, these organizations' accomplishments were not trivial.[1] But the actual state of affairs in Soviet cities during the regime's first decades diverged absolutely from city-builders' visions of carefully planned urban development. The period was one of rapid urban growth: after the depopulation episode during the Civil War, Russian cities gained an average of 2.4 million new residents per year until the onset of World War II.[2] But this redistribution of population around new sites of industrial production was hardly planned. Most discussions of "settlement" during this period referred not to the careful balance of demographic and industrial development but to practical struggles in attracting workers to—and retaining them in—new sites of production. The situation was no better for planning a new city *khoziaistvo* in the Soviet Union's growing industrial centers. Even in cities with plans, planning work lagged behind industrial construction and demographic expansion. To the extent that urbanists and architects influenced developments, they did so largely through the design of central districts and monumental buildings. Little progress was made in building facilities for satisfying daily needs, and in important respects urban conditions deteriorated during the period of Stalin's rule.[3]

The slow progress in city-building needs little explanation. As William Blackwell points out, "no assessment of the pace and scope of Russian urban development can avoid considering the grim fact that during the first three decades of the new regime, from 1917 to 1945 ... the cities of the Soviet Union were suffering frequent and extensive destruction" (1986: 296). Also crucial were conscious decisions to squeeze consumption and social welfare in the name of industrialization and preparation for war, and to focus nonindustrial construction on monumental structures rather than functional designs. What was true of Rodniki in the 1920s was true of most Soviet cities prior to World War II: urban conditions recalled nothing so much as the reckless tropism of the capitalist non-city that Soviet urbanists were so keen to avoid.

All of this began to change after World War II. During the 1950s and 1960s the network of planning institutes expanded, and by the late 1960s plans had been approved for most if still not all Soviet cities.[4] Over the same period the Soviet regime began to direct substantial resources to urban development. Construction capacity expanded in most cities, and the pace of building—not only of apartments but of urban utilities that were a crucial element of a new substantive economy—accelerated. Taking all of this into view, we can say that if the basic conceptual framework of city-building was a product of the 1930s, then it was after World War II that we see the consolidation of city-building as an apparatus of transformation comprised of experts, technical institutes, resource flows, material structures, spatial forms, demographic distributions, and organizational arrangements.

The present chapter traces this consolidation of the city-building apparatus by examining post–World War II developments in Belaya Kalitva, the small industrial city that was discussed in this book's introduction. The first part of the chapter examines the plans that were developed for the city in the early 1960s in order to illustrate how the concepts of settlement and city *khoziaistvo* allowed city-builders to take hold of a specific reality and formulate proposals for its transformation. The second part describes the process through which some of the works anticipated in Belaya Kalitva's plans were actually built, focusing on urban utilities, material and bureaucratic structures, patterns of resource flow, and developments in industrial production. Through this analysis, I will show that city-building provides a window on the process through which a new kind of collectivity was assembled in Soviet cities, as urban populations were linked together and plugged into a new substantive economy. In this sense, the city-building apparatus will be understood as a key dimension of the Soviet social.

Belaya Kalitva: Plans for Settlement

It will be recalled that in the nineteenth century Belaya Kalitva was a small Cossack *stanitsa*, or administrative center. Industry in the city was limited to small food processing facilities that served agricultural producers in the surrounding rural region. The Revolution did not immediately change Belaya Kalitva's status. But just before World War II the Party's Central Committee issued a decree ordering the construction of a new industrial enterprise in the *stanitsa* center. Building began before the war, but little was accomplished prior to the German invasion; and much of that was destroyed, including several barracks that housed early construction workers.[5] Work on the enterprise was taken up again only in 1949, apparently with urgency. Given the enormous task of reconstruction, the delay hardly needs explanation, and the reason for subsequent haste is readily imagined. By the late 1940s, the Soviet Union and the United States faced a new military reality in which air power was a vital strategic factor; Belaya Kalitva's enterprise was an aluminum factory related to defense aviation. The first product rolled off the lines in 1953.

During the first postwar years, scattered communal facilities were built in Belaya Kalitva—three schoolhouses, a stadium, a hospital, and a "house of culture"—alongside some housing for specialists sent to work on the aluminum enterprise.[6] These new buildings were located near the aluminum facility at some remove from the old *stanitsa* center, and were arranged symmetrically in neighborhoods that extended out from a central plaza that would form the core of what locals called the "new city" (see figure 4.1, pp. 98–99). But beyond this rough layout, there is little to suggest that urban development was advancing according to a plan. Most construction took place in the chaotic manner typical of many cities before the war, as newly arrived workers built small huts for their families. For the most part, resources continued to be focused on industrial development, with everything else—as Moshe Lewin (1973: 276) said of the period before World War II—left more or less to its own devices.

This picture did not change in its fundamentals from Belaya Kalitva's liberation to the early 1960s, when three crucial documents were approved that bore directly on the city's future development. The first, approved in 1962, was a plan for settlement or *rasselenie* for Rostov Region, where Belaya Kalitva is located. The second, in 1963, was a plan for settlement for the city itself. The third, in 1964, was a general plan for Belaya Kalitva. These three plans constituted a kind of logical series.[7] Regional and city plans for settlement laid out the future development of industry and population. The general plan proceeded from these parameters to elaborate a detailed, integrated vision of a future city *khoziaistvo*. In examining this progression of plans in some detail, we will see how city-builders formulated a blueprint for future adjustments between processes of production, the development of population, and a new apparatus of social welfare provisioning.

The first plan to formally address Belaya Kalitva's long-term development was a Rostov Region *Plan for Settlement*, approved in 1962 by the Executive Committee of the regional Communist Party.[8] The plan was prepared by *Lengiprogor,* the Leningrad State Institute for the Design of Cities. It was not unusual that planning in peripheral cities was conducted centrally. Though the network of project institutes had expanded by the 1960s, regional institutes were few in number until well into the postwar period.[9] The purpose of this plan was to lay out general parameters for industrial and demographic development for every city in Rostov Oblast'. These parameters were influenced by a range of factors. Most important among these, of course, were plans for industrial development made elsewhere in the Soviet planning apparatus; the future development of cities was dictated by the future development of industry. But in light of the discussion in the prior chapter—concerning urban planners' limited role in setting broad parameters for development beginning in the early 1930s—it is notable that the Rostov *Plan for Settlement* did not simply translate industrial plans "onto the territory," as Puzis had put it in 1930 ("K Probleme Planirovki Sotsgoroda" 1930: 107). Rather, the *Plan for Settlement* balanced existing plans for industrial development with long-standing principles of urban and regional planning, such as spatial balance in regional development, and limits on the growth of existing cities. For example, the regional plan noted that certain cities of Rostov Region, most notably the capital city of Rostov, had already exceeded the desired size. It therefore proposed to limit further growth in these cities and to promote growth in smaller cities. The plan also proposed to correct spatial imbalance in regional development. In the tsarist period industrial development had been concentrated in the region's southwest, due both to the location of Donbass coal and to the commercial activity associated with the capital Rostov and the port city of Azov. The plan proposed, therefore, to focus development in the northeast part of the region. For both reasons, Belaya Kalitva, located on the northeastern extremity of the Donbass, was identified as a desirable center for future growth.

These conclusions in the regional *Plan for Settlement* formed the basis for a subsequent *Plan for Settlement* (*Skhema Rasseleniia*) for Belaya Kalitva itself, that was approved in 1963. This city plan was referred to as an elaboration (*detalizatsiia*) of the regional plan in relation to conditions in Belaya Kalitva. The city *Plan for Settlement* began by describing existing conditions in Belaya Kalitva, based on a survey undertaken by a multidisciplinary team comprised of economists, geologists, architects, transport engineers, and energy specialists. Such multidisciplinary teams were used in Soviet planning since GOELRO (and before that in major tsarist planning efforts, such as the Trans-Siberian railroad) to plan for the interrelated development of energy, industry, transport, and cities in undeveloped regions. Following the general parameters of teleological planning, the purpose of this survey was not to consider ongoing "social" or "economic" processes underway in Belaya Kalitva and to project their future patterns. Rather, it provided what might be called an *inventory* of the city as it existed in the early 1960s: a catalogue of the natural features and the urban and demographic elements that had to be taken into account, and that were available for rearrangement, in planning the city's future.[10]

Belaya Kalitva's *Plan for Settlement* began by describing geologic and topographical features of the city and its environs. It considered: characteristics of the local climate; the tendencies of the rivers that ran through the city, including their volume and seasonal dynamics; the local prevalence of building materials that could be used for construction (including the white—*belaia*—rock that, along with the river Kalitva, gave the city its name); and the appropriateness of land in the city for various uses, including agricultural plots and gardens, industrial and residential developments, open space, and parks. Next, the *Plan for Settlement* catalogued existing industrial facilities. First among these was Belaya Kalitva's aluminum enterprise, referred to in the plan only as "No. 16" since it was a secret military facility. The plan also noted a number of smaller industrial enterprises, including a construction organization and a handful of food processing enterprises. The *Plan for Settlement* then turned to the broader geographic location of the city and the network of external transport to which it was connected. Following the regional *Plan for Settlement*, the city plan emphasized that Belaya Kalitva's growth was desirable for reasons of demographic and industrial balance in the region. It also noted Belaya Kalitva's location on an existing railroad line from Volgograd in the east to the Moscow-Rostov line in the west (see figure 1.1), and the proximity of major construction facilities in the nearby cities of Kamensk (to the northwest) and Novocherkassk (to the south).

Taking all these factors into account, the *Plan for Settlement* recommended rapid growth of the city. Belaya Kalitva's population had more than doubled since World War II, from 12,100 in 1951 (with an additional 14,000 in the large coal mining settlements surrounding the city) to 26,400 in 1963. The *Plan for Settlement* established a target for population growth by the end of the planning period (*raschetnyi srok*[11]) of 120,000. This "target population" (*proektnaia chislennost' naseleniia*) was a crucial figure in city-building practice that guided the planning of all elements of a city *khoziaistvo*. Alongside this target population, the city *Plan for Settlement* drew attention to two further problems concerning the adjustments of population and production that had to be addressed in a future general plan for Belaya Kalitva. First, the city's industrial base, which in 1963 was composed primarily of coal mines in the surrounding countryside and the aluminum factory, did not provide adequate industrial employment for women. Second, since the mines were old, deep, and increasingly unproductive, their closure seemed immanent—at least it did to planners in the early 1960s. As it turned out, thanks to the discovery of new seams, and to the Soviet Union's chronic (perhaps ultimately fatal) inability to shut down old and unproductive industrial endeavors, the mines remained open to the end of the Soviet period. But in the 1960s planners assumed thousands of coal miners would soon be left without work. Consequently, future industrial developments would have to provide adequate employment for women and for displaced male miners in Belaya Kalitva's central city. This process of labor adjustment required that the population in the settlements be relocated. The plan proposed a possible approach: initially, women from mining settlements would commute to new industrial jobs in the central city; as mines closed, and men lost their jobs, families would be resettled in central Belaya Kalitva.

In sum, the plans for settlement established a series of general parameters for Belaya Kalitva's development: a major industrial enterprise with a certain need for industrial labor; a projected total population; relevant features of geography, topography, hydrology, and climate; and future considerations concerning the mutual adjustments between population and production. What remained was to lay out the city *khoziaistvo*, the material and administrative apparatus required for meeting the local population's needs. This problem was taken up by Belaya Kalitva's general plan.

The General Plan—City Khoziaistvo

Belaya Kalitva's general plan was approved in 1964, one year after the city *Plan for Settlement*. It should be clear that when we talk of the general plan of the city, we are referring to a sprawling array of documents: innumerable blueprints for urban utilities and social services, plans for apartment blocks, transportation schemas, and tabulations of different services and facilities that should be provided. This mass of documentation was summarized in a document called the *Poiasnitel'nye Zapiski* (*Explanatory Notes*), which, even in a small city like Belaya Kalitva, ran to hundreds of pages. These *Notes* are of particular interest because they presented the logical steps of the planning process. By examining them, we can understand how the general plan for a Soviet city unfolded like a grand derivation in which every detail of a future city was calculated on the basis of simple initial parameters.

The key mechanisms in this derivation were prescriptive norms (see discussion, chapter 3) that defined the substantive elements required to meet particular human needs. By the period after World War II, a massive range of "Construction Norms and Rules (*Stroitel'nye Normy i Pravila*)" or SNiPs (*SNiPy*) had been elaborated by central technical institutes. SNiPs were arranged in nested hierarchies that defined ratios among all possible elements of a Soviet city. At the top of this hierarchy were "city-building coefficients" that established general equivalencies between industrial laborers and a total city population. One level down were norms that defined the number of health, educational, and housing facilities required to meet this population's needs. For example, the Belaya Kalitva general plan referred to SNiP 41–58, which defined the relationship between the size of the local population and the amount of land in a city that had to be set aside for buildings that housed stores, cafeterias, social facilities, and cultural facilities. Further clusters of norms defined the facilities required in any given domain of city-building activity—communal services, housing, leisure, education, health, and culture—and specified the infrastructure, staffing, and other requirements for these facilities.

In principle, planners could move from any given element in a plan to any other. Since the SNiPs defined substantive or physical equivalencies, one could start with a quantity on either side of a given equation and derive the quantity on the other side. But as the derivation of a new city was laid out in general plans for cities, the process of planning had a definite directionality. Industrial plans provided the baseline: a certain number of workers in "city-forming" production. From there, the plan described the composition of the future population and the apparatus required to meet its daily needs. In sum, if plans for settlement addressed the correlative development of population and production, the general plan for a city laid out a new city *khoziaistvo*.

From Industrial Production to Local Population

The first logical step of general plans was to move from the labor needs of industrial production to a general population. As we have seen, a "control figure"—both a target and a planning baseline—for the population was already established in plans for settlement. The role of the general plan was to determine the size and structure of this population as it developed over time. The derivation began from the number of individuals involved in what was called "city-forming" production. This crucial concept referred to all those organizations and activities—first of all major industrial enterprises—that served an area larger than the city whose planning was in question. City-forming production excluded, meanwhile, enterprises of "local significance" (*mestnoe znachenie*) whose purpose was to serve only the needs of the city itself. This distinction reflected a crucial assumption that was rooted in the earliest discussions in the 1930s: the existence of any given city was justified by its contribution to the broader planned economy—the *narodnoe khoziaistvo*—of the Soviet Union. Everything related to what Miliutin had called the *internal* organization of the city—local mechanisms of need fulfillment—was a separate planning problem that fell in the domain of city-building.[12]

Table 4.1, reproduced from the *Explanatory Notes* for the Belaya Kalitva general plan, summarizes the basic assumptions underlying plans for the correlative development of population and production in Belaya Ka-

TABLE 4.1
Population Calculations—Belaya Kalitva General Plan

Projected Employment in City-Forming Production, Belaya Kalitva General
Plan, 1964

Enterprise	Current employment	First priority (5–7 years)	Plan period (20 years)
BKMZ (Number 16)	4,000	6,000	11,000
Repair shop	286	300	300
Fur Factory	—	2,000	2,000
Knitting Factory	—	1,350	1,350
Stocking Factory	—	1,800	5,350
Meat Factory (old)	160	—	—
Meat Factory (new)	—	300	400
Coal Mining	2,494	2,000	1,000

Distribution of City-Forming Personnel (thousands), Belaya Kalitva General
Plan, 1964

City-forming group	Current	First priority	Plan period
Industry	7.1	15.8	23.4
External transport	1.2	2	2.5
Technical training	0.4	0.7	1.5
Administration	1.3	0.8	0.8
Construction	0.7	3.5	3
Agriculture	0.8	0.6	0.6
Reserve	—	—	3.0
Total	11.5	23.4	34.8

Projected Distribution of Population, Belaya Kalitva General Plan, 1964

	First priority	Plan period
Planned number of city-forming personnel	23,400	34,000
Relative weight of city-forming personnel	29%	30%
Planned population size	80,000	120,000

litva. These tables followed conventional practice in projecting development over two time periods: "first-priority" construction—generally five to seven years—and the planning period—generally twenty years (Khauke and Magidin 1963). It projected an expansion at "No. 16," the aluminum enterprise, from 4,000 in 1963 to 11,000. Employment in local coal mines was anticipated to drop from 2,494 to 1,000. A number of new factories were proposed, presumably to deal with problems noted in the *Plan for Settlement* related to women's employment (the knitting, stocking, and fur factories) and the absorption of labor from closing mines.

The laborers engaged in city-forming production formed the core of a larger group of city-forming personnel (*gradoobrazuiushchie kadry*), which included employees of transport, administrative, and repair organizations, as well as workers in technical institutes directly connected with city-forming production (table 3.2).[13] This group also included a "reserve" population of 3,000 individuals, apparently introduced as an error factor—a rare acknowledgment that the planned adjustments between population and production might not be easily achieved.

The final step was to calculate a total population based on the size of city-forming groups. In addition to city-forming personnel, the total population included those too young, old, or sick to work. It also included workers employed in general education, health, and leisure facilities. In practice, planners simplified these calculations by means of a "city-building coefficient," that established a normative relationship, which might change as a city matured, between "city-forming personnel" and a total population. It was no coincidence that the projected population over the planning period, 120,000, exactly matched the "target population" defined in the city *Plan for Settlement*. The point, after all, was not to adjust the target population in light of local conditions, but to adjust all possible planned elements of a future city in relation to the target population that had been derived from industrial plans.

The City Khoziaistvo

The second step in the *Explanatory Notes* for the Belaya Kalitva general plan was to derive the facilities, infrastructures, and services required to meet the daily needs of the local population—the city *khoziaistvo*. Two major parts of the city *khoziaistvo* were treated separately in general plans. The first—the "social sphere" (*sotsial'naia sfera*)—included health, leisure, and general education facilities. The second—the "communal sphere" (*kommunal'naia sfera*), sometimes referred to as the communal *khoziaistvo*—included all the material elements of the city: housing, roads, electricity, transport, water, gas, heat, and other infrastructures required to support local life. In both areas the plan followed a simple logic: first, it described the inventory of existing facilities; second, it compared existing facilities to normatively prescribed levels of provisioning; and third, it specified additional facilities required to close the gap.

In its discussion of the social sphere, the *Explanatory Notes* described a situation that was not entirely dismal. The number of teachers and doctors in 1964 was not far below normative levels given the size and structure of the population. The network of facilities would simply have to be expanded as the population grew. Plans for this future expansion were formulated using *raschety*, or tabulations. For most domains in which *raschety* were calculated, a basic planning unit was established. These planning units allowed a single element such as a hospital bed or a classroom to stand in for a complex of personnel, equipment, structures, and other resource needs, thus simplifying the adjustments between planning problems in related domains. For example, in the case of health care, *koiki* (hospital beds) were used as a proxy for a cluster of related elements: square meters of hospital space, medical equipment, medical personnel, and demands on infrastructure services such as electricity and heat. Belaya Kalitva's general plan worked off a norm of 11.2 hospital-bed units per 1,000 people. On this basis, it was possible to calculate the number of hospital-bed units required given the projected future growth of the city:

$$(11.2 \ koiki/1{,}000 \ \text{population}) \times (100{,}000 \ \text{population}) = 1120 \ koiki$$

Calculations based on such norms implied adjustments in related areas. The number of hospital-bed units, for example, would have implications for the amount of land devoted to hospitals and clinics, and for the number of doctors and nurses required to staff them. Additional workers and facilities, in turn, required adjustments in housing, social services, and utilities.

The second major area of planning for the city *khoziaistvo*—the communal sphere—presented different challenges. By the early 1960s, development in the social sphere roughly conformed to norms, in large part because the Soviet Union was quite successful in rapidly training large numbers of doctors, nurses, and teachers. By contrast, the communal sphere, including most importantly housing and the technical infrastructure related to it, was basically *un*developed. The Belaya Kalitva general plan recorded 305,000 square meters of housing in the city—far below normative levels given the population at the time—of which 214,000 square meters were accounted for by the single-family "private" houses that dominated construction of the early post–World War II period. Buildings over two stories accounted for only 6,000 square meters of housing; most of the remainder was barracks.

The general plan projected that one million square meters of housing had to be built by the end of the planning period—an increase of more than ten times over 1964 levels. Expansion of the housing stock presented a range of problems related to spatial development in the city. By 1964 Belaya Kalitva's territory was already filled by single-family houses. Two options for claiming more space were explored in the *Explanatory Notes*: first, the demolition of single-family houses; and second, construction of a major new residential region on the far bank of the river Kalitva. The plan also noted that expansion of the housing stock would require local construction capacity of 35,000 square feet per year, a modest volume by the standards of big cities, but a major challenge in Belaya Kalitva. This rate of construction placed requirements not only on equipment but also on construction workers and on facilities for producing construction materials. The expanding communal housing stock would also create new demands for centralized communal services, which were basically nonexistent at the time the plan was prepared. In the early 1960s no centralized system of either sewage or running water served the city, although a few buildings in the new settlement near No. 16 were connected to the enterprise's water system. Gas and centralized heat were available only in a small number of "communal" houses. The plan, thus, called for the construction of centralized infrastructures—heat, water, and sewerage—and of the distribution networks—pipes and wires—required to link these and other infrastructures to the city's housing stock and other buildings. As in the social sphere, planning in this domain drew from standard designs, and tabulations were used to calculate the capacity of utilities based on assumptions concerning the number of users and on norms for provisioning. For example, in the case of centralized heating systems, the required output of heat (*raskhod tepla*) was derived by calculating the need for "heat-energy" in industrial production, in indoor heating, and for hot tap water, thus allowing planners to design a boiler with the capacity required to meet these needs. A similar structure of norms was used to calculate requirements for water consumption, trash collection, wastewater treatment, and so on.

And so it went—in area after area, for facilities large and small—for all the possible elements of a future city. And by the post–World War II period the list of these elements that, together, comprised the city *khoziaistvo*, was expansive. An entry in the 1969 edition of the *Big Soviet Encyclopedia*, that essential bestiary of Soviet life, defined the city *khoziaistvo* as the "complex of services, enterprises, engineering facilities and networks, whose aim is to satisfy the everyday communal ... and social-cultural needs of the inhabitants of cities." These included "the housing *khoziaistvo*, the communal *khoziaistvo*, the enterprises and organizations for meeting the population's daily needs, city transport, communications, trade and communal cafeterias, and ... facilities for education, health care, culture [and] social protection."[14] A Soviet urbanist handbook published in 1977 offered an even more detailed catalog:

- housing and related services (heat, light, water supply, sewage, gas, garbage);
- internal transportation (roads, sidewalks, streetlights);
- services such as dry cleaners, barbers, public baths, pools, street cleaning, general lighting of the city;
- supply of foodstuffs, including organizations for collective food service;
- supply of other consumer goods—such as clothes, shoes, furniture, and cooking supplies;
- repair shops for consumer goods such as clothing, shoes, refrigerators, televisions;
- medical services, including pharmaceutical products;
- organizations for raising and educating children (kindergartens, schools, and so on);
- sports facilities, including stadiums;
- organizations to satisfy the cultural needs of the population, such as theaters, movie houses, concert halls, museums, libraries;
- communications, such as postal service, telegraph, telephone, and radio;
- organizations for the "rational use of free time"—parks, clubs, restaurants, dance halls;
- organizations to ensure order, including the police, fire crews, and so on (Berkhman, F. F. Diderikhs et al. 1977: 8–9).

And so on, indeed. The list is necessarily comprehensive. When engaged in total planning, you have to think of everything.

ENTERPRISE-CENTRISM AND INFRASTRUCTURAL SOCIAL MODERNITY

The remainder of this chapter examines how the planning framework laid out in Belaya Kalitva's General Plan was linked to practical developments. This question may seem to imply a concern with "implementation," but I do not use this term for two reasons, one methodological, the other germane to the practical organization of city-building activity. The methodological reason is that I am not concerned with whether this or that work was actually built, or whether this or that norm was precisely followed. Rather, I am concerned with the broad form of the Soviet social as it emerged during the late decades of the Soviet period. I will have more to say about this point when I address the problem of "assessing" Soviet city-building in the next chapter.

Another reason why it is difficult to address the "implementation" of plans has to do with the practical organization of city-building activity. Like other long-term plans in the Soviet Union, general plans for Soviet cities contained broad timelines and rough estimates of costs. But they generally did not provide detailed construction or investment schedules beyond the most general parameters. Nor were the works anticipated in plans assigned to a specific organization with the resources or bureaucratic power to manage their implementation. Organs of local territorial administration—local soviets—were nominally responsible for questions of "local significance" (*mestnoe znachenie*), including the implementation of city plans. But local soviets were weak, particularly in small cities. Consequently, a range of different organizations—social ministries (education and health), the local government and, most importantly, industrial enterprises, all formally under the supervision and control of local party organs—might take responsibility for the "implementation" of some part of a plan. And as William Taubman showed in *Governing Soviet Cities* (1973), there was little coordination among them, and constant battles over priorities and spheres of influence.[15] In sum, if city-building plans envisioned a unitary space of total instrumental control, then the reality of plan implementation was a tangled mess.

Thus, instead of inquiring into the implementation of plans per se, I want to examine how a new city *khoziaistvo* was actually assembled. The specific institutional configuration of this process, particularly what I will call the "enterprise-centric" pattern of urban development, was not anticipated in city plans, and it sometimes led to outcomes that directly contradicted the wishes of city-builders. But these plans nonetheless allow us to understand the distinctive features of an emerging form of collective life in Belaya Kalitva and hundreds of similar cities across the Soviet Union.

To trace this story, we have to return to the beginnings of Belaya Kalitva's industrial history. Despite the onset of industrial construction before World War II, postwar builders essentially had to begin from scratch. The war, as a local historian wrote years later, "swallowed the work of its predecessors, leaving almost nothing behind ... that would make it possible, somehow, to begin construction."[16] Available evidence indicates that the material conditions were extremely difficult. Major construction facilities in *Rostov oblast'* could be found only in the regional capital, Rostov, and in Novocherkassk, an old Cossack city far to the south. Given the state of transport infrastructure, it took two days to reach Belaya Kalitva from either city, making even the most basic construction a truly daunting task.

The first construction organization to be based in Belaya Kalitva, named AliumStroi (Aluminum Construction), recruited its first workers during the winter of 1950.[17] As its name suggests, AliumStroi's efforts focused on industrial construction, specifically on Belaya Kalitva's city-forming metallurgic enterprise. It also completed the handful of buildings in the "new" settlement near the enterprise, including some barracks and other one- or two-story housing units for industrial workers and technical specialists, along with a stadium, a hospital, and the first schools. But these efforts were limited by scarce resources and by the absence of industrial methods and materials; early communal housing was constructed of wood, brick, or locally available rock. And the vast majority of housing construction after World War II was not communal housing at all but small huts built by individuals or families, whose efforts were encouraged by authorities as a postwar expedient.[18] As late as 1963, when studies were conducted in connection with Belaya Kalitva's general plan, such "individual" housing comprised 56 percent of the total housing stock. The remainder was accounted for by shoddily built "communal" housing, most of which was meant to be temporary.

Real progress in communal construction began only in the 1960s, following a significant shift in the organizational underpinnings of city-building activity. AliumStroi, having completed its central task of industrial construction, turned its attention elsewhere, in particular to the coal settlements around Belaya Kalitva. Meanwhile, Belaya Kalitva's city-forming enterprise No. 16—we can now use its Soviet-era name, The Belo-Kalitvean Metallurgic Factory (Belo-Kalitvenskii Metallurgicheskii Zavod) or BKMZ—emerged as the most important organization in financing and actually building works anticipated in the city plan. As early as 1954, BKMZ organized its own department for housing administration (*domoupravlenie*), a step that was typical of industrial enterprises struggling to attract workers from virtually the beginning of the Soviet period (Kotkin 1993a). BKMZ's first construction project was a kindergarten, and its efforts expanded into housing later in the decade with the construction of Belaya Kalitva's first multistory brick apartment blocks. It is notable that these initial efforts at apartment building did not rely on industrial methods or even, necessarily, on cadres of professional builders. Most early housing was built using the "individual method," so-called not because it involved the construction of single-family houses but because construction was undertaken by BKMZ's workers or their spouses, in return for which they received apartments.[19] This individual method accounted for the vast majority of urban construction during the 1950s and 1960s, including five kindergartens and twenty-three housing blocks. These buildings, collectively, formed the core of the new central district that took shape near BKMZ.

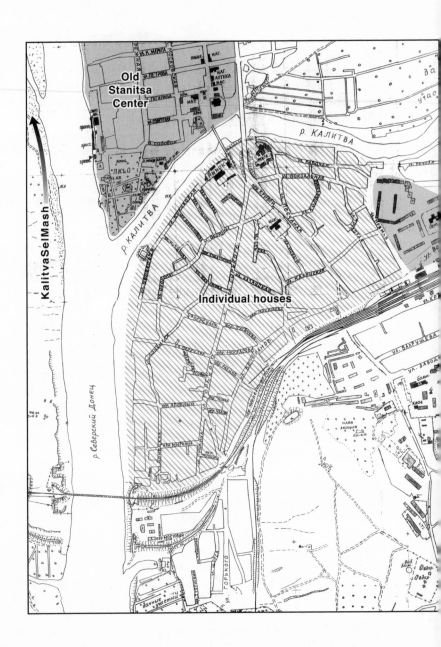

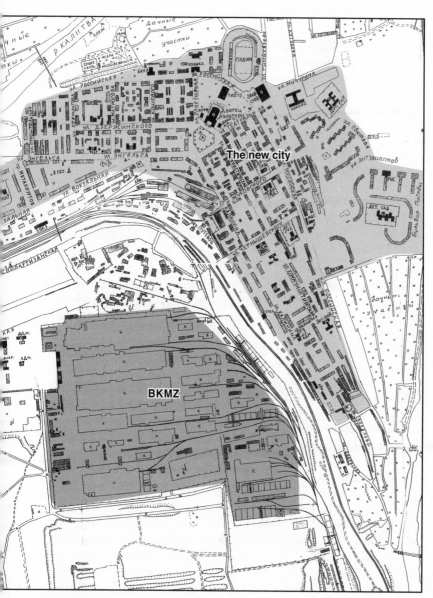

Figure 4.1. Map of Belaya Kalitva. The nineteenth-century *stanitsa* in Belaya Kalitva was located just north of the confluence of the Kalitva and Donets rivers. BKMZ, the city-forming metallurgic enterprise, was built after World War II at some remove from the existing settlement, near a planned "new" city. But most housing built in the early post–World War II period was constructed by individuals in an unplanned settlement across the Kalitva from the old *stanitsa* center. It was only in the 1960s and 1970s that extensive housing construction took place in the new city. In the early 1970s, work also began on a new machine-building enterprise—Kalitvasel'mash—and a new city on the far bank of the Donets, north of the old *stanitsa* center.

During the 1960s BKMZ also began to play a central role in another crucial area of city-building activity: the construction of urban utilities such as water, sewage, and heating systems. The "production" facilities for these utilities—boilers or filtration stations—were generally located on the grounds of the enterprise itself. Over the course of the 1960s and 1970s the pipes that comprised the distribution (or collection) systems for these utilities began to radiate out from BKMZ, winding their way through Belaya Kalitva's growing collection of apartments, schools, kindergartens, clinics, and offices. These urban networks literally assembled the city through new webs of material interconnection, plugging the population—whether in schools, clinics, or apartment blocks—into mechanisms of centralized need fulfillment.

We can illustrate this process by examining one of the most important infrastructures constructed during the late 1960s in Belaya Kalitva: the centralized heating system. In the years following the war most residences were heated either through boilers located in individual apartments and houses or through communal boilers that served small clusters of buildings. One such "local" boiler provided hot water and steam for industrial processes at BKMZ; another served the handful of barracks and other residential buildings that sprang up in the new settlement near the enterprise. In the late 1960s, the small neighborhood boilers were removed, and the existing distribution network was connected to the enterprise boiler, whose capacity was expanded to meet growing need. Over time, the majority of buildings in Belaya Kalitva, and all the buildings in the new central district around BKMZ, were heated by a single industrial boiler comlex and linked to a single heat network (teploset').

It is notable that this centralization of the urban network in Belaya Kalitva took place almost simultaneously with another centralization and "networking" of resource distribution across the Soviet Union. The small boilers constructed in the early years after World War II ran on local coal. But in the late 1960s the enterprise boiler was converted to natural gas. Thus, just as individuals and families were resettled into apartments, and as apartments were plugged into centralized urban networks, the city as a whole was being connected to a rapidly expanding national infrastructure that linked settlements all over the Soviet Union to gas fields in northwest Siberia that were developed after World War II.[20] In this sense, the enterprise boiler (like other urban utilities) became a point of articulation between an urban regime of need fulfillment and a national regime of resource distribution. The new works in the communal sphere were, thus, crucial elements of what Stephen Graham and Simon Marvin have called a "networked" urbanism (2002: 69) They articulated what might be called an "infrastructural" social modernity, both *assembling* the social and allowing it to be managed as an object of government.

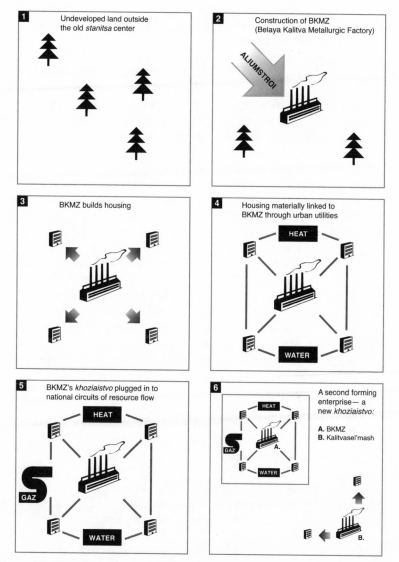

Figure 4.2. Enterprise-centric social modernity. After its construction by an out-side building organization, BKMZ, like enterprises in most Soviet small cities, assumed a dominant role in building housing and urban infrastructure in Belaya Kalitva. Urban infrastructures plugged residents into centralized urban networks of provisioning, such as the heating system. Through the construction of these material infrastructures a new urban *khoziaistvo* was assembled around the city-forming enterprise, and ultimately linked to the *narodnoe khoziaistvo*—the na-tional economy—of the Soviet Union. When construction began on a second city-forming enterprise in the early 1970s the process was repeated: a new enterprise, a new *khoziaistvo*.

Although forms of "networked urbanism" emerged around the world over the course of the twentieth century, the Soviet variant had some distinctive features. One, which will be important in subsequent chapters, concerns the rigidity of the interconnections that were constituted through urban services such as the heating system. Soviet urban utilities were centralized to an unusual degree. The technical setup of heat systems—for example, the fact that they were not fitted with individual control mechanisms, since heat delivery was based on norms—meant that all the users of a given utility were regulated as a single unit of consumption. Another distinctive feature of the Soviet variant of infrastructural modernity concerned its institutional form, in particular the way that, through it, a particular adjustment between population and production was literally hardwired into the material forms of the city. Max Weber famously argued that the changing relationships among the family, processes of production, and mechanisms of need fulfillment were a crucial diacritic of capitalist modernity. If in all noncapitalist forms of organization, commercial businesses tended "to be part of the greater *household* (the *oikos*) of a ruler or landowner," then "[t]he modern rational organization of capitalist business" depended on "the separation of household and business" (2002: 361–62). As we saw in the last chapter, Soviet planners, motivated by the very different imperatives of the Soviet system, imagined a parallel transformation. The development of socialist cities would be part and parcel of the displacement of the *khoziaistvo*—in the double sense of production and need fulfillment—from the household. Production would be taken up by industrial enterprises that were integrated with the national economy—the *narodnoe khoziaistvo*. Need fulfillment would be displaced to the city—the *gorodskoe khoziaistvo*. As Soviet cities developed, this displacement of *khoziaistvo* was, indeed, slowly realized, but it evolved in a direction that urban theorists had not anticipated. Particularly in small cities, *narodnoe khoziaistvo*—the nexus of industrial production—and *gorodskoe khoziaistvo*—the nexus of need fulfillment—were merged in the figure of the city-forming enterprise.

GENERALIZING SOCIAL MODERNITY—
POPULATION AND PRODUCTION

By the late 1960s, a coherent institutional pattern of city-building had emerged in Belaya Kalitva. But it was hardly a completed project. Services in the social sphere, such as health and education, approached the norm-defined levels put forth in the city plan. But the other elements of the city *khoziaistvo*, particularly those that had to be articulated through resource intensive infrastructures, reached only a small minority of Belaya Kalitva's residents. It was only during a third period—one situated surprisingly late in the Soviet period—that the majority of the population was plugged into new regimes of centralized provisioning and, thus, into the matrix of a networked urbanism. In wrapping up this discussion of the Soviet social, I want to briefly consider this *generalization* of infrastructural social modernity in Belaya Kalitva, which can be traced through what may seem initially to be a surprising proxy: the construction of multistory apartment blocks.

Sovietologists have long noted that the changing forms of housing served as an index of urban development in Soviet cities. Blair Ruble observed, for example, that the progression in construction methods over the post–World War II period—from individual houses and barracks to four- and five-story brick apartments, to buildings of nine stories and more made of prefabricated concrete panels—made it possible to date parts of a city through its housing types (Ruble 1993: 238; French 1995: 77).[21] The progression of housing forms was also a crucial indicator of urban modernity. The construction of multistory apartments often coincided with other dimensions of a city's physical development: widened and more carefully planned streets; green space between buildings with benches and playgrounds; neighborhood planning, with schools and kindergartens built in proximity to residential units (French 1995: 81). What is more, as we have already seen, apartment blocks were planned and constructed as living units that were fully integrated into centralized urban infrastructures. Consequently, resettlement of urban populations from barracks or small huts into apartment blocks was simultaneously a process of plugging populations into centralized regimes of communal provisioning. For all these reasons, as a 1984 update to the Belaya Kalitva general plan observed, the average number of stories of housing in a city—what city-builders called *etazhnost'*—was a key indicator of "an urban way of life [*obraz zhizni*]."[22]

With this in mind, it is striking to note how late in the Soviet period mass resettlement into apartment blocks—and, thus, the emergence of an "urban way of life"—took place in Belaya Kalitva. In 1963, buildings of four stories or more accounted for only 6,000 square meters of the housing stock. A decade and a half later, a meager 60,000 square meters of such housing had been built. But after 1976 construction exploded. From 1976 to 1983, 300,000 square meters of new housing was built, a five-fold increase in six years. By the end of the Soviet period, apartment blocks of over four stories accounted for over 470,000 square meters of housing. How is this rapid acceleration explained? The immediate explanation is the adoption of construction using prefabricated concrete panels. When compared to brick construction, which continued to predominate in Belaya Kalitva throughout the 1960s and into the 1970s, concrete panel construction offered tremendous production economies. But here I want to focus not on *technical* developments but on their organizational bases, for the construction explosion was linked to a crucial development in Belaya Kalitva's city-building makeup.

It will be recalled that in the 1963 *Plan for Settlement* and the 1964 general plan Belaya Kalitva's planners anticipated that further adjustments would be required in the city's pattern of settlement—that is, in the adjustments between population and production. Labor freed by the closure of coal mines, and new labor added due to the integration of women into the workforce, would have to be accommodated by expanding local industrial employment. The general plan proposed that added employment could be provided by a number of smaller enterprises including a knitting factory and a meat processing plant. But these plans were scrapped, and instead, by a 1971 decree of the Central Committee, construction was undertaken on a single, large machine-building enterprise called Kalitvasel'mash (Kalitva Agricultural Machine-building Factory). This enterprise was to be a "daughter" (*dochernee*) enterprise of the agricultural machinery producer Rossel'mash, a sprawling giant of Soviet industry that, by the late Soviet period, had such affiliates spread across cities of southern Russia.

The shift to a single large enterprise was indicative of what by the late Soviet period was a mature institutional pattern of urban development. General plans referred to cities as a single unit. But the unit of practical development—particularly in small cities[23]—was the integrated socioindustrial complex of a city-forming enterprise. And it was precisely as such that Belaya Kalitva's new enterprise was planned and, for the most part, built: as an autonomous socioindustrial world. Much as, twenty years earlier, BKMZ had been located at some remove from the city's old administrative center, the new enterprise was built across the river Kalitva on one of two sites identified in the 1964 general plan as possible locations for future development. The social and communal facilities for workers and their families were not integrated into the existing city. Instead, a new heat boiler, schools, and clinics were built around this enterprise to serve a large settlement of concrete-panel apartments. Though it was located within Belaya Kalitva's administrative boundaries, the new settlement was planned as an entirely new city, with its own city-forming enterprise and its own *khoziaistvo* (see figure 4.2).

In 1977, a plan was approved for this new settlement, which was named Zarechnoe (Over-the-river). This plan, and the timing of its implementation, indicates how far Soviet city-building had come from the early 1960s. Twenty-five years passed from the time ground was broken on BKMZ to the first city plan; fifteen years from the resumption of construction after World War II. By contrast, only six years passed from the decree approving Kalitvasel'mash to a general plan for the new settlement. Construction in Zarechnoe was slow, and it encountered problems that, as we see in the next chapter, frustrated city-builders to the end of the Soviet period. But it more closely approximated the coordinated development of population, production, and social welfare—of *rasselenie* and *khoziaistvo*—that city-builders always imagined. It was not just that housing blocks, infrastructures, schools, clinics, and kindergartens rose in tandem with industrial construction. More striking, perhaps, was the fact that this enterprise was built at all. The justification for the construction of Zarechnoe was not that existing plans for industrial development had to be translated "onto the territory" by adjusting populations around it. Rather, it was that an *existing* population needed an industrial enterprise.

The Moral Economy of City-Building

In the next chapter we will see that the development in Zarechnoe is indicative of a broader modulation in the relationship between city-building and industrial planning that can be traced over the arc of the Soviet period. In the early Soviet period industrial development was given absolute priority. By the late Soviet period, plans for industrial development were sometimes bent around an existing urban population's "need" for industrial jobs. Here, however, we will wrap up our discussion of city planning, the city *khoziaistvo*, and the process through which a new form of collective life was assembled in Belaya Kalitva.

By the end of the Soviet period, Belaya Kalitva was progressing toward the ultimately modest future outlined in city-building plans. This was a future of universal social services, of communal housing and therefore of populations plugged in to centralized infrastructures, and of increasingly balanced adjustments between the population and industrial production. The plan's implementation was hardly a model of rule-bound bureaucratic impersonalism. But it is not wrong to say that the tight structure of norms articulated in plans was beginning to find its correlate in a coherent reality, a collectivity that was bound together through material connections, bureaucratic apparatuses, and the curious organizational forms of an enterprise-centric pattern of urban modernity. This complex of elements was one key dimension of what I have called the Soviet social.

Though it is not the focus of my concerns—which are, in their own way, bureaucratic-impersonal—it bears noting that this new collectivity was tied together in another sense as well. The project of city-building— linked, as it was, to postwar reconstruction and to the emerging regime of Soviet social welfare—was "solidarising" in the sense that it forged moral ties based on shared historical experience and shared values. At one level, there is nothing particularly strange or unfamiliar about this dimension of the Soviet experience. As Gøsta Esping-Andersen has pointed out, social welfare states everywhere in rich industrial countries presented "a ray of hope to those who were asked to sacrifice for the common good in the war effort"; they were crucial, in this sense, to the "political project of nation-building" (1996: 2). Similarly, city-building was, in important ways, the most immediate connection many citizens had to the all-important project of postwar reconstruction. In Belaya Kalitva, many residents literally built with their hands, through tremendous exertion and following tremendous sacrifice, a new urban world. This project bound residents to the city and to each other. Writing in the late 1980s of the energy with which Belaya Kalitva's builders worked after the war, a local historian wrote of his own struggle to understand "the enthusiasm of people who had converged on an unknown place from different corners of the country." The straightforward answer was that "all of them came together around one task: they tried to heal the wounds of the war as quickly as possible."[24] The process of city-building was, in this sense, a key feature of the Soviet moral landscape after World War II.

As the postwar period progressed, this new moral landscape was shaped in sometimes surprising ways around the peculiar material, organizational, and normative forms of city-building. Apartment blocks, infrastructures, and social services were pillars of the late Soviet regime that George Breslauer (1978) called "welfare state authoritarianism," to designate a situation in which it was the Soviet system of social welfare, rather than the terror or socialist ideology, that lent durability and legitimacy to a rapidly calcifying authoritarian system. Meanwhile, the enterprise-centric pattern of social welfare provision gave new solidarisms concrete institutional form and sociological embodiment. It was often the directors of city-forming enterprises who were the key figures in the local *khoziaistvo*—who were looked upon, to invoke another crucial term from Russian moral vocabulary, as the *khoziains* of the city (see discussion, chapter 5).[25] These *khoziains* were expected to show a kind of personalistic care for each and every member of the *khoziaistvo*. They glowed with the warmth of industrial paternalism.

All of this may seem rather mundane when compared with the visions of a revolutionary urbanism put forth in the 1920s; or even compared to the more "realistic" vision of the garden city that provided many guiding norms of Soviet urbanism to the end of socialism. It was mundane, certainly. But what, in the end, was the garden city all about? It was an industrial settlement of limited size, that was neither town nor country, but the town-country, as Ebenezer Howard (1965) famously put it: in which industrial life would be built close to the "beauty of nature"; in which the correlative development of population and production would be carefully managed; in which the daily needs of the population would be carefully planned for; and in which, finally, a spirit of cooperation and public-spiritedness pervaded, linking citizens to a common project. And what was Belaya Kalitva by the end—really the *very* end—of the Soviet period? It was a small industrial settlement tucked neatly into a confluence of rivers ranged with pretty white bluffs, with collective farms and individual garden plots just beyond the boundaries that marked the city's modest territory. It was a city in which, from some perspectives, a livable balance between industrial production and residential development had been achieved; in which a moral economy was organized around the *khoziains* of the city, and around the mundane elements of urban infrastructure and social welfare provisioning.

We should not, of course, romanticize the situation. Enough has been written about the scourges of the late Soviet period to know that there is not much to long for in the mature world of the socialist small city. And the products of late-Soviet construction in Belaya Kalitva—the unfinished production facilities of Kalitvasel'mash, rows of decaying apartment blocks in which slight modulation of ornamentation on metal balconies counted as adding diversity and color to the cityscape—remind us that the "goods" this system delivered were not all that great. One knows, finally, that the moral landscape of late socialism also included crippling cynicism about many spheres of official life and about grandiose claims concerning a radiant future. But as Alexei Yurchak (2006) has shown, there were some elements of official life in the late socialist system to which Soviet citizens had deep and genuine connection and commitment. This is true, certainly, of city-building in Belaya Kalitva. For all the inefficiency, corruption, drunkenness, shortage, pollution, disaffection, lethargy, mind-blowing waste, and dreary sameness that must have marked late-Soviet Belaya Kalitva, one understands that there must also have been something affectingly pastoral about life in this actually existing socialist city.

CHAPTER FIVE

Consolidation, Stagnation, Breakup

Assessing Soviet City-building

THE PICTURE OF CITY-BUILDING presented in the prior chapter substantially contradicts the story about urban planning that emerged in Soviet and foreign literature over the last decades of the Soviet period. If through the 1960s Soviet urban planning and local administration were seen to exemplify effective new forms of bureaucratic impersonalism, then by the 1970s this image was being challenged.[1] It was observed that productivist norms created incentives to build in a shoddy way, or to do the minimum required for work to count toward annual production targets. Attention was also drawn to the distortions introduced by bureaucratic politics that limited city planners' ability to influence local developments. Here a particularly important role was played by industrial ministries, which, through their "local" affiliates—city-forming enterprises—emerged as central players in urban development. Ministerial dominance institutionalized the long-standing priority given to industrial versus social or urban development. It also created imbalances within cities—development proceeded faster in some areas than others—that city-builders and local administrators were unable to correct. As William Taubman (1971) points out, all these problems were particularly acute in small cities, where enterprise-centrism was most pronounced.

The distortions introduced by ministerialism were evident at the national level as well. Cities with enterprises attached to powerful ministries developed more quickly. And city planners were not able to exert as much control as they might have liked over patterns of settlement on the regional or national level. Big cities got bigger, and population growth in small cities often fell short of targets. The image that emerges from these accounts is one of industrial suzerainties, not of a bureaucratic-impersonal system that spread the norms and forms of city-building over both local and national populations. City-building plans, in this context, were often judged to be nearly irrelevant. Taubman argued that for many cities general plans were "more or less useless" (1973: 32). And R. A. French concluded that urban development took place "only lightly under the control of plans" (1995: 93).

On their own terms, it is hard to dispute these findings. If our central concern is the relationship between the often vague schedules for construction laid out in plans and the reality of urban transformation, then one is bound to conclude that failures were rife and plans were often ignored. If one asks whether developments were strictly dictated by norms, then one could point to imbalances both within and among cities. These were the questions posed by Soviet city planners, who constantly bemoaned their weak position relative to large enterprises. It is no surprise that Sovietologists—whose understanding was inevitably based on what Soviet planners wrote—came to similar conclusions.[2]

But from the perspective of post-Soviet Russia, we might be less concerned with the ideality of plans and the details of implementation, and more with whether city-building tells us something about the distinctive forms of collective life that emerged in Soviet cities, and about the broad adjustments of population and production over national space. From this broader perspective, it is possible to acknowledge the distortions introduced by ministerial dominance, the imbalances in plan implementation, and the vast universe of unofficial activities of all kinds while still recognizing that certain dimensions of Soviet urban modernity—not only developments within cities but also the urban structure of the country as a whole—can only be understood in reference to the norms and forms of Soviet city-building.

Consider the late-Soviet development of the cities in which I worked, Belaya Kalitva and Rodniki. Certainly the distortions noted by Sovietologists were evident in Belaya Kalitva. Up until the very end of the Soviet period, the social and communal spheres of the city lagged behind industrial developments. Urban construction proceeded more quickly in the "new" region around BKMZ than in the old *stanitsa* center, which, at the end of the Soviet period, was still comprised of individual houses and small lanes and was poorly served by urban infrastructures. But seen more broadly, if one compared Belaya Kalitva's 1964 general plan to the built city at the end of the twentieth century, one would conclude that what *had* been completed conformed to plans: buildings were built where they had been planned; infrastructures ran, more or less, as indicated in diagrams from the 1960s; and the further adjustment of population and production anticipated in the general plan, though delayed and modified, was undertaken with the construction of Belaya Kalitva's second city-forming enterprise and, around it, a new city.

Development in Rodniki was delayed even longer. A city plan was not approved until the late 1960s; and a 1987 review of the plan's implementation, noting works that were left incomplete and imbalances in urban development, concluded that Rodniki's general plan had "not been fulfilled." But it also found that "[o]verall construction took place in accordance with [the general plan's] proposals" and did not violate planning decisions.[3] The Russian researchers G. N. Tumanik and M. R. Kolpakova (1996) have found a similar situation in other small cities.

In sum, we might say that, at least in small cities, to the extent that urban modernity took shape, it conformed to the norms and forms of city-building. Of course there was tremendous scope for activities that were never anticipated in any plan: the unofficial trade in foreign luxury goods, country houses built for Party bosses or enterprise directors, and so on. But if we are talking about the admittedly circumscribed domains of "official" urban and social welfare planning, it is not misleading to say that city-building plans defined what could *be* in Soviet cities: kindergartens, schools, clinics, hospitals, sidewalks, roads, streetlights, stores, cafeterias, barber shops, dry cleaners, bath houses, parks, apartment blocks, houses of culture, stadiums, gymnasiums, heating systems, electrical grids, telephone systems, water systems, sewage systems, and gas distribution networks. Actual developments sometimes disappointed for their omissions but they were not fundamentally at variance with this universe of possible objects.

What of the national scene? What of the distribution of social welfare and communal services over national space and the size-structure of Soviet cities? Here too we observe imbalances and significant deviations from city-building ideals; but we also find patterns that can only be understood in reference to the norms of city-building. Administrative centers and large cities did indeed develop much more quickly than small cities, as is witnessed by the delayed development of urban amenities in cities like Rodniki and Belaya Kalitva. But these imbalances, though persistent, lessened in the late-Soviet period, as the distribution of social services and communal infrastructures was equalized, and more closely approximated levels defined by norms. Crucial in this development were national infrastructures—not only material networks but also bureaucracies such as the Ministry of Finance—that plugged cities into national regimes of resource distribution.

The best-studied example of such equalization is the budgetary system, which was crucial to financing local education and health care facilities. As Donna Bahry (1987) has shown, the distribution of core services in the social sphere displayed a marked equalizing tendency over the late-Soviet period. This equalization is most readily explained, she argued, by a national finance bureaucracy that allocated resources according to the same social norms used in city-building plans. At the same time, she found limited evidence that the political machinations of powerful ministries or Party bosses substantially influenced the distribution of resources.[4] An equivalent study has not been conducted for the works of the communal sphere, but a similar pattern of universalization and equalization can be traced. By the end of the Soviet period, the basic package of urban utilities that went along with the modern apartment block had reached over 90 percent of the urban population. Here too an important factor was the extension of infrastructures—first electricity and then gas—that linked cities to networks of pipes and wires that distributed resources over national territory. Budgets, gas and electricity networks, and urban utilities were thus key elements in articulating an infrastructural social modernity at the *national* level.

What, finally, of the size and spatial structure of the cities that were linked through these national regimes of resource distribution? We have seen that from the very beginning of the Soviet period city-builders emphasized development in relatively small cities in which balance could be maintained between industry and a new *khoziaistvo*. And it became almost axiomatic in Sovietological literature that efforts to control city size failed.[5] On the one hand, the growth of small cities often fell short of plans. Belaya Kalitva's target population, for example, was 100,000 to 120,000. The city's central area peaked at 50,000—though the target number was nearly reached if the surrounding coal mining settlements are taken into account.[6] On the other hand, the big cities of the Soviet Union grew more than planners wanted. Here again ministerialism played its role. Ministries had incentives to locate enterprises in large cities that were close to large populations and to administrative power.

Reflecting these dynamics, Chauncey Harris famously wrote in 1970 that the Soviet Union was a country of big cities. It may have seemed so at the time. The cities that took shape around the industrial works of the Stalinist period, along with the growth of administrative capitals, meant that by that time the Soviet Union had a significant number of industrial cities with populations of more than 500,000 residents. But subsequent experience has cast the Soviet urban experience in a different light. Given the hypertrophic growth of the largest cities in the big countries of the developing world (Brazil, China, India, Mexico, Nigeria), the continued development of urban-suburban agglomerations in the United States, the decline of small industrial cities elsewhere, and the founding of many *new* small industrial cities in the Soviet Union after World War II,[7] two facts about the size structure of Soviet cities stand out. First, the *large* cities of the Soviet Union were notably *smaller* than the biggest cities of other large industrial countries; Russia has, in the language of urban geographers, a flat size-rank curve. Second, in comparative terms, the Soviet Union produced, and, just as importantly, sustained, a large number of small industrial cities like Belaya Kalitva and Rodniki. By the end of the Soviet period, 27.5 million people, or 28 percent of Russia's urban population, lived in industrial cities with populations under 100,000.

Nearly 60 percent of urban residents lived in cities with populations under 500,000.[8] These numbers present a stark contrast to the United States, where today roughly 75 percent of the urban population lives in urban agglomerations of 1,000,000 or more.[9] In sum, by the end of the Soviet period the preponderance of small cities and the relatively small size of large cities were key features of an urban pattern that was, as a 2005 World Bank report noted, "unique to Russia" (World Bank 2005: 28). This unique urban pattern bore the unmistakable imprint of urban and regional planning norms that had been established in the very earliest part of the Soviet period. All of these facts seem best understood by the gradual *consolidation*, rather than failure, of Soviet city-building, whose products comprise one of the fundamental Soviet legacies.

Pyrrhic Success

There is, of course, another perspective from which we might assess Soviet city-building. We would not ask whether, through it, we can understand some distinctive features of urban and social welfare development in the late-Soviet period. Instead, we would ask how these developments related to the broader dynamics that ultimately contributed to the Soviet Union's demise. For what appears as success from the first perspective has a very different valence when considered from the second. Here we might draw an analogy to an argument that has often been made with respect to the Soviet project of industrialization. As Daniel Chirot pointed out in 1991, in some important respects the Soviet industrial experiment, which aimed to overtake the industrial economies of the rich capitalist countries, achieved its goals. By the late twentieth century the system had indeed created "the world's most advanced 19th century economy, the world's biggest, best, most inflexible rust belt." From this perspective, the "tragedy of communism was not its failure but its success" (Chirot 1991: 6–7).

Following Chirot's observation, we might understand Soviet city-building in terms of its Pyrrhic success: what is remarkable is not its failure to create ideal "cities of the future" but its utterly pathological inability to do anything else. Here, again, comparative perspective is instructive. Small, monoindustrial towns were crucial to the development of industrial capitalism everywhere. But they underwent a long process of decline through most of the twentieth century. Soviet small cities, by contrast, were shielded from the waves of creative destruction that devastated the economic bases of most small cities in the leading industrial countries. Rodniki's textile enterprise operated with obsolete technology and a bloated workforce until Soviet breakup, passing unperturbed through a period (covering most of the twentieth century[10]) during which the global textile industry underwent multiple waves of restructuring and spatial reorganization. Similarly, despite longstanding plans to close them, the coal mines around Belaya Kalitva, and the settlements in which miners lived, survived to the very end of the Soviet period.

And not only did these small cities survive! After spending so much of the Soviet period as "non-cities"—industrial enterprises surrounded by rough collections of huts and barracks with only the most limited urban amenities—in the last Soviet decades small cities experienced rapid modernization, as the elements of urban and social infrastructure that had been anticipated at the outset of the Soviet period and specified in post–World War II general plans were built. Here, what is exceptional in the Soviet case is not so much the historical moment at which this regime of social welfare consolidated; as Esping-Andersen has pointed out (1996), in most countries social welfare states reached their apotheosis of universality only in the late 1960s and early 1970s. But in country after country, the rising tide of the welfare state was at least slowed by conjunctural shocks and structural rigidities that spurred reflexive critiques and reforms beginning in the 1970s. Although similar pressures were felt at some level in the Soviet Union, city-building, as a normative rationality for understanding urban life and planning its transformation had no way to detect or respond to them. In the face of financing shortages or construction delays, the only question it could pose was that of plan fulfillment—the success, or failure, to build the future defined by plans. This inability to understand situations except through operations of self-reference became, as we will see, a prime target of neoliberal reformers. But for Soviet planners, the only response was to redouble efforts to reach this future as quickly as possible.

The Biopolitics of Zastoi

It is ironic, but entirely coherent, that the consolidation of city-building coincided with a weakening of the Soviet industrial dynamic as it entered the period from the early 1970s to the onset of *perestroika*, referred to as "stagnation" or *zastoi*. From an economic perspective, *zastoi* is generally associated with declining rates of industrial growth and increasing obsolescence of many Soviet enterprises in world terms. Its roots are traced back to longstanding and long understood dynamics of the Soviet economy. Pressure to shut down obsolete enterprises or lines of production (or, indeed, the economic mechanisms that would be required to know what was obsolete and what was not) was virtually absent. Once a certain form of industrial activity had been organized, the Soviet system had a difficult time letting go.

Zastoi also involved a fundamental shift in the patterns of adjustment between population, production, and social welfare—what Foucault called the biopolitics of population. The Soviet model made remarkable gains when the main developmental task was to organize what might be called "primary" biopolitical adjustments—those that involved inserting "new" labor inputs into industrial production through either the mechanical or natural growth of urban populations. But by the 1970s this dynamic of primary adjustments was tapped out. The shrinking pool of rural inhabitants meant that the flow of rural-urban movement dwindled. If 23.2 million Soviet citizens migrated from the countryside to cities in the 1960s, then in the 1970s the number had shrunk to 17.8 million, and in the 1980s to 9.5 million.[11]

Coincident with this drop in the rate at which labor was added to industry was a shift in the relative priority given to industrialization versus social welfare and communal infrastructure. Beginning in the late 1950s in big cities, resources were increasingly devoted to the various works anticipated in city plans. By the 1960s and 1970s, as we have seen, a surge in construction of housing, urban infrastructure, and social service facilities foreseen in city plans was felt even in small and out-of-the way industrial cities like Belaya Kalitva and Rodniki. As Stephen Kotkin observed in his work on the steel city, Magnitogorsk, this weighty social infrastructure itself made inefficient enterprises difficult to close down or dramatically restructure. Over the long arc of the Soviet period the dominant dynamic shifted, Kotkin observed, from "production for production's sake" ("conspicuous production," as Michael Polanyi once quipped[12]) to "production for employment's sake," and for the sake of an enterprise's social commitments.[13] In a 2008 article, Clifford Gaddy argued in similar terms that "[m]any of the least competitive enterprises—the so-called dinosaurs of Soviet industry—were socially the most important. ... Entire cities depended on them. ... The importance of the manufacturing sector in Russia was an illusion economically but continued to be a political and social reality" (Gaddy 2008).

In sum, the very institutions through which successful "primary" biopolitical adjustments were organized—institutions for building new enterprises and, around them, new cities—contributed to the difficulty of "secondary" adjustments that involved redistributing production from one activity to another and moving people around the country to places where they could engage in more productive economic pursuits. Of course the Soviet Union was still able to organize large movements of population when projects of national priority required it.[14] But the dominant trend was toward increasingly inflexible mutual articulations—both spatial and institutional—between population, production, and a social welfare apparatus. By the late-Soviet period rates of internal migration had dropped to a fraction of those found in the United States or Britain.[15]

What I would like to add to this story concerns the specific dynamics of city-building in the broader context of *zastoi*. For if the period was one of industrial stagnation, city-building remained remarkably dynamic. It is not just that the various elements of the *khoziaistvo* simply *continued* to accumulate. Moreover, in some cases, the imperatives of city-building actually *drove* industrial development. Here, too, a longstanding pattern was effectively reversed. For most of the Soviet epoch new settlements were built as "cities by an enterprise" as the Soviet urban theorist Tat'iana Govorenkova put it. But in the sometimes hallucinatory twilight of the Soviet period, we see instances of the opposite phenomenon: new enterprises were built in existing cities to meet a local population's "need" for industrial labor.

To illustrate we can return to late-Soviet developments in Belaya Kalitva and Rodniki. In both cities, we have seen that in the 1960s planners identified imbalances in the adjustments between population and production that would have to be corrected in the medium term. In Belaya Kalitva and other cities of the surrounding coal mining areas the chronic problem was a lack of industrial employment for women. Rodniki and other textile cities in Ivanovo *oblast'* had the opposite problem. Since the late nineteenth century, when textile work was feminized, the region had a chronic deficit of work for men. A general shortage of jobs was added to this gender-specific imbalance after labor-saving technologies were introduced in the region's manufactories. Planners arrived at an extraordinary solution to these imbalances: build *new* enterprises to provide work for *existing* populations.

Thus, in the coal cities of Rostov *oblast'*, new light manufacturing enterprises—often textile enterprises—were planned to provide industrial work for women.[16] Meanwhile, in Ivanovo *oblast'* machine-building enterprises were planned in the region's many small textile cities. A 1976 regional plan for settlement in Ivanovo anticipated nineteen new enterprises, both large and small, that were to provide 22,000 jobs. The development of these enterprises, the plan noted, had a "double purpose": "on the one hand," they would "satisfy the growing need in light industry for equipment"; on the other hand, they would provide work for men.[17] Processes of adjustment in the two regions were contingently linked: specialists were recruited from Ivanovo to help build and run new textile enterprises in the coal cities of southern Russia.

These new enterprises were hardly a priority for central planners, and their construction proceeded slowly. The decree ordering construction of Kalitvasel'mash was signed in 1971, but by the end of the Soviet period only two of five production units had been completed. Delays were even longer in Rodniki. It was only in 1983 that work was undertaken on an enterprise connected to the Ministry of Defense Production. Planned employment at this new enterprise was set at 4,500. As was the case with Kalitvasel'mash, planners did not anticipate that these workers and their families would reside in the built-up areas of Rodniki. Rather, plans called for a new settlement built for 12,000 inhabitants. This was simply the unit of planned development in small cities during the late-Soviet period—not individual neighborhoods or individual enterprises, but an entire *khoziaistvo*, a unit of production and need fulfillment. Ground was broken in 1983, but, for obvious reasons, progress through the decade was sporadic. As the new city slowly emerged, however, a distinctive pattern of building became apparent. Unlike the works of the Stalinist period, and unlike the enterprises built in the years immediately after World War II, construction on this new city proceeded just as city-builders had always wanted: *kompleksno*, in an integrated fashion, with all elements of industrial and social life developed in careful coordination. First, the physical infrastructure underpinning the enterprise and city was constructed: sewage lines, an electrical substation, gas lines, and a boiler for heat, all planned to accommodate industrial production, housing, and social services. Next came the housing for construction workers—not the barracks or individual houses that accompanied industrial construction before and after World War II, but concrete panel apartment blocks— locals called them "Moscow apartments"—the first to be built in the city. And then a health clinic was completed, then a school and a kindergarten. And then the beginnings of the enterprise: the boxes—*korobki*—in which the productive apparatus would be housed . . .

And then the Soviet Union broke up. Financing for capital construction evaporated as Rodniki's new enterprise was severed from ministerial linkages. The collapse of industrial coordination left innumerable Soviet enterprises stranded, with little experience in organizing external economic ties, and little capacity to adjust to a market economy. For the new enterprise in Rodniki, however, things were particularly dire: *there was no enterprise*, only empty boxes in which industrial equipment was to be housed, as well as the underlying infrastructures into which it would be plugged. What had been completed, or at least what had been begun in a serious way, was the new city. At the moment of breakup, the enterprise employed 1,200 workers, most occupied with construction; the new city had 4,000 inhabitants. The infrastructures underlying it were built to accommodate many more, since growth was planned.[18] Here was an emblem of *zastoi* seen from the biopolitical side. In the first Soviet decades, the characteristic figure—not all that different from the early industrial city in other parts of the world—was an enterprise around which human beings accumulated, without the apparatus required for meeting their basic needs. Over the long threshold of Soviet industrial modernity the biopolitical problem had been reversed: from an enterprise without a city to a city without an enterprise.

THINGS FALL APART: DISARTICULATING KHOZIAISTVO

The collapse of Rodniki's new enterprise was as quick and inconsequential as its rise. The enterprise's top management positions had been filled by Russians who were resettled from an Uzbek metallurgic facility. In the early 1990s, the metallurgic complex acquired the unfinished enterprise in Rodniki. The general director explained in an interview to a local paper that "the Rodniki machine building enterprise found itself in a difficult situation, so the leadership of [the Uzbek facility] decided to create a machine-building enterprise in Rodniki."[19] Perhaps the Russians in Uzbekistan performed a favor for some old friends. But otherwise there was little to be done to save the enterprise—and little for these new arrivals to do. The enterprise had no capital equipment and a few experiments with small production through the 1990s went nowhere.[20]

More problematic was the situation at Bol'shevik, Rodniki's city-forming textile manufactory. Since the Soviet textile complex extended across republican boundaries (cotton producers were located predominantly in Uzbekistan—the double Uzbek connection was a coincidence, so far as I know), Russian textile production depended on a coordinating entity that extended across these lines as well.[21] Already at the end of the Soviet period, increasing republican independence was causing problems in Rodniki. In late 1991, the local paper reported "a difficult situation in the textile industry in Russia in which the cotton producing republics continually break agreements on the delivery of cotton to enterprises in the [textile] sector." The enterprises of Ivanovo region faced the prospect of work stoppage, in which case "many city programs, which are supported and financed by the company, would be under threat, and the local budget would suffer." With Soviet breakup, these fears were realized as inter-republican supply chains broke down. The ensuing collapse was stunningly abrupt, even by the standards of the early 1990s. By early 1992, inputs were acquired increasingly through barter: Uzbek cotton for Russian energy. By March of that year the local paper was reporting work stoppages at other enterprises in the region, as Uzbek suppliers began to demand prepayment for deliveries. By mid-April stoppages spread to Rodniki, as the supply of cotton at Bol'shevik shrunk to less than the amount required for a single day of production. By 1993, production reported at Bol'shevik had dropped to below 25 percent of 1991 levels.[22]

Initially, the gravity of Bol'shevik's troubles was lost on some locals. Several residents told me that at the time of the first stoppages it never occurred to them that short-term difficulties signaled long-term decline. The local paper reported disapprovingly that during the first periods of reduced workweeks some employees welcomed the extra time off. Likewise, managers at Bol'shevik seemed to completely misunderstand the rules of the new economic system in which they operated. Cutoffs in cotton supply were initially interpreted as a short-term difficulty, to be weathered until times turned better. When finished product began to accumulate at the enterprise, and the problem could no longer be attributed only to troubles with acquiring inputs, the commercial director insisted that there was no problem with "demand" for Bol'shevik's products. The problem, he argued uncomprehendingly, was that those who demanded its products did not have any money.

As was true in most cases, privatization transferred most of Bol'shevik's shares to workers. Also typical was the fact that this transfer did not substantially affect the management of the enterprise or its performance. Through the late 1990s, production was based on ad hoc deals that were desperately sporadic and largely cashless. Occasionally, inputs were acquired through one-time administrative arrangements. In 1997, for example, the federal government financed a purchase of cotton from a British company, which was used to fill a clothing order for the Russian military. Bol'shevik, a major producer of camouflage, received a significant portion of the order. But such arrangements did not change the bigger picture. The demise of the enterprise seemed inevitable. According to Bol'shevik's economic director, a team of researchers from the World Bank that visited the enterprise in the mid-1990s "left us for dead."[23] As it turned out, they were dead wrong. The enterprise recovered dramatically after the 1998 devaluation, which shifted the terms of trade in favor of Bol'shevik and much of Russian light industry. But the researchers' assessment was understandable, and a visitor through much of the 1990s might have come to the same conclusion about the city as a whole.

In Belaya Kalitva, too, things deteriorated fast. At its "second" city-forming enterprise, Kalitvasel'mash, the root of the problem lay in total dependence on Rossel'mash, the giant Soviet producer of agricultural combines located in nearby Rostov. After Soviet breakup, production at Rossel'mash collapsed following the disintegration of investment in Russian agriculture, bringing its half-built Belo-Kalitvean affiliate down with it. Things initially seemed more promising for Belaya Kalitva's first city-forming enterprise, the aluminum factory BKMZ. An early investment in compliance with international quality standards brought in some foreign orders. By the mid-1990s, however, the enterprise's prospects had worsened for reasons that were connected to sectoral dynamics in post-Soviet metallurgy. Tax laws gave foreign metal traders incentives to import primary inputs and to export alumina rather than process it through domestic firms like BKMZ. The laws were a boon for smelters, but Russian producers of aluminum products were cut off from Soviet supply chains.[24] Without foreign investment, and given the lack of financing on the domestic market, BKMZ's prospects were grim. By the late 1990s, wages had fallen deeply into arrears and employment had dropped to half its previous level. Though it seemed a prime candidate for success in the global market economy of the late twentieth century, BKMZ hardly fared better than Rodniki's Bol'shevik, a relic of nineteenth-century capitalism.

During the 1990s the severity of Russian industrial collapse was hotly disputed. Many reform-minded observers assumed that official production declines were overstated,[25] and some took the absence of significant layoffs or mass bankruptcies as indications that the process of restructuring was slow. But from any perspective the industrial contraction amounted to a cataclysm for small industrial cities. Due in part to contingencies of industrial structure, things were particularly bad in Belaya Kalitva and Rodniki. But the situation in most small industrial cities by the late 1990s—indeed in the country as a whole—was roughly analogous. Industrial employment in Russia fell from around 32 million in 1990 to less than 20 million by 1999 (World Bank 2005: 6), a scale of deindustrialization that took shape over the entire post–World War II period in the most advanced industrial countries. Perhaps it was not therapeutic; but the shock was undeniable.

Who in the City is the Khoziain?

The problem that industrial collapse presented to small cities was not merely one of employment. We have seen that enterprises were entangled with many aspects of local life, not least of all the provision of social welfare. Residents anticipated that industrial collapse would have ruinous implications for whole cities. Thus, in 1992, a Belo-Kalitvaen wrote to a local paper that "[t]he metallurgic combine ... always took upon itself responsibility for everything [in Belaya Kalitva]: How is industry running? What is being built? How is the people's leisure?"[26] But with the onset of economic crisis, the writer noted, all those questions "bow down before the central problem: How to survive?"[27]

In fact, the disentanglement of production and social welfare—those two inextricably linked elements of the Soviet urban *khoziaistvo*—was foreseen in reforms of the early 1990s. New laws provided enterprises with legal grounds for turning major social and communal responsibilities such as kindergartens, utilities, and apartments over to municipal governments. During the 1990s, progress in this transfer varied across cities.[28] As Veronika Kabalina (1997) has shown in research on enterprise restructuring, where old Soviet directors remained in control a strategy of "balanced conservatism" was typical. General directors sought to keep basic elements of the productive apparatus and the social sphere intact, waiting for external conditions to improve rather than undertaking adaptive restructuring. Where enterprise leadership was replaced by outside owners Soviet general directors were often ousted and replaced by a "manager" (*menedzher*), oriented not to the old problems of enterprise paternalism but to maximizing profit. Such managers often jettisoned enterprises' social commitments.

In Rodniki, the strategy of the last "red" director of Bol'shevik was a precise embodiment of balanced conservatism. An unfortunate figure who was appointed at the very end of the Soviet period, he stood by Bol'shevik's social commitments—the workers, the kindergartens, the collective farms, and the housing stock—notwithstanding the enterprise's dire circumstances. After his dismissal, the local paper defended his tenure in elegiac terms. The former general director

> believed and believes that under any economic conditions you can't deprive a person of the last hope to get normal medical treatment, to raise children ... the last hope to live a dignified life, in the place where that person was born and lived. The economists, the marketeers conducting the Russian reforms are convinced of just the opposite: everything must be destroyed to the foundations, and then— and then come what may. And this approach to reform was taken by many textile plants and other enterprises, and it got to a point where there was no place for the enterprise to have a social sphere (clubs, stadiums, children's camps, and so on), to a point where ... without any particular concern, up to a third of the workers were long ago thrown into the streets, where for kopecks the property of a factory is sold.[29]

It was the great virtue of Bol'shevik's red director to resist the apparently inexorable trend of decline: "All these ten years he was able to hold together the [workers] collective, and the productive capacity of the enterprise."[30] But this story of a virtuous Soviet manager fighting off rapacious capitalists did not capture the whole picture. The red director "held together the collective" in the sense that he never undertook mass layoffs. On the other hand, half of Bol'shevik's workers simply left during his tenure because he had no means to pay them. A more precipitous collapse of industrial employment could hardly be imagined. But in terms of the local moral economy, this was admirable behavior.

His replacement, hired by the holding company that took control of Rodniki's textile factory in the late 1990s, was cut from an entirely different mold: young, an outsider (from Ekaterinburg, the large city in the Urals), and a recent graduate from an economics department. He had little attachment to the state of local life and did not live in Rodniki. This new manager did not undertake layoffs, only because there was no need to. Given the massive attrition of workers over the prior decade, and given that production recovered dramatically under his watch, he was left with a deficit of workers. He did jettison the housing stock, the collective farms, and the kindergartens, to which the red director clung. He had no interest in being at the center of the city *khoziaistvo*.

The withdrawal of the general director from responsibility for the *khoziaistvo* in small cities—whether due to incapacity or abdication—left unoccupied a crucial position in the moral economy of the Soviet and post-Soviet small city: the *khoziain*, that distinctive figure of Soviet neo-traditional authority.[31] With the erosion of enterprise support for the "social" and "communal" spheres, the question was often raised (and still is raised): "*kto v gorode khoziain?*"—who in the city is the *khoziain*? This question means: Who will show concern for the health, welfare, and conditions of existence of each and every inhabitant of the city? Who will take care of our *khoziaistvo*?[32]

The question *kto v gorode khoziain?* is most often posed when those who ought to play the role of the *khoziain* are somehow failing. I caught a glimpse of one such situation in Belaya Kalitva when an audit by the tax inspectorate of Rostov *oblast'* uncovered a number of violations by the city-forming aluminum enterprise. An angry resident wrote a letter to the local paper titled, "A policy of profit dictates [the actions of] the *khoziains*." "What have we come to?" the writer asked. "We have come to a situation in which everyday workers are living on promises [*posulami*] of a salary increase for the third year in a row. ... This question is periodically raised timidly, but the position of the *khoziains* was clearly stated: let them tolerate it [*raz terpiat*], there can be no discussion of an increase." The complaints extended beyond production and employment to the entire city *khoziaistvo*. "The infrastructure, built by the enterprise and supported by it," the letter writer continued, "is abandoned [*ottorgnuta*]," and the company's tax payments had dropped to a miniscule 3 percent of the local budget.[33]

The bankrupt budget; the abandoned infrastructure; the desperate city: all of these were signs of moral codes broken, of responsibilities shunned. The "policy of profit"—management for narrow economic gain rather than collective welfare—was a fundamental betrayal. It was still "the enterprise's infrastructure," the population was still comprised of the enterprise's workers, and Belaya Kalitva was, moreover, the enterprise's city. From the perspective of the local moral economy—criteria for evaluating whether actions are just or exploitative (Scott 1976)—all these remained the enterprise's responsibility. BKMZ's management was hardly unaware of the fact. In the depths of the crisis, the economic director recalled that "[f]rom 1953 when production at the enterprise began, the whole complex for daily life [sotskul'tbyt] was built by the enterprise. That means the kindergartens, the clinics, the hospitals, all the housing in this part of the city. Then there was the collective farms, the sanatoria, the children's camps, the palace of sport, the palace of culture—this was all the property of the enterprise. It was all 'enterprise.'" "We could," he continued, "just drop everything, without any problem. But what are we going to do tomorrow? Because we all live in one city."[34] A touching sentiment. But for all intents and purposes BKMZ *had* dropped everything. Though the enterprise was still vital to Belaya Kalitva's future, its directors were no longer the *khoziains* of the city *khoziaistvo*.

Local Government

In the 1990s another candidate for the *khoziain* of small cities emerged—the head of the local government. As we have seen, local government has not had a happy history in Russia. Before the Revolution there was no local government at all in many industrial settlements, and where it existed, it was weak. Notwithstanding a flicker of autonomy in the 1920s, the pattern changed little in the Soviet period, particularly in small cities dominated by one to a few enterprises. Another fleeting opening took shape in the late Soviet and early post-Soviet period. The 1993 Constitution carved out the juridico-legal framework for self-government, focusing on its independence from higher-standing administrative entities, its formation through elections, and the right to control its own budget and property.[35] A 1995 law clarified some dimensions of the political bases of local government—electoral processes, for instance—and defined its competencies as encompassing all "questions of local significance" that were "related to the direct provision for the vital activity [zhiznedeiatel'nosti—literally "life activity"] of a city's population."[36] Among these were control of the budget; control of municipal property; promotion of the city's socioeconomic development; upkeep of housing; organization and development of health and educational facilities; maintenance of sanitary conditions, water resources, municipal energy, gas, heat, and water supply; and "other questions of local significance not specifically excluded from its consideration by other municipalities or organs of state administration."[37] In this expansive vision local government would be responsible for the entirety of the city *khoziaistvo*.[38]

During the first years of the post-Soviet period a number of excited discussions emerged around local government, ranging from nostalgic turns to the pre-Soviet *zemstvo*—the form of local government instituted with the Alexandrine reforms—to utopic liberal visions of an active post-

Soviet citizenry mobilized around local problems. Citizens groups briefly became active in local affairs.[39] The ability of local governments to respond to citizens' demands, or to take on new roles, ranged widely. Regional capitals tended to fare better than isolated industrial cities, thanks to trade and the appurtenances of political power. So too did a handful of settlements positioned to reap the flood of cash that was injected into isolated corners of the Russian economy after Soviet breakup. But among small cities, these were the rarest exceptions. In most cases reality set in as economic conditions deteriorated and a series of responsibilities previously assumed by major enterprises were unceremoniously dumped on local governments. Housing was transferred, as was responsibility for utility payments. Social services, particularly health clinics and kindergartens, were transferred as well, burdening local governments with increased expenditures just as their revenue base collapsed. In such a context there was little local governments in small industrial cities could do to sustain the "vital activity" of the population on their own. Perhaps they became more adept at dealing with major local enterprises, the practiced power brokers of small cities. Perhaps they became more skillful in their dealings with regional governments upon which industrial cities increasingly depended for budgetary transfers. But collective life deteriorated in their hands. Communal service delivery slumped. Wage arrears for public sector workers swelled. And expectations that city governments would be the focal points for public participation in the affairs of local life were disappointed. As Andrei Chernyavsky and Karen Vartapetov put it in 2004, "[d]eprived of almost any fiscal autonomy, continually disoriented by changes in rules introduced by the centre, powerless and debt-ridden—such self-government simply cannot be of any interest to the citizen, who was supposed to find in it an arena for public activity" (2004: 252).

In sum, enterprises collapsed and turned away from social commitments. Local governments were impotent. In most small industrial cities the answer to the question, "*Kto v gorode khoziain?*"—Who in the city is the *khoziain?*—was: no one.

THINGS HANG TOGETHER

On one level, the observation that small cities lacked a *khoziain* after the passing of socialism reflected the fact that the organization that had previously supported the city's social infrastructure had withdrawn from this responsibility, and the organization that took its place was not up to the job. But behind this, of course, was a more fundamental shift in how government was constituted as a conceptual and practical problem, in the field of objects upon which it worked, and in the forms of reasoning that lent it a specificity and focus. There will be much to say about the character of this shift in the second half of this book, but one dimension is immediately obvious: namely that in important respects the city of city-building was, to suggest an unwieldy term, *degovernmentalized*. What does this mean? We recall that for city-builders the city appeared in its elaborate substantive detail as an object of knowledge and a target of intervention that was oriented to a future imagined in equally elaborate detail. City-building plans may have been perpetually unfinished projects, always distorted, and always behind schedule. But there always *was* a project, a *telos* that made sense of the present in terms of its proximity to, or distance from, a planned future. And the orientation to this *telos* assured those living in Soviet cities that they had a place in the planned future (for all the good and bad that assurance did) and that a certain set of provisions would be made for their livelihood. To say that *this* city was degovernmentalized is simply to say that *this* way of constituting the city as an object of government—of linking the present to a future, of making sense of this peculiar collection of people, apartments, infrastructures, and enterprises—was no more.

What the "degovernmentalization" of the city of city-building does *not* imply is that the elements that comprised the material, spatial, and demographic reality of cities built according to the city-building ideal simply vanished, either as material realities or as governmental problems. The concrete apartment blocks, pipes, boilers, and sewage systems were not going anywhere. Nor, it turned out, was the population. As Clifford Gaddy has observed, a substantial relocation of people across Russian territory during the 1990s mostly originated in the far north, and even that flow has recently tapered off (Gaddy 2007). The small cities of European Russia did not experience a mass exodus of population to larger urban centers. In sum, the elements that comprised the small city remained entangled and stubbornly intransigent. To a somewhat surprising degree, this distinctive urban-industrial form has persisted as a pervasive reality of post-Soviet Russia. It has also remained an intractable political problem, one that was recently thrust back into national consciousness with events in Pikalevo, a small city near St. Petersburg whose residents were left without industrial work—and without hot water—after the "restructuring" of the city-forming enterprise (Kots and Steshin 2009).

There are various reasons for the persistence of the small city and the city *khoziaistvo*. One is that the centripetal forces of marketization and the disintegration of the ministerial system were actively resisted. In small cities, such resistances were particularly evident in the activities of local governments, which, as we will see in later chapters, were preoccupied, with holding together systems that were essential to local life by squeezing transfers out of the regional government or navigating in-kind transactions with local enterprises. A second explanation for the persistence of the city-building *khoziaistvo* was that it was sustained by distribution networks through which resources continued to flow even in the hardest years of the 1990s. These often unnoticed pipes, wires, and budgetary mechanisms that linked individuals and cities to national circuits of resource distribution—delivering pensions, salaries for teachers and doctors, gas, electricity, and heat—became a lifeline upon which small cities depended. Lastly, something happened that few anticipated: just when, in the late 1990s, things seemed most desperate they took a dramatic turn for the better. Rodniki's textile enterprise was purchased by a holding company and, after the devaluation of 1998 dramatically improved terms of trade, production rebounded. In Belaya Kalitva, RUSAL—the Russian metals conglomerate—acquired *BKMZ* (it was later sold again to ALCOA). Its production, too, recovered rapidly.

This, at any rate, was the broad outline of the situation in small cities as they stood on the threshold of the twenty-first century: profoundly shaken by economic upheaval, but initially intransigent, and then surprisingly resilient as economic recovery took hold. For my purposes, at least two directions of inquiry suggested themselves. It would have been possible to trace the trajectory of these small cities after the difficult years of the 1990s, examining how they adapted to somewhat brightened economic circumstances, and tracing out how local government was transformed. This is a rich field of inquiry, as a range of subsequent studies have shown (Clarke 2004; Humphrey 2004; Oushakine 2009; Kharkhordin and Alapuro 2010). I turned in a different direction, one that took me away, at least initially, from the scene of the small city even as I kept the specific problems it presented firmly in view. I wanted to understand what new forms of governmental reflection were emerging to critique and reform these elements of the Soviet city *khoziaistvo*; to use the mundane infrastructures and budgetary routines as exemplary sites for examining how the biopolitics of population—the adjustment between population and production—was being reshaped; and to ask, finally, what any of this had to do with neoliberalism as an important contemporary form through which life and population are being raised as problems of government.

PART II

Neoliberalism and Social Modernity

Figure P.2. Pipes

IN THE FALL OF 1990, a group of Soviet and American specialists began to meet to discuss the future of the Soviet Union and the future of Soviet-American relations. The Soviets in the group were reformers who occupied, at that time, a tenuous political position. After initially backing a plan for rapid economic transformation, Soviet leader Mikhail Gorbachev had been pressured by reactionaries into a partial retreat, leaving the reformers' influence uncertain (Service 1998: 493). The Americans were academics and high-level technocrats with backgrounds in international security and international economics. Among their prominent spokespeople were Graham Allison, an expert on arms control, and Jeffrey Sachs, a specialist on international trade and stabilization.

Over the course of 1991 the members of this group, both individually and collectively, articulated a distinctive position about U.S. policy toward the Soviet Union, and about Soviet transformation. This position was summarized in a report—delivered first to U.S. and Soviet leaders, and then to the G7—entitled "Window of Opportunity: The Grand Bargain for Democracy in the Soviet Union." After a few preliminary chapters establishing the plausibility of Soviet reform and outlining the vital western interest in the Soviet future, "Window of Opportunity" introduced "a program for political and economic transformation" of the Soviet Union. Political matters received passing attention, occupying just over three pages that noted "important strides toward democracy" and concrete steps taken during 1991 to ensure the decentralization of power (Joint Working Group on Western Cooperation in the Soviet Transformation to Democracy and the Market Economy 1991: 29). Economic transformation occupied thirty-eight pages, the bulk of the report. The aim of economic reform, the authors argued, was to "create a *normal market economy* in the Soviet Union." This normal market economy might involve some peculiarities since, they allowed, "[e]ach nation has unique historical and cultural characteristics that lead to distinct economic institutions." But great subtlety in analyzing the varieties of capitalism was not the order of the day. This was, after all, the beginning of a decade in which old ideological antinomies were, in some quarters, declared dead and the proposition was forcefully advanced that human economy spoke a single universal language. "[R]ecognition of historical and cultural identity," the report cautioned, "should not be allowed to raise illusions about the possibility of some 'third way.' The Soviet Union's unambiguous objective must be to create as rapidly as possible a market economy with the commonly shared basic characteristics of the advanced industrial countries" (Joint Working Group 1991: 36).

"Window of Opportunity" proposed what would become a familiar package of policies (indeed it already was familiar to observers of international development): macroeconomic stabilization, price liberalization, privatization, and the freeing of international trade. Implementation was envisioned in two phases. From 1991 to 1993, "the legal and economic institutions of the market economy" would be created, and a considerable portion of state assets privatized. Subsequent reforms, from 1994 to 1997, would focus on "structural adjustment in the economy, accelerating the shifts from public to private ownership, from military to civilian industry, from heavy industry to production of consumer goods and services, and from a closed economy to an open economy" (Joint Working Group 1991: 39).

The proposals laid out in "Window of Opportunity" echoed earlier reforms formulated by Russian economists.[1] The report broke new ground in its vision for the role of Western aid in Soviet transformation.[2] Perhaps due to a healthy comparative perspective (these were not narrow Sovietologists trained in the subtle and hidden arts of Kremlinology), perhaps due to a certain naiveté (that could be attributed, their detractors argued, to the Americans' lack of experience with Soviet affairs), this group proposed that Western countries could encourage Soviet transformation through active engagement and financial support. This policy orientation was linked to a specific mechanism: conditional lending. Allison and Robert Blackwill, another key figure in the working group, described this mechanism in *Foreign Affairs* in the summer of 1991. The terms of aid would be "substantial financial assistance for Soviet reforms *conditional* upon continuing political pluralization and a coherent economic program for moving rapidly to a market economy." Such "conditionality," the authors explained, would "create incentives for leaders ... to choose a future consistent with our mutual best interest by promising real assistance for real reform" (Allison and Blackwill 1991: 95). This "real assistance" was to be of Marshall Plan proportions—$100 billion over four years.

The proposals advanced in "Window of Opportunity" did not reflect consensus opinion in the Western, and particularly in the United States, foreign policy establishment at the time. Thus, a 1991 article in the *New York Times* noted that U.S. officials dismissed the report as "a wooly product of ivory tower thinking" (Redburn 1991). And the report's authors did not initially get what they wanted. Aid from foreign governments and the International Financial Institutions was not immediately forthcoming. But over time this cluster of terms and technical modalities—conditionality, liberalization, stabilization, and structural adjustment—became central to efforts to govern post-Soviet transformation.

The term "neoliberalism" was not frequently bandied about in early discussions of reform. But for the self-conscious keepers of the neoliberal flame, a heterogeneous group of intellectuals, policymakers, and technocrats in think tanks and academic posts, Soviet breakup was immediately understood as the apotheosis of a century-long intellectual battle between advocates of planning and advocates of markets. James Dorn of the CATO Institute thus began a 1991 article about post-Soviet transformation by referring to what some regard as a starting point for a specifically neoliberal intellectual development: the socialist calculation debates. "As early as 1920," Dorn wrote, "the Austrian economist Ludwig von Mises pointed to the inherent difficulties of communism and predicted that rational economic calculation would be impossible without private ownership of the means of production and money prices" (1991: 175). This argument against socialist planning continued in think tanks and departments of economics after World War II. The "intellectual war" over the future of Russian reform was, in Dorn's view, the latest chapter in this battle—perhaps the last, since Soviet collapse demonstrated conclusively that the opponents of planning had won. In the peculiar historiography of conservative libertarian economics, the struggle over post-Soviet reform could be located in a coherent line of liberal and neoliberal thought; and the stakes of post-Soviet transformation could be understood as a battle of markets against planning.

As the 1990s wore on, this conservative, libertarian interpretation found a somewhat unexpected mirror image in the assessment of those who criticized programs of post-Soviet transformation like the one laid out in "Window of Opportunity." These critics found it self-evident that post-Soviet reform was shaped by a tradition of liberal and neoliberal thought, and that neoliberalism, therefore, was responsible for the patterns of post-Soviet transformation.[3] An economic and political gambit like that laid out in "Window of Opportunity"—associated with structural adjustment, shock therapy, the Washington Consensus, or "transition"—exemplified *neoliberal* reform.

Neoliberalism and Great Transformation

This first half of this book examined the distinctive Soviet approach to the biopolitics of population. We saw how, beginning from a framework of total industrial planning, Soviet planners advanced the novel proposition that all elements of a substantive economy could be organized as inputs into productive processes. In this light, cities could be conceptualized as details in regional economic development, and city plans could be approached as logical extensions of economic plans. This kind of planning, and the peculiar organizational mechanisms to which it corresponded, produced a distinctive substantive economy: a pattern of spatial adjustments between population, production, and apparatuses of social welfare, and an organization of need fulfillment that I have analyzed by referring to the Soviet city *khoziaistvo*.

The remainder of this book asks how the norms and forms of Soviet city-building have been taken up as targets of neoliberal reform. Following the pattern of the first half of the book, it begins on the broadest level of the biopolitics of population, considering how neoliberalism relates to the mechanisms of adjustment between population, production, and social welfare. Chapter 6 examines "structural adjustment," the reform paradigm that took up the basic proposals established in "Window of Opportunity"—a vision of transition to a market economy through "shock" liberalization, privatization, and stabilization, backed by large-scale foreign aid. I will show that structural adjustment was not the "emanation of a coherent neoliberal ideology"—to borrow Ganev's phrase (2005: 350)—but the product of conjunctural factors, and that it was hardly as rigid or unchanging as its critics assumed. By the late 1990s, the strategy of structural adjustment was shifting from macroeconomic adjustment and privatization to areas such as social welfare provisioning. The book's last two chapters examine two areas of reform that came into focus during this period and that are particularly important for the "neoliberal" reshaping of Soviet social modernity: budgetary reform (chapter 7) and reform of communal services, in particular centralized heating systems (chapter 8).

In pursuing these topics, I will engage—though often implicitly—with what might be called the "great transformation" view of neoliberalism and neoliberal reform.[4] The term is, of course, borrowed from Karl Polanyi's classic work on the twin births of modern liberal thought and what he called "market society" in Britain at the beginning of the nineteenth century. For many observers of Russia in the 1990s, Polanyi's account provided a penetrating critical guide to the project of post-Soviet transformation. The new liberal project described in "Window of Opportunity"—though of course not originally or only there—was not cloaked in the naturalistic Robinsonades of nineteenth-century political economy. But its faith in equilibrium and the invisible hand recalled early liberalism's "uncompromising ferocity" in promoting laissez faire (Polanyi 2001: 143). And its quixotic quest for "self-regulation and harmony," critics argued, produced a cascade of consequences for which early nineteenth-century analogues could be found. "Neoliberal" policies in Russia disrupted an existing "substantive economy"—those mechanisms of regulation, planning, and social welfare produced by Soviet socialism—resulting in a wrenching upheaval. The collapse in industrial production, the growth of poverty and social misery (without the extraordinary economic expansion that, as Polanyi acknowledged, accompanied the advent of market society in Britain), amounted to what Polanyi called the "demolition of society."

Finally, Polanyi's account illuminated the political dynamics of reform in Russia during the 1990s. Marketization provoked a series of reactions that recalled the second part of what Polanyi called the "double movement" of marketization and self-protection. Everywhere they looked, critics of post-Soviet reform found a thousand acts of resistance to market forces, as mayors, governors, regulators, enterprise managers, and households sought to defend the existing fabric of life. "In reaction to the iron law of market expansion," Michael Burawoy and Katherine Verdery argue, an "iron law of market resistance" took shape (1999a: 7). Against promises of rapid ascent to the prosperous land of the "normal market economy," post-Soviet transformation played out as a series of battles, large and small, that pitted advocates of "the market" against those whose livelihood was tied to the existing organization of society.

Given my specific objects of concern—the small city, Soviet city-building, biopolitics—this "great transformation" account was compelling. As we have seen, the dismemberment of the administered economy ripped the economic heart out of most small cities. The result was not rapid adjustment to new circumstances but a sustained and painful struggle to preserve existing mechanisms of need fulfillment.[5] Indeed, the small city, in its total dependence on one or a few enterprises formerly embedded in the planned economy, seemed to embody the battle of markets versus the existing organization of collective life in nearly ideal purity. Polanyi's analysis also shed light on the contrast between neoliberalism and city-building as governmental forms, and as biopolitical gambits. Polanyi argued that early nineteenth-century liberalism introduced the extraordinary proposition that it was possible to "govern" collective life by disembedding economic action from social and political mechanisms of regulation. The contrast between such a proposal and city-building seems absolute. Against the *substantive* planning of Soviet city-building, which defined every detail of the small city, assigning it a specific place in a planned future, neoliberalism presented the stark *formality* of a governmental rationality that operated exclusively through the calculative choices of free actors on the market. The substantive reality of the city—the object par excellence of city building—appeared, in the lens of neoliberalism, only as an accidental collection of productive factors, a historical artifact and oddity that would now be left to its own devices. Certainly, for those in small cities—fretting about the designs of reformers and marketeers—*laissez faire, passer et aller* seemed precisely the neoliberal creed: let be, let pass, leave to perish, as Polanyi put it with thudding finality, of "death by exposure" (2001: 85).

All of that said, as my research progressed I grew increasingly impressed by the limits of this great transformation story of neoliberalism in Russia and more generally. First of all, this account seemed most relevant to a relatively brief interregnum of post-Soviet history. During the 1990s, reforms focused on liberalization, privatization, and stabilization, and were implemented in a particularly austere economic climate. These conditions made the choice between markets and the existing substantive organization of collective life particularly difficult, producing a political economy of reform that fit the story of great transformation quite nicely. But after 1998 things changed on a number of fronts. Stabilization proved a much less contentious and difficult issue in improved economic circumstances; reform was championed by a president whose popularity rested, at least in part, on his defiance of Western influence; and crucially, as we will see, the substance of reforms shifted.[6]

But there is a second and equally profound problem with the "great transformation" story, to which I referred in this book's introduction: it does not clarify what post-Soviet developments have to do with "neoliberalism" or neoliberal government. In part the issue is that, following Venelin Ganev, policies implemented in these countries were "incoherent, tentative, and contradictory." Consequently, to see "an ideology that is both comprehensive and radical" as the "primary cause of socioeconomic change" in post-Soviet Russia would amount to "committing a grand simplification" (Ganev 2005: 350). But there is a further point to be made: the question of whether developments in post-Soviet Russia can be attributed to neoliberalism is not just a matter of whether reform programs were successfully implemented. More troublingly, as I argued in the introduction, it is simply not clear what reforms should be called "neoliberal." The literature that has explicitly invoked neoliberalism in discussions of post-socialist reform has used the term casually. Even when scholars take the institutional or sociological development of neoliberalism as their explicit object of analysis, it is assumed that neoliberalism—as a form of reflection, as a doctrine—can be associated rather loosely with hostility to the state and affinity for markets, with qualifications generally not considered of conceptual importance.[7] As Taylor Boas and Jordan Gans-Morse (2009) point out, the term is most frequently used in a manner that is appraisive rather than descriptive. "Neoliberal" is a term of derogation, associated with a string of other figures—The Washington Consensus, structural adjustment, "transition," neoclassical economics—to which one is opposed. This is a kind of analysis that, as

Foucault quipped, treats neoliberalism as "always the same thing, and always the same thing but worse" (2008: 130).

The problem is that the relationship of the Washington Consensus, structural adjustment, or neoclassical economics to neoliberalism is exceedingly slippery. As one illustration, consider the comments of John Williamson—the economist renowned for coining (to his later regret) the term "The Washington Consensus"—in a response to his critics in 2002: "[a]udiences the world over," Williamson observed, "seem to believe that [the Washington Consensus] signifies a set of neoliberal policies that have been imposed on hapless countries by the Washington-based international financial institutions and have led them to crisis and misery." The misunderstanding, in his view, lay in the conflation of the Washington Consensus with neoliberalism. "Some of the most vociferous of today's critics of what they call the Washington Consensus," he noted, specifically mentioning the economist Joseph Stiglitz, "do not object so much to the agenda [of the Washington Consensus] as to the neoliberalism that they interpret the term as implying." The Washington Consensus, Williamson insisted, did not include "quintessentially neoliberal" policies such as "capital account liberalization ... monetarism, supply-side economics, or a minimal state (getting the state out of welfare provision and income redistribution)" that never enjoyed consensus support in Washington, "or anywhere much else except perhaps at meetings of the Mont Pelerin Society."

Critics of neoliberalism might be confused by—or just dismissive of[8]—Williamson's contrast between the Washington Consensus and neoliberalism. But most would likely agree with his account of neoliberalism's key tenets: opposition to social welfare programs and income redistribution, adherence to supply-side economics, monetarism, and a minimal state. But what are the grounds for arguing that these are the "quintessentially" neoliberal ideas? Is neoliberalism opposed to welfare provision and redistribution? Does it accept only a minimalist state? We have, in any case, to grapple with this deep confusion, not because we need a stabilized definition of neoliberalism in order to begin inquiry, but because we need ways to constitute neoliberalism as an object of inquiry.

RETHINKING NEOLIBERALISM

As suggested in the introduction, my approach is to reconstruct the field of inquiry by asking how, precisely, developments in Russia are linked to thinkers and to styles of reasoning that could be labeled "neoliberal" in some meaningful sense. Is it possible to identify specific neoliberal thinkers—among the German ordo-liberals or the American neoliberals, for

example—whose thought would allow us to better understand the programs of reform that have actually been proposed in Russia? Through
what set of intermediary steps was their thought brought into relationship with post-Soviet reform? And what did these reforms actually propose to do with the social norms and material forms of the Soviet social?
These questions took me away—indeed, quite far away—from the scene
of the small industrial city and post-Soviet Russia: through long looping
detours to James Buchanan's fiscal contractarianism; to George Stigler's
new neoliberal economics of regulation; to minor traditions of neoliberal thought in which theoretical reflections were joined with sets of
practices in technocratic frameworks of reform; to proposals for post-
Soviet reform formulated by foreign and local experts, and by bureaucrats and policymakers, examining how, finally, these were articulated
onto the existing reality of post-Soviet Russia. In this manner, I worked
my way back to the small industrial city, to Soviet social modernity and
its reform—oriented by different points of reference, and equipped with
different analytical tools.

Through the twists and turns of these detours, the following claims
emerge in the second half of this book: The dominant critical view of
neoliberalism, particularly as it concerns matters of international development, was forged in response to a particular historical conjuncture
that can be dated from the 1970s to the 1990s. The policies articulated
during this period—shock programs of liberalization, stabilization,
privatization, budgetary austerity—were animated by specific events and
problems. They can be meaningfully linked to the specific intellectual and
institutional genealogy of liberalism and neoliberalism, although we have
to be cautious, because they are not the unique emanations of neoliberal
thought but the contingent products of specific historical circumstances.
It is coherent to associate these policies with neoliberalism but we are
not justified in *reducing* neoliberalism to them. We need to specify the
circumstances in which they took shape, and move beyond them, because
new situations, new problems, and new responses have emerged.

Reforms in areas such as fiscal policy and communal services, which
have been central to the Russian government agenda in the 2000s, can
also be linked to minor histories of thought and practice that are meaningfully situated within the liberal and neoliberal traditions, though to
aspects of the neoliberal tradition that have received less scholarly attention, such as its view on government, social welfare, and redistribution.
What we will find, peering into these minor traditions, is that the standard critical account of neoliberalism is deeply unsatisfactory. Neoliberalism is not simply marketization. Neoliberalism is not constitutionally
opposed to social welfare or public value. Neoliberalism does not govern
only through the stark formality of calculative choice. And, finally, the

stakes of "neoliberal reform" cannot be portrayed in Polanyian terms as a battle of markets versus the existing organization of collective life.

Working through the details of pipes and heat boilers, budgets and social norms—those mundane elements through which the Soviet social was assembled—we will discover that neoliberal reforms do not reject the basic value-orientations of Soviet social modernity. Rather, they aim to craft new accommodations between economic efficiency and social welfare, between mechanisms of enterprise and choice and the substantive constraints imposed by existing social norms and material forms. The *nature* of these accommodations is the central concern of the second half of this book.

CHAPTER SIX

Adjustment Problems

IN THE EARLY 1990S, structural adjustment emerged as a key frame through which foreign and domestic reformers thought about, and acted on, post-Soviet transformation in Russia. The searing battles over this policy paradigm and this vision of transformation were burned into the consciousness of critical observers. Structural adjustment came to define the stakes of post-Soviet reform: planning versus markets, substantive provisioning versus formal efficiency, public versus private value. And the great experiment with structural adjustment in Russia stood, for many critical observers, as a paradigm case of neoliberal reform.[1]

My argument in this chapter begins from the observation that, although it has important connections to the neoliberal tradition, and although specific neoliberals played an important role in shaping it, this familiar figure of structural adjustment is not the embodiment or the apotheosis of a coherent neoliberal project. Instead, the form of structural adjustment that became most familiar in debates during the 1990s is best understood as an ensemble of heterogeneous elements, comprising a *lending modality* of conditional budgetary support loans from the International Financial Institutions (IFIs); a *package of policies* promoting stabilization, liberalization, and privatization; and a *model of transformation* defined, in Sachs's (1995a) parsimonious formulation, as the "reallocation of resources in the economy after the introduction of market forces." My strategy in this chapter is to sketch a rough conceptual and historical outline of how these elements were assembled in a particular historical conjuncture. In drawing attention to its contingencies, I hope to loosen the grip that the figure of structural adjustment has on the critical imagination, and to open the space for an analysis of neoliberalism that moves beyond it.

The first part of the chapter draws on primary and secondary sources to trace the genealogy of structural adjustment, focusing on two vectors: first, a longstanding neoliberal critique of state-centered development theory; second, the lending modality generally associated with structural adjustment—fast-disbursing, conditionality-based, general budgetary support loans—invented in response to the debt crises of the late 1970s. These two threads were brought together by a changing problematization of economic crisis. Initially the economic shocks of the 1970s were understood to be short term and "external." But through the early 1980s, as the first generation of adjustment policies failed to resolve critical problems such as Latin American debt, economic crises were understood not as *external* shocks but as the product of *inflexibilities* in *internal* economic organization. Thus, fast-disbursing general budgetary support loans were linked to policies whose aim was the wholesale reform of *domestic* economies.

It was this assemblage of elements that arrived on the Russian scene in the early 1990s and was deployed in the project of "transition." Beginning with proposals advanced in "Window of Opportunity," discussions of structural adjustment in Russia were cast in terms of an epochal transformation from socialism to capitalism. But in fact the emphases of reform shifted rapidly. By the middle of the decade elements of structural adjustment were achieved, including stabilization, large-scale privatization of industrial enterprises, and liberalization of most prices. But growth remained frustratingly elusive for reformers, and they increasingly turned their attention to inflexibilities created by sociotechnical systems such as infrastructures and the government budget that were not easily reorganized through a market mechanism. The problem was still one of structural adjustment—that is, one of correcting the distortions created by the Soviet patterns of urban and spatial development. But this rethought process of adjustment could no longer be conceived in purely formal terms as a market reallocation of productive factors. Instead, we will see that reforms in these domains sought to craft accommodations among the demands of flexibility, Russia's existing urban and demographic structure, and the government's continuing obligation to pursue core aims of public policy such as redistribution and the delivery of essential services. Thus, through a detour that takes us far from the small city, from the city *khoziaistvo*, and from Russia, we will work our way back, tracing how the material forms and social norms of city-building came into view as the *substance* of structural adjustment.

"MARKETIZING" STRUCTURAL ADJUSTMENT: A BRIEF GENEALOGY

In one sense, the story of structural adjustment could be traced back at least to the beginnings of the post–World War II projects of reconstruction and development, when economists were grappling with the tremendous transformation of economic and political life that had been wrought by military mobilization.[2] Thus, in 1953 Walt Rostow (310) wrote of the need to deal with "structural distortions"—in particular excess industrial production—produced by wartime economies in Europe. His proposal for "adjustment" involved a "massive, purposeful, investment program" in the non-communist world. This meaning of structural adjustment—

referring to "purposeful" intervention to correct distortions in economic structure—persisted. In the 1960s, Michael Piori (1968) referred to the problem of retraining workers for new jobs after industrial enterprises closed in Europe as a process of "structural adjustment." A similar meaning can be found in contemporary European Union discussions.[3]

A significant commonality links structural adjustment in these earlier senses to the meaning it came to have in the 1980s and 1990s. In all these cases, structural adjustment refers to a problem of what Ulrich Beck (1992) calls reflexive modernization: one "modern" governmental form—whether industrial, welfarist, developmentalist, or military mobilizational—is identified as pathological. "Adjustment" refers to a correction. The key distinction among these uses lies in the *mechanism* and *telos* of adjustment. Previously, adjustment was the target of "purposeful" government intervention defined in *substantive* terms, implying planning in the broad sociological sense. By contrast, the form of structural adjustment that emerged in the mid-1980s was starkly formal. The *mechanism* of adjustment—and the *telos* to which it was directed—was simply marketization. The genealogy we have to trace, thus, is not of structural adjustment generally, but of this particular "marketizing" variant of structural adjustment that, by the 1980s, was linked to a particular lending modality, a set of policies, and a vision of transformation.

The Neoliberal "Counter-Revolution" in Development Economics

The unavoidable and familiar backdrop to this story is the paradigm of "state-led" development that consolidated after World War II, and the critique of that paradigm, which J.F.J. Toye has called the neoliberal "counter-revolution" in development economics. The state-led model that emerged in complex conjunction with late colonialism, decolonization, the establishment of the Bretton Woods system, postwar reconstruction, and the Cold War, is hardly exogenous to our story, since it was profoundly influenced by the Soviet example. As T. N. Srinivasan has noted, many "pioneers [of the post–World War II development paradigm], particularly those from the relatively advanced developing countries, viewed the problem as one of achieving in one or two generations a level of development that it took several generations to achieve in the developed countries" (1984: 51); "the only experience of such rapid transformation" was the Soviet. Consequently, key assumptions of the Soviet approach were accepted. But outside the socialist world the Soviet model was significantly modified.

One variant of the state-led model emphasized government investment in certain key industrial sectors—most centrally infrastructures—based on the assumption that, due to the complementarities of complex modern economies, an initial push of state investment was required to overcome the failures of markets to provide capital to "backward" countries. It shared the Soviet emphasis on infrastructure development, but assumed that infrastructure would provide the "flywheel" of economic development that was ultimately organized by private entrepreneurs. Another variant, import substitution, was a program of trade controls and selective state investments that favored the development of domestic industry. Here, the key assumption was that deteriorating terms of trade meant that primary commodity producers—which included most poor countries—were at a permanent and worsening structural disadvantage in the world economy. Government intervention would break a pattern of dependent development.

In either case, a key premise was shared with the Soviet theorists of the 1920s: the pathway to modernity for backward countries would have to be different than it was for the advanced industrial countries; markets failed in poor countries, and the state had to play a compensatory role. Outside the socialist orbit these state-led strategies were generally not proposed as permanent economic models. Rather, it was presumed that, after an initial period of intervention, the state would withdraw, and market forces would predominate (Mason and Asher 1973; Colclough 1991: 2). But for reasons that have been exhaustively examined—and that became central to neoliberal criticism of state-led models—institutions of government intervention became entrenched, and continued to structure economies in developing countries.

Almost from the beginning of this project a significant neoliberal countercritique—which can be traced from the socialist calculation debates of the 1920s, through discussions of development in the Mt. Pelerin Society, to the University of Chicago and other key venues of American neoliberal thought after World War II—attacked the very premises of the state-led approach.[4] Critics such as Peter Bauer, Deepak Lal, and Jagdish Bhagwati disputed the "trade pessimism" of postwar development theory, and questioned the need for, and merits, of a "big push" of capital accumulation, arguing that investments by the state would crowd out private capital, and undermine the benefits of comparative advantage realized through free trade.[5] They also pointed to perversities of state-led models, such as the anti-poor and anti-rural bias of investment and trade policies designed to promote industrialization. Most broadly, these neoliberal critics rejected the proposition that a separate field of development economics was required for poor countries, insisting, as W. Paul Strassman put it, that "[a] new body of thought was not needed ... to show that market interest rates would raise and deploy capital in an optimal manner, that flexible exchange rates would solve balance-of-payments problems, that inflation and planning were bad, and competitive profits good" (1976: 278).

This neoliberal critique was one condition of possibility for the emergence of "marketizing" structural adjustment as it took shape in the 1980s. Of particular importance is its identification of the "distortions" introduced by statist policies of development, and its emphasis on allowing markets to correct those distortions. But for a number of reasons it is too simple to read structural adjustment as the unique emanation of this body of neoliberal thought about development. First, although neoliberals contributed key pieces in a mounting edifice of empirical and theoretical arguments, the critique of postwar state-led development was taken up from various directions (Mosley et al. 1991). The neoliberal was only one among a host of critical positions that had emerged by the 1960s and 1970s. Second, the implications to be drawn from these critiques were neither uniform nor unchanging. Some early neoliberal critics of development accepted crucial tenets of the state-led model, such as the emphasis on infrastructure development (Plehwe 2009b: 23). Even trade studies in the 1970s later cited as key to the counter-revolution in development thinking did not uniformly reject "state-led" strategies. Instead, they identified failed elements of these strategies and proposed to revise them as appropriate (Bhagwati 1984: 202).

The third and, for our purposes, most important reason that structural adjustment cannot be simply identified with the neoliberal "counter-revolution" was that the form of structural adjustment that became familiar in the 1980s and 1990s—comprising a lending modality, a package of policies, and a vision of transformation—was the product of conjunctural factors, not the outgrowth of an idealized neoliberal blueprint for reform.[6] As a *lending modality*, structural adjustment was initially a pragmatic attempt to deal with economic crisis rather than an attack on strategies of state-led development that was ideologically driven. And the first structural adjustment programs were not oriented to dismantling the institutions of state-led development. It was only following the failures of a first round of structural adjustment loans to resolve the Latin American debt crisis that adjustment *lending* was linked to the *policy* package implied by the neoliberal critique of postwar development economics.

Vulnerability and Flexibility:
A New Problematization of Economic Crisis

Major accounts of the World Bank and the International Monetary Fund (IMF) have shown that the rise of structural adjustment *lending* was tied to fundamental changes in the mechanisms governing the global economy during the 1970s.[7] The abandonment of the gold standard displaced a central function of the IMF, whose original charge included monitoring country compliance with the Bretton Woods system.[8] It also made the international economy more volatile, and was followed by a series of financial crises in developing countries that challenged the IFIs in their respective tasks relating to stability in the global financial system (the IMF) and development in poor countries (the Bank). The IMF turned to addressing balance of payments crises faced by poor and middle-income countries (previously it had lent overwhelmingly to rich countries). The World Bank also had to confront the fact that its borrowers increasingly faced short-term shocks that had implications for growth and standards of living.

Beginning in the mid-1970s, therefore, first the IMF and then the Bank created new lending facilities for responding to balance of payments crises.[9] These facilities established one key element of structural adjustment as it came to be understood in the 1980s and 1990s: fast-disbursing, concessional, general budgetary support loans that were linked to policy reform. After the oil shocks in 1979, these new facilities were drawn on with greater frequency. But loans from them were not immediately connected to the program of wholesale liberalization and *domestic* reform that was later central to "marketizing" structural adjustment. The IMF's loans from its new facilities, which addressed the "stabilization" side of crisis response, focused on policies derived from its longstanding monetary understanding of balance of payments problems: that they were rooted in domestic credit expansion (Boughton 2001: 559). The World Bank, meanwhile, was from the outset presumed to have the task of dealing with "stubborn imbalances with enduring causes … that called for adjustment in the *structure* of the borrower's production" (Kapur et al. 1997: 509). But in early structural adjustment lending this problem was understood and addressed narrowly. Lending programs focused on correcting *external* imbalances by expanding exports, particularly in the region that was the most important target of lending in the first half of the 1980s, Latin America (Kapur et al. 1997: 506–7). Ernest Stern, at the time the vice-president of operations at the World Bank and a key advocate of the turn to policy-linked adjustment lending, noted later that despite the Bank's reorientation to structural adjustment, in the early 1980s there was little appreciation of, or attention to, distortions in *domestic* economies (1983: 91).[10]

This initial approach was thrown into doubt by the first round of adjustment lending. The debt crisis triggered an expansion in the IFI's role in managing international financial shocks (Boughton 2001: 42). But their program of lending—focused, again, on austerity measures and trade adjustment—was not successful in managing the underlying debt problem. Key policymakers in the IFIs and the U.S. government increasingly recognized that, as Stanley Fischer put it in 1986, stabilization measures "averted financial collapse at the cost of a sharp slowdown in growth and investment in the heavily indebted countries" (1986: 163). Governments were no more able to deal with their debt than before stabilization was begun.[11]

By the mid-1980s a consensus had formed around the proposition that the apparent conflict between stabilization and economic recovery had to be overcome through policies that promoted "adjustment with growth."[12] The suggestion was not that trade liberalization or stabilization measures were inappropriate. Rather, it was that they had to be accompanied, as Stern suggested, by "specific actions ... that were designed to make more effective use of productive capacity and to reduce aggregate demand in ways consistent with development objectives" (1983: 90). If previously the problem had been seen as short-term crises of "liquidity" resulting from external shocks, the new emphasis was on "solvency"—the ability of economies in developing countries to grow out of debt.

As Kapur, Lewis, and Webb observe in their detailed history of the World Bank during this period, the new focus on solvency implied a shift "in the relative weighing of factors internal to a country (economic policies and institutions) and the external circumstances (terms of trade, interest rates, sudden withdrawal of lending) affecting their worsening fortunes" (1997: 617). In part, this was a matter of placing the blame for the debt crisis and its persistence more squarely on the shoulders of developing countries because the root problems were increasingly traced to domestic policy choices rather than external shocks beyond a government's control.[13] But underlying these shifts—from stabilization to adjustment with growth, from liquidity to solvency, from a concern with *external* shocks to an emphasis on distortions in *domestic* economies—was a significant transformation in the *problematization* of economic crisis. In other words, we see the emergence of a new way of constituting economic crisis as a conceptual and practical challenge. The contours of this emerging problematic should be carefully marked.

Adjustment lending, we have seen, was initially shaped in response to problems arising from external flows and balances; intervention focused on trade and stabilization. These concerns did not vanish. For some, Stern among them, the underlying rationale for structural adjustment would always be found in balance of payments issues. But the understanding of the *source* of these imbalances—and the possible avenues for addressing them—shifted fundamentally. Fluctuations in economic conditions were understood to be a permanent condition of the international economy after the abandonment of the gold standard. Consequently, emphasis was placed on the ability—or inability—of economies to flexibly adapt to a constantly changing economic environment and to avoid imbalances that would make them *vulnerable* to inevitable economic fluctuations.[14] Stern concluded in 1984, thus, that attention had to be focused on the "failure of, and need for, flexibility in economic management in a world economy which is not likely to get much less volatile" (Kapur et al. 1997: 617). Economic crisis, from this perspective, was not to be seen as an exceptional circumstance to be addressed through exceptional measures (at least not in the medium term). Rather, economic shocks were seen to be endemic features of the international economic system. The response was to make economies more adaptive and resilient.

In this context, the attention of experts at the international development institutions, in the U.S. Treasury, and also in the finance ministries of many governments facing economic crisis, was increasingly drawn to the inflexibilities that prevented economies from responding dynamically to changing conditions. And it is *here* that we can locate the intersection between structural adjustment *lending* and the ideas that emerged from the neoliberal counter-revolution in development economics. Reformers turned their attention to the institutions of postwar economic development—a vast array of mechanisms such as price controls, licensing regimes, social services, regulatory regimes, and public ownership arrangements—that had been set up in country after country. The "distortions" introduced by these mechanisms had not been entirely neglected previously. But, to repeat Stern's observation, they were not the focus of Bank lending. It was only after the first round of adjustment lending failed to resolve the debt crisis that these *domestic* mechanisms of economic and social regulation became the primary targets of reform. Stern argued, nicely summing up the new orientation, that "[d]istortions in the policy and allocation framework that were undesirable in the 1960s have become unsustainable in the much more difficult international economic environment of the 1980s" (1983: 91).[15] The implication for key figures in the international policy community and in the policy elite of developing countries was that hard choices and a dramatic change of course were required: an extension of liberalization into domestic governance, a focus on the reduction and reform of the state, and a more rigorous and consistent focus on the view of structural adjustment Sachs articulated a decade later—the reallocation of productive factors by market forces.

Shock Therapy and "Transition"

At one level, the shift from a focus on external balance of payment issues to distortions in domestic economies may be seen as a "deepening" of structural adjustment, as liberalization was extended from external trade to domestic governance. But this evolution was complicated, and its tensions should be appreciated. First, the "deepening" of *liberalization* did not necessarily imply an extension of *marketization*. Instead, it pointed to matters of governance in areas that remained in the purview of state administration. These issues—to which we return below—became central to discussions of structural adjustment by the mid-1990s. A second tension, which pertains to the situation in the mid-1980s when marketizing structural adjustment was being assembled, concerned the modality of structural adjustment programs themselves. The shift toward domestic reform was also a shift to ever more encompassing visions of transformation (Boughton 2001: 31). And because the change envisioned was increasingly fundamental, it was also more political, raising questions in particular concerning the pace of adjustment operations. Stanley Fischer noted in 1986 that economic logic "pointed in the direction of gradualism" in the design of structural adjustment programs, since substantive reorganization of the economy took time. But "political logic" suggested accelerating reform, since the short-term pain of stabilization and liberalization might knock reformers out of office before structural reforms were complete (Fischer 1986: 171).[16] This dilemma was basic to discussions in the mid-1980s, and at that time a broad spectrum of reformers and development analysts tended to resolve it optimistically, projecting that the pace of economic transformation could be bent to the dictates of political necessity. This position was supported, in particular, by the World Bank's research department, which produced country studies in the mid-1980s suggesting that rapid structural reform could quickly restore growth (Kapur et al. 1997: 629). Fischer, who became chief economist of the World Bank in 1988, and whose leadership broke from the strong ideological orientation of the early 1980s, nonetheless shared this optimism. He proposed to "apply shock treatment" through measures like devaluation, but to simultaneously prepare for four- or five-year adjustment programs (Fischer 1986: 171).

Thus, in the mid-1980s, we find a political and economic calculus that takes the familiar form we have come to associate with structural adjustment: "shock" stabilization, structural reform, and conditional lending. There is no doubt that a distinctive "neoliberal" influence on this particular assemblage of elements can be traced. Beyond the intellectual contribution of neoliberal thinkers to Washington-based international institutions, economists trained in bastions of neoliberal thought, such as the University of Chicago, the University of Rochester, and UCLA, gained prominent institutional positions as key advocates of, and innovators in, the practice of structural adjustment in many developing countries.[17] Within the World Bank, meanwhile, the shift to an emphasis on domestic economic governance institutions was pushed by the World Bank's research department, which in the early 1980s had spearheaded an ideologically driven and very much radicalized position that saw "any government intervention in markets" as inappropriate (Kapur et al. 1997: 625). That said, we should be careful in calling this form of marketizing structural adjustment "neoliberal" in some straightforward way. Structural adjustment lending was not universally supported in neoliberal circles. For at least some "self-conscious neoliberals"—to recall Plehwe's phrase—development aid per se was the problem. As a formula for massive lending—which is to say, massive *intervention* of a particular type—structural adjustment was criticized by neoliberal thinkers.[18] What is more, as we have seen, the "marketizing" variant of structural adjustment was an assemblage of heterogeneous elements, patched together through the twists and turns of crises and failed responses to these crises. It was hardly the pure expression of ideology or economic theory.

But in both critical and sympathetic histories, the birth of structural adjustment through shock therapy has been given a kind of mythical origin in a few iconic figures and events that are associated with neoliberalism in this domain.[19] First among these is the response to hyperinflation in Bolivia in 1985, when Jeffrey Sachs emerged as a key advocate of structural adjustment policies. Sachs shared with many contemporaries a basic optimism about rapid adjustment operations. "In a decisive action," Sachs argued later, reflecting on the experience with structural adjustment in the early years, "one can end the monetary chaos and get money working again to be able to buy goods, to bring goods to the market, to be able to operate a supply and demand, and normal market exchange. This can happen very quickly, and it seems miraculous" (Sachs 2003).

However it seemed to Sachs (and many other observers), this was not a period of miraculous success. By the late 1980s both internal and external critics were pointing to problems with adjustment programs, including their impacts on social welfare, and their failure—still—to resolve the debt problem (Boughton 2001: 31). But the mood of the time was hardly one of circumspection or retreat. A 1988 World Bank review of adjustment lending, thus, identified myriad problems with adjustment programs, and recognized the need for "improved design ... in the use of this lending instrument." Nonetheless, the report maintained that its findings "reinforce[d] the basic rationale for adjustment lending" (World Bank 1988a: 10). The "structural adjustment apparatus" was, by the late 1980s, consolidating.[20]

These, at any rate, were some of the conditions—the institutional matrix, the repertoire of techniques, the accumulation of past experience—that made a program like that laid out in "Window of Opportunity" possible. Janine Wedel (1998: 21) has written that the challenge of postsocialist transformation presented new problems to the IFIs because the formerly socialist countries had been "'misdeveloped,' not 'underdeveloped.'" But this is surely wrong. Key figures in the world of international development were able to find in the postsocialist cases entirely familiar circumstances.[21] The form of structural adjustment that emerged in the 1980s was distinguished precisely by the fact that it assimilated the critique of misdevelopment that had been articulated by neoliberals and other economists and policy observers. This is not to say that a reform template devised in other countries was simply imposed on Russia. Domestic reformers played an active role in modifying an existing repertoire of interventions to local circumstances.[22] But these reformers, of course, were themselves not sui generis; they had been keenly observing and learning from unfolding events, first in Latin America and then in Eastern Europe. Whatever novelties are traced to the Russian case, no dramatic shift in paradigm was required.

What the post-Soviet experience did add, perhaps, was a kind of rhetorical and imaginative inflation of the project. John Williamson, in outlining the terms of the Washington Consensus, had hailed the end of a development "apartheid"—the premise, fundamental to postwar development economics, that the institutions appropriate for development in the advanced industrial countries would not be appropriate for "underdeveloped" countries (Williamson 2002). But the Consensus was defined in relatively *modest* terms, referring to a "lowest common denominator of policy advice being addressed by the Washington-based institutions" to Latin America, given the exigencies of the debt crises. As the socialist countries entered the picture, however, these policies were increasingly associated with a project of transformation that was cast in *epochal* terms. The World Bank's 1996 *World Development Report*— which focused on problems of the transition countries, but generalized their circumstances to a much broader range of experiences—captured the mood and ambition of the period. "Between 1917 and 1950," the *Report* argued, "countries containing one-third of the world's population seceded from the market economy and launched a vast experiment in centrally planned economies that transformed the economic and political map of the world." The present task was to "bring them back by steering a 'transition' from planning to markets" (World Bank 1996c: 3). For the World Bank, "transition" served, at least for what turned out to be a relatively short interregnum, as an alternative to "development," the rubric that had defined its mission since World War II. If "development" described a transformation from "tradition" to "modernity" (a project that seemed increasingly untenable after almost half a century of "development") then "transition" involved replacing one (pathological) modernity with another, thus suggesting the end of another basic division: between the capitalist and socialist worlds. For supporters and critics alike, the project of structural adjustment gained epochal cast and world-historical significance.

The details of what transpired in the early years of Russia's reform—the attempted application of "shock" stabilization, liberalization, and structural reform—have received exhaustive scrutiny. Like Bolivia's shock stabilization the Russian experience has become an obligatory point of passage for narratives about neoliberalism. Here it bears recalling only a few points. A relatively small group of domestic reformers and foreign advisors—Sachs initially among them—gained influential positions, both formal and informal, in the government in the early 1990s.[23] In the first years of the post-Soviet period, these reformers' signal achievements lay in dismantling industrial ministries, in price liberalization, and in privatization. These measures shook industry in a destructive wave. But it was not the creative destruction for which reformers hoped. And it was not, they argued, enough destruction to begin with. The Central Bank, aligned with industrial interests, propped up enterprises with soft loans, allowing them to postpone restructuring or closure.[24] The soft loans set off an inflationary cycle that, in the view of reformers, introduced growth-stifling uncertainty into the calculations of banks, enterprises, and other economic actors. Economic turbulence was accompanied by constant political turmoil that culminated in the 1993 shelling of parliament by President Boris Yeltsin.

By the early to mid-1990s, these events had already triggered an exploding discussion of "transition," and a series of characteristic debates. For critics early failures were to be hung on the shoulders of structural adjustment policies and misguided neoliberal reformers, who some saw as "all powerful" in the years immediately following Soviet breakup.[25] For defenders of the reforms, meanwhile, things looked much more disjointed: the failures of the early 1990s could hardly be attributed to any given, coherent approach since none had been tried. There is something to this. Sachs—the most prominent foreign advocate of structural adjustment in Russia during this period—spent the first years of the post-Soviet period criticizing foreign donors and cajoling the IFIs to see things his way. He complained of the lack of financing, and criticized the IFIs for insisting on budget deficits that were below those maintained by OECD countries. In any case, by the mid-1990s, Sachs was able to say that despite his entreaties, structural adjustment had not been seriously pursued by the Russian government, and that financing for structural reform "was simply not part of the West's real policy discussion with Russia" in the early years (Sachs 1995b: 55).[26] Of course this defense can be taken too far. Polanyi wrote that the last recourse of the pro-market liberal facing failure was to claim that real marketization was not tried, never that marketization failed. And in his persistent conviction that radical change could be led by a small policy elite, in his disregard for long-term political and institutional costs of such vanguard action, and in his insistence that change could be miraculously fast, Sachs often played the part of a reckless market revolutionary.[27] One could make a lot or a little of this.

I would prefer to simply point out that by the mid-1990s the project of "marketizing" structural adjustment was already being transformed.

REDEFINING GOVERNMENT

As Stefan Koeberle noted in a comprehensive 2005 review of World Bank program lending, the paradigm of structural adjustment underwent significant changes by the mid-1990s. In the 1980s lending conditionalities had focused on "stroke of the pen" measures such as privatization, removal of price controls, and trade liberalization. By the early 1990s, however, conditionalities increasingly focused on issues that were "long term, institutional, and microeconomic," related to the social sector, economic governance, and public sector management.[28] This broader shift was reflected in the evolution of strategic thinking about reform in Russia. Long-term institutional reforms were often mentioned in adjustment programs of the early 1990s, but they received little attention from domestic policymakers or international advisors. Over the next decade, however, such reforms took center stage.

The remainder of this chapter traces this shift in the Russian reform agenda. I will argue that the longer-term institutional reforms that came into focus in the late 1990s and 2000s can still be situated within the broad concern of marketizing structural adjustment: with making the economy flexible and adaptable to changing economic circumstances, and with correcting the "distortions" of Soviet socialism. But they touched upon areas that could not, for a variety of reasons, be dealt with simply through marketization. Structural adjustment had, in this context, to be reconceptualized: not as the "reallocation of resources in the economy after the introduction of markets" but in more *substantive* terms as a tricky accommodation between market mechanisms of allocation, existing patterns of spatial, material, and demographic development, and the continuing social welfare aims of the government. My analysis focuses primarily on the assessments of foreign observers, since for the moment I am interested in the modulation of structural adjustment as a reform paradigm. But it is important to my broader argument that these foreign assessments increasingly converged with Russian government reforms in the 2000s, which are addressed in the next two chapters.

Fiscal Adjustment

The shifting emphases of structural adjustment lending in Russia were reflected in a major World Bank strategy note, initially released on October 16, 1995, and later published in 1996 under the title *Russian Federation: Toward Medium-Term Viability*.[29] *Toward Medium-Term Viability* (hereafter *TMTV*) was situated at an important conjuncture in the evolution of post-Soviet reform. Sachs had withdrawn from his role advising the Russian government toward the end of 1994. In the same year, stabilization policies began to gain traction. Early in 1995, the Russian government and the Central Bank agreed on a stabilization package that was backed by an IMF standby arrangement.[30] Funds began to flow in greater volumes from the IFIs, and supporters of "transition" began to assess the project's chances with greater optimism. *TMTV*'s "Executive Summary" began by reviewing these developments, noting progress on stabilization and, with cautious optimism, projecting that Russian GDP—whose official decline in the period 1990 to 1994 was over 50 percent—had bottomed out, and that growth was poised to resume.

These accomplishments raised a range of new problems related to what *TMTV*'s authors called *fiscal* adjustment. Most immediately, fiscal adjustment referred to a set of by-now familiar problems of fiscal and monetary management. "*To keep the stabilization program viable,*" they argued, "*the Government will have to maintain tight fiscal discipline*" (World Bank 1996b: ix).[31] In the short term, "fiscal discipline" meant financing deficits not through "monetization" but through sale of short-term domestic debt and lending from the IMF; in the medium term, it meant reducing the federal deficit to 1 percent of GDP by 1999.[32] This understanding of fiscal discipline would seem to accord with what many critics have seen as the hard logic of structural adjustment and shock therapy: social welfare sacrificed to the cold facts of scarcity. But if we scratch only a bit beneath the surface, we find that in *TMTV* fiscal adjustment opens out onto a range of *substantive* problems and priorities. "Cutting the deficit and stabilizing inflation," the report's authors argued, "are necessary but not sufficient conditions for restoring sustainable growth. ... A further requirement is the redefinition of the role of government" (World Bank 1996b: xiii). In some areas, they argued, "Russia continues to have 'too much government,'" singling out "too much interference in economic activity through enterprise support and subsidies, as well as a poorly designed tax structure that exacerbates the normal tax burden and discourages productive investment." But in other areas, Russia had "too little government." "Vulnerable groups in society," they recognized, are "not sufficiently protected from adverse shocks during transition" and "too little is invested in critically needed infrastructure and social services." This issue seemed particularly pressing given the fiscal and monetary tightening implied by stabilization, which raised the "the daunting task of further reducing the size and changing the composition of government at a time when social dislocation and restructuring ... have placed a greater demand on public services" (World Bank 1996b: 31).

The bulk of *TMTV* was occupied with specifying this "redefinition of government" by outlining specific policy changes. The report's second section, "Structural Policy Issues for Creating Fiscal Viability," laid out programs for reform in five areas: taxation, intergovernmental finance, enterprise support, housing and utilities, and the social safety net. Taken collectively, the proposals hardly suggested a coherent direction or vision of reform; they were, rather, something of a tangle. The report called for the reduction and eventual elimination of production subsidies in agriculture and coal mining, and of social welfare payments that were not targeted specifically to the poor. At the same time it proposed "continued, but modest, support to enterprises in one company towns." The authors of *TMTV* observed that Russia had perhaps the greatest interregional inequality of any federation in the world, and advocated reforms to make outlays from the federal government's "Equalization Fund" more equalizing so that poorer regions could afford basic social services. Finally, the report argued that due to "widening ... income differentiation and the emergence of pockets of poverty," more would have to be invested in social protection programs, such as "a well functioning housing allowance scheme" to help households pay rising rates on maintenance and communal services such as heat, water, and electricity (World Bank 1996b: xvi, 62).

TMTV's third and final section presented a scenario for fiscal adjustment over the period 1996 to 1999. The scenario was developed using a "flow of funds" analysis, a form of financial modeling that examines money flows between the government, the rest of the domestic economy, and an "external" sector. Derived from accounting techniques, flow of funds models have nothing in common with the abstract economic models—so frequently criticized by critical social scientists—that rest on assumptions about optimality, efficiency, or equilibrium. Rather, flow of funds analyses generate data-rich analytical models whose strength lies in their ability to understand interrelated changes in the financial accounts of various actors in an economy (echoes, despite obvious differences, of Soviet "material balances").[33] This kind of financial modeling was invented in the late 1940s, and was soon adopted by the U.S. Federal Reserve, but was rarely applied to developing countries, in part because the data required was not systematically gathered. But with the fiscal crises of the 1970s, development program modeling—which did not deal with money-flow issues—was found to be inadequate given the demands of fiscally oriented adjustment programs. Flow of funds analyses were adapted for the purpose, making it possible to model structural adjustment neither as a "reallocation of resources in the economy," as Sachs had put it in 1994, nor as a transformation oriented to a concrete vision of future economic activities, as Rostow had imagined after World War II,

TABLE 6.1.
An Adjustment Scenario, 1994–1999, as Percentage of GDP

Total deficit reduction	9.2
Increase in revenues	4.8
Direct taxes	2.2
Indirect taxes	2.3
Non-tax revenues	0.3
Reductions in expenditures	9.8
Public consumption	3.7
Subsidies	6.0
Households	3.5
Enterprises	2.5
Other expenditure reductions	0.1
Increase in expenditures	—5.4
Social safety net	—5.0
Public investment	—0.4

Note: expenditure increases have a negative sign.
Source: (World Bank. 1996, xx).

but as a modulation of market valuation and allocation with substantive goals of government through the mechanism of the *fisc*.

TMTV's adjustment scenario began from assumptions about growth and investment that were exogenous to the model. It then proceeded to project mutually consistent changes for the government budget, the remainder of the economy, and the external sector, taking into account the effect of the reforms outlined in the prior section. On the basis of this analysis, it was then possible to plan changes over time in the revenues and expenditures of the federal government: deficit reduction of 9.2 percent of GDP achieved through increases in tax and non-tax revenues (4.8 percent of GDP), and a net reduction of expenditures (4.4 percent of GDP) achieved through a combination of cuts in subsidies and public consumption and increased outlays in various categories, particularly the social safety net (see table 6.1).

In contrast to the detailed visions elaborated in the general plans produced by Soviet city-builders—to take one possible point of comparison—the vision laid out in *TMTV* is indeed striking for its formality. A massive transformation of the economy and of government is represented in purely numerical terms, through a log of fiscal balances. But it is nonetheless a plan of a certain type: it provides a framework for purposeful intervention by the state. And upon some reflection, it becomes apparent that this vision of fiscal adjustment recalls not the stark antinomies of "great transformation"—the market versus the substantive organization of society—so much as the discussions of the state budget in the Soviet 1920s. The advocates of the "genetic" positions in the Soviet planning debates explored new ways to think about an expanding state, not as a substitute for the market, but as a major sphere of activity that had to be limited and adjusted in relation to the autonomous processes on the market. Reformers of the 1990s began, in some sense, from the opposite end of the problem: How could an already bloated state be disciplined, brought into some kind of general economy with the autonomous activities of private actors? But in both cases planners used "extrapolation" to project the dynamics of economic activity from a known past into an uncertain future; in both cases the concern was with constraining the state within limits imposed by the economy, but also with examining how the state's activity would reshape the functioning of the economy. In both cases the question was one of managing the articulations between markets, administrative arrangements, and mechanisms for need fulfillment in areas such as public utilities, the system of interbudgetary relations, and mechanisms of social welfare. And in both cases the budget was the hinge that linked the autonomous domain of the economy to myriad substantive problems of governing.

The Substance of Structural Adjustment

The guardedly optimistic assumptions underlying *TMTV*'s "adjustment scenario" were disappointed. Even after stabilization in the mid-1990s Russian GDP continued to contract. As Barry Ickes, Peter Murrell, and Randi Ryterman point out, this situation presented a "puzzle to those who claim that liberalization and stabilization are sufficient conditions for economic growth" (1997: 105). Part of the explanation was to be found in macroeconomic conditions. An overvalued ruble made Russian enterprises high-cost producers in world terms. High interest rates made borrowing prohibitively expensive. Continued uncertainty made firms hesitant to undertake adaptive restructuring.

By the late 1990s another interpretation of the puzzling (for economists) circumstance of "stabilization without growth" emerged. Its perspective was not *macroeconomic* but *substantive* in the Polanyian sense. It reconceptualized adjustment in terms of the existing material, demographic, urban, and spatial forms of post-Soviet Russia. This interpretation was initially articulated by critics of "transition"—David Woodruff, for example—and more technocratically minded observers—Clifford Gaddy is prominent, among others—trying to explain the slow pace of adjustment in light of stabilization in the mid-1990s. But this substantive perspective was soon assimilated into World Bank strategy statements about Russia, and ultimately into the rationale for major government reform initiatives in the 2000s.

The starting point for this "substantive" analysis of adjustment was a question that preoccupied many observers of Russian affairs in the mid- to late 1990s, and was central to discussions of "stabilization without growth": Why did struggling Russian industrial enterprises not close or dramatically reorient production? On one level, the question provided its own answer. If loss-making enterprises survived, it was because they did not face hard constraints. Suppliers did not demand payment from purchasers; governments at all levels allowed tax arrears to accumulate; workers worked without wages; and energy producers—most crucially the gas monopoly Gazprom, which acted as a "value pump" (Gaddy 2008) for the rest of the economy—continued to deliver gas, oil, and electricity to firms that had no means to pay for it.[34] The system-wide tolerance for arrears put off the day of reckoning for innumerable Soviet enterprises that stumbled on after Soviet breakup. Although it received less attention, a similar logic could be identified in the public sector. Local and regional governments were not forced to make dramatic cuts in public employment or services thanks to cheap or free gas and electricity, and to budgetary transfers that funneled money from the few value-adding parts of the economy to the overwhelming majority of cities and regions whose industry had contracted precipitously since 1991. If adjustment meant the reallocation of all these factors according to a market logic, then this system of arrears and (generally hidden) subsidies was a vast system of self-protection or *preservation* that, as Michael Burawoy and Katherine Verdery (1999a) have pointed out, could be observed at every level of the Russian economy and polity.

Similar issues arise, of course, in any country undergoing rapid industrial restructuring. But in the late 1990s foreign observers recognized—and it is here that things get interesting—that the stakes of "adjustment" and "preservation" in Russia were particularly high thanks to the peculiar features of Russia's urban and industrial structure. Woodruff trenchantly observed that in Russia "the absence of possibilities for labor mobility, the prevalence of one- or few-factory towns, and the intertwining of 'public' and 'private' physical infrastructures" meant that the survival of enterprises was "coextensive with survival of critical sections of the local community," thus making the imposition of hard constraints particularly difficult (1999: 144). Fiona Hill and Clifford Gaddy wrote in similar terms: Russia, they argued, is in "an entirely different league from other developed states" due to the wide dispersion of "huge cities and massive enterprises and extractive industries" across a vast territory in a cold climate (2003: 100). In fact, as we have seen, it is the preponderance of *small-* and *medium*-sized cities—and the *absence* of huge cities—that really distinguishes the Russian urban pattern.[35] But the key point here concerns the way that the existing substantive arrangement of Soviet cities and industry came into the view of expert reflection about the problem of adjustment. Hill and Gaddy's diagnosis was a universe away from the stark formality of the vision that Sachs had advanced in the mid-1990s—the reallocation of productive factors by markets—or the placid assertion by the authors of "Window of Opportunity" that no special consideration of the Soviet legacy was required to understand the endpoint of post-Soviet transformation. We might also note that these features of the substantive economy that increasingly seemed central to problems of adjustment—the spatial distribution and size structure of cities, the intertwining of production and social services, and the particularly intransigent connections between populations, industrial enterprises, and apparatuses of social welfare— were precisely the inheritance that Soviet city-building bequeathed to post-Soviet reformers.

Initially this substantive analysis was articulated as an explanation for the slow pace of adjustment. But soon it was assimilated into a revised conception *of* adjustment in which post-Soviet transformation was no longer conceived as a "transition" from socialism to capitalism but instead as a complex, path-dependent reconfiguration of the inherited forms of Soviet urban and social modernity. This revised understanding was evident in a 2005 World Bank economic memorandum, whose title—"From Transition to Development"—seemed to suggest that the specifically "postsocialist" problems of Russian transformation were in the past. But this title belied the report's contents, which made it clear that post-Soviet Russia was not on the verge of becoming a "market economy with the commonly shared basic characteristics of the advanced industrial countries"—as the authors of the Grand Bargain had hoped in 1990—or even a "normal middle income country," as Andrei Schleifer and Daniel Treisman (2004) suggested in the more sober atmosphere of the 2000s. The problem of dealing with the socialist legacy was long term. Adjustment had to address not just macroeconomic variables but also the Soviet pattern of spatial development. "[C]entral planning," the report's authors explained, "oversaw the industrialization of Russia but it also, to a large extent, oversaw the country's urbanization. In the period after World War II there was rapid growth of 'artificial' cities, many of them newly founded and located in inhospitable areas to the north and east of Russia." The result was an urban structure that was "unique to Russia" (World Bank 2005: 45). The implication for post-Soviet reform was that "reaction to the socialist legacy" could not consist of a "simple dismantling of that legacy: economic development is bound to be path-dependent, shaped by the urban legacy of the socialist past, and there is no theoretical reason to suppose that urbanization in Russia will snap back to the *status quo ante*" (World Bank 2005: 28).

In this view the spatial allocation of people, of cities, and of the social welfare apparatus required to meet their needs, was *itself* identified as a "monumental misallocation of resources" (Hill and Gaddy 2003: 100).[36] "Structural adjustment" was acknowledged to imply, thus, a monumental *spatial* and *substantive* upheaval. "Successful economic adjustment is predicated," observed the authors of "From Transition to Development," "on vast demographic changes, particularly internal migration across the huge Russian space, reflecting the need for spatial resource reallocation to deal with the socialist legacy" (World Bank 2005: 18).

In fact, during the 1990s "free-market forces" had begun "rectifying the mistakes of the Soviet era" through migration, particularly from the most extreme climes of the far north (Gaddy 2007: 35). But then something rather paradoxical happened. As the economy began to recover after 1998, and as Russian firms began successfully adapting to market pressures—not through mass closures but through the reorientation of their production to real market opportunities—the Russian population became not *more* but *less* mobile. Rates of internal migration declined to levels less than one-third that of the United States or Canada (Gaddy 2007: 36). The reasons are readily imagined. The "easy" spatial adjustments from the most remote and inhospitable areas had already taken place and conditions in many small industrial cities began to improve. Enterprises recovered and resources began to flow in greater volume through the public sector, leading to a decline in public sector wage arrears, and increased stability in communal service delivery.

But for reformers, Russia's urban and industrial structure was still badly distorted. The problem was that, even in good economic times, the viability of these far-flung cities was predicated on a vast universe of tax policies, fiscal transfers, material flows, and tariff regimes that underpinned the Soviet system of social welfare and that shaped the Soviet urban pattern. If previously these material and fiscal flows had followed a logic dictated by the will of planners (or by the bureaucratic power of ministries) then in the post-Soviet period they were dictated largely by the *existing* pattern of settlement. Subsidized gas and electricity flowed where the wires and pipes ran, that is, to the *existing* urban settlements of post-Soviet Russia. Budgetary transfers—from the central government to regions, and from regional governments to cities—were channeled to those localities where pensioners, teachers, or health workers *already* lived. The problem of "spatial resource reallocation" and "internal migration across the huge Russian space" remained, and it implied dealing not only with the private economy, but with the still enormous public sector.

So what form would adjustment *policies* take given this revised understanding of adjustment as a *process*? One option for organizing the spatial repatterning of settlement in Russia, noted the authors of "From Transition to Development," would be to create incentives for people to move from remote cities, or even to organize planned migrations. Predictably, this administrative approach was firmly rejected for classically Misean reasons: "Given the state of our knowledge," economic policies that "try to pre-judge the future geographical 'winners and losers' of long-term population reallocations run the risk of costly mistakes and may hamper growth" (World Bank 2005: 36). Instead, the report proposed that the reform agenda should focus on the patterns of public and quasi-public resource flow and the regulatory regimes that supported the existing urban and industrial structure of Russia. "[S]ubsidies designed to support remote locations, including differential pricing for energy or electricity," the report's authors argued, "are a tax on the more viable sectors and regions of Russia's economy which have to finance them." They therefore proposed reforms that would remove these subsidies and differential pricing regimes, thus eliminating their distortive effects on the allocation of people and cities across the country. Similarly, the report proposed reforms that would make the government budget function in a manner that was more consistent with market mechanisms for allocating people across the country: "[I]ncreased decentralization of taxation and fiscal expenditures," it argued, would help ensure that "the actual economic situation of a particular location is most accurately reflected in households' incentive structure" (World Bank 2005: 36).

In this way, mundane sociotechnical systems like infrastructures and the state budget became critical to the continued project of "adjustment." Reforms aimed to make these systems more flexible, to loosen the spatial dependencies that they produced. But I will be at pains to argue that these reforms do not simply propose deregulation, decentralization, and flexibilization. These systems remain, after all, critical mechanisms through which the Russian government carries out basic social welfare functions. Reformers were thus left to craft accommodations between "flexibility" and the persistent imperatives of social provisioning.

NEOLIBERALISM BEYOND THE WASHINGTON CONSENSUS

This chapter outlined a rough genealogy of structural adjustment. It showed that the "marketizing" variant of structural adjustment that took shape during the 1980s should not be understood as the pure expression of neoliberal ideology. Instead, it was an assemblage of elements that combined policies oriented to correcting distortions in domestic economies with a particular lending modality that was initially forged as a pragmatic response to the debt crises of the 1970s and 1980s. This convergence emerged from a new problematization of economic crisis that focused not on "external" balances but on the flexibility of domestic economies. I also identified a dynamic tension in this problematization of economic crisis: as liberalization went "deeper" it encountered areas of governmental activity that could not be addressed exclusively through "stroke of the pen" reforms that simply removed state controls. Instead, adjustment required a more complex interweaving of market mechanisms, existing substantive features of Russian cities, and the social welfare goals of government. Thus, in post-Soviet Russia, a project of adjustment initially conceived in purely *formal* terms, increasingly ran up against, and had to reflect upon and try to manage, the substantive reality created by city-building.

It bears noting that this evolution in the problematization of adjustment coincided with a significant shift in the alignment between national politics, economic processes, and the reform agenda in post-Soviet Russia. For much of the 1990s, it seemed possible to portray structural adjustment as an imposed project that enriched a tiny few while immiserating the great mass of Russians. External support appeared to be aimed, as much as anything, at propping up unpopular domestic reformers, from the Grand Bargain to Yeltsin's reelection in 1996 to the desperate attempts to stave off devaluation of the ruble in the summer of 1998. But these dynamics changed. The ruble did collapse in August 1998, despite an ill-fated $22.6 billion bailout whose failure turned out to be the coup de grâce for the Western-backed project of transition in Russia. Devaluation was initially seen as a disaster. But the shift in the terms of trade—and a contingent rise in world oil prices—contributed to rapid economic recovery that, among other things, eased the pressures on government finances. One important consequence was a marked loosening of the relationship between the government and IFIs. By the early 2000s, the Russian government had little use for aid from Washington, and Washington's influence in Moscow was, correspondingly, reduced.[37] If in the 1990s critical observers imagined a coherent neoliberal project backed by the United States and the IFIs, then by the early 2000s the specter of the "Washington Consensus" had faded from the scene.

So what has been the fate of neoliberalism in Russia after the devaluation? The presidency of Yeltsin's successor, Vladimir Putin, scrambled the categories that made sense of the 1990s. His policies have been aggressively centralizing and in important respects authoritarian. Putin undermined the autonomy of local and regional governments, curtailed press freedoms, attacked members of the oligarchy that was so crucial to Yeltsin's hold on power (while allowing others to retain or even consolidate their positions), and effectively nationalized some strategic enterprises. But as Dieter Plehwe, Bernhard Walpen, and Gisela Neunhöffer (2006) have argued is true elsewhere, these developments did not mean the abandonment of neoliberal reform. Putin is obviously not a liberal in political philosophy. But his government adhered to important elements of what is usually considered the neoliberal recipe for reform, maintaining a macroeconomic and fiscal policy that—notwithstanding some hand-wringing about resource dependency that seemed increasingly pertinent amidst the economic turmoil of 2008 and 2009—has generally won approval from outside observers. Meanwhile, in areas such as fiscal administration and social welfare the pace of "neoliberal" reform arguably increased. A comprehensive review of the World Bank's role in Russia concluded that its policy recommendations were more widely accepted in Russia after the devaluation than before it (Zanini 2002). This is certainly true of communal service and budgetary reforms, to which I turn presently. Both remain central to the Russian government reform agenda, and both are major areas of cooperation with external donors to the present day.

In short, by the 2000s the problem of neoliberal reform had been detached from the high politics and high economics of the "Washington Consensus." But what followed surely was neither a reversal of neoliberal policies nor an abandonment of a neoliberal approach to government. It would be best to simply say that the 1990s were a rather peculiar historical conjuncture, one whose specificity was often belied by the epochal framings used to describe it. It was shaped by what now appears to be a contingent ensemble of policies, geopolitics, and political personalities. Neoliberalism was associated with certain things in that context; today it is associated with others. The challenge, in this light, is to develop approaches to studying neoliberalism beyond the Washington Consensus. "Beyond" does not necessarily mean "after," since in many cases we are concerned with traditions of neoliberal thought that have long histories. Rather, it refers to dimensions of neoliberal critique and programming that have come into view now that structural adjustment and the Washington Consensus no longer, like Yeats's "vast image out of *Spiritus Mundi*," trouble our sight.

CHAPTER SEVEN

Budgets and Biopolitics

ON SUBSTANTIVE PROVISIONING
AND FORMAL RATIONALIZATION

> Where a planned economy is radically carried out, it must
> further accept the inevitable reduction in formal, calculatory
> rationality which would result from the elimination of money
> and capital accounting. Substantive and formal (in the sense
> of exact calculation) rationality are, it should be stated again,
> after all largely distinct problems. This fundamental and,
> in the last analysis, unavoidable element of irrationality in
> economic systems is one of the most important sources of all
> "social" problems, and above all, of the problems of socialism.
> —Max Weber, *Economy and Society*[1]

"Hey! You! MinFin!"

BEFORE BEGINNING MY FIELDWORK IN RUSSIA, I traveled with a colleague
to Rostov *oblast'*, a relatively rich and populous region in southern Russia. On the way to the small cities in which we planned to conduct research, we passed through the region's capital, Rostov. The stop was
obligatory. Letters had to be signed and permissions granted for fieldwork to begin. Among the officials whose permission we required was
the head of the regional government's Ministry of Finance.[2] The head of
the Ministry was a woman—a circumstance that may seem initially surprising, given the near-total dominance of men in positions of economic
and political power in Russia. But the vast majority of budget officers in
Russia are women. In the Soviet Union money functioned as a unit of account rather than a store of value; it was the allocation of things rather
than the allocation of rubles that mattered. Thus, as Martha Lampland
(2010) has observed, in the occasionally perplexing gendered division of
labor in the Soviet Union, budgeting, considered a low-status occupation,
was regarded as women's work (see also Johnson 2006).

We soon found out, however, that this was not a typical Soviet budget officer but a forceful and fast-talking reformer who, in the course of
our short conversation, offered a spirited defense of reforms that were

being advanced by the regional government to transform the system of "interbudgetary relationships" (*mezhbiudzhetnye otnosheniia*) in Rostov *oblast'*—that is, the system through which revenues and expenditures are distributed among the regional and local governments. As tax collections collapsed in most cities, local governments no longer had sufficient resources to pay for utilities and salaries for teachers and doctors, or to repair deteriorating infrastructures. In Rostov, as in other regions, the regional budget office had responded by transferring resources to cities and rural districts in an attempt to "fill the gap" between local revenues and expenditure "needs" defined by long-established Soviet norms for social provisioning. In the lean years of the 1990s, however, most regional governments did not have enough money to fill the gap entirely. Predictably, transfers became the subject of acrimonious struggles between local and regional governments.

For reformers like the head of the Rostov Ministry of Finance the problem this crisis presented was not one of inadequate budgetary resources per se. Rather, it was that the very effort to perpetuate the old Soviet practice of gap filling created perverse incentives for local governments, and worked against necessary adjustments to new fiscal circumstances. Mayors and city councils did not respond to budgetary shortfalls by cutting services or laying off employees. Instead, they jockeyed for transfers, in some cases by hiring even more teachers, doctors, and communal service workers in the hopes that they might thereby pressure the regional government to send more rubles their way. The solution, in the view of this reformer, was to make local governments in the region's cities and rural districts face the harsh reality of scarce resources. And this is precisely what the reforms in Rostov aimed to do. On the one hand, they proposed that local governments—which had little autonomy in the Soviet period—should be given more freedom to define how they raise revenues and allocate expenditures. On the other hand the reforms imposed constraints on local governments. They proposed to clarify the system of "tax assignments" that determined how much tax revenue collected in the city could be expended by the local government, and to create a system of "formula based financing" that employed a strict quantitative methodology to distribute scarce resources among local governments.[3] In the new system there would be no more jockeying for resources or special pleading about local needs. Mayors and city councils would have to make tough choices to allocate limited resources among competing priorities.

After our meetings in the capital we moved on to conduct interviews in the small cities of Rostov *oblast'*, most of which were based on industries such as coal mining, machine building, and textile manufacturing that had been particularly hard hit by the brutal inflationary recession of the 1990s. We had a memorable conversation with the head of the local government's budget office in Belaya Kalitva. This budget officer, again a woman, presented a stark contrast to the regional reformer. Cut from the classic model of a Soviet finance official, budgeting for her was not about scarce resources and hard choices. Rather, it was about allocating funds to meet norm-defined needs. Her view, to paraphrase what a Ukrainian finance official said to my colleague Lucan Way (2001), was that the purpose of the Ministry of Finance was to finance things.

But this was a difficult time for financing things in Belaya Kalitva. The coal mines around the city, which provided a substantial chunk of local tax revenue, had closed. The city's aluminum enterprise was barely operating. In the Soviet period, Belaya Kalitva had been a relatively prosperous "donor" city—that is, it made a net contribution to the budgetary system. But by the late 1990s it was the region's largest "recipient"—overwhelmingly dependent on transfers from the regional government. As this local budget officer saw things, just as Belaya Kalitva had contributed during better times, it should now receive help. "Our territory is a recipient [dotatsionnaia] territory," she reasoned. "In principle, according to the law on the finances of local government, there are our own revenues and federal revenues. They should, in principle, give everything, as they did in the past."[4] She found, however, that entreaties to reform-minded regional officials who calculated transfers based on strict formulas fell on deaf ears: "[The regional officials] say: we aren't hiding anything from you. ... They make their calculations ... in Rostov—and we suffer. ... And we say: Hey! You! MinFin! But there are new people there. The people who used to be there, they helped somehow. And now they just shrug their shoulders."[5]

In the reflections of these two budgetary officers—one the reformist head of a regional ministry of finance, the other the budget officer in a small, struggling industrial city—we have two entirely different styles of reasoning about budgeting as a technology of government. For the local budget officer, the city appears in the old terms of city-building as a khoziaistvo, a collection of human needs that have to be met. For her, budgeting is a problem of substantive provisioning that, as David Woodruff has observed, presents a kind of "social sine qua non." For the head of the regional ministry of finance, by contrast, the city appears in a different guise: as a collection of calculative actors—mayors and members of city councils—who must be forced to make choices about which needs they wish to meet, and which, given scarce resources, they can neglect. This problem of formal rationalization—of allocating scarce means among different possible ends—seems incompatible with an absolute imperative to meet needs. A "social sine qua non," Woodruff observes, can have no place in the world of "numerical assessments of costs and benefits—it introduces an impossibility, like a division by zero" (1999: 144–5).

BUDGETS AND BIOPOLITICAL GOVERNMENT

During the 1990s this contrast between substantive provisioning and formal rationalization powerfully framed the stakes of reform in post-Soviet
Russia. This was true not only for those who, like the budget officers in
Rostov and Belaya Kalitva, were engaged in practical struggles over local
policies, but also for critical observers trying to conceptualize the relationship between the patterns of provisioning inherited from Soviet Russia and what they generally regarded as neoliberal reform. In this chapter,
using the budget as a test case, I ask whether this contrast between substantive and formal rationalization does in fact offer critical purchase on
the relationship between neoliberal reform and social modernity.

In debates about neoliberalism and neoliberal reform the government
budget is often viewed as a key locus in which it is possible to observe
the absolute antinomy between substantive provisioning and formal rationalization. "Budgetary austerity"—understood as a key component of
structural adjustment and, thus, of neoliberal reform—presents an image
of social welfare goals sacrificed to demands of scarcity (or the demands
of international capital markets). But seen in a somewhat broader view,
it becomes apparent that the government budget, far from being a site in
which these two forms of rationalization are opposed, is among the most
critical sites in which the tricky relationship between formal rationality
and substantive provisioning is constituted as an explicit target of technocratic reflection and management in modern states. On the one hand,
during the twentieth century, as the social state expanded dramatically in
most countries, ever-growing portions of national product cycled through
the *fisc*, and were allocated according to some criterion of substantive
need defined by governments. Budgetary allocations—and the process
through which decisions about such allocations are made—can be thereby read as expressions of "public values" and of the mechanisms through
which these values are defined and realized. On the other hand, the budget has also become a privileged site of formal rationalization—particularly since reforms (from the eighteenth to twentieth centuries) unified
government budgets and professionalized budgetary management. The
budget is thus also the crucial governmental mechanism through which
scarcity is confronted, and through which government is forced to weigh
competing priorities.[6]

Ideally, these formal and substantive dimensions of the government
budget are carefully balanced in a framework of budgetary management.
Through the budget, a government can survey its resources and its diverse aims, and weigh the benefits, costs, and opportunity costs of various courses of action. As Naomi Caiden and Aaron Wildavsky put it in
a classic essay,

[b]udgeting is supposed to aim for economy and the most productive use of resources. It should plan ahead so that funds are available to fulfill needs as they arise. Budgeting provides an accounting for past expenditures and revenues, controls current spending and revenues, and forecasts those of the future. Ideally, it helps to determine the effectiveness of expenditures and allocates resources accordingly. Through its budget, a government may hope to understand its financial position, fix its best course of action, and implement public policy (1986: 146).

Ideally. But inevitably there are tensions between the formal and substantive dimensions of a budget. As Max Weber observed long ago, the substantive orientation of the state introduces an "unavoidable element of irrationality" into allocational decisions. The process of weighing the relative importance of different ends—and of choosing different courses of action that prioritize one rather than the other—cannot be a matter of purely quantitative calculation. This problem is germane first of all to socialism: it is the fundamental and enduring insight of neoliberal critiques of socialist planned economies that they offered no mechanism, equivalent to a market, for expressing competing values in commensurable terms. But as Weber also noted, this "unavoidable element of irrationality" was present any time "social" problems were addressed by government. *Any* approach to budgetary management—including a neoliberal approach—must therefore grapple with the relationship between the imperatives of calculative rationality (since, like it or not, resources are indeed scarce) and the imperatives of substantive provisioning.

And indeed, it turned out that the reforms I first encountered in Rostov were a bit more complicated than was suggested by the heated exchange (through my own intermediation) between regional and local officials, or by the simple antinomy of formal versus substantive rationality. These reforms did aim to make local budgets loci of calculative choice and thus of formal rationalization. But they also reinscribed—in a certain way—the *substantive* ends of Soviet social modernity. The questions were, then: How was this tricky balance between formal and substantive rationalization worked out? What style of reasoning animated these reforms? And what—if anything—did they have to do with neoliberalism?

I discovered that the Rostov reforms were adapted from a template that had been developed in a USAID-funded project on tax reform based in Moscow, which had formulated a framework for reform of interbudgetary relationships. The foreign specialists involved in this project were among a broader universe of economists and technocratic experts who, circulating among institutions such as the World Bank and USAID, made fiscal reform a key area of programming in international development during the 1980s, 1990s, and 2000s. Reading through the technocratic and academic literature that these experts produced, particularly on the critical questions of budgetary transfers and redistribution, I found that a clear line pointed to the work of James M. Buchanan, a central figure in American neoliberalism. In a series of articles written just after World War II, Buchanan identified budgeting as a key area of concern for a new liberal reflection on contemporary government given the rise of the social state. What Buchanan formulated, what the minor tradition of fiscal federal theory elaborated technically, and what the Rostov reforms proposed concretely, was not a program for doing away with the norms of the social state. Rather, it was a program for reconciling the liberal preference for limited and decentralized government with the imperatives of substantive provisioning that are core to the social state. In exploring *how* it proposed to do this, we will get to the heart of fundamental questions about neoliberalism and social modernity: What is the neoliberal position on redistribution? And what do neoliberal reforms propose to do with the norms that articulated the Soviet system of social welfare?

SOVIET BUDGETS AND SOVIET BIOPOLITICS

We have already seen (in chapter 5) that the budget was a critical mechanism of Soviet social modernity, serving to finance a network of social and urban services that were distributed with increasing uniformity over Russian cities as the Soviet period wore on. Here it bears examining the Soviet budget in a bit more technical detail—and considering its transformations in the early *post*-Soviet period—so that we can understand the system that reformers grappled with.

The character of the government budget was hotly contested in the Soviet Union's early years (see chapter 2). Two distinct visions of the budget emerged that corresponded to two visions of the state's role in shaping collective life. The People's Commissariat of Finance, whose position was dominant in the mid-1920s, emphasized the *formal* problem of the fiscal constraints under which the government operated. It developed new techniques for projecting the autonomous dynamics of the economy so that tax collections—and, thus, resources available to the state—could be anticipated. The planning agencies, meanwhile, countered that budgeting should be guided not by fiscal limitations but by the substantive ends of the state. The question was not one of working within limited *financial* resources but of mobilizing *physical* resources toward the *telos* of a planned future. The planners' victory implied a fundamental change in the character of the budget. As planning (or, at any rate, administrative decision making) expanded to cover an ever-greater portion of social and economic life, the range of activities reflected in the budget expanded as well. The state budget accounted not just for a limited state sector but for the entirety of economic processes in the country. Paradoxically, however, as the budget expanded to cover more and more activities, the practice of budgeting declined in importance. The budget no longer functioned as the key instrument by means of which the relationship between scarce resources and substantive goals was worked out. Instead, as Way puts it, the budget was "simply an accounting mechanism for distributional decisions made in other parts of the government" (2001: 55).

How did the state budget relate to the planning for and provision of social welfare goods and urban services and, thus, to the city *khoziaistvo*? In principle, plans for social provisioning in a given city—like plans for population growth, for industrial employment, and for all other aspects of urban development—were unified in a city plan. But there was not a unified budgetary mechanism through which resources for these various activities flowed. Instead, budgeting for local needs was splintered into multiple streams of expenditure that were often only lightly coordinated. Industrial production was planned and budgeted through the hierarchies of industrial ministries. Meanwhile, spending responsibilities for social welfare planning and urban development were divided. Industrial enterprises might take responsibility for funding kindergartens, some roads, clinics, housing, and major elements of urban infrastructure such as water and heat systems as costs of production. Most primary education spending along with some health care and communal services were funded through what can be called "local budgets," since they corresponded to the official organs of territorial administration—local soviets. Particularly in small cities, where industrial enterprises dominated the scene, the scope of activities financed from these local budgets could be narrow. But it bears focusing on them here, for they later became the primary target of post-Soviet reforms.

Local budgets were managed by local offices of the union-wide Ministry of Finance, a vast bureaucracy with offices in every republic, region, and locality.[7] The peculiarity of the system of budgets organized through the Ministry of Finance lay in the relationship between the planning for revenues and the planning for expenditures. In the ideal-typic view of budgeting laid out by Caiden and Wildavsky, revenue constrains expenditures, imposing the fundamental fact of scarcity, and encouraging "economy and the most productive use of resources" (1986: 146). But as Carol Lewis (1976, 1983) has documented, in the Soviet budget system planning for revenue and planning for expenditures were largely independent processes.[8] Plans for revenues were derived from plans for production at major local enterprises, which determined the amount of tax collection that could be expected in a given year. Plans for expenditures, meanwhile, were formulated on the basis of budgetary "needs"—or *potrebnosti*—that were derived from norm-based calculations for social provisioning. The key mechanisms in calculating needs were prescriptive norms—similar to those employed in city plans (see chapter 3)—that defined the concrete elements required to fulfill a given need for a given unit of population: teachers per thousand school-age children; hospital beds per thousand population; heat per square meter of housing, and so on. Officials in the Ministry of Finance then used financing norms to translate these *substantive* needs (for teachers, heat, and hospital beds) into ruble equivalents. By aggregating these ruble amounts, it was possible to calculate the budgetary needs (*potrebnosti*) for a given locality. The result was a quantification of norm-defined needs of a certain population, with a certain demographic structure, living in a locality with certain characteristics (climate, building conditions, transportation infrastructure, and so on).

These two "plans" for the budget were brought into alignment through the mechanism of gap filling that we have already encountered in one of its post-Soviet incarnations (see figure 7.1). Budget officials (whether at the regional, republican, or all-Union level) calculated the difference between locally collected tax revenue and bureaucratically defined requirements for budgetary expenditure in any given city or region. They would then use transfers and adjustments in the system of tax sharing to close the gap between what was raised locally and what was required.[9]

This simplified picture of the Soviet budget system does not tell the whole story, of course. Incrementalism was a powerful determinant of budgetary outlays (that is, prior year "actuals" influenced subsequent year expenditures). Much financing was simply determined by the existing network (*set'*) of facilities rather than by norms. And political influence certainly played its role. Powerful party bosses from big cities were able to grab a disproportionate share of resources. But as we have already noted, the development of the Soviet social welfare system suggests that norms played a crucial role in determining the allocation of resources. This budgetary system promoted substantial equalization—not only of expenditures but also of social goods and services—across the territory of the Soviet Union.[10] In this sense, the Soviet budgetary system was a picture of substantively oriented economic action in nearly ideal purity—and with all its attendant pathologies. A city "showed up" in the budget as a unit of account in a system of mutually articulated norms that shaped the city-building *khoziaistvo*. Normed needs drove fiscal flows. There was no particular incentive to ask whether resources were available to meet these needs, or whether these resources were being used efficiently. There was no question of whether these needs were properly weighted, one in relation to the other, or whether, indeed, they were the right needs in the first place. These simply were the accepted ends of government. The job of the Ministry of Finance was to finance them.

FISCAL CRISIS: PRESERVING THE *KHOZIAISTVO*

With the collapse of industrial production in small cities this system of budgeting was thrust into crisis. Tax receipts declined precipitously and the expenditure burden on local budgets increased, as the responsibilities for financing many social and communal services previously supported by city-forming enterprises were transferred to local governments. One indicator of the depth of the fiscal crisis at the local level was the grow-ing gap between actual expenditures and estimates of expenditure needs. In Belaya Kalitva, for example, expenditures in 1995 still approached 90 percent of "need." By 1998 the number had plunged to a mere 30 percent (Collier 2001: 196–97). Even using more modest estimations of need pro-posed in the Rostov budgetary reforms—discussed in detail below—by the end of the 1990s revenues only came to 66 percent of expenditures in the ten cities of the region where such a "deficit" was found.[11] Another indicator of fiscal crisis was the increasing dependence of small industrial cities on transfers from regional governments. In the Soviet period such cities had generally been "donors": net contributors to central budgets. By the late 1990s they were almost universally net recipients. In Ivanovo *oblast'*, where Rodniki is located, every city other than the capital re-ceived over 40 percent of revenues in transfers by the late 1990s. In Rod-niki the figure stood at 58 percent. In other cities it was as high as 60 or 70 percent (Collier 2001: 195).[12]

So how did local governments respond to these newly austere circum-stances? One possibility would have been to cut services, lay off doctors and teachers, and transfer the burden of paying for communal services to recipients—to adjust, in short, the volume of substantive provisioning in light of hard constrains. But in the 1990s local governments did not take these steps. Instead, they treated support for these existing commit-ments precisely as a social sine qua non and struggled to adjust flows of resources around them, using a variety of strategies to *preserve* an exist-ing set of services and to *preserve* or even augment existing public sector employment.

One such strategy of preservation was to focus resources on "socially necessary expenditures" by, for example, shifting resources from agri-cultural or industrial subsidies to social expenditures such as education and health care.[13] Within these broad categories—education, health care, communal services—local governments also focused on essential items

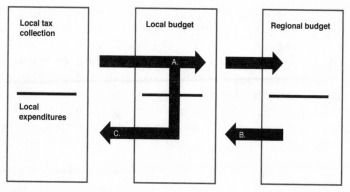

The Soviet interbudgetary system

A. Tax sharing
B. Transfers
C. Potrebnosti (requirements)

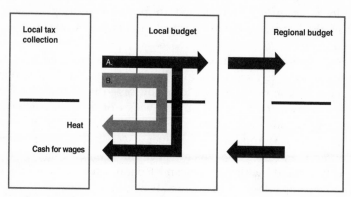

Post-Soviet Preservation—restiching the *khoziaistvo*

A. The cash circuit
B. The material circuit

Figure 7.1. Soviet and post-Soviet gap filling. During the Soviet period, Ministry of Finance officials manipulated tax assignments and transfers to adjust the resources available to local governments so that they matched norm-defined "needs." Although the system was distorted by various factors—including the influence of powerful ministries and tendencies of "incrementalism"—it contributed to the growing equalization of social and communal services across the Soviet Union by the 1970s and 1980s. In the 1990s, this system was rocked by fiscal crisis, as revenues to budgets at all levels declined precipitously. One response of local governments was to manipulate mutual settlements of debt and in-kind payments to meet local needs. The budget thus emerged as a key mechanism of "preservation" in small cities during the most difficult period of economic collapse.

that were required to preserve a basic network (*set'*) of services. For example, wages and utilities were favored at the expense of capital repairs, maintenance, and supplies. By my calculations between 75 and 85 percent of the local budgets in Rodniki and Belaya Kalitva were expended on wages and utilities in the late 1990s (Collier 2001: 202). Another strategy of preservation employed by local governments was to carefully manage two distinct and largely separate flows of resources: one of cash, the other of things. These flows were "particularized" in the sense that resources were not passed from one circuit to another. Each came from certain sources, and each was directed to certain ends, a fact nicely summarized by a local budget officer in Rostov region, who noted that "cash is for wages; everything else—offsets [*den'gi-to tol'ko na zarplatu; ostal'noe— vse po zachetam*]." In other words, any cash was used to pay workers employed by the local government, and everything else was transacted in various forms of material exchange.[14] In examining these two circuits (figure 7.1), we can better understand not only how, in the face of fiscal crisis, local governments managed to preserve existing services but also how the budget served as a critical mechanism in rearticulating the city *khoziaistvo*.

First—the cash circuit. In the 1990s, cash was rare and precious in an increasingly barterized economy. To the extent that local budget offices collected cash revenue from local sources—that is from local enterprises—they used it exclusively to pay wages of doctors, teachers, and administrators. But major industrial enterprises tried to avoid parting with precious cash. And local governments were not necessarily keen to press enterprises for cash payment, since tax revenue collected in cash had to be "shared" with regional and federal levels of government. In any case, the unpaid wages of doctors, teachers, and local administrators were a powerful tool for prying subsidies out of regional governments.[15] Locally collected cash revenues were thereby supplemented with cash transfers from regional governments that acted to "fill the gap"—not between "revenues" and "expenditures," but more specifically between locally collected cash and the wage obligations of local governments.[16]

The other great circuit of resource flow was material. Through it, major local tax payers— industrial enterprises, construction organizations, and so on—extinguished tax debts to the local government by rendering payment in goods and services.[17] For example, enterprises and construction or maintenance organizations might complete projects for the local government such as roadwork or repairs on facades of public buildings. Occasionally, barter transactions were arranged involving the products of industrial enterprises—easy to do when the product was coal, and a local government needed coal to fire a heat boiler; harder when it was rolled aluminum, as in Belaya Kalitva, or camouflage, as in Rodniki. But most frequently, and in truly massive volumes, material flows through the budget involved *heat*—specifically hot water and steam—which enterprises in many small cities produced thanks to the centralized boiler complexes they had built during the Soviet period. In the next chapter we will explore the reasons why these boilers remained in the possession of enterprises after Soviet breakup. Here, the important point is the implication for local budgetary relations. Once responsibility for housing was transferred to local governments, the heat bill became the largest expenditure on local budgets in small cities. Consequently, a substantial proportion—at times more than half—of the local budget was transacted in heat offsets. Tax debts were swapped for hot water.

In sum, instead of adjusting to new circumstances, local governments hunkered down in what Michael Burawoy and Pavel Krotov (1992) have nicely called an "involutionary" response to economic collapse. Local administrators pulled all of the levers at their disposal, carefully routing flows of resources to particular ends, in order to somehow hold the existing substantive economy together. From the perspective of local governments—and, it should be added, of most people who lived in the cities they governed—"preservation" was a virtuous response to hard economic conditions. But for domestic and foreign reformers preservation marked, precisely, the pathology of the Soviet system as it faced the new realities of post-Soviet Russia. Drawing on an entire tradition—a neoliberal tradition—of thinking about fiscal matters, they formulated a new kind of critique and an entirely different programming of the budgetary system. It is to this tradition that we now turn.

BUCHANAN'S FISCAL CONTRACTARIANISM

A comprehensive account of neoliberal thinking about the *fisc* would extend back to a nineteenth-century tradition of continental fiscal theory. But the story I tell here begins as an American story and a twentieth-century story that revolves around the economist and political theorist James M. Buchanan.[18] Buchanan is widely recognized to have made seminal contributions to a neoliberal theory of redistribution. And the Rostov reforms can be understood as a technical elaboration, in the post-Soviet context, of Buchanan's norm of fiscal equity. Buchanan is also of interest because he was embedded in the crucial American experience that is taken to be seminal for neoliberalism more broadly. The rise of American neoliberalism was, of course, a response in part to international events, particularly for those influential recent arrivals (Hayek, Mises, and others) who experienced fascism in Germany and Russia firsthand. But there was also an important domestic context that is more immediately relevant to our story. The U.S. federal government emerged from the New Deal and World War II having assumed new roles in economic regulation and social welfare provisioning. This development was viewed with anxiety by liberal thinkers. What were the implications of a growing central government for American democracy and federalism, or for the system of free enterprise? How might the rise of the "social state" be accommodated to principles of classical liberalism? It is in relation to such questions that we should understand Buchanan's efforts, beginning in the late 1940s, to constitute the budget of the emerging post–World War II social state as a site of neoliberal critique and programming.

Buchanan is known best for his work on "public choice," for which he received a Nobel Prize in 1986. In his first academic papers, however, he explored the narrower problems of public finance, federalism, and redistribution. I will try to show that the *technical* framework Buchanan proposed for a neoliberal economics of public sector budgeting was taken up by subsequent generations of fiscal federal theorists. But I also want to emphasize how these mundane technical considerations were linked to a distinctive *political philosophy* that defines, it seems to me, what is specifically "neo" about Buchanan's liberalism. Buchanan (and other neoliberals) argued that economists had arrived at workable approaches to the private economy but had ignored the analysis of government. This lacuna was particularly problematic at a time when the state was expanding rapidly. In this light, Buchanan revisited basic questions that had been raised by classical liberalism: What kind of a thing is the state, and of what elements is political collectivity comprised? How do we think about the "goods" or "values" produced by the state? The position he developed in his early essays might be labeled a "fiscal contractarianism." It rested on the basic politico-philosophical claim of eighteenth-century liberalism: that government existed and possessed the authority to rule only thanks to the consent of the governed. But he also recognized that the government had a major role to play in addressing growing social inequality and in providing services to citizens based on some criterion of need. The challenge of reconciling these orientations—which, we will see, were often in tension—was the central preoccupation of Buchanan's early reflections on the social state.

Methodological-Ontological Orientations

Buchanan's first work on these themes was a 1949 essay, "The Pure Theory of Government Finance," published in the *Journal of Political Economy*, a crucial outlet of Chicago economics and, more generally, of American neoliberalism. The article addressed the fundamental question concerning the economic analysis of government: How does one think about the value produced—and the burdens imposed—by the activity of government? How does one analyze fiscal choice from an economic perspective? Marginalist economics had provided the grounds for modern economics to conceptualize value as it was produced in markets by replacing the "substance" theory of value found in classical political economy from Ricardo to Marx with a "subjective" theory, which posited that value was derived from the preferences of economic agents.[19] The question was whether an equivalent proposition could be found for the value produced by government. "What," Buchanan asked, "is the common denominator to which the alternative goals of [government] may be reduced for comparative purposes, analogous to the equally vague, but less elusive, 'satisfaction' or 'utility' for the individual?"[20] Could economic reasoning provide a solution to that "unavoidable element of irrationality" (to recall Weber's phrase) introduced by fiscal distributions oriented to some criterion of need?

Buchanan contrasted two approaches to this question. The first was what he called the "organismic" approach, which he associated with the dominant Pigovian public finance economics of the time.[21] It posited that the state was a "single decision-making unit acting for society as a whole," and that government "sought to maximize some conceptually quantifiable magnitude"—an overall "general welfare" or "social utility." In this view "[i]t is the function of the 'fiscal brain,'" Buchanan wrote, referring to Pigou's metaphor that the government was the "brain" of the community, "to select the values of [the] many variables which will maximize social utility." (1949: 496).[22] "The necessary condition for a maximum" could be understood as a kind of equilibrium state for public taxation and expenditure, "produced when … a dollar's tax load upon each economic entity deducts from social utility an amount equivalent to that added by a dollar's expenditure in each line" (1949: 497).[23] The organismic approach thus formulated the problem of public value as an optimization problem; the value to be maximized was "social welfare."

In his later work on public choice, Buchanan exploded this unitary conception of government and its assumption that the state acted in a benevolent way to maximize social utility or general welfare. He analyzed government not as a single "fiscal brain" but as a collection of bureaucrats, policymakers, and interest groups who, Buchanan posited, were no more or less self-interested than any other economic actors. But in his early papers of the late 1940s and early 1950s, Buchanan was occupied with a different problem. It related to what he saw as the "major difficulty" involved in understanding the values that the fiscal brain was supposed to maximize (1949: 496). For Buchanan, the concepts of social welfare economics were fundamentally mysterious. How, he asked, was public interest or social utility defined? What was this "society" or "public" for whom these values were valuable?

Buchanan contrasted the Pigovian "organismic" view of the state to a second—from his perspective, vastly preferable—approach in which "the individual replaces the state as the basic structural unit." This "individualistic" position began from classic liberal contractarian propositions. "The state," Buchanan wrote, "has its origin in, and depends for its continuance upon, the desires of individuals to fulfill a certain portion of their wants collectively. The state has no ends other than those of its individual members and is not a separate decision making unit. State decisions are, in the final analysis, the collective decisions of individuals" (1949: 498). In this individualist view the state was not a coherent actor that maximized anything. And there was, in any case, no "general welfare" function to be maximized since there was no "society" to whose "utility" such a concept might refer. Instead, public finance should be analyzed as part of an exchange, in which citizens traded one value for another. Budgeting was part of the process of politics as conceived in the liberal tradition, through which individuals got together to achieve ends that could not be achieved in isolation. As such, it was a domain in which the social contract was constantly renewed and renegotiated.

For Buchanan this individualistic perspective on the budget provided the orientations required for an economic theory of public finance. It suggested that it was not some mysterious quantity of social welfare but the *balance* in the exchange "between the contributions made and the value of public services returned to the individual" that should be regarded as "the relevant figure" in thinking about the value produced, or taken away, by government. "Each individual," Buchanan wrote, "is subjected to some fiscal pressure; his economic resources are reduced by the amount of tax that he bears. His real income is increased by the benefits that he receives from government services. The allocation of total tax load among individuals must be combined with the distribution of benefits from publicly provided services in any complete theoretical framework" (1949: 499). This individualistic focus had not been entirely absent from the prior economics of the public sector. But the classical approach had addressed only one side of the equation: the problem of "tax incidence," that is, the distribution of the tax burden that government imposed on individuals.[24] The expenditure side—thus, the benefits individuals realized from the activity of the state and, thus, the value *produced* by the state—had been neglected. An economic approach had to consider the "balance between the two sides of the fiscal account" (Buchanan 1949: 499, n. 5).

This balance—which Buchanan called the "fiscal residuum" (1949: 501)[25] —was the critical concept for analyzing what he regarded as the fundamental question of fiscal policy in light of the social state: How did the fiscal system modify the distribution of income? In the "Pure Theory of Public Finance" he laid out three possible orientations for the state's intervention in patterns of distribution. In the first, which he called "aggregative," government policy "increase[s] the inequality in the distribution of real income among individuals." In the second, "status quo," the fiscal system has no net effects on income distribution. In the third, "redistributive," "people in low-income groups receive more benefits than they pay in taxes and the upper-income groups contribute more than they receive in benefits" (1949: 502).

In Buchanan's view, it was not the role of a "fiscal scientist" to decide which among these options were appropriate; the distributional effects of the *fisc* were properly "political" decisions. And the political view of the day was clear. "For the present," he wrote, the "redress of the prevailing income distribution toward greater equality has been accepted as one of the fundamental purposes of the fiscal system in the modern state." In this light, the fiscal scientist could "provide policy-makers with practical guides to action." He or she could determine "roughly the amount of redistribution of real incomes actually accomplished through the fiscal process" and indicate "alternative tax and expenditure allocations which would yield approximately equivalent redistribution results, some of which might result in significantly different effects upon the economy"—reducing, for example, the allocative efficiency of private markets (1949: 504). This was a strictly self-limiting vision of economic science that could have been drawn (indeed, may well have been drawn[26]) from Weber's "Objectivity in the Social Sciences." The role of an economist was to tell politicians which value-ends were being achieved by policy, and what the costs or opportunity costs of that policy might be in terms of *other* values (such as economic prosperity). It was not to determine what the proper aims of government should be.

Federalism and Fiscal Justice

"The Pure Theory of Government Finance" set out what Buchanan called the "methodological-ontological" terms in which a liberal critique and programming of the social state could proceed.[27] It provided an explicit reflection on what government was, how public value should be understood, and what tools were relevant for its analysis. Buchanan's next essay, entitled "Federalism and Fiscal Equity" (1950), turned from these general considerations to the contemporary problems of the social state, addressing in particular those specific institutions involved in intergovernmental distribution in a multilevel federal system.

Federalism was a contentious issue in the United States after World War II. The growth and centralization of the government beginning in the New Deal challenged the autonomy of state and local governments. In the late 1940s and early 1950s, Buchanan was hardly alone in recognizing that these developments raised questions about the U.S. federal system that were entirely beyond the horizon of the constitution's framers.[28] "In 1789," Buchanan wrote, apparently referring to the year in which government under the U.S. Constitution began, "a significant share of economic activity was limited to local markets; there was relatively little areal specialization of production." What is more, a small portion of collective wealth cycled through the governmental system, and "governmental services were performed predominantly by the local units which were drawn up roughly to correspond in area to the extent of local markets" (Buchanan 1950: 584). Under such circumstances, as Buchanan saw it, public finance raised few problems for political liberalism. The preferences of individual citizens would be reflected in the expenditure choices of local governments that were close to their constituents. The production of value by government was limited, and seemed to rest on acceptable contractarian footing.

The situation after World War II was different. Industrialization, specialization, and integration of the national economy had concentrated wealth, creating greater inequality across the United States. Simultaneously, since the 1930s the government had assumed a vast range of new roles, particularly in providing social services and social security. These developments raised a number of problems. The growth of the social state involved "the diversion of greater and greater shares of the total of economic resources through the fiscal mechanism" rather than through markets, raising questions about how state activity affected mechanisms of resource allocation in the economy (Buchanan 1950: 584). The growth of specifically the *federal* government moved mechanisms of collective decision making farther from those who were affected by them, thus undermining a key tenet of local democracy. Buchanan saw in this combination of circumstances a distinctive challenge for the U.S. federal system. "As more government services were provided equally to all citizens, or upon some basis of personal need," Buchanan wrote, "the discrepancies between the capacities and needs of the subordinate units arose" (1950: 585).

For many contemporary observers, the rise of the social state meant that the extant U.S. political system had become "outmoded, and the federal spirit [was] a thing of the past" (Buchanan 1950: 585). They argued that only a unitary state—no longer organized along federal lines—"would resolve the peculiar fiscal problem" that federalism faced when confronted with the imperatives of equality that were central to the social state. Given what we know—or what we think we know—about neoliberalism, we might expect that Buchanan took precisely the opposite position, opposing the new roles of government, particularly in welfare provisioning, preferring to defend markets and autonomous local government. But this was not the case. Buchanan felt that social welfare and central redistribution were unavoidable features of life in a complex industrial society. They were necessary if one wanted to move from a situation of growing inequality to a distribution of wealth that was, as he put it, more "ethically acceptable" (1950: 590). The question was not whether there ought to be a social state but how such a state could be reconciled with the values of individual autonomy, local control, and market organization of the economy. What were the neoliberal grounds for redistribution? And how could the fiscal system serve, in Buchanan's terms, as the "major means" through which unequal distribution was redressed?

In "Federalism and Fiscal Equity," Buchanan approached these questions by focusing on one critical point of intersection between institutions of federalism, public finance, and redistribution—namely, federal grants to states. This may seem a narrow and technical topic, but it was of great political importance at the time. Much of the New Deal had been financed through federal grants, and they featured centrally in discussions of the U.S. fiscal system and, more generally, of social welfare, after World War II. As such, the principles for their allocation were crucial to patterns of redistribution in the United States. Buchanan's analysis began by considering the basic principle of the social state: that government services should be "provided equally to all citizens" or on "some basis of personal need." He did not reject this basic orientation but restated it so that, in his view, it could be reconciled with liberal principles. First, he insisted that the proper question was not whether different states in the U.S. federal system *actually* delivered equal services. It was essential, in his view, to preserve the autonomy of local governments that were "close" to their constituents. Instead, the appropriate principle was equality of fiscal *capacity* of states, which should *be able* "to provide equivalent services at equivalent tax burdens" but might *choose* differing levels of services and taxation (1950: 586).[29]

Buchanan's second modification of the equality principle concerned the relevant units for thinking about equalization: What, precisely, should be equal? "Equal fiscal capacity" was a concept that referred to states (that is, to sub-national governments). But "equality in terms of states," Buchanan wrote, is "difficult to comprehend, and it carries with it little ethical force for its policy implementation." "Is there," he asked, "any ethical precept which implies that states should be placed in positions of equal fiscal ability through a system of intergovernmental transfers?" (1950: 586). Buchanan concluded that principles of redistribution could be placed on firmer ground if the equality of *individuals* rather than that of states was in question. What a fiscal system should provide in a liberal and democratic polity, he argued, is "equal treatment for equals"—equal treatment for "persons dissimilar in no relevant respect." This, for Buchanan, was an "essential ... guide to the operations of a liberal democratic state, stemming from the same base as the principle of the equality of individuals before the law" (1950: 587). But this formulation is not self-evident. It seems clear enough to speak of equality before the law. What does it mean to speak of equality before the *fisc*?

In answering this question, it is helpful to first ask what might be meant by *inequality* before the *fisc*. For Buchanan, the growth of government expenditures had created—or made dramatically more acute—a certain kind of fiscal inequity that could be explained in the following way. Imagine two states, one rich and one poor. In order for the governments of these respective states to provide equal levels of social services, the rate of taxation would have to be much higher in the poor state than in the rich state since taxes are imposed on a lower per capita income of its inhabitants. Thus, in figure 7.2, if the total income in state A ($I_{\text{State A}}$) is greater than the total income of state B ($I_{\text{State B}}$) then the rate of taxation in state B ($T_{\text{State B}}$) would have to be greater than taxation in state A ($T_{\text{State A}}$) in order to collect a certain amount of revenue (R). Now imagine two individuals, equal in all respects, including income; one lives in the poor state, one in the rich state. A given level of public services will come at a higher cost for the individual in the poor state than for the individual in the rich state since the rate of taxation required to pay for such services is higher. This is "fiscal inequity"; a kind of inequity—unequal treatment of equals due to a geographic accident of birth—that offended liberal thought.

With this understanding of fiscal *inequity* in mind we can imagine what Buchanan meant when he spoke of fiscal *justice*. Fiscal justice—equality before the *fisc*—refers to a situation in which states were able to provide "equal services at equal rates of taxation" (Buchanan 1950: 586). This was precisely the equalization of fiscal capacity, but now rooted in firm individualistic grounds. Fiscal justice required a transfer of resources from rich to poor states in sufficient volume that, at a given rate of taxation, an individual with a certain income in a poor state could receive the same services as an individual with the same income in a rich state. Such redistribution could be achieved through various mechanisms: through federal grants to poorer states, or—the alternative that Buchanan thought theoretically preferable but less practicable—by adjusting the federal tax rate applied in each state.

In developing the nearly taken-for-granted liberal formula that equals should be treated equally in the mundane domain of fiscality, Buchanan arrived at an original approach to the problems of the social state, one that would have longstanding implications for the neoliberal programming of government. Its implications are surprising, given our usual understanding of neoliberalism. Although the equalization of "fiscal capac-

Fiscal Inequity

State A   **State B**

Citizen C   Citizen D

T = Tax rate
I = Taxable income
R = Amount of revenue required to deliver a certain level of public services
F = Federal transfer

If $I_{\text{State A}} > I_{\text{State B}}$ then $T_{\text{State B}} > T_{\text{State A}}$ in order to collect **R**.

If **C** and **D** have equal income, **D** must pay more than **C** to enjoy an equal amount of public services.

Fiscal Equity—"Equal Treatment for Equals"

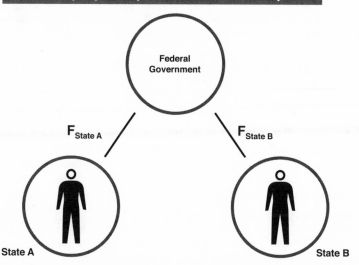

Fiscal equity is achieved through federal transfers (**F**) when

$$(T^*I_{\text{State A}}) + F_{\text{State A}} = (T^*I_{\text{State B}}) + F_{\text{State B}} \text{ at a given tax rate } (T).$$

Figure 7.2. Buchanan's conception of fiscal equity. James Buchanan argued that the only meaningful value that could be produced by government was value for concrete individuals, defined by their own preferences. This individualist-contractarian assumption led him to formulate a striking argument for redistribution in modern societies with large social states that, he thought, was consistent with the tenets of classical liberalism.

ity" referred to subnational governments, it also implied *interpersonal* redistribution since equalization affected both the tax burden imposed on individuals and their "income," understood to include the individual utilities that are realized from government expenditures.[30] Buchanan presented, thus, a principled defense of equalization that, following the classic liberal argument for social welfare, did not rest on any conception of charity. "Inter-area transfers," Buchanan wrote in the conclusion to "Federalism and Fiscal Equity," "do not represent outright subsidization of the poorer areas, do not represent charitable contributions from the rich to the poorer areas. ... The principle establishes a firm basis for the claim that the citizens of the low income states within a national economy possess the 'right' that their states receive sums sufficient to enable these citizens to be placed in positions of fiscal equality with their equals in others states" (1950: 596).

FISCAL FEDERALISM: PROGRAMMING THE SOCIAL STATE

Over the following three decades, Buchanan's work on fiscal contractarianism evolved into a sustained reflection on economic constitutions that was in dialog with major strands of normative theory in the postwar United States. His subsequent theory of public choice became a central framework for a new political economy. But his early work on fiscality and federalism was taken up in another tradition that was quite removed from high theory in political science or economics. This was the field of fiscal federal theory, one of those "minor" traditions of neoliberal thought and practice to which I referred in this book's introduction. It lies, following Michel Callon, at the interstices of "several worlds and institutions" and has compiled "an entire body of knowledge" that, "although hybrid" is "both original and general" (1998b: 28). Prominent academic economists, such as Buchanan, Charles Tiebout, and Wallace Oates, have made major conceptual contributions to this field. But of equal importance are figures who circulate among the domains of academic production, policy research, and consultancies, think tanks, and government ministries: Robin Boadway, Anwar Shah, Jorge Martinez-Vazquez, and Galina Kurlyandskaya, to name only a few contemporary figures, of varying international prominence, whose work is drawn on in the discussion that follows.[31]

The modern theory and practice of fiscal federalism can be traced to the period around World War II. A comprehensive review would consider how its subsequent development has been inflected by episodes such as the "federalism crisis" in the United States in the 1960s and 1970s, the experience with equalizing transfers in Canada, discussions of European

Union federalism and, most recently, the experience of developing and "transition" countries following fiscal crises in the 1980s and 1990s.[32] My aim in this section, however, is not to trace the theoretical or practical development of fiscal federalism per se. Instead, I will show how, through this minor tradition, the conceptual orientations laid out in Buchanan's fiscal contractarianism were turned into an entire programming of the social state that would ultimately shape reforms in post-Soviet Russia.

Microeconomics of the State:
Citizens as Consumers—Government as Enterprise

Fiscal federal theory is a body of economic thought about a multilevel governmental system comprising a central government and at least partially autonomous regional (state) and local (urban or rural district) governments.[33] It is an "economic" theory of the state in the sense that these governments at different levels are conceived as autonomous actors that can be analyzed in terms of their preferences and their calculated choices in the face of incentives created both by constituents (citizens and firms) and by the institutional setup of the governmental system itself. Taxation and expenditure—the classical problems of public economics—are central topics for fiscal federal theory, much of which is concerned with the most basic questions of budgetary programming in a federal system: Which level of government—local, regional, or central—should pay for defense, education, or social welfare services? Which should impose property, income, or sales taxes? How should intergovernmental grants be organized? I will show that these mundane problems are linked to a framework for programming the state through choice, calculation, and enterprise, particularly in light of the functions and value orientations of the social state.

Following Buchanan's orientations, the literature on fiscal federalism assumes that the relevant values in public economics are individual values: costs borne and benefits enjoyed by individual citizens, not by any collectivity whose welfare should be maximized. This conception of public value creates a presumption in favor of decentralization in the programming of fiscal federal relations. If the relevant values are individual values, and individual preferences are not homogeneous (that is, not everyone wants the same things), then it can be presumed that local governments are, as Robin Boadway has argued, "best able to cater to the preferences and needs of their residents (2003: 3)."[34]

Another central preoccupation of fiscal federal theory is the role that the federal system plays in determining the allocation of people, enterprises, and government services across a federal state. Fiscal federal theory analyzes the interactions of citizens, enterprises, and subnational governments in terms of "market-like" adjustments structured by mechanisms of choice, competition, and enterprise. Citizens are understood as consumers—or, as Charles Tiebout (1956) put it in his seminal article," A Pure Theory of Local Expenditures," "consumer-voters"—who can pressure governments to provide the level of taxation and services that they desire, or "vote with their feet" by moving to jurisdictions in which the mix of services and taxes fits their preferences.[35] "In much the same way that consumers purchase private goods," Wallace Oates explained, in a federal system an individual who is "unhappy with the pattern of expenditures and the structure of taxes in his community" can "always move to another community which provides a 'fiscal package' better suited to his tastes" (1968: 48). If citizens and enterprises are understood as discriminating consumers of a "fiscal package," then subnational governments are analyzed in terms of their enterprising efforts to increase their tax base by attracting firms and people and promoting local economic development. Through the appropriate programming of fiscal federal relations, subnational governments can be framed as calculative agencies with "an incentive," as Philip Hanson has put it, "to promote the long-term growth" of the cities or regions that they administer (2006: 193).

Today, this framework may seem commonsensical. But in the 1950s when its foundations were being laid in the work of Thiebout, Buchanan, and others, fiscal federal theory presented a critical revision of then-dominant theories of public finance. The reigning public sector economics, dominated by Richard Musgrave and Paul Samuelson, was restricted to an analysis of a unitary governmental system. In this important respect it shared the assumptions of the organismic theory of the state that Buchanan criticized in 1949.[36] And as Tiebout observed, given that Samuelson allowed for "no 'market-type' solution ... to determine the level of public goods," his approach seemingly left economists and policymakers "with the problem of having a rather large portion of ... national income allocated in a non-optimal way when compared with the private sector" (1956: 416).

As it emerged in the hands of Buchanan, Tiebout, Oates, and others, federal fiscal theory aimed to show that the autonomous adjustments among citizens, firms, and local governments could serve precisely as a "market-type" solution to the production of public services and the definition of public value.[37] In Tiebout's view, the locational decision of firms and residents "replaces the usual market test of willingness to buy a good and reveals the consumer-voter's demand for public goods" (1956: 420).[38] The choices of local governments in providing these goods—and interlocal competition to provide the best "fiscal package"—replaced mechanisms of market competition. In this way, fiscal federal programming was conceived in part as a political technology for "enhanc[ing] the efficiency of resource allocation" in countries in which an increasing volume of national product was being cycled through the *fisc* (Oates 1968: 48). It presented a powerful vision of how the mutual adjustments between populations, production, and systems of social welfare provisioning could be organized through spontaneous, decentralized processes. In it we find what are usually taken to be the classic markers of neoliberalism: government through calculative choice; the extension of market schemas to non-economic domains—here, specifically, the domain of government.

But we should not be too quick to conclude that fiscal federalism is a market model of the public sector, and that this, precisely, marks its neoliberalism. For we have considered only one side of the story. Fiscal federal theory is indeed a theory of government through the dispersed calculative choices of firms, local governments, and "consumer-voters." But it is equally concerned with the functions that *cannot* be fulfilled—or that can only be fulfilled in an inefficient manner—through "spontaneous" or decentralized processes of adjustment, and that have, therefore, to be *centrally* provided.[39] Crucial among these are economic stabilization and national defense—both of which are "pure" public goods. Although spending on social welfare is generally considered to be an appropriate prerogative of local government, distribution, and, thus, *redistribution*, is considered to be an appropriately *central* function. And in managing redistribution, we will see, fiscal federal theory reintroduces problems of substantive provisioning into its formal framework.[40]

Transfers and Equity: Microeconomic Critique and Programming

To illustrate this point we can consider the area of fiscal federal programming in which Buchanan made his most singular contribution and that also happens to be most relevant to the Rostov reforms: the design of redistributive transfers or "equalization grants." At certain moments the topic of equalization grants has received a great deal of attention in the fiscal federalism literature. But the fiscal federal theory of equalization has been *technically* elaborated only in recent decades, indeed, arguably in the last several years.[41] The context—which relates in particular to developing and "transition" countries—is relevant to our story.

As we saw in the prior chapter, problems of fiscal reform were pushed to center stage in developing and transition countries by balance of payments crises that triggered battles over deficits and the volume of government expenditures in the 1970s and 1980s. Initially reforms focused on "rolling back" the state in order to achieve fiscal balance and make domestic economies more flexible given volatile economic conditions. Debates about these reforms focused, therefore, on the *size* of the state relative to the private economy. But by the 1980s and 1990s reforms increasingly focused on the "institutional setup" of fiscal systems. Thus, a 1988 World Development Report on public finance and development called for moving beyond debates about the size of the state—which it considered to be inconclusive and fruitless—to questions about how the state should be programmed as an allocational and distributional mechanism.[42]

When compared to the richer industrial countries, developing and transition countries tended to have highly centralized fiscal systems (World Bank 1988b: 48). This was particularly true of the socialist cases, many of whose budgetary systems were essentially unitary. By the 1990s and 2000s major decentralization initiatives were underway in many of these countries, often supported by external donors such as the World Bank and USAID. For reasons that should be apparent, decentralization was itself a critical dimension of fiscal federal programming. By defining what revenue sources and what expenditure responsibilities belonged to local governments—and, of course, by expanding their autonomy—reformers hoped to make the public sector more efficient, and more responsive and accountable to the diverse preferences of citizens.

At the same time, reformers and policymakers recognized that decentralization raised new problems. Jorge Martinez-Vazquez and R. J. Searle noted that "very often the allocation of expenditure and revenue assignments in a fiscally decentralized nation leads to horizontal fiscal imbalances"—that is, inequalities in the resources available to governments at the same "level"—"because of the different fiscal capacities and expenditure needs of sub-national governments" (2007a: 3).[43] Equalization transfers were thus seen as "a necessary counterpart to decentralization, offsetting its tendency to create disparities among regions in the ability to provide public goods and services" (Boadway 2003: 1).

The programming of redistribution in fiscal federal theory—at least in every formulation I have encountered—begins from the familiar norm of fiscal equity: equals should be treated equally. In the contemporary literature Buchanan is recognized as the source of this norm, which is interpreted as he interpreted it: local governments ought to be able to provide "comparable public services at comparable tax rates" (Boadway 2003: 3).[44] What contemporary fiscal federal theory has added to this broad normative orientation is both a massive technical elaboration of the programming of equalization transfers—to which we turn in a moment—and a critical assessment of the systems of intergovernmental transfers that have emerged since World War II.

In the lens of fiscal federal theory, the postwar experience revealed a number of problems with mechanisms of distribution around the world. In most countries, transfers were calculated on the basis of a "gap filling" mechanism akin to the Soviet system. Central or regional governments calculated the difference between estimated local revenues and the expenditure "needs" of local governments, and then transferred resources to close the gap. Fiscal federal theory recognized that the quantities that defined this fiscal "gap" were calculated in a way that created perverse incentives for local governments. Estimates of revenues were often based on prior-year tax collection. Such an approach, as Richard Bird and Francios Vaillancourt explain, gave local governments "an obvious incentive to impose lower tax rates ... or to make less effort to collect taxes in order to receive higher equalization grants" (2007: 263). A parallel problem arose in calculations of budgetary "need." In many cases, regional or central governments defined a locality's expenditure requirements by referring to the prior year budget, or examining existing "commitments"—the salaries of teachers or health care workers already hired, or the costs of facilities already built. As a result, Le Grand notes, local governments had "an incentive to increase public expenditure" (1975: 535). If equalizing transfers based on gap filling created incentives for a "race to the bottom" when it came to taxation, then when it came to expenditures they perversely incentivized a "race to the top."

This microeconomic *critique* of equalizing transfers implied, in turn, a microeconomic *programming* of local (regional or municipal) governments. To better grasp how this microeconomic programming works, it will be helpful to refer to Michel Callon's framework for analyzing the constitution of "calculative agencies" in markets. Callon focuses in particular on the work of "framing," which serves to "define agents (an individual person or a group of persons) who are clearly distinct and dissociated from one another" and can, therefore, calculatively pursue their self-interest (1998b: 17). It is crucial to underline what Callon notes parenthetically: these agents may be individuals *or* a collective of some size and type, whether a capitalist firm or a city government. The work of framing entails, first of all, clearly delimiting the rights, responsibilities, and scope of autonomy of these agents. It also entails "formatting" the mode of interaction between the calculative agency and its environment. As Callon puts it, "a clear and precise boundary must be drawn between the relations which the agents will take into account ... in their calculations and those which will be thrown out of the calculation as such" (1998b: 16). By externalizing factors that should *not* be taken into account and internalizing those that *should*, framing defines the "possible worlds" among which an actor must choose, and defines, thus, what is at stake (and what is not at stake) in calculative choice.[45] For Callon, thus, calculative actors are technical artifacts whose production can be examined by investigating the work of framing.

In the fiscal federal approach to equalizing transfers, the framing of local governments as calculative agencies works through programming key variables in a fiscal federal system: the distribution of competencies, the assignment of revenue sources, and the calculation of equalization payments itself. Thus, for example, fiscal federal programming will aim, following Callon, to "disentangle" different levels of government, making them "clearly distinct and dissociated from one another" by clarifying their right to levy certain taxes, their claim to some portion of the proceeds from those taxes, and their responsibility for financing certain expenditures. The framing of choice is also achieved by defining which factors will, and which will not, be taken into account in the choices of these calculative agents. Thus, fiscal federal theorists have proposed ways to calculate transfers so that their volume will not, as Le Grand puts it, vary with the "fiscal operations" of a local government (1975: 536). They are "externalized" from a local government's taxation and expenditure decisions.

The details of this "framing" will become clearer in the next section, when we return at last to budget reforms in post-Soviet Russia. In anticipation of that discussion, and in wrapping up the present one, it bears making an observation about fiscal federal theory as a framework of government through calculative choice. Thus far, it has certainly seemed that fiscal federal programming has, following Nikolas Rose, a certain "formal" character. It aims to constitute local governments as loci of calculated choice, where scarce resources have to be rationally apportioned among diverse ends. But the formality of fiscal federal programming goes much further. Fiscal federal theory imagines a system of adjustments based on the autonomous choices of people and firms to locate in one city rather than another, or of local governments to provide a "fiscal package" that will attract them—and not on directed intervention by central government. Even the *normative* orientations of fiscal federal theory—to fiscal equity—are expressed in purely formal terms. Fiscal equity, which requires that individuals *could* enjoy equal services at a given rate of taxation, is a statement of *capacities* that can itself be instituted through a logic of local autonomy and calculated choice. It does not require specific reference to any particular kind of substantive provisioning to any specific individual or group.

But we will see that in order to *operationalize* the principle of fiscal equity a whole series of substantive problems will have to be introduced. The realization of fiscal equity *in practice* requires prior decisions about which services should be provided by government—that is, about the proper *substantive ends* of government. It will also require that the programming of transfers takes into account a range of factors—the demographic structure of a local population, climatic conditions, access to transport, the material organization of welfare provisioning, the rate of poverty, and on and on—that define the "need" for budgetary resources in a given locality. "Fiscal equity" thus opens out onto a vast universe of problems concerning the substantive conditions in which need fulfillment is practically organized. As we will see in examining Russian fiscal federal reforms, the design of equalizing transfers therefore will involve not only the "framing" of calculative action, but also the production of public value.

REPROGRAMMING THE RUSSIAN SOCIAL STATE

The evolution of budgetary reforms over the first two post-Soviet decades followed a pattern that is broadly characteristic of reform dynamics elsewhere. During the 1990s, reformers were consumed with a series of financial crises, and as Jack Diamond has observed, budgetary reform was focused on short-term "firefighting" (2005: 3). But by the end of the decade their attention had shifted to longer-term problems concerning what was often called the "institutional set-up" of the budgetary system. Reform of interbudgetary transfers, which were among the first targets of "second-wave" reform, are exemplary in this development.[46] In 1994, a system of formula-based equalization was instituted on the federal level (concerning transfers from the central government to the regions). But its methodological basis was poorly developed and actual transfers were highly politicized throughout the decade. A parallel system of formula-based financing on the regional level was called for in the 1995 Law on Local Self-Government. But at that time, according to Galina Kurlyandskaya and Natalia Golovanova, "almost no one could grasp the legal meaning of the advanced word 'formula,' and the relevant provision of the Law was simply ignored" (2006: 216). It was only in the late 1990s that a more coherent framework for programming equalization grants was defined. On the federal level, reforms in 1998 established a single system of formula-based transfers (Ministry of Finance 2000b: 4). Reform of regional-local interbudgetary relations, meanwhile, was inaugurated by a USAID backed technical support program. The fiscal federal reforms I encountered in Rostov were part of a pilot project supported by the USAID initiative.

The USAID grant on fiscal reform was administered by the Georgia State University (U.S.) Fiscal Research Center, which created partnerships with Russian experts in the Moscow-based Center for Fiscal Policy (run by Kurlyandskaya). Along with a team of experts from the Russian Ministry of Finance, and with financing from the World Bank and USAID, this group first produced a set of "Methodological Recommendations" (hereafter, *Metodicheskie Rekomendatsii*) in 1999, followed by "Temporary Recommendations" (hereafter *Vremennye Rekomendatsii*) for interbudgetary reform accompanied by an "Explanatory Note"

(*Poiasnitel'naia Zapiska*, hereafter, *Zapiska*) that provided a template for regional reforms with supporting technical materials.[47] The remainder of this chapter explores the framework laid out in these documents—which I refer to collectively as *Recommendations*, with more precise references noted parenthetically.

I want to be explicit about the purpose of this exercise. Its aim is not to provide an account of the actual evolution of the Russian budgetary system—a task to which scholars with other kinds of expertise are better suited (Martinez-Vazquez and Timofeev 2008; Freinkman et al. 2009; De Silva et al. 2009). Nor do I mean to suggest that *Recommendations* presented the only or even the most important framework for budgetary reform, although it is essential to my project that these proposals were taken seriously at the highest levels of government, and that elements of them have, indeed, been adopted. Instead, I am interested in the style of reasoning that animates them, and in the distinctive movement through which fiscal federal theory—as one minor tradition of neoliberal thought and practice—has taken up the Russian social state as a target of critique and programming.

Critique

Recommendations begins with an assessment of the system of interbudgetary relationships as it stood in the late 1990s. The story it tells of fiscal crisis and "preservation" will be familiar. After ruble stabilization in 1994, finances of most local governments collapsed; the disjuncture between the fiscal capacity of the public sector and existing social commitments baldly confronted decision makers at every level. But the response, particularly at the subnational level, was not to reduce expenditures in line with these newly tightened constraints. Instead, regional budget offices responded to fiscal crisis through the old Soviet logic of gap filling— trying to "make up, from the regional budget, the difference between tax and non-tax revenues of the local budget ... and its requirements [*potrebnosti*]" (*Metodicheskie Rekomendatsii*, 10). The size of this gap was calculated in the "traditional" way: based on "actual implementation of the budget for the prior year" and on "normative expenditures" but "without taking into account revenue capacity" (*Vremennye Rekomendatsii*, 5)—that is, without taking into account the resources at the disposal of local governments. "NORMS," wrote *Recommendations'* authors—the capitalization, it seems, a playful reference to Soviet slogans of old— "dictate expenditures [*NORMATIVY—fakticheski diktuiut raskhody*]" (*Zapiska*, 13).

Thus, in the face of fiscal shortage, regional governments did not see local budgets as loci of hard constraints and calculative choices, but as "lists of expenditures [*smety raskhodov*]" that had to be financed: children who had to be educated; sick individuals requiring health care; apartments that, during cold winters, needed to be kept warm (*Zapiska*, 60). Nor did regional governments treat local administrations as autonomous governmental entities that ought to be accountable to the preferences of their citizens. Instead, they were treated as "territorial subdivisions [*territorial'nye podrazdeleniia*]" of the regional government itself, their budgets a mere "transit account [*tranzitnyi schet*]"—a resting place for resources as they made their way in an uninterrupted path from distributional decisions of regional governments to the satisfaction of local needs (*Vremennye Rekomendatsii*, 4). In sum, *Recommendations'* authors diagnosed "preservation" as precisely a reaction to fiscal crisis within the existing institutional routines and norms of the Soviet budgetary system. So how did a critique of this preservation take shape?

Before answering this question we should note what is *not* identified as a problem. The authors of *Recommendations* did not object per se to the norms that regional governments used to define local "needs." Indeed, we will see that they not only *accepted* these norms but argued that, if anything, they were *not applied strictly enough* given the politicization and incrementalism of the post-Soviet budgetary system. Nor did these reformers reject the idea that an important function of central or regional governments should be to support local governments as they endeavored to provide a basic package of social services. What they *did* reject was a system for employing norms and, by extension, for defining needs that simply ignored the basic fact of scarcity, the incentives of local governments, and the preferences of its citizens. And it is around these problems that a microeconomic critique took shape. *Recommendations* began from the presumption that a central motivation of local governments is to "increase their chances of receiving extra funds from higher-standing budgets." It then articulated a critique that examined the city no longer as a collection of needs but as a collection of calculative agencies whose incentives had to be programmed through the system of interbudgetary finance. An entire critical apparatus and a grid of intelligibility for knowing the state, developed over decades in other countries, swung into motion.

The influence of transfers on the incentives of local governments was not trivial. On some accounts, by the 2000s transfers covered almost half the revenues of local governments (Martinez-Vazquez et al. 2006: 145); we have seen that the number was even higher in poor cities. And given the existing system of transfers, *Recommendations* argued, the incentives produced by transfers were perverse indeed. The practice of evaluating available resources on the basis of actual tax collections "decreases incentives to mobilize resources for the local budget," and during the 1990s local governments displayed a "permissive attitude [*popustitel'skoe ot-*

noshenie] attitude toward non-payers of taxes" (*Zapiska*, 14).[48] Meanwhile, on the expenditure side, the system of gap filling encouraged local governments to increase their estimates of revenue "need"—or to simply increase their expenditure obligations by creating "facts on the ground" in the form of public employees whose salaries needed to be paid or services that required funding. Local governments "use all their strength," *Recommendations* explained, to "inflate the staff of budgetary organizations" such as schools and hospitals "and use ineffective technology for delivering budgetary services" such as wasteful water or heating systems that, *precisely in their inefficiency*, served to increase the transfers to which a local budget might lay claim (*Vremennye Rekomendatsii*, 14).

In sum, the efforts at preservation, which from the local perspective seemed so unambiguously virtuous, appeared from the reformers' perspective to waste resources, reduce the efficiency of budgetary management, and distort expenditure decisions. They also disrupted the most fundamental purpose of a budget. Estimates of revenues and expenditures were simply bargaining positions, not clear reflections of scarce resources and the dilemmas involved in their allocation. In this context, noted *Recommendations*, the budget did not "fulfill its basic function—it does not regulate the distribution of resources" (*Zapiska*, 95).

The persistence of gap filling in the context of fiscal crisis had more general implications for the function of local governments as organs of territorial administration. Because the gap between actual revenues and norm-defined needs was never closed entirely thanks to severe and chronic budgetary shortages, actual transfers were ad hoc and unpredictable. "The volume of financial assistance transferred to local budgets was defined by the ability of local officials to reach agreements with higher standing officials [*s vyshestoiashchimi vlastiami*]" (*Zapiska*, 6); local governments therefore devoted an inordinate amount of energy to the constant bargaining, cajoling, and deal-making required to get extra transfers rather than to the proper concerns of government (*Vremennye Rekomendatsii*, 5). This perpetual uncertainty and dependence on the good graces of regional budgetary officials also undermined the accountability of local governments. "[F]or all intents and purposes," *Recommendations* concluded, local governments "do not bear responsibility for the formation and implementation of budgets, and in the final analysis for the quality and quantity for services, since all blame for problems not addressed at the local level can be placed on a higher power" (*Zapiska*, 12). The ideal-typic local government of fiscal federal theory—an autonomous entity with clearly defined rights and responsibilities, accountable and responsive to its constituents, incentivized first of all to increase tax collection, rationalize expenditures, and promote local economic development—was light-years from the reality of local government in post-Soviet Russia.

Programming I: Framing Local Autonomy

After identifying the microeconomic problems introduced by existing interbudgetary relationships, *Recommendations* turned to a new programming of the regional fiscal federal system. This programming began from
a principle that was established in the 1993 Russian Constitution and
reaffirmed in subsequent laws on local government: "governments at different levels possess a certain autonomy in shaping the revenues and expenditures of their budgets" (*Zapiska*, 45). This statement of autonomy
is articulated in the idiom of legal right. But it is also a technical problem,
implying a work of what Callon calls disentanglement—of replacing the
confused and ambiguous distribution of budgetary responsibilities and
functions with "clear and concise boundaries of competencies between
regional and local governments" on a "permanent (or long-term) basis"
(*Zapiska*, 65). As Callon notes in his analysis of market actors, disentanglement does not mean absolute freedom. Instead, it means establishing a "certain" autonomy and a set of budgetary "rights" by adjusting
the assignments of taxation and expenditure functions among different
levels of government.

Let us consider the assignment of expenditure responsibilities—that
is, the question of what functions (education, health care, social welfare
services, and so on) should be carried out by what level (local, regional,
or central) of government. *Recommendations* begins from a familiar first
principle of fiscal federal theory—the principle of subsidiarity: "Given
that local governments are closer to users of budgetary services and know
their needs best" services should be delivered on the "lowest possible
level of the budgetary system" (*Zapiska*, 54). But there are situations in
which the "lowest possible" level is not the local level. *Recommendations* also proposes, therefore, a "principle of territorial correspondence
[*printsip territorial'nogo sootvetstviia*]." This principle, closely related to
the concept of externalities in economics,[49] states that "[r]esponsibility
for delivering a certain budgetary service should be assigned to the governmental level that ... entirely encompasses [*polnost'iu okhvatyvaet*] the
population whose interests are affected by that budgetary service" (*Vremennye Rekomendatsii*, 6; *Zapiska*, 54). For example, primary education and basic health care, which are directed only to a local population,
should be financed by local government. Higher education or a clinic
specializing in a particular disease—whose "constituency" reaches outside the city in which it is located—may be most appropriately financed
at the regional level. In this way, the costs and benefits of public policy
are, again following Callon, "internalized" in the choices of governments
at different levels.[50]

These two principles of subsidiarity and territorial correspondence are
intended to produce a kind of a scalar alignment between public choice

mechanisms and the individual citizens who feel the effects—both costs and benefits—of different aspects of government policy. On the one hand, the principle of subsidiarity devolves choice mechanisms as far as possible in order to create a feedback between the producers and consumers of public services. On the other hand, the principle of territorial correspondence centralizes choice mechanisms up to a point where the costs and benefits of given decisions are fully internalized in the government making those decisions. As such, this scalar adjustment aims to create a structure of accountability around public choice by defining "which level of the budget will answer for the fulfillment of concrete functions and the provision of corresponding services to the population."[51] In so doing, it also creates a decentralized and "spontaneous" solution to the problem of public value by defining local government as a decision-making unit whose choices will feed directly back into its utilities (or disutilities).[52]

Recommendations begins, thus, with a principle of local autonomy that has a certain formal quality: it relates to the framing of calculative choice, not to the substantive ends of government. The question is, What happens when a principle of equity is introduced into this formal programming of the fiscal federal system?

Programming II: Equalization

Like the principle of autonomy, equalization is enshrined in federal legislation, which states that the aim of interbudgetary transfers is to uphold minimum "social standards" [*sotsial'nye standarty*]. But as Jorge Martinez-Vazquez, Andrei Timofeev, and Jameson Boex noted in a review of regional-local fiscal federal reforms, it is unclear whether this standard refers to a "fiscal norm"—that is, a *formal* expression of equality before the *fisc*—or a "service standard"—that is, a level of substantive provisioning (2006: 156, n. 10). The Soviet system—and, in its own way, the post-Soviet system—was organized around the idea that the aim of transfers was to uphold a *service standard*: all individuals should be provided with a certain set of services. The authors of *Recommendations*, by contrast, propose that the appropriate interpretation of federal legislation is that equalizing transfers should provide for fiscal equity, defined in a manner that resembles (though with reference only to the expenditure side of the budget) the one that James Buchanan articulated fifty years earlier: "Every inhabitant of [any given] region," they argue, "has roughly equal requirements for budgetary expenditures and has the right to make a claim on an equal level of services from local government" (*Metodicheskie Rekomendatsii*, 10).[53]

According to this standard, regional fiscal policy should equalize "budgetary provisioning [*obespechennost'*]" (*Zapiska*, 59).[54] Regional governments should aim, therefore, to close "the gap between the expenditure requirements of local budgets for the execution of functions that are assigned to them and their revenue capacity" through transfers from the regional budget. The first step in programming equalization is therefore to assess each locality's "fiscal gap" by measuring its expenditure "requirements" and "revenue capacity." The challenge will be to do so in a way that does not introduce the incentive problems that *Recommendations* identified in the existing system of gap filling.

Take, for instance, the estimation of revenues. We have seen how the practice of basing revenue estimates on *actual* tax collections reduces local governments' motivation "to mobilize the maximum amount of resources" through taxation (*Vremennye Rekomendatsii*, 11). *Recommendations'* solution is to measure the fiscal gap by reference to factors that are "objective" [*ob"ektivnye*] in the sense that they are external to—that is, not taken into account in—the decisions of local government to levy and collect taxes, and to report those taxes that they do collect. The report's authors propose, therefore, a measure of tax *potential*—based, for example, on local economic activity—that is "as much as possible free of the influence of tax collection effort on the part of municipalities" (*Zapiska*, 77),[55] thus making it "irrational" for local governments to reduce tax collections or "hide or understate the actual receipt of revenues" (*Vremennye Rekomendatsii*, 11). We see, thus, how a microeconomic perspective not only provides a critical visibility of the state but also suggests a form of programming.

A similar approach was developed on the expenditure side, which deserves more detailed treatment, for it is here that the framing of local government as a calculative actor touches on the substantive *ends* of the state. Once again, the technical challenge will be to define an "objective" metric for calculating needs that cannot be influenced, at least in the short term, by the activities of a local government, and that will not, therefore, be taken into account in its choices. One parsimonious solution, *Recommendations* notes, would be to use the size of the population of a given city to measure its budgetary requirements. This approach seems to correspond neatly to the proposition that each citizen has a roughly equal need for government services. The problem is that, for a variety of reasons, equal abstract needs do not translate into an equal need for concrete services. First, the cost of delivering services will depend on local prices. Second, *per capita* need may vary in relation to "particularities of the territory [*faktory, otrazhaiushchie spetsifiku territorii*]" (*Vremennye Rekomendatsii*, 14) on which a city is located, such as its climate, features of the pattern of settlement (e.g., its density), and the material organization of services such as heat and water. It may also vary in relation to the structure of the local population: municipalities with a large number of schoolchildren or elderly citizens, for example, will have higher needs for expenditures on education and health care.

In order to calculate "need," therefore, *Recommendations* proposes to incorporate various factors relating to the character of the local population, the territory on which that population resides, and the mechanisms through which its needs are fulfilled.[56] Implicit in this proposition is a prior understanding about which services should be provided by government. For how, precisely, could one take into account the implications of a cold climate or a dispersed urban territory without having already determined that a local government ought to provide heat and transport services to people residing on that territory? Here *Recommendations* proposes a curious calculative device called a "representative system of expenditures." This device—which was developed in the mid-1990s by Canadian federal fiscal experts in response to a constitutional mandate for equalizing transfers[57]—involves creating a *hypothetical system of local budgets*.

To create this hypothetical system of budgets, regional governments are instructed to undertake an exercise of budgetary planning for every local government in their region. This planning exercise begins with the assumption that "all municipalities provide their population with the same collection of budgetary services" but that the "need for these services in different municipalities is different" due to the various factors just noted (*Zapiska*, 89). "A critical moment," therefore, is the "selection of indicators that make it possible to measure the objective requirements for budgetary services in different municipalities" (*Zapiska*, 89). The first step in defining these "objective" requirements is to identify the "specific group of users [*tselevuiu gruppu potrebitelei*] that is to be served for each type of government service" and to make "adjustments for the demand that each group makes on a service" (*Zapiska*, 89). To do so, regional budget officers are to calculate not only the number of users of a given service—thus, for example, for primary education, the number of school age children—but also to make adjustments for the different "need" for services of different subgroups of the city population. The result is an estimate of a number of "standardized users ['*uslovnykh' potrebitelei*]," which are distinguished from physical persons by the fact that they have a "single, standardized demand for budgetary resources."[58] This number of standardized users, in turn, will allow budgetary planners to adjust the "needs" of different subgroups of the population (retired persons, children, and so on) using an "inflator coefficient" [*povyshaiushchii koeffitsient*].

For example, in the case of health care, *Recommendations* proposes to calculate the number of standardized consumers as the sum of four variables: the number of unemployed, children, and pensioners, and the total population. Each of the last three variables is adjusted by a coefficient (k1, k2, k3)—calculated either by examining statistics on health provision or by soliciting expert opinion—that reflects the amount of *additional* expenditures required for individuals in each group beyond that of the "average [*srednestatisticheskii*] inhabitant of the region" (*Zapiska*, 93).[59] Thus:

$$\text{USERS(HLTH)}_{\text{CityX}} = \text{POP}_{\text{CityX}} + (\text{k1})\text{UN}_{\text{CityX}} + (\text{k2})\text{CH}_{\text{CityX}} + (\text{k3}) \text{PEN}_{\text{CityX}}$$

Where: USERS(HLTH) = Standardized users of health services
POP = Population of the city
UN = Unemployment
CH = Children under the age of 16
PEN = Population of pension age

A second set of adjustments is related to the cost of providing a given service in a given municipality. In the case of communal services, for example, *Recommendations* incorporates federal cost norms calculated annually by the Federal Ministry of Finance for its own system of interbudgetary redistribution. These Federal norms incorporate coefficients for wage levels, consumer prices, transportation costs, climatic conditions, and the cost of producing communal services.[60] Each of these is derived through a *further* set of calculations that take into account everything from the construction materials used to build houses in a given city (that determine their thermal properties), to the climate, to the technical setup of communal service systems.

A final step: On the basis of these calculations of standardized demand for each kind of service, regional governments are to calculate an "index of budgetary expenditure" for every category on the standard list of services (education, health care, communal services, and so on). This index defines the *proportion* of budgetary need for a particular service for *all* municipalities in a region that is accounted for by a *given* municipality. Thus, for example, one municipality might have 8 percent of the regional "need" for education expenditure, while another might have 13 percent of the regional "need" for expenditure on heating communal housing. Indices for different items of expenditure are then added together—with weights assigned to each—to arrive at an overall index of budgetary expenditures that indicates the amount of *total* need in a region for which a *given* municipality accounts:

$$\text{IBR}_{\text{CityX}} = (\text{K}_{\text{ED}}) \text{ x } (\text{ED}_{\text{CityX}}/\text{ED}_{\text{ALL}}) + (\text{K}_{\text{HLTH}}) \text{ x } (\text{HLTH}_{\text{CityX}}/\text{HLTH}_{\text{ALL}}) + (\text{K}_{\text{CS}}) \text{ x } (\text{CS}_{\text{CityX}}/\text{CS}_{\text{ALL}}) \ldots \text{etc.}$$

Where: ED = "Need" for expenditure on education
HLTH = "Need" for expenditure on health care
CS = "Need" for expenditure on communal services
IBR = Index of Budgetary Expenditures
K = Weight of each service in total "need"

From Normed Needs to Fiscal Flows

It should be apparent that this procedure for creating a representative budget bears more than a little similarity to budgetary planning under socialism. In both cases, a hierarchy of norms is used to measure the needs of a population—based on a mass of geographic, economic, demographic, and climatic information. And in both cases, these normed needs are used to calculate the distribution of equalizing transfers. This point should be underlined. The difference between the Soviet and "neoliberal" models of budgetary redistribution does *not* lie in whether they take into account the substantive organization of need fulfillment. Nor do they differ in their assumption that a definite range of needs should be met by the state.

Instead, the difference between the Soviet and neoliberal systems for interbudgetary redistribution lies in how normed needs are translated into fiscal flows. In the Soviet period, we have seen, this process began with norms that *Recommendations* refers to as "natural indicators [*natural'nykh pokazateliakh*]," which defined the supplies, utilities, personnel, and other elements required to satisfy the substantive needs of an urban population (*Zapiska*, 19). Next, employing cost norms, these material requirements were translated into a ruble amount that defined a municipality's *budgetary* needs. In a final step, regional offices of the Ministry of Finance made adjustments through taxation and transfers in order to close the gap between these needs and revenue available to local governments. In this system of calculation—which *Recommendations* calls a "direct account" [*priamoi schet*]—it was possible to make *direct* translations: from a population to needs; from needs to means of want satisfaction; from means of want satisfaction to budgetary requirements; from budgetary requirements to budgetary adjustments. Through it, a right of social citizenship was defined through the *fisc* as the right to specific goods and services.

The system of "representative budgets" proposed in *Recommendations* also begins with an assessment of a population's needs, taking into account geographic, demographic, and economic factors. Although some details diverge, the system of representative budgets does not differ from the Soviet system of budgetary planning in the way that it calculates budgetary need in *substantive* terms. But it incorporates them into a logic of budgetary distribution that is, as *Recommendations*' authors observe, "fundamentally different" from the Soviet approach. The representative budget, to repeat, is a *hypothetical* budget. Its purpose is *not* to list expenditures that should *actually* be made. Rather, it is a *calculative* device. The "Index of Budgetary Expenditures" derived from this hypothetical system expresses "the *relative* requirements of individual municipalities" for financing each kind of service (*Zapiska*, 61). This index defines the *proportion* of regional "need" that is accounted for by a given municipality, and thus, the *proportion* of total expenditure in a given region on a given service to which citizens in a given municipality can lay claim. The standard of equity, after all, is not that equal services are actually delivered but that the level of "budgetary provisioning" [*obespechennost'*] in each municipality "is equalized *based only on the volume of resources allocated to this purpose*" (*Zapiska*, 91). And *here* lies the distinction between the Soviet and neoliberal approaches to public value. Gone is the pretense of plentitude, the technological assumption—if often not, it should be underlined, the material reality—that resources will be available to meet normatively defined needs. The "right to make a claim on an equal level of services from local government" is not a claim on a definite level of financing; there is, indeed, no guarantee that any of these needs will be met. We might say that the *absence* of such a guarantee is the sine qua non of neoliberal reform. Scarcity, as Karl Polanyi observed long ago, is the (neo)liberal economist's "anthropological constant."

But we are not quite done. We have yet to address the critical question of how the volume of scarce resources allocated to pay for functions assigned to local governments is defined. *Recommendations* proposes another standard mechanism of fiscal federal theory: an equalization fund [*fond vyravnivaniia*] that regional governments will create with a certain portion of regional budgetary revenues. *Recommendations* identifies a range of options for determining the size of this fund. At one extreme, a large part of the financial resources of a regional budget may be used for redistribution so that budgetary provisioning is highly equalized across municipalities. This approach would lead to budgetary outcomes that approximate the norm that citizens should be able to demand equal services at equal rates of taxation.[61] But equalization has costs. "The more resources are redistributed to 'poor' municipalities the greater is the tax burden of 'rich' and more economically developed municipalities, which not only removes [*lishaet*] their incentive to develop their tax base but may compromise [*podorvat'*] the economic development of the region as a whole." A relatively small fund, by contrast, would theoretically increase the incentives of local governments to develop their tax base, since it would increase the marginal return on increased revenues (*Zapiska*, 60).[62]

Notably, *Recommendations* does not indicate a correct path among these options. "The decision about what volume of resources should be allocated to the equalization of local budgets," conclude the report's authors, "is not so much a question of economic rationality [*ekonomicheskoi tselesoobraznosti*] as it is a question of political choice that assumes various compromises between the imperative to equalize and the imperative to finance other expenditures by the regional government" (*Zapiska*, 60).[63] The most appropriate variant "should be chosen by regional governments on the basis of the priorities of regional socioeconomic policy and the existing differentiation in the tax base of individual municipalities" (*Metodicheskie Rekomendatsii*, 53). This is straight Buchanan, and straight Weber: The task of the economist is to clarify what is at stake in alternative policies, not to tell politicians what their values ought to be.

CONCLUSION: NEOLIBERALISM, BUDGETING, AND THE BIOPOLITICS OF POPULATION

In concluding this chapter, it bears returning to a question from which we began: What does neoliberal reform imply for the system of substantive provisioning that contemporary Russia inherited from the Soviet period? And what does budgetary reform imply for those peculiar adjustments between population, production, and social welfare provisioning—exemplified in the figure of the small industrial city—that the Soviet system produced? One answer—and perhaps it is the answer that reformers would give—is that budgetary reforms have had disappointingly little impact. Regional and local governments have not been quick to take up the recommendations formulated by federal authorities or by foreign and domestic experts. "Public servants," Martinez-Vazquez, Timofeev, and Boex observe, "continue to think and act as they did under the previous regime," employing "budgetary practices inherited from the Soviet system" (2006: 148). Regional level redistribution is still driven by "annual negotiations on the basis of historical tax collections and expenditures," and even where formulas are used they employ expenditure norms that are "mostly based on ... existing facilities' capacity rather than service need."[64] More progress has been made on the use of redistribution formulas on the federal level. By the late 2000s, 70 percent of federal-regional transfers were being cycled through a redistribution mechanism akin to the one we have just outlined, and other federal-regional redistribution mechanisms also worked on a formula-based principle (Freinkman et al. 2009: 5).

But these improvements in redistributive mechanisms have been accompanied by a massive assault on the autonomy of subnational governments during the presidency of Vladimir Putin. This assault has been felt most acutely in the institutions of local democracy, as elections for regional executives have been eliminated. But it resonates in the fiscal sphere as well. As Kurlyandskaya and Golovanova have found, although a large portion of public expenditures is accounted for by the local level—suggesting a certain level of fiscal decentralization—"a more thorough qualitative analysis shows that subnational budgets have little or no fiscal autonomy" since, as in the Soviet period, local governments have little control over these expenditures (2006: 213). Stripped of meaningful local democracy, the current fiscal federal system in Russia bears little relationship to Buchanan's vision of decentralized democratic decision-making.[65] It is not particularly illuminating, therefore, to call the current Russian fiscal federal system "neoliberal" in some straightforward sense. That said it would be analytically debilitating to try to understand it without reference to neoliberalism, since elements of the fiscal system derive from a tradition of thought and practice that can only be understood as neoliberal. This, at any rate, is the rather fine methodological line that it seems to me we must walk.

So where are things headed? Perhaps a strengthened system of formula-based redistribution will be embedded in a fiscal federal system that is relatively decentralized in the sense that a large proportion of expenditures are "local" but in which there is very little local autonomy. Such a fiscal system—a kind of neoliberal-welfarist-authoritarian formation of government—might be highly redistributive, and highly oriented to fulfilling a basic set of needs through the public sector.[66]

This kind of budgetary system would also have curious implications for the existing spatial adjustments between populations, production, and the provisioning of social welfare in Russia. During the Soviet period, we have seen, the budgetary system helped to fix enterprises, local governments, human populations, and social services in given spatial and institutional relationships. In the 1990s, as officials in the Ministry of Finance and other government officials engineered the "preservation" of basic services, the budget continued to play this role. Indeed, one goal of budgetary reform was precisely to reduce this persistent distortion-preserving function of the interbudgetary system. We recall that the 2005 World Bank report, "From Transition to Development," anticipated that "increased decentralization of taxation and fiscal expenditures" would help ensure that "the economic situation of a particular location is most accurately reflected in households' incentive structure" (World Bank 2005: 57). But developments over the past decade—limited decentralization combined with some progress in reform of redistributive mechanisms—may not have had the effects that the reformers desired. After all, the "system of representative budgets" works by coding the *existing* spatial distribution of cities and people into a funding formula. To the extent that the federal government and regional governments distribute their resources through such a formula, fiscal flows will follow normed needs, and normed needs, of course, can be found precisely where people and cities already are—that is, where Soviet city-building and industrial planning put them. "Preservation," from this perspective, is not just a problem that neoliberals try to address. It may also turn out to be the product of neoliberal reform.

CHAPTER EIGHT

The Intransigence of Things

> DH [centralized district heating] systems in CEE/FSU
> were designed to be robust and reliable in the sense that
> the systems would deliver heat to the end-user under all
> circumstances. In the communist period, heat was considered
> an elementary need (and as such it still is) that has to be
> provided in abundance for little or no cost.
>
> —The World Bank/UNDP, "Increasing the
> Efficiency of Heating Systems in Central and
> Eastern Europe and the Former Soviet Union"[1]

> The [Housing and Communal Services] sector is one of the
> most inefficient sectors in the Russian economy and one of
> the last sectors that requires serious reforms if Russia is to
> complete the transition to a market economy.
>
> —The World Bank,
> *Housing and Communal Services in Russia*[2]

> *Технические вопросы переливаются на социальные вопросы.*
> (Technical questions overflow into social questions)
>
> —First Deputy of Transport, Energy,
> and Construction, Rodniki *Raion*[3]

PIPES MATTER

Anyone who has spent time in Russian cities has been struck by the ob-
trusive presence of pipes. Some are yellow gas pipes, usually visible only
for a short distance among apartment blocks or suspended along the
borders of yards between small, single-family homes. Most of the visible
pipes, however, are heating pipes. In some areas these pipes are buried
or otherwise out of view, running discretely along fences or buildings.
Elsewhere, they emerge suddenly from the ground, in the midst of a park
or walkway, often two in parallel, up to a few feet in diameter, leap-
ing over driveways and roads, sometimes with shreds of insulation or
metal wrapping hanging off them. These visible pipes are small segments
of sprawling arrays called *teploseti* or heat-networks that branch out to
capillaries that extend through radiators in apartments, schoolhouses,
and hospitals, or—via transfers that heat-filtered water—to running hot

water in bathrooms and kitchens. In Rodniki, where only half the small city's population of 33,000 is connected to the *teploset'* (those in separated houses generally use gas, coal, or wood for heating), the network is 20 kilometers long; one estimate places the length of the total Russian *teploset'* at 260,000 kilometers (OECD/IEA 1995: 252).[4] *Teploseti* carry hot water or steam from industrial boiler complexes. A single boiler complex may provide heat for all the apartments, administrative buildings, schools, hospitals, and industrial enterprises in small cities. Most boilers run on natural gas, which is delivered through another network of pipes that extends from the massive deposits of northwestern Siberia to virtually every settlement in Russia.[5] These two great networks of pipes—for gas and for heat—link a critical mechanism of social provisioning to broader patterns of resource distribution.

The heating system was a key element of the Soviet variant of "infrastructural" social modernity (see chapter 4). As a 2000 World Bank/ UNDP report noted, Soviet planners recognized heat as an "elementary need"; through pipes, boilers, transfers, and radiators the norms of social modernity were hard-wired into the very material structure and spatial layout of Soviet cities. After the collapse of socialism, the material infrastructure was still there; and "as such," as the same report observed, heat remained an elementary need. Indeed—Russia, as such, is still pretty cold. But the systems of regulation in which heat systems were embedded have been thrust into crisis. As local governments faced mounting deficits, household incomes fell, and the national gas company enjoyed expanded opportunities to sell its gas to users with more money, shortages became chronic and breakdowns more frequent. But during the Soviet period the provision of heat to the Russian population had been established as a basic responsibility of the state. It is no surprise that as the character of that responsibility was called into question, heat became the topic of contentious debate and urgent political concern. By the early 2000s, as Oleg Kharkhordin (2010) observes, it was widely recognized that Russia faced an "infrastructure crisis" that was simultaneously financial, technical, political, and social. Heat was at its center.

David Woodruff, in his book *Money Unmade* (1999), described one kind of political drama that took shape amidst this "infrastructure crisis"—the showdowns between regional officials and the federal government or energy companies over winter energy deliveries. The most famous of these transpired in Primorskii Krai, a region of Russia's Far East. In 2001 (after Woodruff's writing) the governor used the threat of shutoffs to pry subsidies out of the federal government. The gambit did not pay off. Regional authorities were ultimately not able to procure inputs for heat (in Primor'e this meant coal, not gas), resulting in shutoffs that froze and destroyed substantial chunks of the heating system. Primor'e's governor was sacked by President Vladimir Putin, an early blow in Putin's assault on local governments. The political lesson was clear: an intransigent governor lost out to the even more intransigent imperatives of heat provision.[6]

Heat was a constant concern in the small industrial cities where I worked. In the fall, local newspapers ran articles that nervously reported on the progress of preparations for the "heating season" (*otopitel'nyi sezon*). Battles over heat between mayors, governors, and directors of major industrial enterprises (that, for reasons we will explore, often controlled boilers in small cities) were a rite of winter. And, of course, there was the matter of indoor temperature. I was in Rodniki during a very cold snap when temperatures in the central industrial region of European Russia hovered around minus 30 degrees Celsius for over a week. In Moscow, where heat flows in abundance, residents sometimes crack windows in winter to allow a thin stream of frigid air to cool overheated apartments. Not so in Rodniki, where it was cold *everywhere*. In the evening, the family in whose apartment I rented a room, gathered in their small kitchen—doors closed, with burners on the stove turned all the way up. I recall one particularly chilly evening when the mother of the family rapped the tepid kitchen radiator with her knuckles, glared out across 1.5 kilometers that separated her apartment block from the boiler complex, clearly visible across a snowy field through the kitchen window, and exclaimed "they just aren't heating at all! [*voobshche ne topiat!*]." It was not exactly true. A column of smoke extended stiffly from the boiler's massive chimney. But she pointed to a key element of the moral economy of post-Soviet Russia. "They" were the powers that be who were failing so miserably in what seemed obviously to be their responsibility. Indoor temperature in Russia is, indeed, a biopolitical problem of national significance and the highest stakes.

Urban heating systems have also been wrapped up in broader debates about post-Soviet transformation. They impose a tremendous economic burden on Russia as both a gigantic financial liability and, in the eyes of reformers, an impediment to market adjustments of productive factors. Their reform was therefore addressed from the very onset of the post-Soviet period. During the 1990s, however, little progress was made in this sphere, as attention was fixed on stabilization and churning political crisis. In 2003 the World Bank argued that the communal sector—of which heat is the most important component—was among the last sectors that had to be reformed for Russia to "complete the transition" to a market economy. And in the somewhat calmer climate of the 2000s heat production and delivery became the target of focused government reforms, and a major area of cooperation among international experts, funding organizations, domestic policymakers, and local officials. Technical projects and lending programs continue to the present day, with a loan agreement for a $200 million World Bank project signed in September 2009.

In this chapter I take up heat reform as another privileged site for studying neoliberalism and social modernity. As is true of budget reforms and the image of "austerity," infrastructure reform has often been identified as a key example of how neoliberalism shatters existing regimes of social welfare. Through privatization and deregulation of such infrastructures, the argument goes, governments abandon their commitment to providing basic services either free or at low, uniform rates. As in the case of budget reform, a closer look suggests a much more complicated story.

INFRASTRUCTURE AND SOCIAL MODERNITY: BUNDLING AND UNBUNDLING

In focusing on the Russian heating apparatus, I follow a growing literature in the social sciences that has turned to infrastructures as objects of investigation. In a valuable agenda-setting essay, Paul Edwards argues that infrastructures—and here he means both material networks and systems of standards—"simultaneously shape and are shaped by—in other words, co-construct—the condition of modernity" (2002: 186).[7] Whether we are concerned with the mechanisms of what Michael Mann calls the "infrastructural power" of the absolutist state (particularly what were called "communications" such as roads and canals), with the great material works of modern industrial countries (railroads, telecommunications, electricity grids), or with more contemporary processes of network construction (the internet, for example), the creation and extension of infrastructure is intimately bound to modernization. And a modern society, from one perspective, is precisely a form of collective life that is articulated by infrastructures. We should add that the construction of infrastructures is central to the history of modern biopolitics: they have been key mechanisms through which the health, welfare, and conditions of existence of populations have been constituted as objects of governmental management.

But to note that infrastructure and modernity are intimately related provides only a general orientation. Infrastructures can be understood and programmed in different ways, not only as purely material technologies but also as sociotechnical systems that are linked to different kinds of projects: of development, social welfare, or military mobilization. Thus, we might say that there are many forms of infrastructural modernity, and the crucial question will be how infrastructure is mobilized as a political technology: What tasks are infrastructures meant to accomplish? What styles of reasoning are deployed to assess and program infrastructures?

One recent contribution to thinking about these questions is Stephen Graham and Simon Marvin's 2002 study, *Splintering Urbanism*, which draws a valuable contrast between two moments of infrastructural modernity. In a first period—that can be traced from the mid-nineteenth century through much of the twentieth century—governments played a central role in building, standardizing, and consolidating infrastructural systems in projects of economic regulation and social provisioning. During this period projects of infrastructural modernization were normatively oriented to an "infrastructural ideal" that emphasized the *universality* of infrastructures—that is, their connection to all members of a national population—and the *equalization* of infrastructure provision across national populations, through common and generally low tariffs. Institutionally, the infrastructure ideal was realized by *bundling* different functional parts of infrastructures—production, distribution, and tariff setting—in unitary regulatory regimes. Although the Soviet variant is distinct in a number of respects, we will see that Graham and Marvin's story nicely describes how infrastructures, in particular heat, were linked to the broader project of Soviet social modernity.

In a second period—associated with the fiscal crises of the 1970s (and beyond), and with the rise of neoliberalism—Graham and Marvin identify a "splintering" of the infrastructural ideal. A crucial element of neoliberal reform, they argue, has been the *unbundling* of infrastructure: unitary systems of regulation are replaced by more differentiated governance regimes that introduce liberalization and marketization in certain segments of infrastructure sectors. Focusing on the "most advanced and dramatic" variant of unbundling, in which an infrastructure is opened to market competition, Graham and Marvin conclude that neoliberal transformation has often resulted in the "reduction of the status" of infrastructure services as "quasi-public goods to be consumed by all, at similar, generalized tariffs" (2002: 167, 102). It has also resulted in the "dramatic reshaping of cities" with the emergence of new patterns of inclusion and exclusion (2002: 177). Taking the postsocialist cases—and, specifically centralized heat systems—as key examples, Graham and Marvin conclude that "state owned infrastructure monopolies have been widely privatized and transnational infrastructure firms have been invited in to lay new networks which often tend to 'bypass' the technically obsolescent legacies of the old systems," and create islands of private provisioning accessible only to those able to pay market prices (2002: 99).

How does this story about infrastructure, social modernity, and neoliberal reform fit the case of Russian heating systems? There have been, of course, notable breakdowns of infrastructure in Russia, significant bypasses of public infrastructures, and growing spatial differentiation of service provision. And many observers—both foreign and domestic—have understood infrastructure reform as part and parcel of the project of liberalization and privatization associated with structural adjustment and "transition." Thus, following the announcement of a government reform package in 2001, the *Jamestown Monitor* published an article entitled "Coming Soon: Shock Therapy Part II?," implying that the measures included in the package extended the project of liberalization, marketization, and privatization pursued in the 1990s. Among the "far reaching economic measures" the government proposed, the article reported, "[s]ome of the most controversial ... hide behind the innocuous title of 'communal services reform'" ("Coming Soon: Shock Therapy II" 2001). Similarly, *Kommersant* wrote on March 20, 2001 that "in the last week the government once more established that the communal sector of the country is on the verge of bankruptcy. The battle with chronic underfinancing was dealt with through the method of shock therapy" (Kuz'minskii 2001).

But this picture does not capture the whole story. First, notwithstanding disruptions, periodic crises, and at times chilly indoor temperatures, it could plausibly be argued that the "big" story of heat in post-Soviet is its *preservation* as a universal service provided on a relatively equal basis to virtually the entire population. Through the worst moments of economic downturn, heat was among the critical systems that served to hold the substantive economy of many Russian cities together. Second—and more central to my concerns—this image of reform as the continuation of a radical project of privatization and marketization does not fit post-Soviet reforms of heat systems or, more generally, of the communal sector. These reforms propose, indeed, to "unbundle" heat systems by separating different elements of production, rate setting, and distribution. But this does not imply privatization and the abandonment of social welfare goals. Instead, reforms aim to reprogram heat systems by deploying what I have proposed to call "microeconomic devices"—while working within the stubborn material framework of heat systems. What is more, they retain the basic proposition that heat meets an essential need, and that its provision has, at the end of the day, to be guaranteed by government.

This chapter seeks to understand how, precisely, such reforms propose to reshape the inherited forms of Soviet social modernity, and to clarify what, precisely, they have to do with neoliberalism. As in the prior chapter, these questions will direct us to key figures in the development of American neoliberalism, to a "minor" tradition of neoliberal thought and practice—in this case, one relating to economic regulation and infrastructure—and back, finally to post-Soviet Russia. First, however, we have to take a closer look at Soviet heating systems.

BUNDLING UP: INFRASTRUCTURE AND SOVIET SOCIAL MODERNITY

We saw in chapter 2 that beginning with GOELRO, the Leninist project of electrification, infrastructure development was central to Soviet bio-politics. GOELRO is usually discussed as a key episode in the development of Soviet industrial planning. But it was also central to the incipient Soviet project of social modernity, as the promise of electricity became one important "good" that the young Soviet state had to offer its citizens.[8] Electricity, thus, emerged as the first Soviet example of a nationally articulated infrastructure that was linked both to the distribution of cities and industry and to social welfare provisioning, establishing, as Foucault wrote of railroads and electricity in other countries, new "links between the exercise of political power and the space of a territory or the space of cities" (1984: 243).

The heat apparatus was the product of a later episode of infrastructure construction in the Soviet Union. If we include in the heat apparatus the national gas distribution network, then heat can be numbered among the great projects of infrastructural modernization of the post–World War II period—and it had special significance for Soviet social modernity. Extending the analysis presented in chapter 4, I will use the case of Rodniki to show how the heat apparatus "bundled" the Soviet social, not only linking the production, distribution, and consumption of heat in a common regulatory regime but also binding together the industrial enterprises, social welfare systems, and material conditions of habitation that comprised the city *khoziaistvo*.

Before the beginning of large-scale city-building in Rodniki, heating was largely an individual affair. Most residents lived in huts that were heated by stoves that burned wood, peat, or coal. Industrial heat boilers fed the looms of the textile factory, Bol'shevik, but they were not connected to the city housing stock. As apartment blocks were constructed, replacing individual houses, small boilers were constructed in residential areas. But most residents remained "unplugged" from the heating system until a new boiler complex was built in 1963. This boiler was initially used to meet industrial needs, but in 1969 it was linked to the expanding urban heat network, which connected the textile enterprise, apartment blocks, and social facilities. In Rodniki and other cities, the centralization of urban heat systems was the crucial technical development in what Graham and Marvin call the "quantum leap toward ubiquity" of infrastructure provisioning (2002: 73). By the 1970s nearly 75 percent of all "heat-energy" in the Soviet Union was produced by centralized boilers with a capacity of over 20 gigacalories per hour rather than by individual boilers in houses or buildings.[9] These centralized boilers, as we have already seen, became the points of articulation between an emerging *national* system for distributing gas and a *local* system for producing and distributing heat.

Centralized heat production facilities built during the Soviet period were of two basic types. In the largest cities, the vast majority of heat-energy was (and is) produced in *Teplo-Electro Tsentraly* (*TETs*)—cogeneration facilities that heat water and produce electricity.[10] A single *TETs* can serve hundreds of thousands of urban residents and scores of enterprises. The second type of boiler, more typically found in small cities, were heat-only facilities called *kotel'nye*. *Kotel'nye* (the singular is *kotel'naia*) are composed of several furnaces (*kotly*) that are housed in an industrial facility. Though not as large as a *TETs*, a *kotel'naia* can provide heat for tens of thousands of urban residents and a major enterprise.

One important distinction between *kotel'nye* and *TETs* concerns the patterns of administrative control that pertained to each. *TETs* were generally built and controlled by local governments or by the Soviet energy ministry. Meanwhile, the smaller (but still very large) *kotel'nye*, which were more typical of cities like Belaya Kalitva and Rodniki, were often built and maintained by city-forming enterprises. As such, *kotel'nye* were an important part of the "enterprise-centric" pattern that characterized urban development in small cities (see chapter 4). Heat distribution systems established a *material* link between industrial production and the city heating system. For example, in Rodniki the new boiler built in the 1960s was situated at some remove, upwind of the city, so that emissions would blow away from settled areas. But from there the distribution of heat was routed *through* the city-forming enterprise Bol'shevik. Two major pipes traversed 1.8 kilometers before reaching the grounds of the enterprise, where a significant portion of heat was diverted to the enterprise's steam looms. Another portion was run through transfers that heated filtered water for hot water taps in the city. The remainder was distributed through the arterials and capillaries that carried heat through radiators in houses, schools, hospitals, and offices. Finally, it returned to the enterprise and back to the boiler, completing the circuit.

This, then, is one sense in which heating systems "bundled" Soviet social modernity: they materially linked industrial enterprises to the housing stock, to social service facilities, and to every other element of a city. Another has to do with the way that the production, distribution, and consumption of heat were planned and regulated. We have seen that plans for heating systems were developed by establishing chains of equivalency between a population, its needs, and the material elements, resource flows, and technical arrangements required to meet those needs. These chains were articulated by norms that defined appropriate indoor temperatures, thermal properties of buildings constructed with certain

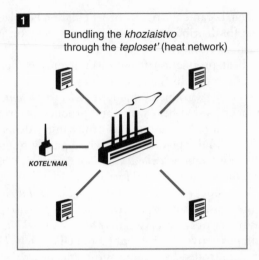

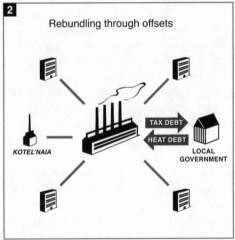

Figure 8.1. Bundling and re-bundling social modernity. During the Soviet period residents of Soviet cities were "bundled" in uniform regimes of social service provisioning that were often financed by enterprises. After Soviet breakup this system was thrust into crisis, as enterprises transferred the substantial burden of providing these services to cash-strapped local governments. Through mutual cancellation of heat debt for tax debt—and due to extraordinary political pressure on gas and heat providers—local governments were able to keep houses warm, at least most of the time.

materials, average temperatures in various temperature zones of the Soviet Union, and heat output for different types of boilers. Since the number of residents, the number and profile of enterprises, and the number
of other urban facilities were determined in city plans, and since norms
made it possible to estimate heat requirements for each of these planned
elements, simple calculations could be used to determine the heat output
required to meet the needs of a developed city.

The control mechanisms for heat systems were also simple. Controls
had only to keep supply temperature at a certain level, and were located, therefore, at the boiler houses themselves. Heat *consumption*,
meanwhile, was determined exclusively by the amount of heat operators
sent through the system and by the fixed parameters of the pipes leading to the radiator in an apartment.[11] No control valves were placed in
apartments since "need" was assumed to be adequately defined by the
very norms that had been used to design the technical elements of the
system and that were already (and automatically) taken into account in
the centralized adjustments made by operators. If, in the budget system,
normed needs drove fiscal flows through distribution formulas applied
by bureaucrats in the Ministry of Finance, then in the heating apparatus
normed needs were inscribed into the very material parameters of the
system itself. A city's population, in such a system, showed up not as a
collection of consumers with individual levels of "demand" for heat but
as a mass known only through normed needs that were derived through
simple formulae. From the perspective of Soviet heating systems, *anthropos* was a warm body—or a mass of warm bodies, materially aggregated—in a very cold country.[12]

In one sense, such "bundling" was hardly exceptional. In most other
countries—socialist and otherwise—infrastructure systems were central to the spatial pattern of urban development.[13] And in most Eastern
European socialist countries (and in some nonsocialist northern European countries) centralized infrastructures were, and remain, important
sources of heating for urban residents. But nowhere else was such a large
percentage of a national population plugged into a service as vital and as
centralized as heat in Russia. Nowhere else did infrastructures inscribe
a distribution of population and production characterized by such a remarkable preponderance of small, geographically dispersed industrial
cities. Nowhere else were these networks so rigidly fixed by a technical
framework that lacked mechanisms for differentiated delivery or user
control. And in no other large industrialized country is it so cold.

As we will see, for post-Soviet reformers the heating system created in-
tolerable inefficiencies and inflexible spatial dependencies. But it made a
kind of sense in the world of Soviet city-building. From its spatial layout
over national territory to the smallest details of system design, the heating

Table 8.1
Russia: Cold and Centralized (UNDP/World Bank 2000)

	% of dwellings with centralized heat (national)	Heating Degree-days*
Bulgaria	25	3,000 (Sofia)
Poland	34	3,450–4,000
Romania	31	2,900–5,150
Russia	80	5,071 (Orenburg#)
Ukraine	65	3,430
Denmark	49	N/A
Finland	46	4,300–6,500

   * Degree days refers to the target inside temperature minus the average outside temperature during the heating season multiplied by the number of days of the heating season.
   # Orenburg is a relatively southerly Siberian city.

apparatus was based on fixed assumptions about the future of individual Soviet settlements, and about their place in the big Soviet *khoziaistvo*. Through it, productive activities and human settlements were bundled together, oriented toward a future that was, if not radiant, then at least reliably warmed.

CRISIS, PRESERVATION, STUCKNESS

But that future is past. With the fiscal crisis that rocked enterprises and local governments in the 1990s, funds for capital investment and repairs quickly dried up. The salaries of communal sphere workers often went unpaid. Arrears for gas, coal, and heat accumulated rapidly, even though tariffs were kept at a fraction of production costs. One consequence was that indoor temperatures did indeed drop in many cities. Official records in Rodniki, for example, showed a sharp decline in the heat output of Bol'shevik's boiler in the 1990s, partly explained by the collapse in textile production (the looms ran on steam) but also by declining heat deliveries to apartment blocks (in which "need," if not "demand," presumably remained constant). But to a surprising degree, heat continued to flow through the kilometers upon kilometers of pipes that wind their way through Russian cities, and apartments were kept livably—though often not comfortably—warm.

This *preservation* of the heating apparatus began from the provision of energy inputs. Gazprom, the Russian gas monopoly, continued to deliver gas at tariffs significantly below market rates to boiler operators that were deeply in arrears.[14] Local governments—which assumed responsibility for heating schools, hospitals, and housing blocks—did not substantially raise rates and did not take harsh measures against an ever-growing number of households and other users that were in arrears for heat. The broad result was a massive cross-subsidy for consumption in the communal sphere—dominated by heat, but including some other areas such as maintenance—that, according to one estimate, constituted 7.5 percent of GDP by the mid-1990s (World Bank 1996a).[15] With economic recovery this subsidy declined, as tariffs were raised consistently over the decade following the devaluation. But in the depths of crisis, when the Russian population was least able to pay for its basic needs, the heat apparatus channeled an enormous volume of public (and, in the case of Gazprom, quasi-public) resources to keep the population warm.

We have seen (in chapter 6) that the theme of preservation was much discussed in the 1990s, usually with reference to industrial enterprises, but also in reference to systems of social welfare. Most discussions referred to the choices of politicians and regulators who were unwilling to take measures that might bankrupt uncompetitive enterprises that depended on cheap energy. Woodruff, thus, referred to a social "sine qua non" that compelled regional governments to shield Russian enterprises from the ravages of the market. A similar logic clearly applied in the case of heat. Most local administrators I spoke to thought that shutoffs were precluded by this fact alone: because heat delivery is a matter of life and death, and because the Russian government, when pressed, can tap domestic gas supplies, it is difficult—for the state, for private boiler operators, for gas and coal producers—to forgo the material possibility of providing heat. Indeed, the imperative to provide heat was in some sense even more absolute than the imperative to protect industrial enterprises. Amidst all the hand wringing about the slow pace of enterprise restructuring, it was sometimes forgotten that Russian industrial employment contracted by nearly half during the 1990s—an extraordinary transformation over such a short time by any measure. By contrast, the number of shutoffs of heat systems, particularly in larger cities, was very small. If there was a social sine qua non in Russia in the 1990s, it was the provision of heat, not the protection of industrial enterprises.

But this sine qua non cannot be explained only by social norms in actors' heads. It was also shaped by the material features of the heating apparatus, which structured actors' choices in a certain way. From this perspective, we may want to reverse the usual approach, to ask not how human actors allocate resources and make choices among alternative ends, but how nonhuman actors—pipes, control systems, the weather—structure the choices of human actors such as managers in gas companies, enterprise directors, and local administrators.[16] Take, for example, gas or coal producers, faced with the choice of shutting off boiler operators—usually enterprises or local governments—who could not pay their bills. The material structure of heating systems made a "hard constraint" difficult to impose, for a shutoff would not simply imply temporary inconvenience and discomfort. If gas is cut off in the middle of winter when the system is still filled with water, pipes will freeze and burst, resulting in large-scale destruction. With enough time, one can empty a *teploset'* and shut the system off without the attendant destruction. But given the centralized and technically integrated character of the system, this remains a high-stakes measure—a collective punishment that is administered not to individual nonpayers but to all the recipients of heat from a given boiler complex. Similar issues shape the interactions between boiler operators and the recipients of heat. Since there are no individual controls—and since individual radiators are situated on risers that pass through many apartments in a vertical series—it is extraordinarily difficult to punish individuals for nonpayment. In the 2000s, local governments very occasionally took steps to evict residents who fell deeply in debt for communal service payments, but this is for obvious reasons a costly option and is rarely taken.

The nonhuman "actors" in heating systems also served to stifle initial efforts at reengineering the institutional setup of this system. We have seen that reforms passed early in the post-Soviet period aimed to pry apart the various elements of the Soviet *khoziaistvo*, and in particular to separate industrial enterprises from social welfare functions, which would be left to the public sector. Recalling Callon again, this was in part a matter of "disentangling" actors and framing their calculative choices. A federal directive called for the transfer of apartment blocks and social facilities from the "balance" of enterprises to local governments—a process that unfolded at different rates in different cities.[17] But in many cities this disentangling did not entail a clean break in old relationships, and not everything was transferred. Housing was usually transferred, as were social facilities (kindergartens and clinics). So too were the distribution networks for heat—the pipes that run from boilers through every building in a small city. But many *kotel'nye* that were operated by city-forming enterprises were *not* transferred. The reason, simply, was that they served both social needs *and* the needs of industrial production.

This partial transfer of communal infrastructure served to retie old knots that reformers meant to untangle. With the transfer of housing—and, thus, of financial responsibility for housing—the fiscal burden on local governments increased dramatically. Heat emerged as by far the largest single item on local budgets in small cities; in Rodniki it accounted for over 50 percent of local government expenditures in the 1990s, and that sum did not cover the entire heating bill, since arrears were mounting fast. Here was the interesting twist: local governments' swelling heat bill was owed directly to enterprises, which still owned the city's heat boilers. Cash-strapped local governments like that of Rodniki did not have resources to pay for this new burden, since *the very same enterprises*, which were the largest taxpayers by far, had no money to pay taxes.[18] Consequently, in one of the multifarious forms of nonmonetary exchange that characterized the Russian economy in the late 1990s, local governments and city-forming enterprises swapped tax debts for heat. In small cities, such transactions could account for the majority of the expenditure *and* revenue sides of local budgets (see figure 8.1 p. 210).

This, then, was the legacy of a form of social modernity in which infrastructure "bundled" the relationships between people, local government, and industrial enterprises: hot water and steam cycled through material networks, leaving behind a trail of debts that actors had to negotiate, and that bound them together through legal and financial obligations, social norms and, of course, intransigent material linkages. City-forming enterprises were stuck with an industrial boiler attached to households through pipe networks. Local governments, regional governments, and the quasi-public gas monopoly were stuck with a given distribution of people and cities that were plugged into this network of pipes, plugged into an existing apparatus of boilers, and plugged into a massive reserve of gas that, at the end of the day, the state controlled. Modifying a term proposed by Michael Storper (1995), the post-Soviet small city might be thought of as a sticky "nexus" of material, spatial, and institutional dependencies.[19] And this sticky nexus is, of course, the city-building *khoziaistvo*.

Neoliberalism and Infrastructure

If as was the case, for example, in post-Soviet Georgia, nonpayments had led to shutoffs, and shutoffs had led to the destruction of heating systems due to freezing or widespread looting (of pipes and radiators for scrap metal), heat would not have been an important problem of post-Soviet reform.[20] Instead, to adapt a phrase from Way (2001), we would have had a kind of "marketization by default." But in Russia heating systems were preserved through the hardest years of economic downturn in the 1990s. As a consequence, when the economic and political crises that gripped the country in the 1990s subsided, these systems—still centralized, still technically integrated, still a huge fiscal burden, and still providing an essential service—became the target of an ever growing mass of technical studies, schemas for reform, and government initiatives. The remainder of this chapter tries to make sense of these reforms by situating them in a tradition of thought, an entire accumulation of past experiences and problems, and a toolkit of techniques and mechanisms of programming that have been assembled over many decades. This story—at least as I will tell it—begins with the Ordo-Liberal critique of the economics of natural monopoly, proceeds through a new economics of regulation that was developed at the University of Chicago after World War II, turns then to a "minor" tradition of neoliberal thought about regulation and infrastructure that took shape in the United States in the 1970s and 1980s, and lands, finally, back where we started: with the reform of heat in post-Soviet Russia.

The (Neoliberal) Critique of (Liberal) Arguments for Economic Regulation

Neoliberal thinking about infrastructure has to be understood as a response to a prior paradigm of economic reasoning about the conditions under which a state could intervene in a market economy, particularly in constructing, managing, or regulating what were previously called "public works." Following Dieter Helm and George Yarrow (1988), three rationales for government intervention dominated economic reasoning from the early nineteenth century to the first half of the twentieth century when the role of states in economic and social life expanded dramatically. First, *natural monopoly* arguments began from the observation that in certain sectors of a modern economy—networked infrastructures such as telephony and railroads are key examples—maximum technical efficiencies can be gained only through monopoly production, which allowed for scale economies and avoided redundancies. The problem was that equilibrium price for a monopolized sector was higher than for a competitive sector, thus yielding a welfare loss that would be borne by rate-payers (the public).[21] This welfare loss provided a rationale for either state ownership or regulation, in which government controlled entry, exit, and price levels. A second argument for state involvement concerned the *complementarities* of infrastructure investment. Infrastructure services could be shown to be productivity-enhancing inputs to most other activities in an economy. But because these positive externalities of infrastructure investment could not easily be "captured" by private firms—at least not in the short term—infrastructure would tend to be undersupplied by markets, thus justifying state provision.[22] If the first two rationales were related to cases of market failure then the third rationale, concerning what Richard Musgrave (1959) called "merit goods," was related to social provisioning. For a variety of reasons, the argument ran, a government may want to supply infrastructure services—electricity, heat, transportation—at a higher rate than that at which the market would supply them. Such rationales were particularly important in justifying governments' efforts to achieve norms of spatial equity and universal provisioning that were central to the infrastructural ideal.

These arguments underpinned a vast expansion of regulation in many countries in the interwar period and after World War II. This expansion encompassed a range of interventions relating specifically to infrastructures: major construction programs designed to promote economic development; regulatory frameworks for private monopolies; and social welfare projects to extend infrastructure services to poorly served populations (in rural areas or slums, for example). It bears noting that in one sense these rationales for intervention were based on a distinctively *liberal* political ontology and style of governmental reasoning. They began from a presumption against government intervention, and assumed that exceptions to this rule required specific argument. Their point was not to displace private initiative. Rather, government was to play a compensatory role when markets failed to produce efficient outcomes, or to yield certain desirable collective goals.

This underlying *liberal* character of arguments for government intervention in various domains, particularly in the construction and management of public works, helps us understand why, when such forms of intervention were becoming dominant in the 1930s and 1940s, they enjoyed the support of economists in institutions that we customarily associate with *neo*liberalism. As Dieter Plehwe (2009b: 22) has shown, some members of the Mt. Pelerin Society wrote in favor of government infrastructure investment in poor countries.[23] And major figures at the Chicago School before World War II supported public ownership of networked infrastructures in the United States.[24]

That said, it was precisely *against* this edifice of liberal argumentation that first the ordo-liberals and Austrians in Europe, and subsequently the American neoliberals, directed their critique of government intervention. The initial target was the theory of natural monopoly, the lynchpin of liberal rationales for government intervention from the late nineteenth century through the middle of the twentieth century. The dominant wisdom of the period was that monopoly was the long-term result of free market competition—suggesting a fundamental contradiction in the pattern of capitalist development. This contradictory tendency provided the justification for regulation: public authorities had to save capitalism from itself. Key figures among the ordo-liberal and Austrian economists accepted the premise that monopoly was a primary danger to the capitalist system, but their diagnosis ran in the opposite direction. As Foucault summarizes their position, the ordo-liberals saw monopoly as the result not of capitalist development but of the "intervention of public authorities in the economy." And they were skeptical of the need for regulation since they saw "the economic process" as "the bearer in itself of a regulatory structure in the form of competition" that would take care of natural monopoly problems if it were allowed to "function fully" (Foucault 2008: 134–35, 137).[25] Many ordo-liberals, thus, categorically rejected natural monopoly arguments for regulation, and focused on interventions that stressed formal rules of competition.

The broad ordo-liberal suspicion about natural monopoly arguments was most prominently taken up in a tradition of economic thought about regulation that developed in the decades after World War II by economists at the University of Chicago. This tradition can, as Robert Van Horn (2009) has shown, be traced to the early 1950s, as key figures such as Aaron Director, Milton Friedman, and George Stigler, adjusting their own previously held positions, questioned the broad scope granted to regulation in the dominant economics of the period. Although these thinkers took up key elements of the ordo-liberal arguments against natural monopoly, their emphasis was different. As Foucault observes, the ordo-liberals saw monopoly as an archaic phenomenon—a holdover from the privileges and protective customs conferred by monarchical states; the remnants of a "predatory neo-feudalism" (2008: 134). The Chicago economists, by contrast, focused specifically on the institutions of modern government. Their position is best understood as a reflexive critique of infrastructural modernity.

George Stigler and the Critique of Regulation

Regulation was a likely site for neoliberal reflection on infrastructure in the United States due to a peculiarity of American government. In contrast to many European countries, American government involvement in economic and social life focused overwhelmingly on regulation of private monopolists (and other private actors), not on public enterprises. Consequently, regulation emerged as a crucial topic in the political landscape shaped by the New Deal. Harry Trebing (1984: 228) has identified 1962 as a crucial year for the development of a direct challenge to the New Deal consensus on regulation.[26] Among other things, that year saw the publication of three documents that were, each in their own way, crucial to the subsequent critique of regulation. The first was an article in the *American Economic Review,* "The Firm under Regulatory Constraint," by Harvey Averch and Leland Johnson (1962), two RAND Corporation economists whose work foreshadowed a powerful intersection between the economics of the firm and the new economics of regulation. The second was Milton Friedman's popular tract, *Capitalism and Freedom* (1962), in which he famously wrote that among the "evils" of public monopoly, public regulation, and private monopoly, he preferred the last.

The third was an article in the *Journal of Law and Economics*, entitled "What Can Regulators Regulate?" by Clair Friedland and George Stigler, a key figure in the neoliberal approach to regulation whose work we consider in some detail here.[27]

Like James Buchanan, Stigler is rarely mentioned in critical discussions of neoliberalism. But he played a decisive role in both intellectual and institutional developments.[28] Stigler was—like Buchanan—a student of Frank Knight at Chicago (one of only a handful). After short stints in the National Resource Planning Board and the Statistical Research Group at Columbia during World War II, and in a few departments of economics after the war, Stigler returned to Chicago. There, in the department of economics and in the business school, he was an at times pointedly ideological advocate of the "Chicago" view of things. He was also an important presence in the Mt. Pelerin Society, both as a founding member and as president from 1976 to 1978. Like Buchanan, Stigler was a new liberal in a specific and meaningful sense. He was explicitly concerned with classic liberal political and economic thought (his dissertation was a work of intellectual history), and with the problem of updating classical liberalism in light of recent developments, most centrally, the rise of the social state. As he explained in a 1964 essay, "[t]he economists have, until recently, been preoccupied with the workings of a comparatively unregulated economic system—what is loosely described as laissez-faire" (Stigler 1975a: 31). But as the state became an important allocator of resources—both directly through the fiscal mechanism and indirectly through regulation—it was imperative to think about government in economic terms: to constitute it as an object of empirical analysis; to disarticulate the black box of the state and, in the distinctively neoliberal move, to break it down into the calculating actors that comprised it.

Stigler worked on a range of topics, including the theory of the firm, the economic theory of information, and the history of economic thought. But his best-known work was on the economics of regulation, developed in a series of articles from the early 1960s through the 1970s. As a later commentator in the field put it, the effect of Stigler's work in this area was like a "shotgun blast"—"an explicit, sometimes effective challenge to the assumptions and institutions that historians associate with the Progressive Era, the New Deal, and the Great Society" (McCraw 1976: 297).[29] Stigler was, indeed, engaged in an unabashedly political project that aimed to take back for the market territory that the prior economics of regulation had claimed for the federal government.

Like many figures of the Chicago School, Stigler's analysis began from a critique of the "public interest" theory of intervention. The public interest school, on his account, proposed that when markets failed to maximize general welfare, government should intervene. In Stigler's view, public interest theory rested on a number of unjustified assumptions, some avowed, some not: that problems of market failure were pervasive, that the state *could* intervene to regulate sectors in which such problems pertain, and that the state *should* intervene—in other words, that intervention served the public interest.[30] Scrutinizing these assumptions was precisely the aim of Friedland and Stigler's 1962 article on electricity regulation. The article addressed a crucial premise of the public interest school: that regulation of a natural monopoly sector would lower prices by preventing monopolies from taking excess profits. Friedland and Stigler tested this relationship by comparing prices before and after regulation was imposed on electricity tariffs by individual U.S. states. The narrow result—that regulation did *not* lower prices—was important in itself, though later critics found Stigler and Friedland's empirical analysis to be flawed and the study's implications overdrawn.[31] But it was the empirical questioning of the effects of regulation *itself* that constituted the article's real novelty and contribution. As Stigler himself wrote a few years later, despite the fact that electricity regulation had spread to two-thirds of the U.S. states by 1915, nearly fifty years later, when he and Friedland began their study, they were "the first investigators ever to do so on even a moderately comprehensive scale" (Stigler 1975b: 27).

Stigler's influence in this area was significant; or, at least, he and Friedland were on the front end of a significant wave. According to Paul Joskow and Nancy Rose, "[s]ystematic analysis of the effects of economic regulation originated with Stigler and Friedland's 1962 paper" (1989: 1495).[32] Before the article's publication there were almost no empirical studies of the effects of regulation. In the ensuing decade hundreds were conducted. The verdict in this rapidly growing literature was not one-sided. What seems important is that it suggested a new approach to posing the question of regulation, a new "site of veridiction" in which regulation could be assessed. In the liberal economics of public interest theory, the "answer" to the question of whether there should be regulation was to be found in the market. If a market diverged from some measure of efficiency—the Paretian condition was often applied—intervention was assumed to be justified. Stigler's critique began from the apparently straightforward proposition that the relevant comparison was not between a monopolistic market and some "imaginary" Paretian state (as Ronald Coase once put it) but between an *actually existing market* and *actually existing regulation*. The implication was that one had to test not only market failure but *regulatory* failure. As Randall Holcombe explains, "if Pareto efficiency is used as the benchmark for success, then government can fail to allocate resources efficiently in the same way that markets can. Thus, one would have to compare market versus government production by evaluating the real-world institutions in each case, rather than comparing the theoretical efficiency of Pareto optimality with the real-world performance of markets" (1997: 5).

This point should be underlined, since it does not necessarily accord with the usual critical understanding of neoliberalism. Whatever his policy convictions, Stigler's critique did *not* begin by rejecting, outright, the proposition that the state ought to pursue collectively agreed upon goals through intervention.[33] It did *not* propose *de*regulation based on fantasies of perfectly efficient markets. Indeed, it criticized public interest theory *precisely* for assuming that the efficiency of unregulated monopolies should be judged against some standard of optimality. Stigler simply insisted on studying whether those values being pursued by regulation were actually achieved (were tariffs lowered? were social goods delivered?) and whether they were being achieved more successfully—more efficiently, more equitably—than they would be in an unregulated market.[34] In a 1964 essay, Stigler proclaimed "much more faith in the long run benefits of the practice of demanding evidence of the effects of various economic policies than ... in the beneficial effects of the policies that you or I now prefer" (1975b: 37). "This," he continued, "is my fundamental thesis. We do not know how to achieve a given end. We do not know the relationship between the public policies we adopt and the effects these policies were designed to achieve" (1975b: 24). The role of economic science was to find out. At his best moments, Stigler was another good Weberian.

The Microeconomics of Regulation: Critique and Programming

In the first instance, then, Stigler's approach to regulation simply insisted on examining the actual effects of government intervention. Beyond this orientation to empirical tests—one that was, as Overtveldt (2007) has pointed out, broadly characteristic of Chicago economics—two extensions of Stigler's work on electricity came to be associated with the Chicago position on regulation. The first related to what would later be called the political economy of regulation: if many regulations do not achieve their intended results, why do they persist? In whose interest is failed regulation? For Stigler, public interest theory had no answer to this question, since it posited a benevolent, technocratic state. His response was a new theory of "regulatory capture," initially laid out in a 1971 article called "The Theory of Economic Regulation" (Stigler 1971). In it, Stigler argued that regulatory decisions would largely be driven by the incentives of policymakers and, thus, by their most mobilized and powerful constituencies, the *producers* in regulated industries. It was often not, therefore, the "public" interest that was served by regulation but, rather, the interests of large corporations. This thesis suggested profound pessimism about regulation, and asserted a presumption in favor of market power rather than regulatory power.[35] The argument was hugely influential. As Peltzman writes, within a decade "the benign view of regulation as a promoter of the general interest had been mainly abandoned. The ascendant image was of the regulator captured by the regulated" (1993: 822).

A second extension of Stigler and Friedland's work on electricity concerned the theory of natural monopoly itself: Were there as many markets with natural monopoly properties as had been assumed? Did natural monopolies produce the problems with which they had been associated? In the electricity study, Friedland and Stigler had found that, from the perspective of consumer prices, outcomes in unregulated industries were no worse than those in regulated industries. In seeking to explain this finding, they hypothesized that excess pricing was limited because unregulated electric utilities were "not possessed of any large amount of long-run monopoly power."[36] This argument extended the older ordoliberal contention that, as Peltzman put it, in "a basically competitive economy with substantial long-run resource mobility" natural monopoly effects were likely to be limited (1993: 821). Stigler posited that competitive markets for narrowly defined product categories provided too limited a frame for thinking about natural monopoly. Mechanisms such as intermodal competition, competition for monopolized markets, and technological change meant that in many monopoly sectors excess profits would be wiped out.[37]

These arguments about regulatory capture and natural monopoly were elaborated by other key Chicago figures: Harold Demsetz on competition for the market; Richard Posner on the welfare costs of natural monopoly; Sam Peltzman on the economic analysis of regulatory politics. This group was recognized to form the core of a Chicago approach that occupied an important and distinctive position in discussions of regulation.[38] If one were to identify a distinctly neoliberal school of thought about regulation, this would be it. But in the late 1960s and 1970s, when this school of thought was consolidating, these neoliberal arguments converged in sometimes surprising ways with a broader field of political activists and economic or technocratic experts (Canedo 2008). On the political front, the Chicago economists were only one voice in a broader movement that drove the major episode of deregulation in the United States during the 1970s. Their attacks on corporate capture of the regulatory process resonated with the positions of progressive reformers such as Ralph Nader and Edward Kennedy, both of whom played crucial roles in the campaign to reform the U.S. regulatory state. Thus, Frederick C. Thayer, a supporter of the "public interest" view of regulation, lamented in 1984 that "[t]he 'capture' theory turns up in Supreme Court decisions written by the liberal Justice William Douglas, in the criticisms of the conservative economist George Stigler, and in the muckraking of Ralph Nader, and is so widely accepted in academe that anyone believing otherwise is thought to be 'hopelessly naïve or disingenuous'" (Thayer 1984: 150).[39] The Chicago neoliberals contributed, thus, to the deregulation crusade, but as a political movement deregulation was not only neoliberal, nor could it be located at one given point on the political spectrum.

Of more central importance to our own story is the fact that the *style of economic reasoning* articulated by the Chicago theorists of regulation was not tightly bound to a particular ideological agenda, nor was it limited to Chicago economists, who provided only one contribution—albeit a critically important one—to a minor tradition of thinking about regulation that was taking shape in the late 1960s and early 1970s. One crucial gathering point for this minor tradition was the *Bell Journal of Economics and Management Science*, later renamed the *RAND Journal of Economics*, first published in 1970.[40] In the journal's first issue the founding editor, Paul MacAvoy, wrote that "despite the growing importance of the regulated sector, very few articles appear each year on the economic theory of the regulated firm or the economic effects of regulation" (1970: 5). But the *Bell* journal (along with Chicago's *Journal of Law and Economics*) would soon be at the center of an exploding literature. It ran a number of foundational articles that articulated the Chicago position on regulation; Stigler, Posner, Demsetz, Coase, and Peltzman all published in its early issues. But the work published in the journal hardly conformed to any Chicago orthodoxy, and the contributors often disagreed with the Chicago economists on particulars. But they shared a style of analysis and a toolkit of techniques for a new kind of critique and programming of regulatory regimes. The distinctive move of this style of analysis was to break down the key actors in the regulatory game—the state, regulated firms, and the "public" that was both the consumer of services and the supposed beneficiary of regulatory intervention—and to analyze them as calculative agents whose incentives were structured both by market signals and regulatory institutions: incentives for regulated industries to produce efficiently (or not); incentives for users to economize their use of services (or not); incentives for regulators to act in the public interest (or not).

Participants in this discussion of very different ideological stripes also shared with the Chicago economists a conviction that competitive markets—that is, markets with multiple firms competing to provide the same service—provided far too narrow a frame for thinking about the scope of natural monopoly. Microeconomic analysis showed, as William Baumol said of his theory of "contestable" markets, that the "invisible hand holds sway" in many more situations than had been previously assumed, and through a range of mechanisms *other than* competitive markets (1982: 2).[41] The contributors to this minor tradition also generated an extraordinary range of proposals for a new *programming* of regulatory systems through mechanisms of calculative choice, competition, and price based on supply and demand: markets in social "bads"; new approaches to regulatory price setting; voucher schemes; peak load pricing; and metering. These were not quite what Callon called "market devices," since what was being crafted by these programmers of regulation was not always a market. Rather, the originality of their contribution lay in their proposals to deploy "microeconomic devices" in areas where competitive markets could not function.[42]

Much of this will become clearer and more concrete in a moment, as we turn to one particular domain—infrastructure reform—in which this new style of thinking was applied. Here it bears emphasizing that the new economics of regulation did not simply negate the old. It did not simply call for deregulation where previously regulation had been accepted. And it did not categorically reject arguments about market failure—relating to natural monopoly problems, economic complementarities, or merit good issues—that had previously been uncritically accepted. It is true that this new form of critique and programming emerged in response to a prior form of liberal reasoning that posited a very broad scope for intervention; and it is true that the new economics of regulation concluded that the regulatory state governed too much. But having begun from an empirical assessment of regulation's effects, the neoliberal "turn" is best understood as a kind of orthogonal movement that cut across the existing alternatives of regulation and deregulation to understand how each could be critically assessed and programmed using microeconomic tools.

The Economics of Infrastructural Transition: Reflexive Modernization

The economics of regulation—and the deregulation movement in the United States—addressed government intervention in many areas, including in networked services such as telecommunications, transport, and energy. But what we have come to call *infrastructure* over the second half of the twentieth century was carved out as an object of reflection primarily in the economics of development (as well as in military contexts).[43] Although the objects of these two fields overlapped, each problematized these objects in different (though interrelated) ways. Discussions of economic regulation, as we have seen, centered on a tradition of economic thought focused on problems of natural monopoly, and in particular on problems of inefficient pricing. In economic development, by contrast, a key justification for state involvement was that infrastructures might be underprovided by private markets. Thus they would hold back processes of industrialization and modernization. In a liberal-developmentalist view that took shape after World War II, government investment in infrastructure was to function not as the backbone of economic planning, as in the Soviet case, but as a target of state investment that would, as Rosenstein-Rodan put it in a classic essay, "have the maximum catalytic effect" in mobilizing the autonomous efforts of citizens and entrepreneurs.[44] The key question for this *liberal* developmentalist view concerned the volume of infrastructure capital required to stimulate modernization. The *neo-liberal* approach to the reform of infrastructure involved remapping the critical vocabulary of the new economics of regulation onto this adjacent domain, whose central problematic shifted from infrastructure *modernization*—that is, investment in infrastructure to stimulate industrialization and urbanization—to the *reflexive modernization* of already "infrastructural" forms of modern society.

I can only plot a few key points of reference in this story, which begins, again, in the United States, but passes quickly into the sphere of international development. One trigger for revisiting economic thinking about infrastructure was what Graham and Marvin call the "infrastructure crisis" of the 1970s. Around the world, breakdowns in infrastructure systems—from blackouts to bridge failures to the decay of roads—lent urgency to concerns that infrastructures were deteriorating. This crisis triggered a multipronged critique of state regulation or ownership of infrastructures.

Initially an attempt was made to map the infrastructure crisis back onto the existing, dominant critical vocabulary for thinking about infrastructure and development. To illustrate, we can take just one exemplary document of the American infrastructure crisis: a 1981 publication entitled *America in Ruins* by Pat Choate and Susan Walter.[45] The study, commissioned by the Council of State Planning Agencies, played a crucial role in drawing public attention to the infrastructure crisis. Following its publication, Roger Vaughan observed, "[a]lmost overnight, the press took [the problem of infrastructure] up with a vengeance," thus demonstrating how a "seemingly obscure and certainly dreary topic ... can become a central focus of public policy debate" (1984: xvii). A major purpose of the report was to document the decrepit conditions of bridges, roads, and energy networks. But its authors did not portray the "crisis" as simply a matter of deteriorating material structures. Choate and Walter argued that declining rates of infrastructure investment were a key culprit in the falling rates of productivity growth that preoccupied economists in many countries during the 1970s. Citing a 1977 RAND study that reported on the results of input-output analyses of the American economy, Choate and Walter

(1981: xi) advanced a structural interpretation of productivity decline: the problem was capacity idled by bottlenecks in chains of industrial production. They proposed to address these bottlenecks through a large-scale program of investment in infrastructure. "[B]y careful planning," they insisted, "government *can* target benefits to help both people and specific industries," proposing, along these lines, to develop a capital budget for the United States that would make it possible to rationally apportion infrastructure spending (Choate and Walter 1981: 27). Their plan can be situated in a long line of attempts—the Soviet central among them—to approach economic management as a logistical optimization problem, to respond to economic crisis by expanding government control, by placing, as Lewin said of the Soviet 1920s, "more hands on more levers."

Choate and Walter's call of alarm was followed by congressional hearings, a range of academic studies, and reports by think tanks and industry groups that triggered a significant debate about infrastructure investment during the 1980s in the United States and internationally. One key question in this debate was whether it was possible to empirically demonstrate basic assumptions that underlay Choate and Walter's argument: that declining government infrastructure investment could be linked to an infrastructure "shortage" that was, in turn, slowing productivity growth. The discussion was catalyzed by a series of articles, most notably by David Alan Aschauer, an economist at the Chicago Federal Reserve, which indicated a very robust relationship between declining economic productivity and a shortage of infrastructure investment and capital. Aschauer's work was answered by a cascade of studies that debated both the results and the methods used to pose the question.[46] What was at stake in this debate was not whether, *ceterus paribus*, infrastructure increased productivity—this was certainly true. Rather, the questions were: Could a government role in infrastructure investment be justified relative to a private role? And did the United States in fact have an infrastructure "shortage"?

For most observers, the discussion was inconclusive. No consensus was reached concerning the correlation between government infrastructure investment and productivity, or even about how to empirically test a relationship that had been more or less taken for granted for most of the twentieth century in developing and rich countries alike.[47] But the most interesting conclusion to the debate was not whether the findings concerning the correlation were positive, negative, or simply difficult to establish. Rather, it was that "infrastructure shortage" had been the wrong question all along. In 1994, the World Bank's World Development Report, referring to discussions of Aschauer's work, argued that infrastructure policy could not be a "simple numbers game of drawing up inventories of infrastructure stocks and plotting needed investments" (World Bank 1994: 1). The economist Edward Gramlich came to a similar conclusion:

"Not only have previous studies not provided very convincing answers to whether there is or has been an infrastructure shortage, but they may not have even focused on the right question in the first place" (1994: 189).[48] The point is not that the question of infrastructure shortage or the appropriate levels of investment disappeared. But different problems—shaped, I will show, by the new economics of regulation—dominated discussions in the 1990s and much of the 2000s.

We can trace this new problematization of infrastructure through the aforementioned 1994 World Development Report, entitled *Infrastructure for Development*, which summarized the current state of thinking and laid out a program for reform. The report began by reasserting a premise that had been central to Bank strategy throughout its history: that infrastructures were, "if not the engine, then the 'wheels' of economic activity" (World Bank 1994: 13–14). As such it saw a very broad scope for state intervention. But the crucial questions to be addressed had shifted. Though some countries still had significant infrastructure "deficits," coverage had "increased significantly in developing countries over the past several decades" (World Bank 1994: 13). In countries of the "second" (communist) world, massive programs of infrastructure construction were drawing to completion; in poorer countries, where the "quantum leap to ubiquity" had not taken place, there was, nonetheless, a significant accumulation of infrastructure stock.

The "numbers game," *Infrastructure for Development* implied, had been appropriate for the first wave of infrastructure *modernization* when the central problem was one of assembling an "infrastructural" form of collective life. By contrast, the crucial contemporary problems (as of the 1980s and early 1990s) were those generated in a form of collective life *already* assembled through infrastructures. The central concern in these cases was not the amount of infrastructure but the fact that "the full benefits of past investments were not being realized due to inefficiencies that resulted in a waste of resources and lost economic opportunities" (World Bank 1994: 13). The critique of infrastructural modernization that unfolded in *Infrastructure for Development* followed a pattern that was borrowed from the new economics of regulation: first, an *assessment* of current infrastructure policies (Do they meet their self-proclaimed goals?); second, a *diagnosis* of the failures of infrastructure modernization through a microeconomic analysis; third, a new *programming* of infrastructure through mechanisms of calculative choice, competition, and enterprise.

First: the assessment. *Infrastructure for Development* presented a mass of evidence indicating that if the point of government intervention in infrastructure was to increase economic productivity and to promote equal access to infrastructure services as "merit goods," it was failing on many counts, particularly in poor countries. The deterioration of infrastructure meant that the technical efficiency of some systems (such as power plants) was actually declining. Poor countries facing enormous fiscal shortfalls thanks to the economic shocks of the 1970s and 1980s were literally throwing money away; infrastructures, far from being flywheels of economic development, were sources of fiscal drain. Even more damning, "merit goods" arguments for state involvement in infrastructure were often not supported by practical experience. This was particularly true in poor countries, where infrastructures such as water and electricity—crucial to providing for basic needs—were found to provide high quality and low cost (indeed, often heavily subsidized) services to rich or middle-class urban populations, while poorer areas were often not connected to infrastructure networks and had to rely on higher cost and lower quality services delivered by small entrepreneurs on the market.[49] For much of the world, particularly in poor countries, the infrastructural ideal was never actual.

Second: the diagnosis. Previously, infrastructure planning and policy had focused on project-level, cost-benefit analysis that examined the overall economic impact of infrastructure investment, or used substantive technical measures to assess existing infrastructure levels—what *Infrastructure for Development* called the "numbers game." In both cases, emphasis was placed on the "macro" relationships among economic aggregates (capital investment, output, welfare provisioning). As Francois Bourguignon, then the chief economist at the World Bank, observed in 2006, such approaches had an "underlying planning character" in the sense that they were oriented to definite substantive ends and understood productivity-enhancing investments in terms of input-output relationships. Meanwhile, they ignored "behavioral responses from both beneficiaries and bureaucrats," that is, the choice structures of the calculative actors of which these systems were comprised (Bourguignon 2008: 282). And these "behavioral" problems—"incentives embodied in the institutional arrangements for providing infrastructure services" (World Bank 1994: 13)—were precisely what the report found decisive in understanding why infrastructure investments often failed to achieve their ends. Extensive research demonstrated that providers had little incentive to deliver efficient or high quality service since inputs and outputs were "not closely measured, monitored, or managed," and suppliers did not depend "on user satisfaction for reward" (World Bank 1994: 33). Managers had ambiguous imperatives: they were obliged to protect bloated workforces, and were rarely rewarded for more efficient production. Meanwhile, pricing structures—such as low levels of cost recovery, flat fees, and "cost-plus" pricing—gave recipients of infrastructure services little incentive to economize their use, and producers little incentive to pursue greater efficiencies.

Third: a new programming. We might expect that, given the problems with state involvement in infrastructure, World Bank economists would propose the market as an alternative mechanism for allocating infrastructure capital. But the story that emerges from *Infrastructure for Development* is different. The report concluded that classical arguments for state involvement in infrastructure construction and provisioning were overstated, but not irrelevant. The public sector would continue to have "*primary* responsibility for infrastructure services in most countries and most sectors in the foreseeable future." The reasons given were classic: due to the public good characteristics of some infrastructures and because "governments have objectives other than profits" that would not be achieved by markets, a significant government role in many infrastructure sectors was essential (World Bank 1994: 37). On the one hand, then, we have a remarkably strong affirmation of a government role in building, managing, and regulating networked infrastructures. On the other hand, the report's authors argued, the special characteristics of infrastructures could not "explain or justify the fact that governments and public sector agencies have dominated almost all aspects of [infrastructure provisioning] in developing countries in recent decades" (World Bank 1994: 24). In this light, the report proposed a movement that was fundamentally similar to the one observed in the economics of regulation: not a turn from intervention to its opposite—nonintervention, privatization, or deregulation—but a new microeconomic approach to assessing and programming infrastructure.

This microeconomic critique and programming implied, first of all, reframing the question of intervention. Previously, the question of intervention or nonintervention was posed for an infrastructural sector as a whole. Regulations had "bundled" together diverse activities—production, distribution, social protection—in "monolithic organizations." In response, *Infrastructure for Development* argued, it was imperative to *unbundle* infrastructure, by which it meant "pry[ing] open monolithic infrastructure sectors," pulling apart their diverse functions in order to rationalize each according to its specific characteristics. Services that "create externalities or produce essential services to captive users" may warrant some regulation, but in an unbundled sector regulation could be focused on "market imperfections while permitting wide scope for competition in other components of the sector." Thus, for example, "activities in which economies of scale are not important" could be separated from those in which they are (World Bank 1994: 52). A similar point was made about merit goods arguments: "[w]here a minimum level of consumption of a particular service (such as water, heating, or power) can be identified as a 'lifeline' for some users, society may judge that they should not be excluded if they cannot afford to pay" (World Bank 1994: 24). Unbundling, thus, involves first of all opening up monolithic sectors in order to pose the question of regulation in a more precise and specific fashion.

In some cases this "unbundling" then opens the way for marketizing specific functions or opening them to competition—by, for example, introducing auctions for market access. In other cases it allows reformers to reengineer specific functions through a microeconomic programming: instituting "incentive" pricing; commercializing maintenance; creating user choice, whether through technical controls (such as valves) or by allowing multiple providers to offer a given service; and so on.[50] In all these respects, the insights recently developed in the economics of regulation and in rich countries were crucial. The report's authors recognized that "the past decade marks a watershed. ... The diffusion of novel ideas such as sector unbundling, competitive entry, and incentive regulations from industrial to developing countries has occurred at a remarkable speed" (World Bank 1994: 71). "Recent changes in thinking and technology," they continued, "have revealed increased scope for commercial principles in infrastructure provision. These offer new ways to harness market forces even where typical competition [that is, competition among many firms providing the same good] would fail" (World Bank 1994: 13). What they proposed was not so much the marketization and deregulation of infrastructure, but a patterning of microeconomic interventions with other regulatory forms in what remains a crucial area for a government's attempt to realize certain substantive ends. It is precisely this kind of critique and programming of infrastructure that, in the 1990s and 2000s, was turned to the sticky problems of Russian heating systems.

Reprogramming the Russian Heat Apparatus

We have seen that reform of Russian heating systems—and, more broadly, of the "housing and communal sector" (the standard and rather unsatisfying translation of *zhilishchno-kommunal'noe khoziaistvo*[51])—was among the "second generation" reforms that were perceived to be crucial "for sustainable long-term growth once macroeconomic stability [had been] achieved" (World Bank 2003: 8). By the early 2000s, as a 2003 World Bank report put it, this was the "largest sector of the Russian economy operating along non-market principles" (World Bank 2003: 6). And a Russian government report recognized in 2001 that delay in reform of the communal sphere posed a "threat to the social and economic development of the country" (Government of the Russian Federation 2001: 5). By the early 2000s a slew of technical studies—some addressing the communal sphere broadly, some heat in particular—had been produced by the World Bank, the UNDP, the OECD, and Russian think tanks like the Institute for Urban Economics. The Russian government also issued a series of reports and reform programs, including a 1997 policy framework and, more consequentially, a 2001 program on the *Reform and Modernization of the Housing and Communal Complex* ("Government of the Russian Federation"), which laid out a plan for sectoral transformation for 2002–2010.

Following the approach in prior chapters, my aim in this final section is not to trace the development of reforms or the political battles around contentious aspects of heat reform, such as the monetization of subsidies, that took shape during the 2000s. Instead, by focusing on various technical studies and reform proposals—most importantly the government's program on *Reform and Modernization of the Housing and Communal Complex* (hereafter, *Program*), but also an array of reports and reform proposals by foreign and domestic experts—I examine how heating systems were constituted as a conceptual and practical problem. These studies and proposals varied in some important respects, placing emphasis on different parts of the reform program. But communal sector reform was a major area of cooperation between the Russian government and the World Bank in the 2000s.[52] Consequently, domestic and foreign reformers speak in a common language; they share a common mode of critique, and a common repertoire of techniques for intervention that is typical of neoliberalism in this domain.

The Problematization of Infrastructure Crisis— ## Unbundling the Khoziaistvo

The various reform programs and technical studies that began to emerge in the late 1990s and early 2000s started from a common point: a diagnosis of problems with the existing heat apparatus. We have seen that reforms in the early post-Soviet period proposed to shift the costs borne by local governments and enterprises to recipients of communal services. But as the government's 2001 *Program* noted, the "social and economic situation" during the 1990s—the severe inflationary recession that created a dramatic new landscape of social and economic vulnerability—meant that users could not bear higher costs. Or, at any rate, local governments were unwilling to impose higher tariffs. Communal service enterprises had nonetheless to keep delivering essential and expensive services, most centrally heat. They were caught in a fiscal vice.[53] Heat and other utilities were effectively "paid" for through arrears for energy inputs and—crucially—through deferred maintenance and repairs. As the government *Program* observed, the housing and communal sphere thus served to cushion "the social impacts of price liberalization," both through cross subsides and through the depreciation of its massive base of fixed capital. If economic reform was supposed to provide a therapeutic "shock," then the communal sector played the role of a "shock absorber" (2003: 5).[54] Reformers, too, recognized the critical role heat played in preserving the substantive economy of Russian cities.

How, then, did reformers diagnose this troubled situation? It is notable that the problem was not, initially, understood to be one of financing. Government and foreign assessments were of one voice in concluding that the ills of the communal sector could not be cured by throwing more resources its way.[55] Rather, as a 2003 draft of a government heat reform program put it, the crisis had to be traced to the fact that "[t]he transition to free prices" in energy inputs took place "practically without any change in the technical base of heat supply" or in the "organizational structure" of heat production" that had been inherited from the Soviet period.[56] Resolution of the crisis, as a UNDP/World Bank report argued, required not more financing but "interrelated changes in the technologies and in the organizational structures for the supply and demand of heat" (2000: 21). As had been the case in the United States in the 1980s, attention shifted from volumes of financing to the underlying technical, organizational, and normative structure of infrastructures as sociotechnical systems. Let us watch, therefore, as these reforms peel back the exigent circumstances of the 1990s to examine the prior "governmentality" upon which Soviet heating systems were built. We will find that reformers provide a most comprehending account of the Soviet heating system and of its post-Soviet transformation.

The central fact of the programming of Soviet heating systems, according to a particularly perceptive study by the UNDP/World Bank Energy Sector Management Assistance Program, was that heat was regarded as an "elementary need ... that had to be provided in abundance." The main requirement of heat systems, therefore, was that they be "robust and reliable in the sense that [they] deliver heat to the end-user under all circumstances." On a technical level, these assumptions meant that all elements of production, distribution, and consumption were regulated through a unitary system "that [could] be controlled and maintained easily from the heat production plant by keeping the supply pressure and temperature at the required levels" (UNDP/World Bank 2000: 17). Productive and social welfare functions were linked together in blanket regimes of subsidization that provided virtually free heat to all residents of cities.

The problem reformers identified with this Soviet system did not concern its *values*. Report after report affirmed, along with the 2001 government *Program*, that heat was an essential need whose provision had to be guaranteed by the state (the *form* of this guarantee is a complicated question, to which we return). Nor did reformers object to the basic fact of centralized heat production. It may be surprising that pumping hot water or steam through tens of thousands of kilometers of pipes in subfreezing temperatures for months on end could be an efficient way to keep apartments warm. But as Eric Martinot, a resource economist who conducted studies of Russian heating systems in the 1990s, notes, "well-maintained district heating systems ... are usually more efficient than autonomous heat sources" (1998: 11). For this and other reasons, the UNDP/World Bank report concluded that district heating "is not a dinosaur that is likely to disappear soon" (2000: 8). Instead, reformers traced the problems with Soviet heating systems to a series of microeconomic issues that were entirely foreign to the Soviet style of reasoning about social welfare, problems related to the incentives of the various actors—communal service enterprises, local governments, and "users" of services—that make up the heating system.

During the Soviet period these incentives had been not so much mismanaged as ignored. Local governments, communal service enterprises, and users were embedded in fixed material relationships and a unitary regulatory regime. Reforms thus proposed that the monolithic structure of the Soviet heating apparatus had to be *unbundled*. This meant first of all that the different organizations involved in the sector should be pulled apart, their distinctive functions clarified. Thus, the 2001 government *Program* argued that local governments should not be directly involved in economic functions such as heat production or maintenance, but should limit their activities to establishing the "rules of the game" by setting norms, enforcing contracts, and overseeing the administration of social protection measures (*Program*, 17). Communal service enterprises, meanwhile, should be oriented exclusively to efficient economic production by introducing incentives through competition and pricing mechanisms, and by freeing them from the fetters of social welfare obligations. The recipients of heat, meanwhile, should be treated not as passive "subjects of need" but as sovereign consumers who would be given "control over the volume and quality of housing and communal services" (*Program*, 8).

This proposal for unbundling may sound like a program for marketization or for government through the calculative choices of autonomous actors. And reformers used precisely the language of markets and competition to describe their proposals. One World Bank report after another during the 2000s—mechanically repeating the commonplaces of the 1990s—proclaimed that communal service reform was the "last sector that will require serious reform if Russia is to complete the transition to a market economy" (World Bank 2003: 5). Similarly, the government's *Program* referred to the introduction of "market mechanisms of functioning" and increasing consumer control as the critical elements of its reform program (*Program,* 19). But if we push past these loose generalities about markets and choice, efficiency and autonomy, we will find that the concrete proposals laid out in these reports are not best understood in such terms. "Unbundling," we have already seen, is not so much a policy framework or a definite course of action as a mode of critical questioning that asks to what extent sectors with significant natural monopoly or merit good properties can be programmed through mechanisms of choice, enterprise, and competition. In doing so, it identifies sites for a micro-economic programming of the heating system, but simultaneously—and this is the crucial point—recognizes the *limits* of such programming, imposed by the material setup of the heating apparatus, and by the social welfare imperatives that it must fulfill. In the case of Russian heat systems, these limits are strict indeed. Consequently, proposals for neoliberal reform take shape as highly selective and ultimately quite limited deployments of microeconomic devices within the material and normative framework of heating systems. Here we examine this unbundling of heat systems by examining three crucial areas that are addressed in all reform proposals: heat supply, consumption, and the system of subsidization and social protection.

Heat Supply

Let us turn first to heat supply—that is, to the production of hot water and steam in boilers, the distribution of heat through the *teploset'*, and the maintenance of the heat apparatus. We have seen that during the Soviet period heat supply was oriented to meeting norm-defined "needs," not responding to "demand." In this context, boiler operators, maintenance organizations, and natural resource producers were governed through a fixed technico-normative regime that defined the outputs they had to produce, the costs associated with these outputs and, therefore, the amount of financing they should receive. Since user tariffs were low, this financing largely came through subsidies. Beginning in the late 1990s, cost recovery from users rose rapidly and the relative share of subsidies declined.[57] But rising tariffs did not change the structure of supply and demand. Instead, they simply rearranged the distribution of costs. Consequently, as reformers noted, problems in the organization of heat supply inherited from the Soviet period persisted into the first decade of the twenty-first century. Communal sphere enterprises were still monopolists with little incentive to make their production more efficient. And their management priorities were confused by competing demands for economic efficiency and social protection. "At the heart of the management problems that have been typical of [communal service enterprises]," noted a 2003 World Bank report, "is the contradiction between the enterprise's function as a commercial entity providing economic services and the use of the enterprise as a vehicle for delivery of ill-targeted social protection" (World Bank 2003: 21). The result was a familiar litany of problems, including grotesque technical inefficiencies and bloated workforces.

The 2001 government *Program* proposed that reforms should be oriented first of all to introducing "market mechanisms of functioning" into the supply of heat (*Program*, 19). What this meant in practice, however, was a differentiated assessment of the need and appropriate scope for intervention in the specific areas of production, distribution, and maintenance. For example, systems of heat distribution—the *teploset'* through which heat or hot water is delivered—had natural monopoly characteristics, and fell, therefore, "in the purview of regulation [*podlezhit regulirovaniiu*]" (*Program*). No "marketization" there. Meanwhile, both domestic and foreign observers were more optimistic concerning maintenance. Although competitive markets with many firms vying to provide the same service were unworkable, it was feasible to have "competition for the market"—or Demsetz competition—through regular competitive tenders for maintenance concessions.

Finally, the government *Program* proposed that the supply of heat to the *teploset'*—that is, the operation of the massive centralized boilers themselves—might be made competitive in some cases. Where multiple boilers could deliver heat over a common network, it reasoned, private investors might be enticed to compete with existing producers (*Program*, 9). But the *Program* acknowledged that such competition was feasible only in large cities. In small cities, monopoly conditions would likely prevail since many were served by a single boiler complex, or by multiple boilers that were not linked in a common distribution network (as was true in both Belaya Kalitva and Rodniki). And even hopes for competition and private investment in large cities were disappointed. Based on the experience of the previous decade, a World Bank report concluded in 2008 that private capital was unlikely to play a significant role in the sector due to high risk and low potential return.[58] Most observers acknowledged that heat production would remain monopolized and regulated, and discussions of production shifted to problems of regulatory pricing. The same report pointed out that the system of pricing inherited from the Soviet era was based on "economically justified" tariffs derived largely by calculating producers' costs. This system—basically a form of "cost-plus" pricing, which had been a central target of criticism in the new economics of regulation—had the perverse effect that providers were "'punished' for efficiency gains" because lower costs might translate into lower tariffs and, thus, lower revenue (World Bank 2008: 25). One proposed alternative was to use tools of incentive regulation to allow producers to capture economies in production (Institute for Urban Economics 40).

The tally of marketization thus far: heat production—regulated monopoly (with, perhaps in the future, incentive pricing); maintenance—Demsetz competition, but not a competitive market; distribution—regulated monopoly.

Consumption: The Constitution of "Demand"

What of the "demand" side? What programming did reforms propose for the *consumption* of heat? It should be evident that the concept of demand was absent from Soviet heating systems. The very notion of a sovereign consumer whose preferences defined requisite levels of heat production and patterns of distribution was not considered in designing systems that were oriented to meeting norm-defined needs. This fact had crucial implications for the technical setup of the Soviet heat apparatus. As the UNDP/World Bank report noted, because norms defined the amount of heat to be delivered to an apartment, "the end-user needed no control devices, not even radiator valves, to influence the supply of heat." Soviet heat systems were based, therefore, on "constant water flows through all parts of the network," with controls installed only at the most aggregated level (UNDP/World Bank 2000: 17).

Into this system, with its sanguine assumptions about a stable and technocratically defined "need" for heat, reformers introduced entirely new questions and problems. Part of the issue was, indeed, one of consumer sovereignty—of allowing individual consumers to define how much heat they really needed (or were willing to pay for) and, thus, to "directly influence the volume and quality of housing and communal services," as the 2001 government *Program* put it (8). But efficiency issues were also at stake. As Martinot observed, in the absence of apartment level controls—and in the absence of a mechanism for charging based on use—"[h]ouseholds face zero marginal costs for their energy consumption and thus have no incentive to conserve" or invest in energy-saving improvements (1998: 5). The government *Program*, therefore, underlined the importance of introducing measures that would "stimulate energy saving" by users (*Program*, 8).

How could heat systems be reengineered to transform subjects of need into sovereign consumers who suffer the costs and enjoy the benefits of the choices that they make? How could a system be created in which calculative choice drives production and distribution? The remedy *seems* simple: install meters and control valves in individual apartments; charge households on the basis of use; let expressed utilities define the "demand" for communal services; let communal service organizations adjust heat supply to the resulting variations in demand—allow a self-regulating mechanism, thereby, to determine the production and distribution of heat. But as these various expert observers were well aware, things are *not* so simple.

An initial problem, as the OECD report explained, had to do with the piping of heating systems in apartment blocks. "The typical residential building," it noted, "is plumbed in series via vertical risers." Consequently, it would be impractical to "modulate flow at the level of the individual radiator (even if control devices were available), since any attempt to limit heat flow through a given radiator would affect the entire vertical series"—that is, it would change the temperature in all apartments directly above it. There are technical fixes for this problem. It is expensive but possible, for example, to install valves on side flows such that controls on one radiator would not affect an entire vertical series. But complications persist. Since "each radiator within a given apartment is served by a different vertical series" the usage of each apartment would not be recorded on a single meter (OECD/IEA 1995: 254).[59] Again, there are potential fixes. One could record usage for multiple meters in each apartment and add them up. In this case, a genuine concept of individual consumption could be programmed into the system. But this step would raise a problem for which Soviet heating systems were not equipped: the specter of *variable demand*. "Once consumers install heat regulating devices on their premises," the OECD report continued, "the system switches to variable flow at the consumer level and the supply side has to be adjusted accordingly." In other words, once users' diverse preferences are "revealed" through valves and meters, heat must be delivered differentially to various points in the distribution network. But in a constant flow regime, controls only allow "macro" adjustments between an aggregate "need" and the vicissitudes of outdoor temperature, making response to variable demand impossible: "The lag-time of heat delivery between send-out and consumption can vary by hours, depending on the customer's location in the system" (OECD/IEA 1995: 253); hours pass before centralized adjustments affect the heat delivered to a given apartment. Response to variable demand is impossible.

For all these reasons, and notwithstanding tireless exhortations about incentivizing users and allowing calculative choices to define the values relevant to production and consumption, reformers have more or less abandoned the idea that the effective demand of sovereign consumers can drive the supply and distribution of heat. Martinot's early studies recognized that individual metering would be impractical, and the World Bank concluded that installing valves and metering use in individual apartments is "technically difficult and prohibitively expensive" (2003: 19)

Without a technical overhaul of entire heating systems involving massive capital investment—which is for the moment unanticipated and quite unlikely—there is not, and will not be, a sovereign consumer of heat in Russia. Consumption will be based on the fixed technical parameters of heating systems. And tariffs will be assessed based on norms rather than on actual use. The marginal cost of heat use for households will continue to be what it has always been: zero.

It bears noting, as a coda to this discussion of demand, that foreign experts have advocated an alternate approach to these problems. Beginning in the early 2000s the World Bank supported pilot programs in which metering at the *building* level was combined with a system of "exchanges." These exchanges, located at many points throughout a city, take in water that has already been warmed by a centralized boiler and then heat it further to temperatures dictated by norms. In this system, which has been studied in detail by the Russian sociologists Olga Bychkova and Evgeniia Popova (2010), the scale economies of centralized heat are captured, while fluctuations in demand for heat at the margins are met by adjustments in the exchanges, thus addressing the daunting technical problem of variable demand. These mechanisms, which create the technical possibility for a kind of calculative agency at the level of *apartment blocks*, require a corresponding social technology—a homeowners association[60] —that could "share out costs to individual apartments" and pressure individual owners to make efficiency upgrades in order to lower costs for the entire association, thus "getting closer to charging users for actual consumption" (World Bank 2003: 19). Bychkova and Popova found that the initial experience with these systems has not been promising.

Subsidization

Let us turn to a final major area addressed by reforms: subsidization and social protection. We have seen that the orientation to basic need fulfillment in Soviet heating systems was practically realized through subsidies that allowed communal service enterprises to deliver heat at low and uniform costs. These most frequently took the form of cross subsidies such as low tariffs on gas or differential tariffs for industrial and residential users. After the collapse of the Soviet Union, such "blanket" subsidies— so-called because they treated all users the same—were not abolished, although they did cover a diminishing portion of the sector's costs thanks to declining government financing and rising input prices. But blanket subsidies were supplemented by another system of "categorical" subsidies—originally established in the Soviet period but vastly expanded in the 1990s—directed to specific groups such as the handicapped, veterans, and victims of repression.[61] Both foreign and domestic reforms noted a variety of problems with this existing system of subsidization. By lowering prices it reduced users' incentives to economize—though this problem was irrelevant in the case of heat since users have no control over how much heat they use and do not pay more for additional consumption. It also contributed to the financial difficulties of the communal sphere, since categorical subsidies imposed as unfunded mandates simply added to the losses of communal service enterprises.[62]

But more fundamentally, reformers articulated a critique of the very conception of public value that was embedded in systems of blanket subsidies. This critique resonated both with James Buchanan's proposal to understand "public" value in terms of individual costs and benefits, and with George Stigler's insistence that the value produced by the state should actually be made an object of economic analysis. Soviet heating systems, we have seen, were organized based on the assumption that a single public value—a normative heating level—could be defined for all citizens and that the state should provide this value to all in abundance. Post-Soviet reforms took aim not at this basic value proposition—that heat was a basic need whose provision, as the government *Program* wrote, should be "guaranteed"—but at the veneer of equality and social protection under which it claimed to operate. Reformers examined the *actual* distributional implications of subsidies by breaking up the "public" (in the Russian case, the more relevant concept would be "population" [*naselenie*][63]) whose needs were purportedly being met, and examining the costs and benefits that subsidies bestowed upon individuals and households differentially situated in an unequal social and economic field.

What reformers found is that the existing system had uneven and in many cases regressive effects. Blanket subsidies, as the World Bank noted, "benefit better-off households disproportionately," in large part because richer households tended to live in larger apartments with higher norm-defined levels of consumption. Consequently, they received bigger subsidies in absolute terms (World Bank 2003: 12). Meanwhile, as the *Program* noted, the beneficiaries of categorical subsidies were "not only citizens with low income [*maloimushchie grazhdane*] but also groups of citizens with high and middle incomes" (*Program*, 7). Confirming this observation, a 2005 study by Ellen Hamilton, Sudeshna Ghosh Banerjee, and Maka Lomaia (2005) showed that the richest two quintiles of households benefited more from subsidies than the poorest two quintiles.[64]

In this light, the government *Program* proposed to reprogram social protection by overhauling the system of subsidization along two axes. First, it proposed that "all budgetary resources ... dispersed to subsidization of the sector, will be taken from communal service enterprises and given to citizens"—"the actors [sub"ekty] most interested in [these resources'] effective expenditure"—in the form of monetary grants (*Program*, 7).[65] Second, it proposed to reorient the system of subsidization from categorical or blanket subsidies to targeted [*adresnye*] subsidies. The proposed technical mechanism for targeting was a means test that took a familiar form. It established a maximum percentage of household income that could be spent on communal services, and compensated households for normatively justified expenditures on communal services in excess of that amount. As in the definition of "need" incorporated into distribution formulas in budget reforms, discussed in the previous chapter, the technical definition of "normatively justified" expenditures on communal services is critical. The government did not propose to consider the amount a given family *actually* expends on communal services but the amount that *would* be expended on the *normative* level of communal services for an apartment of the *normative* size for a household consisting of a certain number of people. As a consequence, the program would reduce subsidies to small households living in large apartments (generally the rich), and would increase subsidies to large households living in small apartments (often the poor). In establishing normative expenditures, the reforms also proposed to take into account the costs of communal service provision in a given region, which varied in relationship to the local climate, transportation costs, the thermal qualities of the housing stock, heating technology, and so on.

After all: ". . . to each according to his [norm defined] needs"!

The gambit in such reforms of social protection was that subsidies—allocated initially *to* citizens, and then *by* citizens, who thereby "control the expenditure of budgetary resources"—would be allocated in a market-like way. They would be embedded in mechanisms of supply, demand, and price, rather than effectively canceling those mechanisms out. All of this is familiar. What is less familiar here—not because it is foreign to this broader category of technical interventions but because it has been largely ignored by critical scholars—is that this approach entails a very significant critique of received orientations to public value. It rejects the proposition that the core of the infrastructural ideal of low and equal prices for all is an acceptable way to think about distributional justice. It replaces the maxim of equal services at equal prices with a principle that mirrors Buchanan's much more *progressive* (in the sense of more redistributive) and *decidedly neoliberal* conception of fiscal equity. The role of the state is to equalize the burden that a certain socially necessary good imposes on households at different levels of income, residing in different kinds of housing, and in different parts of the country.

Conclusion: Possible Futures

So what have been the outcomes of reforms thus far? From any perspective, the results have been modest. Over the 2000s, reformers grew increasingly pessimistic about the possibility of introducing private capital or competition into the supply of heat, and discussion was limited to competitive tenders for maintenance concessions. Meanwhile, the Russian researchers Valentin Andrianov and Sergei Sivaev (2003) have found that tariff setting continues to function as it did in the Soviet period: on a cost-plus basis. On the demand side, the aforementioned experiments with building-level heat exchanges have been implemented in only a handful of cities; building-level metering is more widespread, though most observers agree that the institution of homeowners associations—essential to make building-level metering work as a social technology—remains weak and ineffective. Otherwise the structure of demand has not changed in its fundamentals. Reform of subsidization has been similarly halting. Though monetization has been implemented in some regions (in most it has not), Anastassia Alexandrova and Raymond Struyk found in 2007 that "not a single regional government has introduced targeting of categorical social assistance to low-income people or households" (2007: 160). A 2008 World Bank report argued that targeting has been difficult to implement because "wealthy consumers are trying to hold on to their perks"—echoing the claim of Chicago regulation theorists that in many cases the persistence of failed regulation is best explained by regulatory "capture" by powerful constituencies. Taking all this into account, the same World Bank report was able to repeat the conclusion that reformers had arrived at several years earlier: that the housing and communal sector was the largest unreformed part of the Russian economy—a vestige of socialism that persisted almost two decades after that system's demise—and that its reform was (still!) essential for "completing the transition to a market economy" (World Bank 2008: 26).

What are we to make of this state of affairs? One approach might argue that neoliberal reformers have run up against a variety of local resistances—political opposition, material structures—that they could only poorly perceive and could not ultimately manage. Certainly there is something to this. Observers agree that an "impressive array of legal and regulatory acts" passed by the Russian government has not been matched by shifts in regional and local governance (World Bank 2008: 7). It is also true that the limitations imposed by the inherited material structure of Soviet heating systems have loomed ever larger in estimates of the possible scope of reform. To read the succession of reform documents and technical reports on heat over the first two decades of the post-Soviet period is to trace a gradual process through which ambitions were dialed back, and the scope of intervention narrowed. By the late 2000s the program had been reduced to changes in regulatory pricing, targeting social protection, and competition for maintenance; not insignificant changes, but a modest program when compared to the sweeping terms in which these reforms were previously discussed (indeed, in many cases still are discussed) by proponents and detractors alike. Certainly, this is an area in which "actually existing neoliberalism" has been shaped by intransigent facts on the ground: facts of geography, demographic structure, and established routines of provisioning.[66]

Certainly, all that is true. But I have tried to tell a different kind of story about neoliberalism. It is not a story about how neoliberal reform was blocked by the stubborn stuff of post-Soviet Russia. I am not arguing that material objects and political realities elude these experts. And I do not take the accommodations and compromises that have emerged during the course of the 2000s to suggest that we are dealing with a qualified neoliberalism, a neoliberalism that was initially one thing, a pure and ideal thing, hatched in the minds of misguided ideologues, economists, or reformers, and that has, in its contact with "reality," become something else.

I am not saying all these things because I do not see neoliberalism as a set of policies that are implemented or not, as a project that is successfully pursued or not, or as a generalized logic that is realized or not. Instead, it seems to me that the accommodations and shifts we find in heat reforms—the specific movement we observe in their successive articulations—can be understood in terms of the form of problem making that defines the neoliberal style of reasoning about infrastructures and economic regulation. Neoliberal critique and programming in these domains, we have seen, developed *precisely* to address situations in which normal mechanisms of competitive markets were unworkable, either due to the material characteristics of production, to the structure of certain markets, or to the characteristics of "merit goods." The tools of the new economics of regulation were invented *precisely* as a new form of critical visibility through which intransigent things, embedded norms, and patterns of social provisioning could be brought into view, down to minute technical details, as the product of a prior governmentality that had to be rationalized. And this rationalization is designed to take shape *precisely* through the selective and in some cases quite limited deployment of what I have proposed to call microeconomic devices. These microeconomic devices depend on formal mechanisms of free choice, calculation, and enterprise. But their aggregate functioning does not add up to a market, in which allocations are driven by mechanisms of supply and demand. Rather, we have a complex ensemble of material structures, allocative principles, and value-generating mechanisms. To characterize some elements of this ensemble as "marketlike" or to note that they involve mechanisms of calculative choice is not so much wrong as it is incomplete; it constitutes only a first step in the analysis. We have then to understand how, in neoliberal reforms, they are articulated with and accommodated to fixed material structures, existing patterns of provisioning, and, crucially, norms of social welfare.

In making these observations I want to be clear that my claim is not that we can take the reform of post-Soviet heating systems to be paradigmatic of a broader neoliberal project. They do not tell us what neoliberalism "really" is. Indeed, for reasons I laid out at the very beginning of this chapter, the Soviet heating apparatus presents a kind of limit case: an extremely inflexible and centralized system that is particularly difficult to reform through microeconomic devices. As such, it brings certain problems into relief in an ideal-typic and one-sided way. But this extreme case provides a useful counter and foil to *another* extreme case that has completely dominated the critical imagination of neoliberalism, but that is of more limited descriptive and diagnostic value than is generally realized. Critical scholars have been transfixed by the image of rapacious multinationals swooping in to reap profits from infrastructure privatization in poor countries while essential needs go unmet. However well or poorly this image portrays what actually happens after privatization, the simple fact is that such privatizations have been surprisingly rare, as Antonio Estache and Marianne Fay (2007) found in a recent survey of developing countries. Most networked infrastructures remain in public hands, and their reform has to be analyzed, therefore, using the much more nuanced analytical vocabulary that I have been proposing. The situation is no clearer in the "neoliberal heartland"—the rich countries of Europe and North America. Though of course it is possible to find examples of marketization of infrastructure and dramatic new patterns of exclusion, they do not necessarily present a typical picture. Joseph Kearney and Thomas Merrill, in an extensive legal review of U.S. regulatory transformation, have noted that "[c]hanges [in infrastructure governance] are typically referred to as 'deregulation.' But if 'deregulation' means that a system of public regulation is abolished and replaced by exclusive reliance on market transactions, this is an inaccurate characterization of what is happening" (1998: 1325–26).

A revised understanding of neoliberal reform would also require a revised assessment of the processes of transformation that we associate with neoliberalism, and the kinds of futures that neoliberal reform implies. In Russia, even if reforms were implemented as both foreign and domestic reformers imagine them, heat would still be regulated as a natural monopoly; profits would be determined by regulatory decision making; and users would still be governed as subjects of need, not as sovereign consumers. If reformers managed to push toward full-cost recovery closely coupled with a more efficient system of subsidization, pressure on many households would increase (as it has throughout the 2000s), thus spurring, perhaps, processes of adjustment of populations across Russia's vast territory, as reformers hoped it would (see chapter 6). But a strengthened redistributive mechanism would limit the impact on the most vulnerable households—both poor households and, critically, households in the coldest parts of the country, where heating costs are the highest.[67] Thus, if the elimination of cross-subsidies would create pressure for "adjustment" of populations and industry away from the coldest, highest-cost parts of the country, then targeted subsidies would relieve this pressure.

But perhaps a future in which reforms are fully implemented is not the one that should be realistically anticipated. After almost total stasis during the 1990s, the improved economic conditions of the 2000s made reformers optimistic that a push to deeper transformation could proceed. As late as 2008 the authors of a World Bank report on a new lending program for the communal sector (ultimately agreed upon with the Russian government in late 2009) were able to write that "sound economic conditions" provided a "window of opportunity" (yet another!) for pushing reform (World Bank 2008: 1). But in fact the progress of reform during the 2000s was quite modest, despite these auspicious circumstances. And the economic turmoil of 2008 and 2009 serves as a reminder that such circumstances are, in any case, always tenuous. When another shock comes, incomes will fall and arrears will again mount, and the sine qua non of heat delivery will, no doubt, assert itself. After all, Russia ultimately does have enormous reserves of gas; ultimately it can deliver gas to boilers; and ultimately, with rare exceptions, these boilers will deliver heat even to residents who cannot pay for it. Reformed or not, the heat apparatus will serve as a great shock absorber during economic downturn, weaving together the elements of the city-building *khoziaistvo* as a sticky nexus of pipes, hot water, and warm bodies, in what remains, as such, a very cold country.

An Ineffective Controversy

> When you talk about contemporary neo-liberalism … you generally get three types of response. The first is that from the economic point of view neo-liberalism is no more than the reactivation of old, secondhand economic theories. The second is that from the sociological point of view it is just a way of establishing strictly market relations in society. … [T]he third response is that from a political point of view, neo-liberalism is no more than a cover for a generalized administrative intervention by the state which is all the more profound for being insidious and hidden beneath the appearances of a neo-liberalism. You can see that these three types of response ultimately make neoliberalism out to be nothing at all, or anyway, nothing but always the same thing, and always the same thing but worse. … Now what I would like to show you is precisely that neoliberalism is really something else.
>
> —Michel Foucault, *Birth of Biopolitics*[1]

> The controversy between conservatives and liberals … is so ineffective that it is not serving the purposes of controversy.
> —George Stigler, "The Unjoined Debate"[2]

IN AN IMPORTANT ESSAY on the theme of governmental reason, Colin Gordon provocatively argued that Michel Foucault's 1979 lectures identified neoliberalism as "a considerably more original and challenging phenomenon than the left's critical culture has had the courage to acknowledge" (1991: 6). Gordon's comment referred, in part, to Foucault's prescient recognition that neoliberalism was profoundly reshaping how government was constituted as a conceptual and practical problem in the last decades of the twentieth century. But he also pointed to Foucault's deepening dissatisfaction with certain tendencies in the discourse about liberalism and neoliberalism.[3] Foucault suggested that critics tended to *over*value neoliberalism by turning it into a kind of general diagnosis of power relations; by finding neoliberalism everywhere they turned it into "nothing at all" or, rather, into something so general and abstract that it either could not be studied empirically, or could be studied only through the endless multiplication of local variations on global themes: the insidious spread of administrative control; the establishment of "purely market relations in society"; or the workings of neoliberal hegemony. At the same time, critics *under*valued neoliberalism to the extent that they analyzed it as a static worldview, the passive reflection of a coherent ideology whose essence could be read from the "projections it has been led to formulate by its analyses and criticisms"—such as the utopia of a self-regulating market.

Thirty years later, Foucault's reflections feel absolutely contemporary. In some ways they may ring truer today than they could have in the late 1970s, when critical discussions of neoliberalism were only beginning to take shape. The explosion of writing on neoliberalism in the 2000s has, indeed, been dominated by what Foucault called an "inflationary" critique that sees neoliberalism everywhere and behind everything. But in reading much contemporary scholarship on neoliberalism, one is equally struck that this ubiquitous thing remains elusive, and one cannot help but feel that it is taken to be one thing when in fact, as Foucault suggested, it is really something else.

In the course of researching and writing this book, I constantly encountered large and small ways in which assumptions about what neoliberalism is simply break down when confronted with particular individuals or programs for reform. It is taken for granted, for example, that neoliberalism holds an unbending belief in the ability of markets to produce optimal outcomes; that utopic faith in "harmony and self-regulation," as Karl Polanyi put it in an oft-cited phrase, is the alpha and omega of the liberal creed. But the neoliberals I examined rejected economic analysis that made reference to an "imaginary" optimum condition as the standard against which either markets or the state should be judged; they rejected the very concept of a "maximum" of general welfare. Critics often insist that neoliberalism is blind to the substantive reality that it takes up and aims to reform. But what struck me in examining the work of Buchanan and Stigler, and the broader streams of thought of which they were a part, is precisely that they invented a new empiricity, a new principle of reality, which made it possible to grasp the minute details of bureaucratic arrangements or material infrastructures in a new and productive way. It is repeated with great assurance that neoliberalism is inextricably tied to a conservative and corporate agenda. But if we examine areas in which specific neoliberals weigh in on matters of policy the story gets tangled. George Stigler, in his crusade for deregulation, was aligned with Teddy Kennedy and Ralph Nader (Ralph Nader!), with whom he shared a conviction that the interests of corporations and other powerful groups, rather than the public interest, often drove the regulatory agenda. It is taken for nothing less than apodictic certainty, finally, that neoliberalism is opposed to social protection, that increasing inequality, to recall David Harvey's claim, is structural to the entire neoliberal project. But we have seen that James Buchanan offered a powerful defense of redistribution that today provides the conceptual and practical orientations for "neoliberal" reforms around the world.

One can readily imagine the response to these observations: This is only the surface, the screen, the ruse. The real neoliberalism should be sought out not in the justifications and rationalizations made by neoliberal thinkers but in broad structural transformations, in deep shifts of class power, in the implementation of neoliberal reforms, and in the real processes of transformation at the local level. No doubt there is something to this, and in this book I certainly have not tried to skirt the question of how economic or politico-philosophical reflections are translated into concrete proposals for reform; indeed, I have tried to trace these connections with some care. The problem, however, is that in too many analyses the "real" neoliberalism of which local developments are taken to be manifestations is always receding: found in suggestive interpersonal or institutional connections or in structural effects; or, alternatively, gratuitously singled out as the decisive factor in complex fields of power and processes of historical change. A critique of neoliberalism built on such foundations, can never find its mark, and can only ever be ineffective, to recall George Stigler's nice phrase, for it has no addressee.

It might be tempting, in light of the apparent difficulty of pinning neoliberalism down, to conclude that the game is not worth the candle. We could abandon any discussion of neoliberalism and simply continue various pursuits of intellectual history, studies of policy implementation, structural analyses, and so on. But this path is not satisfactory. As an analytical term, neoliberalism draws meaningful conceptual interconnections among a range of historical experiences and contemporary problems in a way that is essential; methodologically speaking, we need it. What is more, it remains a crucial form through which problems of government are thought out today. We also need, therefore, an effective controversy about neoliberalism. The question is: What is required to get critical inquiry back on track?

In this book I have pursued three strategies for, as I see it, making a critical discussion of neoliberalism more effective, some of which have been taken up by other scholars in recent years. The first is simply to develop greater critical consciousness about dominant narratives of neoliberalism—where they come from, and what their effects are likely to be.

As I have suggested, and following a related observation of Emma Roth-schild (2001), the dominant interpretation of neoliberalism was shaped by a conservative libertarian historiography that linked classical liberal-ism to neoliberalism to the waves of liberalization and reform that took shape in the 1970s to the 1990s. For *critical* scholars, this interpretation roughly fit an emerging narrative about neoliberalism as a pervasive force in shaping world affairs during a historical period defined by Thatcher-ism and Reaganism, the debt crises and structural adjustment in Latin America and Africa, the Washington Consensus, and the project of "tran-sition" in the postsocialist countries. In this context critical scholars not only accepted but advanced the conservative libertarian view of things, providing it with broader historical scope and, for those of a certain cast of mind, acceptable political credentials.

The problems with this story begin from the fact that, as an alternative historiography of classical liberalism pioneered by Rothschild, Stephen Holmes, and others has shown, it is simply wrong; we cannot find in the history of liberalism—or, for that matter, of neoliberalism—a coherent doctrine, coherent politics or, indeed, consistent views on almost any-thing. Instead, we find a diversity of positions articulated in response to specific historical circumstances. But this diversity and changeability of liberalism—both historical and contemporary—has been obscured by standard critical accounts. The antidote is to better understand the historical conjunctures in which particular stories about neoliberalism seemed to make sense—developing more discerning critical accounts of the Washington Consensus, structural adjustment, and so on—in order to think beyond them.

The second strategy, related to the first, is to turn greater attention to the flexibility of many elements of neoliberal reforms, and to the relation-ships they may have to diverse political projects. Here I have in mind an argument similar to the one advanced recently by Dani Rodrik that "first order economic principles ... do not map into unique policy packages" and that their application is "a lot more flexible" than is generally recog-nized (2007: 15).[4] It is true that neoliberalism—at least in its American variant—was initially aligned with a trajectory of conservative thought and was forged as a critical (though not, I have tried to show, rejection-ist) response to the rise of the social state. But however one evaluates this response or its politics, this circumstance concerning the birth of neoliberal reflection tells us nothing about its current forms. And it seems to me debilitating—an unwarranted submission to a logic of origins— to simply assume that those politics will be everywhere and always the same. Indeed, we might posit that the formality of neoliberal techniques of governing have given them a certain mobility and flexibility that allow them to be deployed in a range of different circumstances, in various political projects, and various institutional contexts (Collier 2005; Collier and Ong 2005; Ferguson 2010).[5] Tracing how that works seems an essential contemporary task.

The third and final strategy I have pursued is simply to take more seriously the question of what makes a particular tradition "neoliberal"; to ask in what, precisely, its neoliberalism consists. This does not mean focusing only on the effects of neoliberal policies, on neoliberalism's characteristic techniques, or on the implementation of neoliberal reforms. It does not mean being content to read popular writings (Milton Friedman's endlessly scorned and, in a technical sense, not particularly "serious" speech acts in *Capitalism and Freedom*). It does not mean seeing neoliberal writing as cover for a hegemonic project. Rather, it means taking neoliberalism seriously in nothing other than the usual anthropological sense: carefully considering the arguments neoliberals have made and trying to understand their coherence by reconstructing the problems that animated them and the styles of reasoning that made them possible. Here, too, Foucault's ethos of inquiry diverges from the balance of critical thinking on the topic in a salutary fashion. As Gordon observes, Foucault's accounts of liberal and neoliberal thinkers "are devoid of the implicit pejorative sarcasm" that many impute to his earlier work, and even "evince a sense of ... intellectual attraction and esteem" (1991: 6). In a similar way, it did seem to me that the thought and proposals not only of Buchanan and Stigler but also of a multitude of lesser-known experts, technocrats, and policymakers—including those who were reasoning through the mundane details of pipes and budgetary routines from a "neoliberal" perspective—were worthy of esteem as serious attempts to grapple with serious problems.

Lest this last point be misunderstood, it should be underlined that I am not offering an *apologia* for neoliberalism. If most critical scholarship has conceptualized neoliberalism in a manner that is "appraisive" (Boas and Gans-Morse 2009)—a judgment, and in this case always a negative judgment, is built into the very definition of a term—I am not simply proposing to reverse the evaluative valence. Certain aspects of neoliberal thinking and writing seem to me quite attractive (for example Buchanan's arguments about redistribution and fiscal justice). But others are most unattractive (his increasingly virulent opposition to state intervention as such). Similarly, if there is much in the "neoliberal" agenda in Russia of the 2000s that seems to me valuable—a potential contribution, dare we say, to a more just society—the post-Soviet experience also provides abundant material for criticizing reforms, individual thinkers, and economic doctrines that can be meaningfully associated with neoliberalism. Indeed, no one who spent significant time in the country in the last twenty years—particularly outside the centers of political power, particularly in small cities like the ones I worked in—could fail to see that critical scholarship has, in this sense, gotten many things right. But the point is that if all these things are simultaneously true—if neo-liberalism does not have a coherency and constancy across its articulation in diverse times and places—it makes no sense to be for it or against it in some blanket way. As with the old tiresome debates about whether the Soviet Union was "really" socialist—and whether, therefore, its pathologies were intrinsic to socialism—it is simply unproductive to evaluate the essence of neoliberalism on the basis of any one of these experiences. Neoliberalism simply is what it becomes, in critical reflection and in programs of reform. We can assess it only by studying these in their actuality.

Behind these methodological orientations to a more nominalistic approach to neoliberalism lies an argument about what we ought to expect from critical discourse about neoliberalism, and about what, indeed, makes critical discourse critical. The vast majority of work on neoliberalism has taken the shape of what Foucault called an "imperative" discourse ("love this, hate that, this is good, that is bad, be for this, beware of that") that begins from the presumption that the political stakes of neoliberalism are clear: we know who the bad guys are (the neoliberals); we know who the good guys are (those who suffer at the hands of neoliberal reforms, or resist these reforms); and we know what the right political commitments are (more social welfare, more solidarity, more equalization, more justice). In this view, controversies about neoliberalism are, in large part, controversies about value: those who care about inequality versus those who do not; those who care about the poor versus those who do not; and so on.

But such a discourse reaches its limits when the important distinctions in a field are not obviously or immediately about conflicting values. If both James Buchanan and the critics of neoliberalism are for equity and justice, what precisely is the problem? How can a controversy around such values proceed? A more productive pursuit would be to ask how these values are elaborated in practical terms, and how they are at stake in particular reforms, institutions, and forms of reasoning about the problems of distribution, substantive provisioning, and calculative rationality that have persistently preoccupied governmental reflection in modern states. Such a practice would be close to what Max Weber (1949: 53) called "technical criticism." Its role is resolutely not to assert values—to engage in "imperative discourse"—or to choose among values. Instead, it entails a labor of critical clarification of values; a labor of assessing the "significance" of a given value-end, as Weber put it, and of clarifying its meaning in a particular context. The question, from this perspective, might not be whether one is for or against equalization or for or against social provisioning, but how these values are specified—What is "justice" in Buchanan's hands? What kind of equality is relevant and what is a "right" to certain services for a citizen of a modern social state?—how they are at stake in different courses of political action, and what other values are sacrificed in pursuing them. Such an approach reverses the stance of an imperative discourse. "Critical inquiry," in this view, is not inquiry motivated by a politics, but inquiry in which the terrain of politics is itself at stake and in question.

Notes

1. Foucault 2008.
2. For a review of work that invokes Polanyi to analyze post-Soviet transformation, see Woodruff 1999.
3. Contributions to the enormous critical literature on "transition" include Stark 1990; Burawoy and Krotov 1992; Verdery 1996; Cohen, et al. 1998; Burawoy and Verdery 1999b; Cohen 2001; Stiglitz 2002.

CHAPTER ONE: INTRODUCTION

1. Foucault 2008: 319–20.
2. Major studies of big Soviet cities include Ruble 1990; Kotkin 1991; Colton 1995; Kotkin 1995; Ruble 1995. Studies of "out of the way" towns include Humphrey 1983, Vagin 1997, and Kharkhordin and Alapuro 2010.
3. In some cases—such as post-Soviet Georgia—they simply collapsed. See Collier and Way 2004.
4. On the trend of limited migration, see Gaddy 2007.
5. The term "common things" is borrowed from Latour and Weibel 2005.
6. On this "guarantee," see also "Poiasnitel'naia Zapiska k Kontseptsii Federal'nogo Zakona 'O Teplosnabzhenii.'" Komissiia Soveta Federatsii po Estestvennym Monopoliiam, March 2003 (www.rosteplo.ru/zaktep/pzap.htlm).
7. For example, the analysis of heat reforms presented in Bychkova and Popova 2010.
8. In recent years various scholars have articulated dimensions of the critique I am suggesting here. See Ganev 2005; Hoffman, et al. 2006; Rose, et al. 2006; Boas and Gans-Morse 2009; Brenner, et al. 2009; Ferguson 2010.
9. Mirowski and Plehwe 2009. I thank Adam Leeds for discussions on this point.
10. Exceptions include the contributions to Mirowski and Plehwe 2009. On "serious speech acts" see Dreyfus and Rabinow 1982.
11. For a similar critique see Rose, et al. 2006.
12. Their assessment of the critical literature on post-Soviet Russia is damning: "Few authors critique particular World Bank projects, but instead critique the ideas of the 'Washington Consensus' or 'Neo-Liberal Economic Ideology' that they perceived framed foreign aid strategy in post-communist countries. Critics rarely distinguish between different international organizations and actors" (Kogut and Spicer 2004: 3).
13. An exception is Amadae's (2003) study of Buchanan.

14. For reviews of the substantial literature that has drawn on Foucault's work to analyze contemporary neoliberalism see Larner 2000 and Rose et al. 2006. Foucault's relevance to Russia, meanwhile, has been debated episodically, beginning with Laura Engelstein's article, "Combined Underdevelopment" (1993), which posited that the historical schema of power Foucault proposed could not be applied to the Russian case, and that Foucault's critical attitude was only possible given the legal protections of liberal democracies. Following Koshar (1993) and Goldstein (1993), the question of "applicability" seems to me misplaced, since Foucault proposed neither a theory of power nor a fixed historical schema of development, but rather a series of analytical orientations to the study of power. It might be added that Engelstein's critique was derived from a rather narrow reading of the Foucault of *Discipline and Punish* (which encompasses the first volume of the *History of Sexuality* and the lectures of 1976 at the Collège de France) and seems particularly unconvincing in light of the subsequently published lectures of 1978 and 1979, which address liberalism and neoliberalism directly. On the shift in Foucault's method and critical orientation during the late 1970s, see Collier 2009b. For a more recent commentary on Foucault and Russia (which revives, in qualified form, the question of "applicability"), see Plamper 2002.

15. If one were interested in pursuing this theme a starting point might be to compare Marc Raeff's essay on "The Well-Ordered Police State" (Raeff 1975) with Foucault's discussion of the mercantilist treatment of population in his 1978 lectures.

16. He continues: "[W]e see the sudden emergence of the problem of the 'naturalness' of the human species within an artificial milieu. It seems to me that this sudden emergence of the naturalness of the species within the political artifice of a power relation is something fundamental, and to finish I will just refer to a text from someone who was no doubt the first great theorist of what we could call biopolitics, biopower" (Foucault 2007: 21–22).

17. This point has been made by Tobias Rees (personal communication).

18. [T]he theme of man, and the "human sciences" that analyze him as a living being, working individual, and speaking subject, should be understood on the basis of the emergence of population as the correlate of power and the object of knowledge. After all, man ... is nothing other than a figure of population. Or let us say again: If, on the one hand, it is true that man could not exist, and that only the juridical notion of the subject of right could exist when the problem of power was formulated within the theory of sovereignty, on the other hand, when the populations becomes the *vis-à-vis* of government, of the art of government, rather than of sovereignty, then I think we can say that man is to population what the subject of right was to the sovereign. There you are, all wrapped up and all loose ends tied (Ibid.: 79).

The constitution of modern Man at the "finitudes" of life, labor, and language is discussed in Foucault 1970.

19. On Foucault's analysis of the Physiocrats as "proto-liberal," see Collier 2009b.

20. Rabinow notes the distinction between Foucault's earlier emphasis on "systems of thought" and this later emphasis on thinking as a situated practice.

21. My italics. In this particular lecture, Foucault associated the forms of analysis and programming invented by liberalism with a "political technology of security," but soon dropped the term.

22. On the distinction between "society"—the object of sociological knowledge—and "the social," see Deleuze 1979. For a discussion of "the social" in the Russian context, see Hoffman 2000.

23. The best known example of the first is Agamben 1998.

24. Studies focused on the subject and power, include Engelstein 1994; Kharkhordin 1999; Yurchak 2003; on "cultural modernity," see Kotkin 1993b, 2001; and the chapters collected in Hoffmann and Kotsonis 2000.

25. Of course a tremendous amount of work has been done on Soviet planning, social welfare, and urbanism, and on the intellectual formation of those individuals who shaped the Soviet system. But these analyses have not been cast in terms of a Foucaultian problematic.

26. Soviet critics themselves described developments in the liberal cases as "spontaneous" and therefore as chaotic and uncontrolled.

27. They are examples of "reflexive modernization" in the sense of Beck 1992.

28. I thank Martha Lampland for pushing me to clarify this point.

29. Here I modify Callon, Millo, and Muniesa's term, "market devices," because these mechanisms of calculation and choice may not be programming a market (Callon, et al. 2007). See discussion in chapters 7 and 8.

30. This formulation is found in Peck and Tickell 2002.

31. On "styles of reasoning," see Hacking 2002.

32. That said, precisely the same lessons could be drawn from other traditions. For example, similar "anti-sociological" arguments can be found in Weber 1949; Wagner 1991; Luhmann 1998; Rabinow 2003; Foucault 2007.

33. On "problematic situations" as sites of inquiry, see Rabinow 1999; Collier and Lakoff 2005.

34. For an argument along these lines, see Collier 2009a.

35. For more on this critique of Actor-Network Theory, see Collier 2009a.

PART I: SOVIET SOCIAL MODERNITY

1. In fact, Miliutin distinguished his conception from the "linear" city. As Meerovich points out, Miliutin's conception owed more to Henry Ford than to Soria y Mata (Meerovich 2007).

2. On Miliutin's pragmatism, see Kopp 1970.

3. This point has been recently made by Hoffman 2004.

4. Classic statements on Russian backwardness include Von Laue 1964; Gerschenkron 1966; Szporluk 1988.

5. "[I]f it is true that the outline of the very complex technology of security appeared around the middle of the eighteenth century, I think that it is to the extent that the town posed new and specific economic and political problems of government technique" (Foucault 2007: 64).

6. Major studies on liberalism in the frame of governmental rationality include Rabinow 1989, Rose 1999, and Foucault 2007, 2008.

7. Material on Rodniki's history is drawn from documents in Rodniki's city library, particularly *Istoriia Goroda i Raiona* (Folder) and a report by the local soviet, *Rodnikovskii Raion k Desiatiletiiu Oktiabr'skoi Revoliutsii* (Rodniki, 1927).

8. On "householding," see Polanyi 1968.

Chapter Two: The Birth of Soviet Biopolitics

1. Foucault 2008: 92–93.

2. This teleological position built on the critique of liberal political economy articulated in the early 1920s by Bukharin and Preobrazhenskii in *The ABCs of Communism* and by Bukharin in his *Economics of the Transitional Period* (Treml 1969).

3. On these "limits" of sovereign power, see Raeff 1975; Foucault 2007.

4. For example, Russia was the world's largest iron producer in the latter decades of the eighteenth century (Blackwell 1968: 56).

5. "In the schema of the artificial town we find again the disciplinary treatment of multiplicities in space, that is to say, [the] constitution of an empty, closed space within which artificial multiplicities are to be constructed and organized according to the triple principle of hierarchy, precise communication of relations of power, and functional effects specific to this distribution, for example, ensuring trade, housing, and so on" (Foucault 2007: 17).

6. Proprietorship was often a matter of compulsory service. See Gerschenkron 1970.

7. See Lappo 1997. For example, the provincial reform of 1775 aimed to establish cities as the focal point of a strengthened apparatus of state territorial administration that, Hittle notes, "depended on the presence of a large number of cities, ideally spaced across the vastness of European Russia. In fact," he continues, "there were not enough cities available in the right places, so it became necessary to create them" (1976: 64).

8. From this point of view it is significant that institutions that *drove* urban reform and autonomy in other cases—such as guilds—were *created* by the state in the interest of strengthening tsarist power in Russia, as in the municipal Charter of 1785 (Hudson 1989: 134).

9. Foucault made a similar point about the Western European cases in which, he argues, an emerging governmentality was "blocked" by an "excessively large, abstract, and rigid framework of sovereignty as a problem and an institution" (Foucault 2007: 102).

10. For a review of these developments, see Blackwell 1968.

11. Ellison notes that in 1815, 95 percent of labor in the cotton-textile industry was free labor (1965: 526).

12. Scholars debate the relative importance of private entrepreneurs during this period. For a revision of the Gerschenkronian thesis on the centrality of the state, see Gatrell 1994.

13. On American railroad building and bond markets, see Chandler 1977. On differing forms of capital accumulation for industrialization, see Gerschenkron 1966.

14. Blackwell 1970: 33. "Austere disciples" in the original is clearly an error.

15. For a discussion of this succession of finance ministers, see Von Laue 1963; Hedlund 2005.

16. On the influence of List in Russia, see Szporluk 1988.

17. Hedlund notes that two-thirds of government expenditure was directed to economic development in the years 1892–1900. The majority of that went to railroad construction (Hedlund 2005: 229).

18. "By a policy of public works, above all by means of railroad construction, the government [would] stimulate individual enterprise in the exploitation of the vast but idle resources of Russia" (Von Laue 1963: 76).

19. Blackwell argues that the rate of economic change in the last tsarist decades provides "clear evidence that Russia was undergoing ... the fundamental economic change or 'take-off' that is associated with an industrial revolution" (1970: 44).

20. On rural developments after the great reforms, see Gerschenkron 1968. On the comparative growth of cities, see Blackwell 1986. On industry-led urban development in southern Russia, see Thiede 1976.

21. A related point can be found in Kotsonis 2000.

22. On tsarist wartime planning, see Davies and Catrell 1991: 151.

23. For a detailed description of the Commission's work, see Cummins 1988.

24. On the integration of national grids in other countries, see Hughes 1983; Graham and Marvin 2002. On Russian electrification, see Coopersmith 1992. On the relationship between infrastructure and new understandings of the national economy, see Mitchell 2006 and Collier and Lakoff 2008.

25. We might distinguish three terms in a conceptual series: first, the "communications" of absolutist power; second, "public works," which suggests a liberal orientation to market failure and public good; and third, "infrastructure," which is linked to an emerging understanding of the economy as an ensemble of vital systems whose functioning was a central problem of government.

26. "By 1892 the basic pattern of the Russian network had been completed. ... In the 1890s, apart from the Siberian road, the main job consisted of improving and increasing the rail network in European Russia" (Von Laue 1963: 89). In the case of the Trans-Siberian, lands along the route were undeveloped. Planners had to anticipate the mutual development of industry and infrastructure in a fashion that anticipates the approach found in GOELRO and in the five-year plans.

27. Krzhizhanovsky Power Institute 1936: 16. Italics original.

28. The aptness of the word "planning" to describe the Soviet system is long-debated by Sovietologists, who pointed out that plans were not simply translated into reality. On the early Soviet period, see Lewin 1973. On the late Soviet period, see Rutland 1985 and Whitefield 1993. I will continue to refer to "planning" as the "native" term.

29. Erlich (1960) is generally regarded as the classic treatment of the planning debates. However, as Davies (1961) points out, the discussion there is largely abstracted from practical developments. Here, therefore, I draw more heavily on

Carr and Davies (Carr 1950; Carr 1958; Davies 1958; Carr and Davies 1969), who focus on the relationship of the planning debates to practical developments.

30. See chapter 1 of Woodruff 1999, which summarizes debates over the character of money in the early Soviet period.

31. "From 1919, money accounts, even when accurate, ceased to reflect the real processes of the economy; behind the budgets there lay the material input and output of the state, taking place as a rule directly in physical terms" (Davies 1958: 38–39).

32. One Narkomfin planning skeptic wrote that

> [t]he question of the dimensions of our budget … depends in a large measure on the dimensions of the tax burden on the peasant, i.e. on the question of the proportional relation between state economy and peasant economy. … It is on the basis of this growth of the peasant economy that the market for our industry can develop in the future, and on the basis of the growth of the peasant economy that our state budget can also develop (quoted in Carr 1958: 457).

33. For discussions of the debate, see Lange 1945; Carr 1958: 496–500; Chandra 1967; Treml 1969; Rutland 1985.

34. Apparently the term "genetic" was used in Austrian economics. Thus, Cubeddu writes of Menger's methodological procedure that "[j]ust like other 'exact laws,' then, theoretical economics will be called upon to investigate 'the concrete phenomena of the real world as exemplifications of a certain regularity in the succession of phenomena, i.e., genetically'" (1999: 3).

35. Most commentators agree that genetic and teleological described two necessary components of planning under any circumstances. Some have simply ignored the debate, as did Ehrlich in his classic study. For an account that is closer to my own view, see Dobb 1948: 324.

36. Scholars continue to disagree about whether NEP could have been adapted to the needs of a quickened program of industrial development. See, for example, Nove 1992.

37. Quoted in Carr 1958: 505.

38. Cited in Carr and Davies 1969: 815.

39. Cited in ibid., 793.

40. For a discussion of the teleological conception of balance, see ibid., 798–801.

41. "This transformation would be brought about through engineering projects involving a system of realistic and inter-connected quantitative targets which strictly corresponded to available resources, and were built up by combining, in 'successive approximations,' the draft plans of each industry or economic sector" (ibid., 790).

42. Lampland (2010: 389) has recently made a related point: "Under its mandate to plan and run the economy, the new socialist regime would grant itself the authority to intervene in the most minute details of accounting and accountability."

43. On foreign influence on Soviet planning, see Carr 1950: 360–83; Szporluk 1988.

44. Krzhizhanovskii, *Ekonomicheskaia Zhizn'*, July 10, 1927, quoted in Carr and Davies 1969. Jowitt 1974 provides a classic analysis of such mobilization strategies in Leninist regimes.

45. Pyatakov, cited in Carr and Davies 1969: 792–93.

46. The treatment of "society" in totalitarian theory is discussed in Edele 2007. For Soviet planners, dealing with what they perceived to be crippling backwardness, the problem was that "society" was so backwards, or that its intrinsic dynamics and laws were so constraining, that it had to be simply abolished, overcome, or remade in new terms. What was brought into governmental view was "society" not in the liberal sense but in the sense Arendt defined it in *The Human Condition*: "the forms in which the fact of mutual dependence for the sake of life and nothing else assumes public significance and where the activities connected with sheer survival are permitted to appear in public" (1998 [1958]: 46).

47. For example, Engelstein 1994. For an argument closer to my own, though not framed primarily in a Foucaultian problematic, see Holquist 2000.

48. I use the term "totalizing" rather than "totalitarian" to distinguish my concerns from the questions of political regime. I do not mean to suggest, thereby, that the term "totalitarian" is inappropriate in describing the Soviet system. A similar use of "total planning" is found in Caldeira and Holston 2005.

CHAPTER THREE: CITY-BUILDING

1. Canguilhem 1989: 247.

2. Meerovich writes that developments in city-building of this period "have not been the topic of a deep and multi-sided history as a single complex phenomenon" (Meerovich 2007).

3. On the prescriptive norm in discipline, see Foucault 2007.

4. On urban administration during this period, see Gleason 1976; Hamm 1976a; Hamm 1976b; Hanchett 1976.

5. For a comparative view of conditions in late-tsarist cities, see Hamm 1976a; Blumfield 1993.

6. On "feminization," see Husband 1990.

7. On this depopulation episode, which took place in many cities see Koenker 1985.

8. On the persistence of itinerant labor into the late 1920s and early 1930s, see Kotkin 1993a.

9. On these waves of administrative reform, see Lappo 1997.

10. *Otchet o Rabote Rodnikovskogo Raionnogo Ispolkoma za 1925–1926 God*, 1926, Rodniki Public Library.

11. According to Bliznakov, pre-Soviet architecture and urbanism lacked a tradition of avant-garde experimentation equivalent to that found in the figural arts (Bliznakov 1971).

12. Much but not all of the substantial literature on these topics has focused on aesthetics and design. Major studies include Kopp 1970; Bliznakov 1971; Clark 1993; Hudson 1994; Cooke 1995; Paperny 2002; Khmel'nitskii 2007. For

historiographical reflections on Russian writing about the history of Soviet architecture, see Khmel'nitskii 2003.

13. Most accounts trace the assault on the avant-garde to a 1930 editorial in *Pravda* that warned of the "extremely harmful efforts ... to overcome in a single leap those barriers on the road to the socialist reconstruction of daily life that are rooted, on the one hand, in the economic and cultural backwardness of the country, and, on the other hand, in the necessity at the current moment to concentrate all resources on the rapid industrialization of the country" (O Rabote Po Perestroike Byta 1930: 3).

14. Thus, Hudson writes that "[t]he plan, published in the spring of that year, called for the construction of two hundred new industrial towns and some one thousand agricultural ones. Given this demand ... it is understandable that a major debate regarding theoretical concepts, planning schemes, and design developed within the architectural community and in the press at large" (Hudson 1994: 62). For Kopp these projects presented Soviet urbanists with a problem that was to remain "essentially theoretical" for urbanists elsewhere until after World War II: that of the "deliberate, planned construction of new cities on virgin land" (Kopp 1970: 164).

15. The relevant section of the Communist Academy was, at the time, linked to members of OSA (Glazychev 1989).

16. The reference, evidently, was to official interventions in architecture—the *Pravda* editorial on the reconstruction of daily life (see note 13, p. 260) was ominously reprinted just above the editors' comments.

17. "Between the urbanism of Ginzburg and the de-urbanism of Okhitovich there are considerably more similarities than differences" (Paperny 2002: 37). See also Meerovich 2007.

18. According to Glazychev (1989), the Central Committee decree on the reconstruction of daily life was already written when this conference took place, but was unknown to the participants.

19. Khmel'nitskii points out that although Miliutin played a quite prominent role in architecture in the late 1920s and early 1930s, he is a mysterious, poorly understood, and somewhat paradoxical figure. His concept of the linear city and his book *Sotsgorod* are among the better-known contributions of the architectural avant-garde (Khmel'nitskii 2007). But he did not refrain from the more vulgar attacks on the avant-garde in the early 1930s (e.g., Miliutin 1932).

20. See, for example, Bater 1980: 26.

21. See also Glazychev 1989.

22. Similarly, Shaw notes that the urban planning simply became a "device to support industrialization" (Shaw 1991: 127).

23. See also Starr 1971; Hudson 1994; Kotkin 1995; Hoffmann 2003.

24. For a discussion of Miliutin's evolution, see Collins and Sprague 1974.

25. For discussion of the relationship between regional planning and city plans, see Baranov 1962: 47.

26. See, for example, Kotkin 1993a.

27. This attack on "statistical" methods echoed attacks on the genetic planners, many of whom employed sophisticated statistical techniques: "In line with

the 'liquidationist tradition' [i.e., of the early Bukharin], the official position was that the science of statistics, i.e., the discipline studying unorganized mass data and random phenomena, was incompatible with the orderly processing and collation of information of a centrally planned economy. Thus the very word 'statistics' was banned" (Treml 1969: 198).

28. "The population as the source of wealth, as a productive force, and disciplinary supervision are all of a piece within the thought, project, and political practice of the mercantilists" (Foucault 2007: 69).

29. Quoted in Colton 1995: 253.

30. This was the Section for Socialist Settlement and for the Construction of Housing and Daily Life (*Zhilishchno-Bytovogo Stroitel'stva*) of the Institute of Economics in the Communist Academy.

31. This is not to say that architects had no role in these other areas. In fact, the journals of the time are filled with designs for clubs and houses of culture and even for factories. But they were reduced to purely architectural concerns, and were detached from problems of settlement or the revolution in daily life as the avant-garde of the 1920s had conceived it.

32. For a discussion, see Buchli 1999.

33. As David Hoffman (2003) has pointed out, this was hardly a consensus position at any point. But the invocation of these extreme positions in the charged atmosphere of 1931 allowed Miliutin to pivot from the utopic problem of creating new kinds of people and new social relations to "processes of daily life."

34. Hoffman has analyzed a broader reinvestment in the institution of the family in the 1930s: "[n]ot only did [the Soviet government] see strong families as a means to maximize the birth rate, but they had come to believe the family could instill Soviet values and discipline in children, and thereby serve as an instrument of the state" (Hoffmann 2003: 106).

35. For another recent discussion of *khoziaistvo* and its companion term *khoziain*, see Rogers 2006.

36. Oxford English Dictionary, online edition (dictionary.oed.com), accessed February 21, 2010.

37. According to Glazychev, the work on "complexes" during the 1920s was among the relatively few innovations of urban planning of that period (Glazychev 1989).

CHAPTER FOUR: CITY-BUILDING IN BELAYA KALITVA

1. On the development of planning institutes in the early 1930s, see Iiun'skii Plenum TsK VKP(b) Ob Organizatsii Gorodskogo Khoziaistva 1931: 2. On planning efforts in large cities during this period, see Ruble 1993; Colton 1995; Kotkin 1995.

2. This growth was accounted for by large-scale reclassification of cities and by rural-urban migration (Bater 1980: 60).

3. For example, average housing per person in cities dropped in the period 1928 to 1952 from six to five square meters per person (Cattell 1976). See also Bater 1980 and Kotkin 1995.

4. In 1953, Parkins (1953: 98) reported that most city plans were produced by either *Giprogor* or another institute called *Gorstroiproekt* (see also Baranov 1962). By the 1970s, regional project institutes were proliferating and completing their own plans (see Shaw 1983; Shaw 1991; French 1995).

5. *Zavety Il'icha*, July 30, 1988.

6. Details of Belaya Kalitva's development prior to the 1960s are taken from the *Skhema Rasseleniia Beloi Kalitvy* (Leningrad, Rosglavinstroiproekt), and from issues of the local newspapers, *Metallurg* and *Zavety Il'icha*.

7. On this nested hierarchy of plans see Baranov 1962: 45–48; Shaw 1991: 396.

8. *Skhema Rasselenia Beloi Kalitvy*, Leningrad, Rosglavinstroiproekt, 1963.

9. On the shortage of regional planning institutes in the 1960s, see Baranov 1962.

10. On the inventory as a technique in the very different context of catastrophe modeling, see Collier 2008.

11. Literally "period of account"—the period for which planning calculations are made.

12. "City-forming production" might include universities or even leisure facilities, assuming that they had "extra-local" significance.

13. On city-forming personnel, see Berkhman, et al. 1977.

14. *"Predpriiatiia i organizatsii bytovogo obsluzhivaniia naseleniia"* (Klopotov 1969).

15. See also DiMaio 1974: 63. The problem of diffused executive authority for the implementation of plans was the topic of repeated administrative reforms. See Baranov 1962: 238–41; Cattell 1976.

16. *Zavety Il'icha*, July 13, 1987.

17. *Metallurg*, August 16, 1996.

18. Enterprises and local Soviets provided materials for such construction, and instructions for a limited number of standard designs were disseminated widely. See Blumenfeld 1942: 28; Sosnovy 1954.

19. *Zavety Il'icha*, July 1, 1988.

20. In 1940 only 4.6 percent of the urban population had gas hookups (Sosnovy 1954: 141).

21. Kotkin has noted that housing was a crucial medium through which "the relationship between individuals and the state was negotiated" (1993b: 174).

22. 1984 update to the Belaya Kalitva *General Plan*. Also see Bater 1986 on the urban *"obraz zhizni."*

23. Things were different in larger cities, where plans might focus on residential microregions that did not include industrial enterprises (Ruble 1990: 248).

24. *Zavety Il'icha*, July 31, 1987. A related point about Soviet city construction as a locus of shared historical experience has recently been made in Kharkhordin and Alapuro 2010.

25. For a discussion of *khoziain*, see Rogers 2006.

CHAPTER FIVE: CONSOLIDATION, STAGNATION, BREAKUP

1. On this shift, see Shaw 1983: 393. For a classic statement of the "bureau-cratic impersonalism" thesis, see Hough 1969. Notable examples of the revision that focus on local government include Taubman 1973 and Bater 1980.

2. Thus, for example, Bater wrote that "The Soviet city ... has been developed according to normative planning criteria. Because this is so, we have an oppor-tunity to assess how successful the planning process has been in terms of norm fulfillment" (1986: 96).

3. *Rodniki General'nyi Plan,* Lengiprogor, Leningrad, 1987.

4. "Once we add in variables capturing the differences in level of economic development and population among regions, the political attributes of a republic still show no correlation with success in the battle for funds" (Bahry 1987: 123).

5. See, for example, French 1995: 72–73.

6. The reasons for this slow growth were various: coal mines around the city continued to operate; in-migration from the countryside decelerated; and construction was slow at the "new" city-forming enterprise, which was to draw population to the city's central district.

7. Virtually all the "big" cities founded during the Soviet period were created during the early five-year plans. Virtually all the cities founded after World War II were small cities.

8.

TABLE 5.1
Size Structure of Russian Cities (Statisticheskii Ezhegodnik Rossii, Goskomstat, Moscow, 1999).

	1926	1939	1959	1970	1979	1991
0–99,000	7,481	12,639	20,480	23,451	24,563	27,510
(% of urban population)	(54%)	(41%)	(39%)	(34%)	(30%)	(29%)
100,000–499,000	2,807	10,080	15,459	23,316	26,791	28,900
	(20%)	(33%)	(30%)	(33%)	(32%)	(30%)
Urban residents	13,928	31,012	52,164	69,998	82,948	96,010

9. The question of whether the Soviet Union had an equivalent to the U.S. ag-glomeration has been discussed in the literature on Soviet urban geography. At the most, there were *industrial* agglomerations, meaning urban settlements with interlinked industrial processes. What did *not* exist (with a few exceptions) were urban agglomerations of the U.S. type in which populations spread over many municipalities were integrated into common labor pools. The Soviet small city was, in this sense, entirely different from the American suburb. It was dependent on industrial production and integrated into the national economy, but relatively autonomous as a unit of need fulfillment—that is, as a *khoziaistvo.* Lappo, who makes a similar argument about the Soviet "agglomeration," points out that for

this reason even many medium-sized Russian cities may be best seen as big "small cities" (Lappo 2001).

10. The decline of U.S. textile towns began at the very beginning of the twentieth century.

11. Data from Freeze 2002: 458.

12. Quoted in Kaser 1964: 145.

13. "In short the steel plant was not really a business; rather, it was an industrial welfare agency" (Kotkin 1991: 17–18).

14. Though it did so at increasing cost, as in the massive resettlement to the far north connected to oil and gas development in northwest Siberia (Collier 2001).

15. "[A]bout 5 percent of the Soviet population moved annually with less than half of those moves between republics or economic regions. The 5 percent figure places mobility in the Soviet Union well below that of developed countries. [T]he Soviet figure is strikingly low when compared to the 17.5 percent of workers in the US and the 9.6 percent in Great Britain who changed place of residence during an average year" (Mitchneck and Plane 1995: 272).

16. Belaya Kalitva, where the "new" enterprise was a machine-building enterprise, was an exception.

17. *Korrektirovki po Skheme Raionnoi Planirovki Ivanovskoi Oblasti*, Goskom po Grazhdanstroiu, TsNIIP Gradostroitel'stvo, Moscow, 1976.

18. Interview, General Director, RUP, December 17, 1999. RUP is an acronym for the meaningless name *Rodnikovskoe Upravlenie Predpriiatii* (Rodniki Administration of Enterprises).

19. *Rodnikovskii Rabochii*, October 31, 1991.

20. In other cities of Rostov *oblast'* these "second" enterprises became important industrial concerns. Of particular importance were textile enterprises in coal cities, which flourished after the 1998 devaluation and supported many cities in which the coal industry simply vanished.

21. For this reason, textile enterprises were unable to pursue one of the major defensive strategies of the 1990s: reestablishing old supply chains within Russia. For a discussion, see Clarke 2004.

22. *Rodnikovskii Rabochii*, September 12, 1991, March 31, 1992, April 18, 1992.

23. Interview, January 26, 2000.

24. On the aluminum sector in post-Soviet Russia, see Sokolov and Iagol'nitser 1997.

25. Many observers argued that production declines were overstated by enterprises as a means to avoid taxes, and that, given overstatement of Soviet production, the drop-off was less than official statistics indicated (Schleifer and Treisman 2004).

26. *Perekrestok*, December 10, 1992.

27. Ibid.

28. On the transfer of social assets, see Healey, et al. 1999.

29. *Rodnikovskii Rabochii*, February 6, 1999.

30. Ibid.

31. This shift in the relationship between enterprise management and the social sphere was by no means universal: "In several enterprises the remaining

'unproductive' social and welfare facilities have been handed over to the municipality, or spun off into separate enterprises. However, in almost every case the traditional social and welfare benefits and social guarantees, much reduced during the 1990s, have been retained and in some cases even enhanced" (Clarke 2004: 413).

32. Tat'iana Govorenkova (1989) wrote an article by this name raising many of the issues discussed here.

33. "Politika 'vygody' diktuet khoziaev." *Perekrestok.* February 25, 2000. Through machinations involving a local branch of a regional bank, BKMPO managed to exempt itself from local payroll taxes.

34. Interview, Economic Director, BKMPO, June 1999.

35. *Constitution of the Russian Federation,* article 130.

36. *Russian Federation, Law on Local Self-Government,* article 1.1.

37. *Russian Federation, Law on Local Self-Government,* article 2.

38. Although some of these functions were officially assigned to local governments during the Soviet period, they had little autonomy in carrying them out, particularly in small cities (Taubman 1973).

39. The question of citizen mobilization around urban issues has been poignantly taken up in the context of early twenty-first century Russia in Kharkhordin 2010.

Part II: Neoliberalism and Social Modernity

1. For a discussion of these prior plans, see Aslund 2000.

2. The prior 500-day plan, formulated by Russian economists, "had made no presumption that [western] aid was either necessary or sufficient for transforming the Soviet Union into a free and prosperous nation" (Dorn 1991: 187).

3. On this assumption that postsocialist transformation could be hung on the shoulders of "neoliberalism," see Kogut and Spicer 2004; Ganev 2005.

4. Polanyi 2001. Examples of work on post-Soviet transformation in Russia that have powerfully drawn on the Polanyian framework, include Burawoy and Verdery 1999b; Woodruff 1999; Reddaway and Glinski 2001.

5. Along with the analyses in the following chapters, see Collier and Way 1999.

6. Some authors suggest that structural adjustment continues to be pursued under Putin (Reddaway and Glinski 2001). My point is not that it has been abandoned, but that it has changed.

7. This critique has been advanced in Kogut and Spicer 2004 and Ganev 2005.

8. Thus, Plehwe (2009a) has recently argued that many aspects of the Washington Consensus can be traced back to the neoliberalism of the Mt. Pelerin Society. His point, it seems, is that contrary to Williamson's claims, the Washington Consensus is thereby "really" neoliberal.. My analysis, by contrast, understands the Washington Consensus as a historically situated ensemble of practices, styles of reasoning, institutional developments, and economic processes. The stakes of my analysis are thus not to tie any particular historical experience to a "real" neoliberalism, but to make the forms of neoliberalism as a kind of critique and programming available for inquiry.

CHAPTER SIX: ADJUSTMENT PROBLEMS

1. The assumption that structural adjustment defines the essence of neoliberalism is made by both critical scholars (Toye 1987; Mosley, et al. 1991; Rapley 1996; Wedel 1998; Harvey 2005; Klein 2007) and by authors more sympathetic to neoliberalism (Dorn 1991; Yergin and Stanislaw 1998).

2. Although the term "structural adjustment" is thus not new, a JStor search indicates that use of the term exploded in the 1980s.

3. Kapur et al. note that this meaning was in wide informal use at the World Bank in the 1970s (Kapur, et al. 1997: ff105, 509).

4. On the socialist calculation debates, see Bockman and Eyal 2002. On development discussions at the Mt. Pelerin Society, see Plehwe 2009b. On development thinking in Chicago economics, see Strassman 1976 and Overtveldt 2007.

5. On this literature see Rapley 1996 and Toye 1987.

6. Some authors dispute this point, arguing that the strong ideological turn to a "counterrevolutionary" position took place *before* the shift to adjustment lending (e.g., Mosley, et al. 1991). But other interpreters have emphasized the contingent and pragmatic character of structural adjustment when it first emerged. Thus Rapley argues "One could liken the early experiments with adjustment to the early experiments with ISI. Both were responses to circumstances that were not necessarily thought to be long term, and neither was necessarily linked to an overarching and radically new vision of what development should entail" (Rapley 1996: 63). A similar argument is made in the authoritative study by Kapur, et al. 1997: 511.

7. See in particular Kapur et al. 1997 and Boughton 2001.

8. At the same time, the increasing volume of private finance capital meant that the IMF was no longer required to provide short-term credit to grease the wheels of global trade.

9. The first was the IMF Trust Fund, formed in 1976, followed in 1979 by a similar fund at the Bank. The sale of the IMF's gold stocks—no longer needed following the abandonment of the gold standard—was used to capitalize the first concessional lending facility (Boughton 2001: 19).

10. Stern later recalled that "When we started ... we were quite naïve about just how profoundly distorted the development strategies of many of the developing countries were. ... The problem had been neglected not only in our own analysis but also in much of the economic literature of the time" (Stern 1991: 1).

11. "The precipitous decline in production ... was one of the most underestimated consequences of the crisis associated with orthodox stabilization programs" (Kapur, et al. 1997: 611).

12. This shift in emphasis was found at both the World Bank and the IMF (World Bank 1988a: 23; Boughton 2001: 44).

13. This new emphasis on domestic governance has been regarded critically by careful observers of the IFIs. Thus, Kapur et al. observe that "[d]uring this period the [World Bank's] eloquence on policy failures by developing countries ... was remarkable. However, the simultaneous prudence demonstrated by the institution with regard to the international causes of the debt problem appears in retrospect to be equally remarkable" (Kapur, et al. 1997: 622).

14. From this new perspective, the initial response of some developing countries to the debt crisis seemed profoundly contradictory.

> Some developing countries postponed domestic policy reforms, or introduced them only slowly, and relied instead on increased external borrowing. In others, government sought to offset constraints imposed by external factors or uncertainty on the part of private investors through increased deficit financing to expand public sector investment programs. But as economic activity slowed down, and external capital flows ... became less buoyant, the costs of such partial adjustments became increasingly severe. This was reflected in growing expenditures on subsidies and in unsustainable budget deficits. To limit inflation and control the balance of payments deficit, some of the countries then resorted to price controls and import restrictions, which led to a misallocation of resources and to an incentive system biased against exporters (Stern 1983: 88).

On the genealogy of "vulnerability," see Collier 2008 and Collier and Lakoff 2008.

15. See also Boughton 2001: 24.

16. This question was considered particularly crucial as economic liberalization shifted from authoritarian to democratic countries.

17. On these connections in Chile, see Valdés 1995; in Eastern Europe, see Bockman and Eyal 2002.

18. For example, Oberstfeld 1994. In this light, the position of key Chicago figures—particularly Milton Friedman—who were skeptical of governments' ability to manage economic crises (including currency crises) should be *contrasted* with the position held by key architects of structural adjustment—particularly Cambridge-area economists including Lawrence Summers, Stanley Fischer, Kenneth Rogoff, and Jeffrey Sachs—who advocated massive government *intervention*. The Cambridge-centrism of economic thinking about postsocialist transition has been noted (Murrell 1995; Kogut and Spicer 2004) but I am not aware of an analysis that has examined the division between "Chicago" and "Cambridge" as a fundamental fissure that divides two groups usually considered "neoliberal."

19. See, e.g., Yergin and Stanislaw 1998; Harvey 2005; Klein 2007.

20. Here I adapt the phrase "development apparatus" from Ferguson 1994.

21. An extensive literature examined the applicability of structural adjustment to the Soviet cases (e.g., Corbo 1991).

22. For example, Russian reformers pushed a more rapid pace of liberalization and privatization than had been proposed by the IFIs (Kogut and Spicer 2005; Bockman and Eyal 2002).

23. For contrasting perspectives on the role of external consultants, see Wedel 1998 and Boycko et al. 1995.

24. On this early alignment of political forces, see Reddaway and Glinski 2001.

25. The "all-powerful" claim is found in Bockman and Eyal 2002.

26. According to Sachs, international aid organizations delivered only $3 billion of an announced $19 billion of support in 1992–1993.

27. Nonetheless, to call Sachs a market Bolshevik (e.g., Reddaway and Glinski 2001) is to fail to make distinctions among things that are obviously different.

28. Koeberle advances an argument about structural adjustment that is consistent with my basic claim in this chapter: "Criticisms of conditionality often claim that a standard blueprint—presumably based on the Washington consensus—is used in all borrowing countries regardless of their circumstances. Although the Bank's current operational policy contains prescriptive passages, this interpretation ignores the profound changes in World Bank policy-based lending over the past two decades" (Koeberle 2005: 62).

29. In examining *TMTV* here, I do not advance any specific claim concerning its influence—although many elements of the reform program it presented were central to government policy by the early 2000s. It is significant because it shows how the problem of structural adjustment was modified as it moved beyond the basic tasks of stabilization and liberalization.

30. For a similar review of developments during this period, see Odling-Smee 2004.

31. Italics in the original.

32. "Monetization" meant reducing the deficit by creating money.

33. John Dawson notes that flow of funds analyses should be contrasted to formal models in academic economics that combine "more and more theory with less and less fact" (Dawson 1996: 5).

34. On "work without wages," see Desai and Idson 2001. For analyses of barter in industry as a mechanism of preservation, see Woodruff 1999 and Nesvetailova 2004.

35. Comparative studies have also demonstrated that Soviet *enterprises* were not particularly "huge," at least not by the standards of late twentieth century or early twenty-first-century capitalism. Soviet gigantism lives on, largely as a myth.

36. Thus, a series of studies examined the "cost of the cold" (e.g., Mikhailova 2005).

37. The contrast with Russia's desperate circumstances of a decade ago is striking, but perhaps the most consequential change has hardly been noticed: [policy] choices are no longer being made in response to the demands and reproaches of other governments and international financial organizations. Disagreements on such matters often dominated Russia's relations with major Western countries in the 1990s. Today they no longer burden these relationships—they are, for the most part, no longer even discussed. To its own and others' relief, Russia makes these decisions—often wisely, sometimes not—on its own (Council on Foreign Relations 2006: 11).

CHAPTER SEVEN: BUDGETS AND BIOPOLITICS

1. Weber 1978: 11.

2. Departments in the Rostov regional government are, atypically, called ministries.

3. Russia has a single tax collecting authority that shares revenues among local, regional, and federal levels of government according to what are called "tax assignments."

4. Her reference is to the system of tax assignments (see prior note).

5. Interview, head of budget office, Belaya Kalitva, June 14, 1999.

6. For a comprehensive review of both developments, see Webber and Wildavsky 1986.

7. In principle local budget offices were subject to "dual' control by local soviets and the Ministry of Finance. In fact, the Ministry of Finance played a dominating role in planning local revenues and expenditures. For overviews of the Soviet budgetary system, see Taubman 1973; Lewis 1976, 1983; Bahry 1987; Way 2001.

8. Lewis observes that this system worked with two distinct conceptions of revenue. "*The total revenue* [revenue$_2$] *appears generally independent of actual revenue sources* [local tax collection—revenue$_1$], with adjustments made to keep revenues within the established norms" (1976: 10, italics in original).

9. In the Soviet period, modification of assignments rather than interbudgetary transfers was the predominant mechanism for adjusting the resources available to local governments (Bahry 1987).

10. See discussion, chapter 5.

11. Information provided by Rostov Oblast' Ministry of Finance, 1998.

12. In principle, regional governments could also adjust sharing rates, making the significance of data about absolute transfers hard to assess. Analyses of total net transfers taking all these factors into account have been conducted by Lavrov and Makushkin 2000.

13. "Expenditure shifting" from military and industrial subsidies to social protection was a key tenet of the Washington Consensus (Williamson 1990).

14. Interview, head of budget office, City of Donetsk, Rostov *oblast'*, May 25, 1999.

15. According to budgetary officials in each city, of locally collected revenues, only 33 percent and 41 percent in Rodniki and Belaya Kalitva, respectively, was collected in cash.

16. Although it has a different status as an "off-budget" item of expenditure—and, thus, is not organized through the Ministry of Finance—a similar logic could be found in the system of pension payments. Here, too, a small percentage of local "requirements" (referring to the volume of monthly pension liabilities in a given locality) were raised from local taxes. Here, too, regional pension offices acted to "fill the gap" between local resources and requirements. Transfers accounted for 80 percent of pension expenditures in both Rodniki and Belaya Kalitva (Collier 2001: 206).

17. The literature on this topic distinguishes between offsets—settlements of mutual debts—and barter, referring to a "natural" exchange requiring a mutual coincidence of wants (see Desai and Idson 2001).

18. For a review of Buchanan's oeuvre, see Borcherding 2002 and, in a more critical vein, Amadae 2003.

19. On this distinction, see Mirowski 1984.

20. "A common denominator is necessary as a starting point in order that any one 'configuration of the economic system' may be regarded as better or worse than any other, or indifferent" (Buchanan 1949: 496–97).

21. Arthur Cecil Pigou was a British neoclassical economist and major figure in public economics. Frank Knight, Buchanan's graduate advisor at Chicago, attacked Pigou for his assumptions about a benevolent unitary state, thus anticipating Buchanan's arguments.

22. Pigou's *reformulation* of the equilibrium condition as an ideal for government allocation of resources should be compared to Oscar Lange's work on the optimization of a planned economy. On the other side, Buchanan's *rejection* of the equilibrium construct as an approach to thinking about public value was consistent with a critique running from Ludwig von Mises to Milton Friedman. In this sense Buchanan's critique of Pigou reprised a neoliberal argument that could be traced from the socialist calculation debates.

23. Pigou wrote that "[i]f a community were literally a unitary being, with the government as its brain, expenditures and taxes could be pushed up to the point where marginal benefits and costs are equal" (quoted in Musgrave 1969: 797).

24. For a similar assessment of the evolution of the economics of public finance, see Musgrave (ibid.).

25. Various approaches to accounting for the "benefit" side of the fiscal balance have been articulated.

26. Foucault (2008) documented the Weberian influence on the German ordo-liberals, and Overtveldt (2007) has documented the profound Weberian influence on Frank Knight and the pre–World War II Chicago School.

27. On "methodological-ontological individualism," see Buchanan 1975. It should be underlined that for Buchanan this individualism entailed no psychological or anthropological assumptions about whether individuals were "really" rationally self-interested (Buchanan and Tullock 1962: 1).

28. Other contemporary commentaries on these developments and their implications for federalism include Carey 1938 and Benson 1941. George Stigler (1965 [1957]) also wrote on questions of federalism and the social state.

29. As Boadway points out, in this individualist perspective "social welfare maximization may entail that like persons in different regions are treated differently" precisely because they have divergent preferences (Boadway 2003: 4).

30. For a detailed exposition of the claim that "fiscal equity" also implies significant interpersonal equalization, see Oates 1968: 47.

31. Boadway is a Canadian economist who has been involved in discussions of Canadian federalism and in broad discussions of fiscal federal theory. Anwar Shah has worked on Canadian fiscal federal issues but also written extensively for the World Bank on equalizing transfers. Martinez-Vazquez is a researcher at the Georgia State University (U.S.) Fiscal Research Center. Kurlyandskaya is the head of the Russian Center for Fiscal Policy and a leading Russian expert on fiscal federalism.

32. On the U.S. federalism crisis, see Porter and Porter 1974. On the Canadian experience, see Shah 1994.

33. Recent reviews of the field include Oates 1999 and Boadway 2003. Oates (1968) notes that in contrast to discussions of political federalism—which refer

to a narrow range of cases—fiscal federalism refers to any system in which there is some distribution of resources, choices, and responsibilities among levels of government.

34. See also World Bank 1988b: 154, 157.

35. Enterprises, too, could be analyzed as they make locational decisions based on the "fiscal package" that suits them.

36. The Samuelson-Musgrave position diverged from Pigou in crucial respects. Samuelson and Musgrave both accepted the proposition that it was individual preferences rather than some function of collective welfare that should—in principle—be maximized. Samuelson noted that he did not assume any "mystical collective mind that enjoys collective consumption goods" (1954: 387). Meanwhile, Musgrave wrote that "the community is not a unitary being, and benefits must be valued ... in terms of the preferences of consumers" (1969: 797). The problem lay in defining some mechanism for efficiently "revealing" individual preferences. What Tiebout and others noticed is that despite the "individualist" bases of his assumptions, Samuelson ended up quite close to Pigou, but for practical rather than conceptual reasons. As Samuelson wrote, "[g]iven sufficient knowledge the optimal decisions can always be found by scanning over all the attainable states of the world and selecting the one which according to the postulated ethical welfare function is best. The solution 'exists'; the problem is how to 'find' it." Musgrave tried to meet this challenge by developing sophisticated techniques of cost-benefit analysis that did, indeed, assume a general welfare function. The great parsimony of Buchanan's approach, by contrast, is derived from the fact that it takes the benefit side into account without having to determine individual utilities.

37. They were "autonomous" in the sense that their actions are not dictated by a central government, not in the sense that they are outside the state.

38. On the shift in economic thinking about public finance toward the position articulated, in different ways, by Buchanan and Tiebout, see Quigly and Rubinfeld 1986.

39. On the scalar distribution of functions in fiscal federal theory, see Oates 1999: 1120. Oates observes that some foreign advisors to the postsocialist countries took up fiscal federalism as simply a prescription for decentralization, but that this advice fundamentally misinterpreted the lessons of fiscal federal theory.

40. As liberal economists have recognized since the British Poor Laws, local redistribution creates a host of distortions.

41. In the area of equalization transfers, some important developments can be traced to the early 1990s (e.g., Shah 1994). Nonetheless, in 2004 Boadway observed that the economics literature on equalization was "surprisingly dormant" (2004: 11). A significant amount of work on grants is found in subsequent years (e.g., the chapters in Martinez-Vazquez and Searle 2007b).

42. The report noted that research into the effect of a larger or smaller state had been inconclusive and that emphasis should be placed on directing state activity to those areas where it could provide goods more efficiently and equitably than the market rather than on questions concerning the size of the state per se (World Bank 1988b: 51).

43. In this and other respects these countries faced circumstances similar to those Buchanan observed much earlier in the United States. Central government

budgets in developing countries grew from around 5 percent of GDP at the end of the colonial period to well over 20 percent of GDP by the 1970s; subnational governments made the public sector share even larger (ibid.).

44. For subsequent formulations of fiscal equity that echo Buchanan, see Le Grand 1975: 532 and Bird and Vaillancourt 2007: 260. Recent reviews of this literature recognize Buchanan's early papers as seminal in the field (Shah 1994; Boadway 2003; Bird and Vaillancourt 2007).

45. Callon's analytics of framing is indistinguishable from Max Weber's definition of the substantive prerequisites of formal rationalization (Weber 1978). In his discussion of the capitalist enterprise, Weber noted three requirements for formal rationalization: first, the clear definition of distinct decision-making units; second, the formal freedom of these units; third, a system of valuation that clearly defines the benefits, costs, and opportunity costs of choices made by these units. Similar formulations are conventional in economics as well, for example the quote from Samuelson in note 36, p. 271.

46. According to Kurlyandskaya and Golovanova (2006: 216–17) the system of intergovernmental transfers was among the first areas to undergo significant changes.

47. See Ministry of Finance 1999, 2000a, 2000b. Observers of Russian fiscal reforms saw this process as critical in reformulating regional fiscal federal relations (Martinez-Vazquez, et al. 2006: 150). All of these documents were technically "recommendations" because, under the constitution, it was the prerogative of regional governments to dictate the structure of interbudgetary relationships at the local level.

48. This was particularly problematic given the Russian system of tax sharing (see note 3, p. 269), since a "permissive" attitude to tax collection at the local level reduces regional and federal tax collection as well.

49. The fiscal federalism literature refers to "cost/benefit spillovers" (Shah 1996), a concept that is closely related to Callon's "overflowing" (Callon 1998a).

50. A third principle mentioned in *Recommendations* is the principle of "maximal effectiveness," which relates to the economies or diseconomies of centralized provision (*Zapiska*, 54).

51. Italics original. *Zapiska*, 12.

52. Precisely this apparent correspondence between political autonomy and economic rationality made decentralized government an attractive solution to the problems of the social state for Buchanan, Stigler, and other neoliberals.

53. This principle is repeated in a variety of formulations. Although I cannot justify the point here, I would argue that all ultimately amount to roughly the same thing.

54. *Obespechennost'* usually refers to material provisioning or the "security" of that provisioning. Thus, its meaning is usually *substantive*. Here it is formal, referring to the ratio between available resources and expenditure requirements.

55. A more complete discussion would address the "representative system of taxation" proposed in the report, parallel to the representative system of expenditures examined in the text.

56. As Freinkman et al. put it, "The formulae are very advanced and complicate because they intend to consider many aspects of the 'need' of regions" (2009: 5, n. 2).

57. Anwar Shah (1994) proposed this device as a correlate to an existing representative system of taxation.

58. "*Uslovnyi*" might be more directly translated as "hypothetical" or "normalized." In this context, however, "standardized" better communicates the sense of the term. This is a different Russian word than the one used in the subsequent phrase—"*standartnyi*" (*Zapiska*, 90).

59. In fact, all of these equations are calculated in per capita terms. I leave this factor out for the sake of simplicity.

60. Thus, for 2000 they are found in *Metodika Raspredeleniia Sredstv Fonda Finansovoi Podderzhki Sub"ektov Rossiiskoi Federatsii na 2000 g.*

61. In the medium term, notes *Recommendations*, this approach would "make it possible to equalize the access that populations of different municipalities have to basic budgetary services [*k bazovym biudzhetnym uslugam*]" (*Vremennye Rekomendatsii*, 13).

62. The less equalizing variant may *not* meet Buchanan's standard of fiscal equity if it does not transfer sufficient funds such that all local governments could pay for equal levels of services at equal rates of taxation.

63. On this point my argument should be contrasted with Amadae (2003), who claims that for Buchanan formal equations somehow dictated the proper orientations and policy choices of government. In the case under consideration here, precisely the opposite is true. Buchanan proposed formula-based distribution *precisely* as a mechanism to pursue equalization *without* making political decisions that he considered to be the proper function of democratically elected government—preferably local government.

64. They continue: "While implementation varies by region, generally it merely 'repackages' the Soviet gap-filling approach" (Martinez-Vazquez, et al. 2006: 147).

65. The tension between this development and the assumptions of fiscal federal theory has been emphasized in Freinkman et al. 2009.

66. For recent analyses of the level of equalization that results from both federal-regional and regional-local interbudgetary systems in Russia, see Martinez-Vazquez and Timofeev 2008 and De Silva et al. 2009.

CHAPTER EIGHT: THE INTRANSIGENCE OF THINGS

1. UNDP/World Bank 2000: 17.
2. World Bank 2003: 5.
3. Interview, January 16, 2000.
4. The *teploset'* in Belaya Kalitva has over 110 kilometers of heat pipes. *Statisticheskii Sbornik. Kommunal'noe Khoziaistvo Rostovskoi Oblasti za 1994–1997 gody* (Rostov-on-Don: Goskomstat Rossii, Rostovskii Oblastnoi Komitet Gosudarstvennoi Statistiki, 1998).

5. The major exception is the Far East, where heat boilers mostly run on coal.

6. On the this episode, see Wines 2001; Humphrey 2003.

7. See also Bowker and Star 1999.

8. On the social welfare aims of GOELRO, see Coopersmith 1992.

9. *Narodnoe Khoziaistvo SSSR*, Moscow, 1987.

10. In English they are called Combined Heat-Power or CHP units.

11. Pumps were used to maintain pressure, but in general they were not designed to serve as control points.

12. A similar point has been made by Bychkova 2010.

13. See also Brenner 2004.

14. Debts did accumulate, but not nearly at the rate they would have had tariffs approached those that Gazprom could have fetched on the European market.

15. This number includes direct subsidies, cross-subsidies, and accumulated debts.

16. Here, of course, I draw on the perspective of Actor-Network Theory.

17. On the transfer of "social assets," see Kabalina and Sidorina 1999, Leksin and Shvetsov 1999.

18. With the transfer of housing, the balance of this mutual obligation swung decisively in favor of enterprises in many small cities, resulting in mounting debts of local governments to enterprises. Thus, in Rodniki, where housing was transferred in mid-1998, we see the following picture:

TABLE 8.2.
Heat Payments in Rodniki, 1998, 1999

	1998 (1/2 yr.)	1999	Total
Heat purchased by the city from Rodtekst (kcal)	34,566	109,791	144,357
Heat purchased by the city from Rodtekst (rubles)	6,058,226	20,303,565	26,361,791
Payments by local government to Rodtekst (rubles)		11,552,856	11,552,856
Debts of local government to Rodtekst (rubles)	6,058,226	8,750,709	14,808,935

A similar situation was found in Belaya Kalitva (*Belo-Kalitvinskii Metallurg*, February 18, 2000) and elsewhere, as the Russian sociologist Ol'ga Fadeeva (personal communication) confirmed to me. See also Shtop 1997.

19. Storper referred to the "nexus of untraded interdependencies" that bind high-tech firms together in high-cost areas of the world economy. Though the context could not be more different, the concept of untraded interdependencies seems valuable in describing the Russian case.

20. On Georgia, see Collier and Way 2004.

21. Other problems with pricing under natural monopoly include discriminatory or predatory pricing (see Berg and Tschirhart 1988: 2).

22. This argument can be traced to Adam Smith, who referred to the problems of "great public works, which, though they may be in the highest degree advantageous to a great society," would be unlikely to be provided privately (cited in Bychkova 2010: 80).

23. See also Strassman 1976.

24. Thus, in his *A Positive Program for Laissez Faire* (1949), Henry Simons expressed deep concern with natural monopoly problems, and argued in favor of public ownership in some cases. Simons was seen as conservative at the time, but did not look so in light of later developments.

25. Foucault's discussion refers to Wilhelm Ropke, Alexander Rustow, Walter Eucken, and Ludwig von Mises, among others.

26. Trebing was a Wisconsin institutionalist, a key exponent of the "public interest" approach to regulation, and a persistent critic of the Chicago position on regulation. For his account of the Chicago School position on regulation, see Trebing 1976.

27. Accounts of Stigler's life and work include Stigler 1988; Peltzman 1993; Overtveldt 2007. Other major Chicago figures made important contributions to the theory of regulation, including Frank Knight, Ronald Coase, Richard Posner, and Gary Becker, but it is most closely associated with Stigler.

28. Overtveldt suggests that Stigler was on a par with Friedman in contributing "to the way in which economics at the University of Chicago developed between the early 1950s and the late 1970s" (Overtveldt 2007: 27).

29. McCraw was critical of the Chicago position, making his assessment of Stigler's importance all the more significant.

30. These assumptions of the public interest school are laid out in Peltzman 1993.

31. On the problems with Stigler and Friedland's study, see ibid. and McCraw 1976.

32. A similar observation has been made in subsequent surveys of literature (e.g., Winston 1985).

33. According to Peltzman Stigler privately held an extreme antipathy to regulation during the 1960s but his views were later moderated (Peltzman 1993).

34. Here, again, Stigler's position was close to Coase, who wrote that "government actions (such as government operation, regulation or taxation, including subsidies)" may indeed "produce a better result than relying on negotiations between individuals on the market. Whether this would be so could be discovered not by studying imaginary governments but what real governments actually do" (quoted in Overtveldt 2007: 208).

35. See, for example, Newbery 1999: 398.

36. Quoted in McCraw 1976: 300.

37. "Intermodal competition" refers to different ways of producing the same good, such as transportation services provided by rail or truck. "Competition for the market" refers to situations in which monopolistic positions

are routinely put up for competitive bidding. Technological change was significant because it meant that in many infrastructure sectors (telecommunications is an obvious example) new technologies undermine the position of monopolists.

38. See Horowitz 1989 for a critical review.

39. He is quoting James O. Wilson. In light of these observations one would have to question the frequent assumption that the infrastructure deregulation agenda was largely pro-corporate. In fact, deregulation was often championed by anti-corporate crusaders, and many corporations (indeed, entire industries) were hurt by deregulation. On the peculiar alignment of political forces favoring the deregulation movement in its early years, see Canedo 2008.

40. It was one of those loci of American postwar intellectual developments in which one could find academic economists and experts from private research groups such as the Bell Labs and the RAND Corporation.

41. The theory said that "contestability"—including competition *for* the market rather than *in* the market—rather than "competition" was the proper metric for thinking about the need for regulation.

42. Some critics suggest that Chicago economists of regulation were never deeply interested in improving regulation; they were primarily concerned with reducing it. Though this may have been true, one can find an enormous range of suggestions for new regulatory schemas in Chicago writing, and it is necessary to appreciate how Chicago thinkers cleared the conceptual grounds for a microeconomic programming of regulation.

43. In discussions of economic development, the word "infrastructure" seems to have become widespread only toward the end of the 1950s. By the 1960s it is ubiquitous. On some of the military contexts in which the term developed, see Collier and Lakoff 2008.

44. "[T]he purpose of an international program of aid to underdeveloped countries is to accelerate their economic development up to a point where a satisfactory rate of growth can be achieved on a self-sustaining basis. ... Thus the general aim of aid ... is to provide in each underdeveloped country a positive incentive for maximum national effort to increase its rate of growth" (Rosenstein-Rodan 1961: 107).

45. Choate was a prominent government economist who gained notoriety as the running mate of Ross Perot in the 1996 American Presidential elections

46. On different methods for assessing this relationship, see Gramlich 1994.

47. Gramlich 1994. The World Bank concluded a review of the literature as follows: "[W]hether infrastructure investment causes growth or growth causes infrastructure investment is not fully established. Moreover, there may be other factors driving the growth of both GDP and infrastructure that are not fully accounted for" (World Bank 1994: 14–15).

48. See also Winston and Bosworth 1992: 291.

49. "The poor often consume fewer infrastructure services and pay higher prices than do the non poor. For example, households obtaining water from vendors pay much more than those households connected to water systems" (World Bank 1994: 5–6).

50. For a more comprehensive analytics of "unbundling"—largely borrowed from the same World Bank report—see Graham and Marvin 2002.

51. As should be evident from prior discussions (for example in chapter 3), the problem is that "sector" does not capture the meaning of *khoziaistvo*.

52. One result of this cooperation is that World Bank and government proposals on reform during this period substantially converge, and World Bank comments on the government's program are strongly positive. For recent summaries of the reforms see Alexandrova and Struyk 2007; World Bank 2008; Bychkova and Popova 2010.

53. Of course the quality (and, in some cases, the quantity) of services declined precipitously. But as I have already argued, in cases like heat the overwhelming fact is that of preservation in the face of fiscal crisis.

54. According to a study of the Institute of Urban Economics, heating systems are among the best maintained urban infrastructures, but the percentage of material stock in a deteriorated condition was still estimated to be over 50 percent in the mid-2000s (Institute for Urban Economics n.d.: 5).

55. See for example *Kontseptsiia Reformy Zhilishchno-Kommunal'nogo Khoziaistva v Rossiiskoi Federatsii*. Approved by Presidential Decree, April 28, 1997.

56. Federal'noe Sobranie Rossiiskoi Federatsii. *Poiasnitel'nye Zapiski k Kontseptsii Federal'nogo Zakona "O Teplosnabzhenii,"* p. 1.

57. Studies have shown that, aside from a pause in 1998 that corresponded to the financial crisis, tariffs for communal services as a whole have risen in step with—though at a rate below—the federal standard for cost recovery, reaching 80 percent of officially determined costs. Cost recovery levels for heat have been significantly lower than those for the sector as a whole. See, for example, Institute for Urban Economics n.d.: 12.

58. "[R]apid increases in private investment are unlikely partially due to high investment risk, low profit potential, the lack of a solid legal and regulatory framework, and widespread political interference" (World Bank 2008: 3, 24).

59. In some new buildings, meters and valves are installed for individual apartments.

60. On homeowners associations, see also Vihavainen 2010.

61. For a discussion of these subsidies, see Alexandrova and Struyk 2007; Wengle and Rasell 2008.

62. Communal service providers were forced to accept discounted payments from users, but did not receive compensation.

63. My observation is that Russian officials always speak of the "population" (*naselenie*), which is generally understood as a subject of need. The concept of "public" in the complex sense of western political theory is basically missing from such discussions. For an excellent and multisided analysis of this issue, see the contributions to Kharkhordin 2010.

64. See also Institut Ekonomiki Goroda 2008; World Bank 2008: 22.

65. For a thoughtful analysis of monetary grants in the very different South African context, see Ferguson 2010.

66. On "actually existing neoliberalism," see Brenner and Theodore 2002.

67. On proposals for targeting, see Institut Ekonomiki Goroda 2008: 10.

EPILOGUE: AN INEFFECTIVE CONTROVERSY

1. Foucault 2008: 130.

2. Reprinted in Stigler 1975a: 13.

3. During the period in which Foucault was working on liberalism and neoliberalism, his dissatisfaction with left politics was growing (Eribon 1991).

4. Rodrick was referring to neoclassical economics, which many critical scholars—mysteriously—conflate with neoliberalism. The economics of Stigler and Buchanan is better understood as a reaction *against* a dominant neoclassicism.

5. On the flexibility and mobility of such "formal " mechanisms, see Collier and Ong 2005.

References

Agamben, Giorgio. 1998. *Homo Sacer: Sovereign Power and Bare Life*. Stanford, CA: Stanford University Press.

Alexandrova, Anastassia and Raymond Struyk. 2007. "Reform of in-Kind Benefits in Russia: High Cost for a Small Gain." *Journal of European Social Policy* 17, no. 2: 153–66.

Allison, Graham and Robert Blackwill. 1991. "America's Stake in the Soviet Future." *Foreign Affairs* 70, no. 3: 77–97.

Amadae, S. M. 2003. *Rationalizing Capitalist Democracy: The Cold War Origins of Rational Choice Liberalism*. Chicago: University of Chicago Press.

Anderson, Perry. 1979. *Lineages of the Absolutist State*. London: Verso.

Andrianov, Valentin, Sergei Sivaev et al. 2003. *Russia's Winter Woes: Tariff Setting for Local Utilities in a Transition Economy*. Washington, D.C.: Urban Institute.

Arendt, Hannah. 1998 [1958]. *The Human Condition*. Chicago: University of Chicago Press.

Aslund, Anders. 2000. *Russia and the International Financial Institutions*. Washington D.C.: Carnegie.

Averch, Harvey and Leland L. Johnson. 1962. "Behavior of the Firm under Regulatory Constraint." *American Economic Review* 52, no. 5: 1052–69.

Bahry, Donna. 1987. *Outside Moscow: Power, Politics, and Budgetary Policy in the Soviet Republics*. New York: Columbia University Press.

Baranov, N. V. 1962. *Sovremennoe Gradostroitel'stvo: Glavnye Problemy*. Moscow: Gosstroiizdat.

Bater, James H. 1980. *The Soviet City: Ideal and Reality*. London: E. Arnold.

———. 1986. "Some Recent Perspectives on the Soviet City." *Urban Geography* 7, no. 1: 93–102.

Baumol, William J. 1982. "Contestable Markets: An Uprising in the Theory of Industrial Structure." *American Economic Review* 72, no. 1: 1–15.

Beck, Ulrich. 1992. *Risk Society: Towards a New Modernity*. London: Sage.

Benson, George Charles Sumner. 1941. *The New Centralization: A Study of Intergovernmental Relationships in the United States*. New York: Farrar and Rinehart.

Berg, Sanford V. and John Tschirhart. 1988. *Natural Monopoly Regulation: Principles and Practice*. Cambridge: Cambridge University Press.

Berkhman, E. I., F. F. Diderikhs, and E. Iu. Faerman. 1977. "Gorod i Planirovanie Ego Razvitiia." In *Voprosy Planirovaniia Gorodskogo Razvitiia*. Moscow: Tsentral'nyi Ekonomiko-matematicheskii Institut.

Bhagwati, Jagdish N. 1984. "Comment on Raul Prebisch." In *Pioneers in Development*, edited by Gerald M. Meier and Dudley Seers. New York: Oxford University Press.

Bird, Richard and Francois Vaillancourt. 2007. "Expenditure-Based Equalization Transfers." In *Fiscal Equalization: Challenges in the Design of Intergovernmental Transfers*, edited by Jorge Martinez-Vazquez and R. J. Searle, 259–90. New York: Springer.

Blackwell, William L. 1968. *The Beginnings of Russian Industrialization, 1800–1860*. Princeton, NJ: Princeton University Press.

———. 1970. *The Industrialization of Russia: An Historical Perspective*. New York: Crowell.

———. 1986. "Modernization and Urbanization in Russia: A Comparative View." In *The City in Russian History*, edited by Michael F. Hamm, 291–330. Lexington: University Press of Kentucky.

Bliznakov, Milka Tcherneva. 1971. "The Search for a Style: Modern Architecture in the U.S.S.R., 1917–1932." Ph.D. diss., Columbia University, New York.

Blumenfeld, Hans. 1942. "Regional and City Planning in the Soviet Union." *Task* 3: 33–52.

Blumfield, William Craft. 1993. "Building for Comfort and Profit: The New Apartment House." In *Russian Housing in the Modern Age: Design and Social History*, edited by William Craft Brumfield and Blair A. Ruble. Cambridge: Cambridge University Press.

Boadway, Robin. 2004. "The Theory and Practice of Equalization." *CESifo Economic Studies* 50, no. 1: 211–54.

Boas, Taylor and Jordan Gans-Morse. 2009. "Neoliberalism: From New Liberal Philosophy to Anti-Liberal Slogan." *Studies in Comparative International Economic Development* 44, no. 2: 137–61.

Bockman, Johanna and Gil Eyal. 2002. "Eastern Europe as a Laboratory for Economic Knowledge: The Transnational Roots of Neoliberalism." *American Journal of Sociology* 108, no. 2: 310–52.

Borcherding, Thomas E. 2002. "The Contributions of James M. Buchanan to Public Finance and Political Economy." *Public Finance Review* 30, no. 6: 646–66.

Boughton, James M. 2001. *Silent Revolution: The International Monetary Fund, 1979–1989*. Washington, D.C.: International Monetary Fund.

Bourguignon, Francois. 2008. "Closing Remarks." In *Rethinking Infrastructure for Development. Annual World Bank Conference on Development Economics—Global*, edited by Francois Bourguignon and Boris Pleskovic. Washington D.C.: The World Bank.

Bowker, Geoffrey C. and Susan Leigh Star. 1999. *Sorting Things Out: Classification and Its Consequences*. Cambridge, MA: MIT Press.

Boycko, Maxim, Andrei Shleifer, and Robert W. Vishny. 1995. *Privatizing Russia*. Cambridge, MA: MIT Press.

Brenner, Neil. 2004. *New State Spaces: Urban Governance and the Rescaling of Statehood*. Oxford: Oxford University Press.

Brenner, Neil, Jamie Peck, and Nik Theodor. 2009. "Variegated Neoliberalization: Geographies, Modalities, Pathways." *Global Networks* 10, no. 2: 182–222.

Brenner, Neil and Nik Theodore. 2002. "Cities and the Geographies of 'Actually Existing Neoliberalism'." *Antipode* 34, no. 3: 349–79.

Breslauer, George W. 1978. "On the Adaptability of Soviet Welfare-State Authoritarianism." In *Soviet Society and the Communist Party*, edited by Karl W. Ryavec, 3–25. Amherst: University of Massachusetts Press.

Buchanan, James M. 1949. "The Pure Theory of Government Finance: A Suggested Approach." *The Journal of Political Economy* 57, no. 6: 496–505.

———. 1950. "Federalism and Fiscal Equity." *The American Economic Review* 40, no. 4: 583–99.

———. 1975. *The Limits of Liberty: Between Anarchy and Leviathan.* Chicago: University of Chicago Press.

Buchanan, James M. and Gordon Tullock. 1962. *The Calculus of Consent: Logical Foundations of Constitutional Democracy.* Ann Arbor: University of Michigan Press.

Buchli, Victor. 1999. *An Archaeology of Socialism.* Oxford: Berg.

Burawoy, Michael and Pavel Krotov. 1992. "The Soviet Transition from Socialism to Capitalism: Worker Control and Economic Bargaining in the Wood Industry." *American Sociological Review* 57, no. 1: 16–38.

Burawoy, Michael and Katherine Verdery. 1999a. "Introduction." In *Uncertain Transition: Ethnographies of Change in the Postsocialist World,* edited by Michael Burawoy and Katherine Verdery, 1–18. Lanham, Md.: Rowman & Littlefield.

———. 1999b. *Uncertain Transition: Ethnographies of Change in the Postsocialist World.* Lanham, Md.: Rowman & Littlefield.

Bychkova, Olga. 2010. "Categories of Goods in Economic and Public Choice Literature Applied to Heat and Water Utilities." In *Reassembling Res Publica: Reform of Infrastructure in Post-Soviet Russia,* edited by Oleg Kharkhordin and Risto Alapuro. London: Routledge.

Bychkova, Olga and Evgeniia Popova. 2010. "Things and People in the Housing and Utility Sector Reform in Russia, 1991–2006." In *Reassembling Res Publica: Reform of Infrastructure in Post-Soviet Russia,* edited by Oleg Kharkhordin and Risto Alapuro. London: Routledge.

Caiden, Naomi and Aaron Wildavsky. 1986. "The Poor and the Uncertain: Low-Income Countries." In *Budgeting: A Comparative Theory of Budgetary Processes* by Aaron Wildavsky. New Brunswick, NJ: Transaction Books.

Caldeira, Teresa and James Holston. 2005. "From Total Planning to Democratic Intervention." In *Global Assemblages: Technology, Politics, and Ethics as Anthropological Problems,* edited by Aihwa Ong and Stephen J. Collier. Malden, MA: Blackwell.

Callon, Michel. 1998a. "An Essay on Framing and Overflowing." In *The Laws of the Markets,* edited by Michel Callon. Malden, MA: Blackwell.

———. 1998b. "Introduction: The Embeddedness of Economic Markets in Economics." In *The Laws of the Markets,* edited by Michel Callon. Malden, MA: Blackwell.

Callon, Michel, Yuval Millo, and Fabian Muniesa. 2007. *Market Devices.* Oxford: Blackwell.

Canedo, Eduardo Frederico. 2008. The Rise of the Deregulation Movement in Modern America, 1957–1980. Ph.D. diss., Columbia University, New York.

Canguilhem, Georges. 1989. *The Normal and the Pathological.* New York: Zone Books.

Carey, Jane Perry Clark. 1938. *The Rise of a New Federalism: Federal-State Cooperation in the United States.* New York: Columbia University Press.

Carr, Edward Hallett. 1950. *The Bolshevik Revolution, 1917–1923 v.II.* London: Macmillan.

———. 1958. *Socialism in One Country, 1924–1926.* London: Macmillan.

Carr, Edward Hallett and R. W. Davies. 1969. *Foundations of a Planned Economy, 1926–1929.* London: Macmillan.

Cattell, David T. 1976. "Cities and Consumer Welfare Planning." In *The City in Russian History*, edited by Michael F. Hamm. Lexington: University Press of Kentucky.

Chandler, Alfred Dupont. 1977. *The Visible Hand: The Managerial Revolution in American Business*. Cambridge, MA: Belknap Press.

Chandra, N. K. 1967. "Long-Term Economic Plans and Their Methodology." *Soviet Studies* 18, no. 3: 296–313.

Chernyavsky, Andrei and Karen Vartapetov. 2004. "Municipal Finance Reform and Local Self-Governance in Russia." *Post-Communist Economies* 16, no. 3: 251–64.

Chirot, Daniel. 1991. "What Happened in Eastern Europe in 1989?" In *The Crisis of Leninism and the Decline of the Left: The Revolutions of 1989*, edited by Daniel Chirot. Seattle: University of Washington Press.

Choate, Pat and Susan Walter. 1981. *America in Ruins: Beyond the Public Works Pork Barrel*. Washington, D.C.: Council of State Planning Agencies.

Clark, Katrina. 1993. "Engineers of Human Souls in an Age of Industrialization: Changing Cultural Modes, 1929–41." In *Social Dimensions of Soviet Industrialization*, edited by William G. Rosenberg and Lewis H. Siegelbaum, 248–64. Bloomington: Indiana University Press.

Clarke, Simon. 2004. "A Very Soviet Form of Capitalism? The Management of Holding Companies in Russia." *Post-Communist Economies* 16, no. 4: 405–22.

Clifford, James. 1988. *The Predicament of Culture: Twentieth-Century Ethnography, Literature, and Art*. Cambridge, MA: Harvard University Press.

Cohen, Stephen F. 2001. *Failed Crusade: America and the Tragedy of Post-Communist Russia*. New York: W.W. Norton.

Cohen, Stephen S., Andrew Schwartz, and John Zysman. 1998. *The Tunnel at the End of the Light: Privatization, Business Networks, and Economic Transformation in Russia*. Berkeley, CA: International and Area Studies.

Colclough, Christopher. 1991. "Structuralism Versus Neoliberalism." In *States or Markets? Neo-Liberalism and the Development Policy Debate*, edited by Christopher Colclough and James Manor. Oxford: Oxford University Press.

Collier, Stephen J. 2001. "Post-Soviet City: The Government of Society in Neoliberal Times." Ph.D. diss., University of California, Berkeley.

———. 2005. "The Spatial Forms and Social Norms of 'Actually Existing Neoliberalism.'" Graduate Program in International Affairs Working Paper 2005–04. The New School. New York. www.gpia.info/files/u1/wp/2005-04.pdf.

———. 2008. "Enacting Catastrophe: Preparedness, Insurance, Budgetary Rationalization." *Economy and Society* 37, no. 2: 224–50.

———. 2009a. "*Reassembling the Social: An Introduction to Actor-Network Theory* (Review)." *Contemporary Sociology* 38, no. 1: 81–83.

———. 2009b. "Topologies of Power: Foucault's Analysis of Political Government Beyond 'Governmentality.'" *Theory, Culture, and Society* 26, no. 6: 78–108.

Collier, Stephen J. and Andrew Lakoff. 2005. "On Regimes of Living." In *Global Assemblages: Technology, Politics, and Ethics as Anthropological Problems*, edited by Aihwa Ong and Stephen J. Collier, 22–39. Malden, MA: Blackwell.

———. 2008. "The Vulnerability of Vital Systems: How Infrastructure Became a Security Problem." In *Securing 'the Homeland': Critical Infrastructure, Risk and (in)Security*, edited by Myriam Dunn and Kristian Soby Kristensen. London: Routledge.

Collier, Stephen J. and Aihwa Ong. 2005. "Global Assemblages, Anthropological Problems." In *Global Assemblages: Technology, Politics, and Ethics as Anthropological Problems*, edited by Aihwa Ong and Stephen J. Collier. Malden, MA: Blackwell.

Collier, Stephen J. and Lucan Way. 1999. *Preserving Social Institutions after Socialism: Fiscal Crisis and Local Government in Russia*. National Council for East European and Russian Research.

———. 2004. "Beyond the Deficit Model: Reflections on the Georgian Case." *Post Soviet Affairs* 20: 258–84.

Collins, George R. and Arthur Sprague. 1974. "Introduction." In *Sotsgorod: The Problem of Building Socialist Cities*, by Nikolai Miliutin. Cambridge, MA: MIT Press.

Colton, Timothy J. 1995. *Moscow: Governing the Socialist Metropolis*. Cambridge, MA: Belknap.

"Coming Soon: Shock Therapy II." 2001. *Jamestown Monitor* 7, no. 121.

Cooke, Catherine. 1995. *Russian Avant-Garde: Theories of Art, Architecture, and the City*. London: Academy Editions.

Coopersmith, Jonathan. 1992. *The Electrification of Russia, 1880–1926*. Ithaca, NY: Cornell University Press.

Corbo, Vittorio. 1991. *Report on Adjustment Lending II: Lessons for Eastern Europe*. Washington, D.C.: The World Bank.

Council on Foreign Relations. 2006. *Russia's Wrong Direction: What the United States Can and Should Do*. New York: Council on Foreign Relations.

Crisp, Olga. 1976. *Studies in the Russian Economy before 1914*. London: Macmillan.

Cubeddu, Raimondo. 1993. *The Philosophy of the Austrian School*. London: Routledge.

Cummins, Alex G. 1988. "The Road to NEP, the State Commission for the Electrification of Russia (Goelro): A Study in Technology, Mobilization, and Economic Planning." Ph.D. diss., University of Maryland, College Park, MD.

Davies, R. W. 1958. *The Development of the Soviet Budgetary System*. Cambridge: Cambridge University Press.

———. 1961. "Review of Ehrlich." *Soviet Studies* 13, no. 1: 108–10.

Davies, R. W. and David T. Catrell. 1991. "The Industrial Economy." In *From Tsarism to the New Economic Policy: Continuity and Change in the Economy of the USSR*, edited by R. W. Davies. Ithaca, NY: Cornell University Press.

Dawson, John C. 1996. *Flow-of-Funds Analysis: A Handbook for Practitioners*. Armonk, NY: M. E. Sharpe.

Deleuze, Gilles. 1979. "The Rise of the Social." Foreword to Jacques Donzelot, *The Policing of Families*. New York: Pantheon Books.

Deleuze, Gilles and Felix Guattari. 1986. *Kafka: Toward a Minor Literature*. Minneapolis: University of Minnesota Press.

Desai, Padma and Todd Idson. 2001. *Work without Wages: Russia's Nonpayment Crisis*. Cambridge, MA: MIT Press.

De Silva, Migara O., Galina Kurlyandskaya, Elena Andreeva, and Natalia Go-lovanova. 2009. *Intergovernmental Reforms in the Russian Federation*. Washington, D.C.: The World Bank.

Diamond, Jack. 2005. "Reforming the Russian Budget System: A Move to More Devolved Budget Management?" IMF Working Paper 05/104. Washington D.C.: The International Monetary Fund.

DiMaio, Alfred John. 1974. *Soviet Urban Housing: Problems and Policies*. New York: Praeger.

Dobb, Maurice. 1948. *Soviet Economic Development since 1917*. London: Routledge & Kegan Paul.

Donzelot, Jacques. 2008. "Michel Foucault and Liberal Intelligence." *Economy and Society* 37, no. 1: 115–34.

Dorn, James A. 1991. "From Plan to Market: The Post-Soviet Challenge." *Cato Journal* 11, no. 2: 175–93.

Dreyfus, Hubert L. and Paul Rabinow. 1982. *Michel Foucault: Beyond Structuralism and Hermeneutics*. Chicago: University of Chicago Press.

Edele, Mark. 2007. "Soviet Society, Social Structure, and Everyday Life: Major Frameworks Reconsidered." *Kritika* 8, no. 2: 349–73.

Edwards, Paul N. 2002. "Infrastructure and Modernity: Force, Time, and Social Organization in the History of Sociotechnical Systems." In *Modernity and Technology*, edited by Thomas J. Misa, Philip Brey, and Andrew Feenburg. Cambridge, MA: MIT Press.

Ellison, Herbert J. 1965. "Economic Modernization in Imperial Russia: Purposes and Achievements." *The Journal of Economic History* 25, no. 4: 523–40.

Engelstein, Laura. 1994. "Combined Underdevelopment: Discipline and the Law in Imperial and Soviet Russia." *The American Historical Review* 98, no. 2: 338–53.

Eribon, Didier. 1991. *Michel Foucault*. Cambridge, MA: Harvard University Press.

Erlich, Alexander. 1960. *The Soviet Industrialization Debate, 1924–1928*. Cambridge, MA: Harvard University Press.

Esping-Andersen, Gøsta. 1996. *Welfare States in Transition: National Adaptations in Global Economies*. London: Sage.

Estache, Antonio and Marianne Fay. 2007. "Current Debates on Infrastructure Policy." Policy Research Working Paper 4410. Washington, D.C.: The World Bank.

Evans, Peter. 2008. "Is an Alternative Globalization Possible?" *Politics and Society* 36, no. 2: 271–305.

Ferguson, James. 1994. *The Anti-Politics Machine: 'Development,' Depoliticization, and Bureaucratic Power in Lesotho*. Minneapolis: University of Minnesota Press.

———. 2010. "The Uses of Neoliberalism." *Antipode* 41, supplement 1: 166–84.

Fischer, Stanley. 1986. "Issues in Medium-Term Macroeconomic Adjustment." *World Bank Research Observer* 1, no. 2: 163–82.

Foucault, Michel. 1970. *The Order of Things: An Archaeology of the Human Sciences*. New York: Vintage.

———. 1984. *The Foucault Reader*. New York: Pantheon Books.

———. 2000. "The Risks of Security." In *The Essential Works of Michel Foucault, 1954–1984*, edited by Paul Rabinow, 365–81. New York: New Press.

———. 2007. *Security, Territory, Population: Lectures at the Collège De France, 1977–78*. New York: Palgrave Macmillan.

———. 2008. *The Birth of Biopolitics: Lectures at the Collège De France, 1978–79*. New York: Palgrave Macmillan.

Freeze, Gregory L. 2002. "From Stalinism to Stagnation, 1953–1985." In *Russia: A History*, edited by Gregory L. Freeze. Oxford: Oxford University Press.

Freinkman, Lev, Konstantin A. Kholodilin, and Ulrich Theissen. "Incentive Effects of Fiscal Equalization: Has Russian Style Improved?." DIW Berlin Discussion Paper, no. 912. Berlin.

French, R. A. 1995. *Plans, Pragmatism and People: The Legacy of Soviet Planning for Today's Cities*. London: UCL Press.

Friedman, Milton. 1962. *Capitalism and Freedom*. Chicago: University of Chicago Press.

Gaddy, Clifford. 2007. "An Impossible Trinity? Resources, Space, and People." *Foreign Service Journal* 84, no. 4: 32–38.

——— 2008. "Russia's Virtual Economy." In *New Palgrave Dictionary of Economics*, edited by Steven N. Durlauf and Lawrence E. Blume. New York: Palgrave Macmillan.

Ganev, Venelin I. 2005. "The 'Triumph of Neoliberalism' Reconsidered: Critical Remarks on Ideas-Centered Analyses of Political and Economic Change in Post-Communism." *East European Politics and Societies* 19, no. 3: 343–78.

Gatrell, Peter. 1994. *Government, Industry, and Rearmament in Russia, 1900–1914: The Last Argument of Tsarism*. Cambridge: Cambridge University Press.

Gerschenkron, Alexander. 1966. *Economic Backwardness in Historical Perspective: A Book of Essays*. Cambridge, MA: Belknap Press.

———. 1968. "Russia: Agrarian Policies and Industrialization, 1861–1914." In *Continuity in History, and Other Essays*. Cambridge, MA: Belknap Press of Harvard University Press.

———. 1970. *Europe in the Russian Mirror: Four Lectures in Economic History*. London: Cambridge University Press.

Glazychev, Viacheslav Leonidovich. 1989. Rossia v Petle Modernizatsii: 1850–1950. http://www.glazychev.ru/books/petlya/petlya.htm (accessed September 15, 2007).

Gleason, William E. 1976. "The All-Russian Union of Towns and the Politics of Urban Reform in Tsarist Russia." *Russian Review* 35, no. 3: 290–302.

Goldstein, Jan. 1993. "Framing Discipline with Law: Problems and Promises of the Liberal State." *The American Historical Review* 98, no. 2: 364–75.

Gordon, Colin. 1991. "Governmental Rationality: An Introduction." In *The Foucault Effect: Studies in Governmentality*, edited by Graham Burchell, Colin Gordon, and Peter Miller. Chicago: University of Chicago Press.

Goskomstat. 1999. *Statisticheskii Ezhegodnik Rossii*. Moscow.

Gosplan. 1964 [1925]. "Kontrol'nye Tsifry Narodnogo Khoziaistva na 1925/1926 god." In *Foundations of Soviet Strategy for Economic Growth*, edited by Nicolas Spulber. Bloomington: Indiana University Press.

Gosudarstvennaia Komissiia po Elektrifikatsii Rossii. 1960. *Trudy Goelro: Doku-menty i Materialy*. Moskva: Izdatel'stvo Sotsial'no-ekonomicheskoi Literatury.

Government of the Russian Federation. 2001. Postanovlenie O Podprogramme 'Reformirovanie i Modernizatsiia Zhilishchno-Kommunal'nogo Kompleksa Rossiiskoi Federatsii' Federal'noi Tselevoi Programmy 'Zhilishche' Na 2002–2010 Gody.

Govorenkova, Tat'iana. 1989. "Kto v Gorode Khoziain?" *Kommunist* 16.

———. 1996. "Kto Zakazyvaet Zastyvshuiu Muzyku." *Stolitsa* 16, November: 10–15.

Graham, Stephen and Simon Marvin. 2002. *Splintering Urbanism: Networked Infrastructures, Technological Mobilities and the Urban Condition*. London: Routledge.

Gramlich, Edward M. 1994. "Infrastructure Investment: A Review Essay." *Journal of Economic Literature* 32, no. 3: 1176–96.

Gupta, Akhil, and James Ferguson. 1992. "Beyond 'Culture': Space, Identity, and the Politics of Difference." *Cultural Anthropology* 7, no. 1: 6–23.

Hacking, Ian. 2002. *Historical Ontology*. Cambridge, MA: Harvard University Press.

Hamilton, Ellen, Sudeshna Ghosh Banerjee, and Maka Lomaia. 2005. *Exploring Housing Subsidies to Households in Russia*. Washington D.C.: The World Bank.

Hamm, Michael. 1976a. "The Breakdown of Urban Modernization: A Prelude to the Revolutions of 1917." In *The City in Russian History*, edited by Michael F. Hamm. Lexington: University Press of Kentucky.

Hamm, Michael F. 1976b. *The City in Russian History*. Lexington: University Press of Kentucky.

Hanchett, Walter. 1976. "Tsarist Statutory Regulation of Municipal Government in the Nineteenth Century." In *The City in Russian History*, edited by Michael F. Hamm. Lexington: University Press of Kentucky.

Hanson, Philip. 2006. "Federalism with a Russian Face: Regional Inequality, Administrative Capacity and Regional Budgets in Russia." *Economic Change and Restructuring* 39: 191–211.

Harris, Chauncy Dennison. 1970. *Cities of the Soviet Union: Studies in Their Functions, Size, Density, and Growth*. Chicago: Rand McNally.

Harvey, David. 2005. *A Brief History of Neoliberalism*. Oxford: Oxford University Press.

Healey, Nigel M., Vladimir Leksin and Aleksandr Shvetsov. 1999. "The Municipalization of Enterprise-Owned 'Social Assets' in Russia." *Post-Soviet Affairs* 15: 262–80.

Hedlund, Stefan. 2005. *Russian Path Dependence*. London: Routledge.

Helm, Dieter and George Yarrow. 1988. "The Assessment: The Regulation of Utilities." *Oxford Review of Economic Policy* 4, no. 2: i–xxxi.

Hill, Fiona and Clifford G. Gaddy. 2003. *The Siberian Curse: How Communist Planners Left Russia out in the Cold*. Washington, D.C.: Brookings Institution Press.

Hittle, J. Michael. 1976. "The Service City in the Eighteenth Century." In *The City in Russian History*, edited by Michael F. Hamm. Lexington: University Press of Kentucky.

Hoffman, David L. 2000. "European Modernity and Soviet Socialism." In *Russian Modernity: Politics, Knowledge, Practices*, edited by David L. Hoffman and Yanni Kotsonis, 245–60. Ithaca: Cornell University Press.

———. 2003. *Stalinist Values: The Cultural Norms of Soviet Modernity, 1917–1941*. Ithaca: Cornell University Press.

———. 2004. "Was There a 'Great Retreat' from Soviet Socialism? Stalinist Culture Revisited." *Kritika* 5, no. 4: 651–74.

Hoffmann, David L. and Yanni Kotsonis. 2000. *Russian Modernity: Politics, Knowledge, Practices*. New York: Macmillan Press.

Hoffman, Lisa, Stephen J. Collier, and Monica DeHart. 2006. "Notes on the Anthropology of Neoliberalism." *Anthropology News* 9, no. 6: 9–10.

Holcombe, Randall G. 1997. "A Theory of the Theory of Public Goods." *Review of Austrian Economics* 10, no. 1: 1–22.

Holmes, Stephen. 1995. *Passions and Constraints: On the Theory of Liberal Democracy*. Chicago: University of Chicago Press.

Holquist, Peter. 2000. "What's so Revolutionary about the Russian Revolution? State Practices and the New-Style Politics, 1914–21." In *Russian Modernity: Politics, Knowledge, Practices*, edited by David L. Hoffman and Yanni Kotsonis. Ithaca: Cornell University Press.

Horowitz, Robert Britt. 1989. *The Irony of Regulatory Reform: The Deregulation of American Telecommunications*. New York: Oxford University Press.

Hough, Jerry F. 1969. *The Soviet Prefects: The Local Party Organs in Industrial Decision-Making*. Cambridge: Harvard University Press.

Howard, Ebenezer. 1965 [1989]. *Garden Cities of To-morrow*. Cambridge, MA: MIT Press.

Hudson, Hugh D. 1989. "Catherine II's Charter to the Towns: A Question of Motivation." *Canadian-American Slavic Studies* 23, no. 2: 129–49.

———. 1992. "Terror in Soviet Architecture: The Murder of Mikhail Okhitovich." *Slavic Review* 51, no. 3: 448–67.

———. 1994. *Blueprints and Blood: The Stalinization of Soviet Architecture, 1917–1937*. Princeton, NJ: Princeton University Press.

Hughes, Thomas Parke. 1983. *Networks of Power: Electrification in Western Society, 1880–1930*. Baltimore: Johns Hopkins University Press.

Humphrey, Caroline. 1983. *Karl Marx Collective: Economy, Society, and Religion in a Siberian Collective Farm*. Cambridge: Cambridge University Press.

———. 2003. "Rethinking Infrastructure: Siberian Cities and the Great Freeze of January 2001." In *Wounded Cities: Destruction and Reconstruction in a Globalized World*, edited by Jane Schneider and Ida Susser. Oxford, New York: Berg.

———. 2005. "Ideology in Infrastructure: Architecture in Soviet Imagination." *Journal of the Royal Anthropological Institute* 11, no. 1: 39–58.

Husband, William B. 1988. "Local Industry in Upheaval: The Ivanovo-Kineshma Textile Strike of 1917." *Slavic Review* 47, no. 3: 448–63.

———. 1990. *Revolution in the Factory: The Birth of the Soviet Textile Industry, 1917–1920*. New York: Oxford University Press.

Ickes, Barry W., Peter Murrell, and Randi Ryterman. 1997. "End of the Tunnel? The Effects of Financial Stabilization in Russia." *Post-Soviet Affairs* 13, no. 2: 105–33.

Institut Ekonomiki Goroda. 2008. *Mery Sotsial'noi Podderzhki (Measures for Social Support)*. Moscow.

Institute for Urban Economics. n.d. *Infrastructure Financing Options for Russia: Background Paper on Financing of Municipal and Communal Services*. Moscow: Institute for Urban Economics.

Jasny, Naum. 1972. *Soviet Economists of the Twenties: Names to Be Remembered*. Cambridge: Cambridge University Press.

Johnson, Juliet. 2000. *A Fistful of Rubles: The Rise and Fall of the Russian Banking System*. Ithaca, NY: Cornell University Press.

Joint Working Group on Western Cooperation in the Soviet Transformation to Democracy and the Market Economy. 1991. *Window of Opportunity: The Grand Bargain for Democracy in the Soviet Union*. New York: Pantheon Books.

Joskow, Paul L. and Nancy L. Rose. 1989. "The Effects of Economic Regulation." In *Handbook of Industrial Organization*, edited by Richard Schmalensee and Robert D. Willig. New York: Elsevier Science Publishers.

Jowitt, Kenneth. 1974. "An Organizational Approach to the Study of Political Culture in Marxist-Leninist Systems." *American Political Science Review* 68, no. 3: 1171–91.

"K Probleme Planirovki Sotsgoroda." 1930. *Vestnik Kommunisticheskoi Akademii* 42: 109–47.

Kabalina, Veronika. 1997. *Transformatsiia Predpriiatii: Issledovatel'skie Podkhody i Rezul'taty*. Moscow: ROSSPEN.

Kabalina, V.I. and T. Iu. Sidorina. 1999. "Predpriiatie-Gorod: Transformatsiia Sotsial'noi Infrastructury v Period Reform." *Mir Rossii*, no. 1–2: 167–98.

Kapur, Devesh, John Prior Lewis, and Richard Charles Webb. 1997. *The World Bank: Its First Half Century*. Washington, D.C.: Brookings Institution.

Kaser, M.C. 1964. "Welfare Criteria in Soviet Planning." In *Soviet Planning: Essays in Honor of Naum Jasny*, edited by Jane Tabrisky Degras and Alec Nove. Oxford: Basil Blackwell.

Kearney, Joseph D. and Thomas W. Merrill. 1998. "The Great Transformation of Regulated Industries Law." *Columbia Law Review* 98, no. 6: 1323–1409.

Kharkhordin, Oleg. 1999. *The Collective and the Individual in Russia: A Study of Practices*. Berkeley: University of California Press.

———. 2010. "Res Publica: How Things Matter with Publics." In *Reassembling Res Publica: Reform of Infrastructure in Post-Soviet Russia*, edited by Oleg Kharkhordin and Risto Alapuro. London: Routledge.

Kharkhordin, Oleg and Risto Alapuro, eds. 2010. *Reassembling Res Publica: Reform of Infrastructure in Post-Soviet Russia*. London: Routledge.

Khauke, M. O. and I. N. Magidin, eds. 1963. *Spravochnik Proektirovshchika: Gradostroitel'stvo*. Moscow: Gosudarstvennoe Izdatel'stvo Literatury po Stroitel'stvu, Arkhitekture, i Stroitel'nym Materialam.

Khmel'nitskii, Dmitrii. 2003. "Istoriia Sovetskoi Arkhitektury kak Lzhenauka." Presentation at the internet conference "Science and the Media." http://www.port-folio.org/part 65.htm. Accessed on August 27, 2010.

———. 2007. *Arkhitektura Stalina: Psikhologiia i Stil'*. Moskva: Progress-Traditsiia.

Klein, Naomi. 2007. *The Shock Doctrine: The Rise of Disaster Capitalism*. Toronto: Alfred A. Knopf Canada.

Klopotov, K. K. 1969. "Gorodskoe Khoziaistvo." In *Bol'shaia Sovetskaia Entsiklopediia*, edited by A. M. Prokhorov. Moscow: Izdatel'stvo Sovetskaia Entsiklopediia.

Koeberle, Stefan. 2005. "Conditionality: Under What Conditions?" In *Conditionality Revisited: Concepts, Experiences, and Lessons*, edited by Stefan Koeberle. Washington, D.C.: World Bank.

Koenker, Diane. 1985. "Urbanization and Deurbanization in the Russian Revolution and Civil War." *The Journal of Modern History* 57, no. 3: 424–50.

Kogut, Bruce and Andrew Spicer. 2004. "Critical and Alternative Perspectives on International Assistance to Post-Communist Countries: A Review and Analysis." OED Background Paper, October 2004. Washington D.C.: World Bank, Operations Evaluation Department.

———. 2005. *Taking Account of Accountability: Academics, Transition Economics, and Russia*. Paris: INSEAD.

Kondrat'ev, N.D. 1964 [1927]. "Kriticheskie Zametki o Plane Razvitiia Narodnogo Khoziaistva." In *Foundations of Soviet Strategy for Economic Growth*, edited by Nicolas Spulber. Bloomington: Indiana University Press.

Kopp, Anatole. 1970. *Town and Revolution: Soviet Architecture and City Planning, 1917–1935*. New York: Braziller.

Koshar, Rudy. 1993. "Foucault and Social History: Comments on 'Combined Underdevelopment.'" *The American Historical Review* 98, no. 2: 354–63.

Kotkin, Stephen. 1991. *Steeltown, USSR: Soviet Society in the Gorbachev Era*. Berkeley: University of California Press.

———. 1993a. "Peopling Magnitostroi: The Politics of Demography." In *Social Dimensions of Soviet Industrialization*, edited by William G. Rosenberg and Lewis H. Siegelbaum. Bloomington: Indiana University Press.

———. 1993b. "Shelter and Subjectivity in the Stalin Period: A Case Study of Magnitogorsk." In *Russian Housing in the Modern Age: Design and Social History*, edited by William Craft Brumfield and Blair A. Ruble. Cambridge: Cambridge University Press.

———. 1995. *Magnetic Mountain: Stalinism as a Civilization*. Berkeley: University of California Press.

———. 2001. "Modern Times: The Soviet Union and the Interwar Conjuncture." *Kritika* 2, no. 1: 111–64.

Kots, Aleksandr and Dmitrii Steshin. 2009. "Zhiteli 25-Tysiachnogo Pikaleva, gde Ostanovilis' Vse Predpriiatiia: 'Myi—Gorod Krepostnykh, Kotorykh Tol'ko na Koniushne ne Poriut.'" *Komsomol'skaia Pravda*, May 26.

Kotsonis, Yanni. 2000. "Introduction: A Modern Paradox—Subject and Citizen in Nineteenth- and Twentieth Century Russia." In *Russian Modernity: Politics, Knowledge, Practices*, edited by David L. Hoffman and Yanni Kotsonis. Ithaca: Cornell University Press.

Krzhizhanovskii, Gleb Mikhailovich. 1964 [1927]. "Prospective Development of the National Economy of the USSR from 1926/1927 to 1930/1931." In *Foundations of Soviet Strategy for Economic Growth*, edited by Nicolas Spulber. Bloomington: Indiana University Press.

Krzhizhanovsky Power Institute. 1936. *Electric Power Development in the U.S.S.R.* New York: International Publishers.

Kurlyandskaya, Galina and Natalia Golovanova. 2006. "Decentralization in the Russian Federation." *Economic Change and Restructuring* 39: 213–33.

Kuz'minskii, O. 2001. "Kommunalka Federal'nogo Masshtaba." *Kommersant*, March 20: 8.

Lampland, Martha. 2009. "Classifying Laborers: Instinct, Property, and the Psychology of Productivity in Hungary (1920–1956)." In *Standards and Their Stories: How Quantifying, Classifying, and Formalizing Practices Shape Everyday Life*, edited by Martha Lampland and Susan Leigh Starr. Ithaca, NY: Cornell University Press.

———. 2010. "False Numbers as Formalizing Practices." *Social Studies of Science* 40, no. 3: 377–404.

Lange, Oscar. 1945. "Marxian Economics in the Soviet Union." *The American Economic Review* 35, no. 1: 127–33.

Lappo, Grigorii Mikhailovich. 1997. *Geografiia Gorodov*. Moscow: VLADOS.

———. 2001. "Urbanizatsiia v Evropeiskoi Rossii: Protsessy i Rezul'taty." In *Gorod i Derevnia v Evropeiskoi Rossii: Sto Let Peremen*, edited by P. M. Polian, T. G. Nefedova, and A. I. Treivish. Moscow: O.G.I.

Larner, Wendy. 2000. "Neoliberalism: Policy, Ideology, Governmentality." *Studies in Political Economy* 63: 5–26.

Latour, Bruno. 2005. *Reassembling the Social: An Introduction to Actor-Network-Theory*. Oxford: Oxford University Press.

Latour, Bruno and Peter Weibel. 2005. *Making Things Public: Atmospheres of Democracy*. Cambridge, MA: MIT Press.

Lavrov, A. M. and Alexei G. Makushkin. 2000. *The Fiscal Structure of the Russian Federation: Financial Flows between the Center and the Regions*. Armonk, NY: M. E. Sharpe.

Le Grand, Julian. 1975. "Fiscal Equity and Central Government Grants to Local Authorities." *The Economic Journal* 85, no. 339: 531–47.

Lenin, V. I. 1967 [1921]. "Ob Edinom Khoziaistvennom Plane." In *Sobranie Sochinenii V.I. Lenina*. Moscow: Izdatel'stvo Politicheskoi Literatury.

Lewin, Moshe. 1973. "The Disappearance of Planning in the Plan." *Slavic Review* 32, no. 2: 271–87.

Lewis, Carol M. 1983. "The Economic Functions of Local Soviets." In *Soviet Local Politics and Government*, edited by Everett M. Jacobs. London: Allen & Unwin.

———. 1976. *The Budgetary Process in Soviet Cities*. New York: Center for Government Studies, Graduate School of Business, Columbia University.

Lotareva, Rena. 1993. *Goroda-Zavody Rossii. XVIII-Pervaia Polovina XIX Veka*. Ekaterinburg: Izdatel'stvo Ural'skogo Universiteta.

Luhmann, Niklas. 1998. *Observations on Modernity*. Stanford, CA: Stanford University Press.

MacAvoy, Paul W. 1970. "From the Editor." *The Bell Journal of Economics and Management Science* 1, no. 1: 5.

Mann, Michael. 1986. *The Sources of Social Power*. Cambridge: Cambridge University Press.

Markusen, Ann. 1996. "Sticky Places in a Slippery Space: A Typology of Industrial Districts." *Economic Geography* 72, no. 3: 293–313.

Martinez-Vazquez, Jorge and R. J. Searle. 2007a. "Challenges in the Design of Fiscal Equalization and Intergovernmental Transfers." In *Fiscal Equalization: Challenges in the Design of Intergovernmental Transfers*, edited by Jorge Martinez-Vazquez and R. J. Searle. New York: Springer.

———eds. 2007b. *Fiscal Equalization: Challenges in the Design of Intergovernmental Transfers*. New York: Springer.

Martinez-Vazquez, Jorge, Andrey Timofeev, and Jameson Boex. 2006. *Reforming Regional-Local Finance in Russia*. Washington, D.C.: The World Bank.

Martinez-Vazquez, Jorge and Andrey Timofeev. 2008. "Regional-Local Dimensions of Fiscal Equalization." *Journal of Comparative Economics* 36: 157–76.

Martinot, Eric. 1998. "Energy Efficiency and Housing-Sector Transitions in Russia." *Perspectives in Energy* 4, no. 3: 295–310.

Mason, Edward Sagendorph and Robert E. Asher. 1973. *The World Bank since Bretton Woods*. Washington: Brookings Institution.

McCraw, Thomas K. 1976. "Regulation, Chicago Style." *Reviews in American History* 4, no. 2: 297–303.

Meerovich, Mark G. 2007. "Neoffitsial'noe Gradostroitel'stvo: Tainyi Aspekt Sovetskoi Industrializatsii, 1928–1932 Gg." http://meerovich.livejournal.com/1738.html (accessed April 24, 2010).

Mikhailova, Tatiana. 2005. "The Cost of the Cold: The Legacy of Soviet Location Policy in Russian Energy Consumption, Productivity, and Growth." Mimeo. Cambridge, MA: Davis Center for Russian and Eurasian Studies.

Miliutin, Nikolai Aleksandrovich. 1931. "Zhilishchno-Bytovoe Stroitel'stvo SSSR." *Sovetskaia Arkhitektura* 1–2: 2–4.

———. 1932. "Vazhneishie Zadachi Sovremennogo Etapa Sovetskoi Arkhitektury." *Sovetskaia Arkhitektura*: 3–9.

———. 1974. *Sotsgorod: The Problem of Building Socialist Cities*. Cambridge, MA: MIT Press.

Ministry of Finance, Russian Federation, Department of Interbudgetary Relationships. 1999. "Metodicheskie Rekomendatsii po Regulirovaniiu Mezhbiudzhetnykh Otnoshenii v Sub"ektakh Rossiiskoi Federatsii."

———. 2000a. "Poiasnitel'naia Zapiska k Vremennym Metodicheskim Rekomendatsiiam Sub"ektam Rossiiskoi Federatsii po Regulirovaniiu Mezhbiudzhetnykh Otnoshenii."

———. 2000b. "Vremennye Metodicheskie Rekomendatsii Sub"ektam Rossiiskoi Federatsii po Regulirovaniiu Mezhbiudzhetnykh Otnoshenii." .

Mirowski, Philip. 1984. "Physics and the 'Marginalist Revolution.'" *Cambridge Journal of Economics* 8, no. 4: 361–79.

Mirowski, Philip and Dieter Plehwe. 2009. *The Road from Mont Pèlerin: The Making of the Neoliberal Thought Collective*. Cambridge, MA: Harvard University Press.

Mitchell, Timothy. 2006. "Rethinking Economy." *Geoforum* 39, no. 3: 1116–21.

Mitchneck, Beth and David A. Plane. 1995. "Migration and the Quasi-Labor Market in Russia." *International Regional Science Review* 18, no. 3: 267–88.

Mosley, Paul, Jane Harrigan and J.F.J. Toye. 1991. *Aid and Power: The World Bank and Policy-Based Lending*. London: Routledge.

Mumford, Lewis. 1934. *The Culture of Cities*. New York: Harcourt.

Murrell, Peter. 1995. "The Transition According to Cambridge, Mass." *Journal of Economic Literature* 33: 164–78.

Musgrave, Richard A. 1959. *The Theory of Public Finance: a Study in Public Economy*. New York: McGraw-Hill.

———. 1969. "Cost-Benefit Analysis and the Theory of Public Finance." *Journal of Economic Literature* 7, no. 3: 797–806.

Naim, Moises. 1994. "Latin America: The Second Stage of Reform." *Journal of Democracy* 5, no. 4: 32–48.

Nesvetailova, Anastasia. 2004. "Coping in the Global Financial System: the Political Economy of Nonpayment in Russia." *Review of International Political Economy* 11, no. 5: 995–1021.

Newbery, David M. G. 1999. *Privatization, Restructuring, and Regulation of Network Utilities*. Cambridge, MA: MIT Press.

Nove, Alec. 1992. "Some Thoughts on the End of NEP." In *Economy and Society in Russia and the Soviet Union, 1860–1930: Essays for Olga Crisp*, edited by Linda Harriet Edmondson and Peter Waldron. New York: St. Martin's Press.

"O Rabote po Perestroike Byta." 1930. *Sovremennaia Arkhitektura*, no. 1–2: 3.

Oates, Wallace E. 1968. "The Theory of Public Finance in a Federal System." *The Canadian Journal of Economics/Revue Canadienne d'Economique* 1, no. 1: 37–54.

———. 1999. "An Essay on Fiscal Federalism." *Journal of Economic Literature* 37, no. 3: 1120–49.

Oberstfeld, David. 1994. "The World Bank and the IMF: Misbegotten Sisters." In *The Collapse of Development Planning*, edited by Peter J. Boettke. New York: New York University Press.

Odling-Smee, John. 2004. *The IMF and Russia in the 1990s*. Washington D.C.: The International Monetary Fund.

OECD/IEA. 1995. *Energy Policies of the Russian Federation: 1995 Survey*. Paris: International Energy Agency/Organization for Economic Cooperation and Development.

Okhitovich, Mikhail. 1930. "Zametki po Teorii Rasseleniia." *Sovremennaia Arkhitektura* 1–2: 7–16.

"Ot Redaktsii." 1930. *Sovremennaia Arkhitektura* 1–2: 3.

Oushakine, Serguei Alex. 2009. *The Patriotism of Despair: Nation, War, and Loss in Russia*. Ithaca, NY: Cornell University Press.

Overtveldt, Johan van. 2007. *The Chicago School: How the University of Chicago Assembled the Thinkers Who Revolutionized Economics and Business*. Chicago: Agate.

Paperny, Vladimir. 2002. *Architecture in the Age of Stalin: Culture Two*. New York: Cambridge University Press.

Parkins, Maurice Frank. 1953. *City Planning in Soviet Russia*. Chicago: University of Chicago Press.

Peck, Jamie and Adam Tickell. 2002. "Neoliberalizing Space." *Antipode* 34, no. 3: 380–404.

Peltzman, Sam. 1993. "George Stigler's Contribution to the Economic Analysis of Regulation." *Journal of Political Economy* 101, no. 5: 818–32.

Piore, Michael J. 1968. "On-the-Job Training and Adjustment to Technological Change." *The Journal of Human Resources* 3, no. 4: 435–49.

Plamper, Jan. 2002. "Foucault's Gulag." *Kritika* 3, no. 2: 255–80.

Plehwe, Dieter. 2009a. "Introduction." In *The Road from Mont Pèlerin: The Making of the Neoliberal Thought Collective*, edited by Philip Mirowski and Dieter Plehwe. Cambridge, MA: Harvard University Press.

———. 2009b. "The Origins of the Neoliberal Economic Development Discourse." In *The Road from Mont Pelerin: The Making of the Neoliberal Thought Collective*, edited by Philip Mirowski and Dieter Plewhe. Cambridge, MA: Harvard University Press.

Plehwe, Dieter, Bernhard Walpen, and Gisela Neunhöffer. 2006. *Neoliberal Hegemony: A Global Critique*. London: Routledge.

Polanyi, Karl. 1968. *Primitive, Archaic, and Modern Economies. Essays of Karl Polanyi*. Garden City, NY: Anchor Books.

———. 1977. "The Two Meanings of Economic." In *The Livelihood of Man: Studies in Social Discontinuity*, edited by Karl Polanyi and Harry W. Pearson. New York: Academic Press.

———. 2001. *The Great Transformation: The Political and Economic Origins of Our Time*. Boston, MA: Beacon Press.

Porter, David O. and Teddie Wood Porter. 1974. "Social Equity and Fiscal Federalism." *Public Administration Review* 34, no. 1: 36–43.

Puzis, G. 1931. "O Metodakh Ischisleniia Naseleniia v Planirovke Naselennykh Mest." *Sovetskaia Arkhitektura*, no. 3: 4–7.

Quigly, John M. and Daniel L. Rubinfeld. 1986. "Budget Reform and the Theory of Fiscal Federalism." *The American Economic Review* 76, no. 2: 132–37.

Rabinow, Paul. *French Modern: Norms and Forms of the Social Environment*. Chicago: University of Chicago Press.

———. 1999. *French DNA: Trouble in Purgatory*. Chicago: University of Chicago Press.

———. 2003. *Anthropos Today: Reflections on Modern Equipment*. Princeton, NJ: Princeton University Press.

Rabinow, Paul, George E. Marcus, James Faubion, and Tobias Rees. 2008. *Designs for an Anthropology of the Contemporary*. Durham, NC: Duke University Press.

Raeff, Marc. 1975. "The Well-Ordered Police State and the Development of Modernity in Seventeenth- and Eighteenth-Century Europe: An Attempt at a Comparative Approach." *The American Historical Review* 80, no. 5: 1221–43.

Rapley, John. 1996. *Understanding Development: Theory and Practice in the Third World*. London: Lynne Rienner Publishers.

Redburn, Tom. 1991. "Authors Find No Buyers for USSR 'Bargain'" *International Herald Tribune*, July 6, 1991.

Reddaway, Peter and Dmitri Glinski. 2001. *The Tragedy of Russia's Reforms: Market Bolshevism against Democracy*. Washington, D.C.: United States Institute of Peace Press.

Rodrik, Dani. 2007. *One Economics, Many Recipes: Globalization, Institutions, and Economic Growth*. Princeton, NJ: Princeton University Press.

Rogers, Douglas. 2006. "How to Be a *Khoziain* in a Transforming State: State Formation and the Ethics of Governance in Post-Soviet Russia." *Comparative Studies in Society and History* 48, no. 4: 915–45.

Rose, Nikolas. 1999. *Powers of Freedom: Reframing Political Thought*. Cambridge: Cambridge University Press.

Rose, Nikolas, Pat O'Malley, and Mariana Valverde. 2006. "Governmentality." *Annual Review of Law and Society* 2: 83–104.

Rosenstein-Rodan, P. N. 1961. "International Aid for Undeveloped Countries." *The Review of Economic Statistics* 43, no. 2: 107–38.

Rostow, W. W. 1953. "Notes on a New Approach to U.S. Economic Foreign Policy." *World Politics* 5, no. 3: 302–12.

Rothschild, Emma. 2001. *Economic Sentiments*. Cambridge: Harvard University Press.

Rowland, Richard H. 1976. "Urban in-Migration in Late Nineteenth Century Russia." In *The City in Russian History*, edited by Michael F. Hamm. Lexington: University Press of Kentucky.

Ruble, Blair A. 1990. *Leningrad: Shaping a Soviet City*. Berkeley: University of California Press.

———. 1993. "From *Khrushcheby* to *Korobki*." In *Russian Housing in the Modern Age: Design and Social History*, edited by William Craft Brumfield and Blair A. Ruble. Cambridge: Cambridge University Press.

———. 1995. *Money Sings: The Changing Politics of Urban Space in Post-Soviet Yaroslavl*. Cambridge: Cambridge University Press.

Rutland, Peter. 1985. *The Myth of the Plan: Lessons of Soviet Planning Experience*. London: Hutchinson.

Sachs, Jeffrey D. 1994. "Russia's Struggle with Stabilization: Conceptual Issues and Evidence." *Proceedings of the World Bank Annual Conference on Development Economics 1994*: 57–80.

———. 1995. "Why Russia Has Failed to Stabilize." In *Russian Economic Reform at Risk*, edited by Anders Åslund. New York: St. Martin's Press.

———. 1996. "The Transition at Mid-Decade." *The American Economic Review* 86, no 2: 128–33.

———. 2000. "Interview for the Program 'Commanding Heights.'" http://www.pbs.org/wgbh/commandingheights/shared/pdf/int_jeffreysachs.pdf (accessed April 23, 2010).

Samuelson, Paul A. 1954. "The Pure Theory of Public Expenditure." *The Review of Economics and Statistics* 36, no. 4: 387–89.

Scott, James C. 1976. *The Moral Economy of the Peasant: Rebellion and Subsistence in Southeast Asia*. New Haven: Yale University Press.

Sektor Arkhitektorov Sotsialisticheskogo Stroitel'stva. 1931. "Na Novom Etape." *Sovetskaia Arkhitektura*, no. 1–2: 97–102.

Sellenart, Michel. 2007. "Course Context." In *Security, Territory, Population: Lectures at the Collège De France, 1977–78* by Michel Foucault. New York: Palgrave Macmillan.

Service, Robert. 1998. *A History of Twentieth-Century Russia*. Cambridge, MA: Harvard University Press.

Shah, Anwar. 1994. *A Fiscal Needs Approach to Equalization Transfers in a Decentralized Federation*. Washington D.C.: The World Bank.

———. 1996. "On the Design of Economic Constitutions." *The Canadian Journal of Economics/Revue Canadienne d'Economique* 29, Special Issue, Part 2: S614–S618.

Shaw, Denis J. B. 1983. "The Soviet Urban General Plan and Recent Advances in Soviet Urban Planning." *Urban Studies* 20: 393–403.

———. 1991. "The Past, Present and Future of the Soviet City Plan." *Planning Perspectives* 6, no. 2: 125–38.

Shleifer, Andrei and Daniel Treisman. 2004. "A Normal Country." *Foreign Affairs* March/April.

Shtop, V. V. 1997. "Biudzhet Goroda." *EKO* 5: 140–42.

Simons, Henry. 1949. *A Positive Program for Laissez Faire: Some Proposals for a Liberal Economic Policy*. Chicago: University of Chicago Press.

Sokolov, V. M. and M. A. Iagol'nitser. 1997. "Tollingovyi Platsdarm Rossiiskogo Aliuminiia." *EKO* 8: 73–92.

Sosnovy, Timothy. 1954. *The Housing Problem in the Soviet Union*. New York: Research Program on the U.S.S.R.

Srinivasan, T. N. 1984. "Comment on Lord Bauer." In *Pioneers in Development,* edited by Gerald M. Meier and Dudley Seers. New York: Oxford University Press.

Stark, David. 1990. "Privatization in Hungary: From Plan to Market or from Plan to Clan?" *East European Politics and Societies* 4, no. 3: 351–92.

Starr, S. Frederick. 1971. "Writings from the 1960s on the Modern Movement in Russia." *The Journal of the Society of Architectural Historians* 30, no. 2: 170–78.

———. "The Revival and Schism of Urban Planning in Twentieth-Century Russia." In *The City in Russian History*, edited by Michael F. Hamm. Lexington: University Press of Kentucky.

Stern, Ernest. 1983. "World Bank Financing of Structural Adjustment." In *IMF Conditionality*, edited by John Williamson. Cambridge: MIT Press.

———. 1991. "Evolution and Lessons of Adjustment Lending." In *Restructuring Economies in Distress: Policy Reform and the World Bank*, edited by Vinod Thomas, Ajay Chhibber, Mansoor Dailamiet al. Oxford: Published for the World Bank by Oxford University Press.

Stigler, George J. 1965 [1957]. "The Tenable Range of Functions of Local Government." In *Private Wants and Public Needs: Issues Surrounding the Size and Scope of Government Expenditure*, edited by Edmund S. Phelps. New York: W. W. Norton.

———. 1971. "The Theory of Economic Regulation." *Bell Journal of Economics* 2, no. 1: 3–21.

———. 1975a. *The Citizen and the State: Essays on Regulation*. Chicago: University of Chicago Press.

———. 1975b. "The Tactics of Economic Reform." In *The Citizen and the State: Essays on Regulation*. Chicago: University of Chicago Press.

———. 1988. *Memoirs of an Unregulated Economist*. New York: Basic Books.

Stigler, George J. and Claire Friedland. 1962. "What Can Regulators Regulate? The Case of Electricity." *Journal of Law and Economics* 5: 1–16.

Stiglitz, Joseph E. 2002. *Globalization and Its Discontents*. New York: W. W. Norton.

Storper, Michael. 1995. "The Resurgence of Regional Economies, Ten Years Later: The Region as a Nexus of Untraded Interdependencies." *European Urban and Regional Studies* 2, no. 3: 191–221.

Strassman, W. Paul. 1976. "Development Economics from a Chicago Perspective." In *The Chicago School of Political Economy*, edited by Warren J. Samuels. East Lansing: Michigan State University Press.

Strumilin, Stanislav Gustavovich. 1964 [1927]. "Perspektivnaia Orientirovka na 1926/27–1930–31." In *Foundations of Soviet Strategy for Economic Growth*, edited by Nicolas Spulber. Bloomington: Indiana University Press.

Szporluk, Roman. 1988. *Communism and Nationalism: Karl Marx Versus Friedrich List*. New York: Oxford University Press.

Taubman, William. 1973. *Governing Soviet Cities: Bureaucratic Politics and Urban Development in the USSR*. New York: Praeger.

"Tezisy Doklada 'O Sotsialisticheskoi Planirovke Rasseleniia.'" 1930. *Sovremennaia Arkhitektura*, no. 6: 1–2.

Thayer, Frederick C. 1984. *Rebuilding America: The Case for Economic Regulation*. New York, NY: Praeger Publishers.

Thiede, Roger L. 1976. "Industry and Urbanization in New Russia from 1860 to 1910." In *The City in Russian History*, edited by Michael F. Hamm. Lexington: University Press of Kentucky.

Tiebout, Charles M. 1956. "A Pure Theory of Local Expenditures." *The Journal of Political Economy* 64, no. 5: 416–24.

Timasheff, Nicholas S. 1946. *The Great Retreat: The Growth and Decline of Communism in Russia*. New York: E. P. Dutton & Company, Inc.

Toye, J.F.J. 1987. *Dilemmas of Development: Reflections on the Counter-Revolution in Development Theory and Policy*. Oxford: Blackwell.

Trebing, Harry M. 1976. "The Chicago School versus Public Utility Regulation." *Journal of Economic Issues* X, no. 1: 97–126.

———. 1984. "Public Utility Regulation: A Case Study in the Debate over Effectiveness of Economic Regulation." *Journal of Economic Issues* 18, no. 1: 223–50.

Treml, Vladimir G. 1969. "Interaction of Economic Thought and Economic Policy in the Soviet Union." *History of Political Economy* 1, no. 1: 187–216.

Tsing, Anna Lowenhaupt. 1993. *In the Realm of the Diamond Queen: Marginality in an out-of-the-way Place*. Princeton, NJ: Princeton University Press.

Tumanik, G. N. and M. R. Kolpakova. 1996. *Otechestvennoe Gradostroitel'stvo: Sovremennye Problemy Razvitiia Sibirskogo Goroda* Novosibirsk: Novosibirskaia Gosudarstvennaia Arkhitekturno-khudozhestvennaia Akademiia.

"Iiun'skii Plenum TsK VKP(b) Ob Organizatsii Gorodskogo Khoziaistva." 1931. *Sovetskaia Arkhitektura* 3: 1–3.

UNDP/World Bank. 2000. *Increasing the Efficiency of Heating Systems in Central and Eastern Europe and the Former Soviet Union*. Washington D.C.: Joint UNDP/World Bank Energy Sector Management Assistance Program.

Vagin, V. V. 1997. "Russkii Provintsial'nyi Gorod: Kliuchevye Elementy Zhizneustroistva." *Mir Rossii* 1997, no. 4: 53–88.

Valdés, Juan Gabriel. 1995. *Pinochet's Economists: The Chicago School in Chile*. Cambridge: Cambridge University Press.

Valverde, Mariana. 2008. "Beyond *Discipline and Punish*: Foucault's Challenge to Criminology." *Carceral Notebooks* 4.

Van Horn, Robert. 2009. "Reinventing Monopoly and the Role of Corporations: The Roots of Chicago Law and Economics." In *The Road from Mont Pelerin: The Making of the Neoliberal Thought Collective*, edited by Philip Mirowski and Dieter Plehwe. Cambridge, MA: Harvard University Press.

Vaughan, Roger J. 1984. *Rebuilding America's Infrastructure: An Agenda for the 1980s*. Durham, NC: Duke University Press.

Verdery, Katherine. 1996. *What Was Socialism, and What Comes Next?* Princeton, NJ: Princeton University Press.

Vihavainen, Rosa. 2010. "Common and Dividing Things in Homeowners' Associations." In *Reassembling Res Publica: Reform of Infrastructure in Post-Soviet Russia*, edited by Oleg Kharkhordin and Risto Alapuro. London: Routledge.

Viola, Lynn. 2003. "The Aesthetics of Stalinist Planning and the World of the Special Villages." *Kritika* 4, no. 1: 101–28.

Von Laue, Theodore H. 1963. *Sergei Witte and the Industrialization of Russia*. New York: Columbia University Press.

———. 1964. *Why Lenin? Why Stalin? A Reappraisal of the Russian Revolution, 1900–1930*. Philadelphia: Lippincott.

Wagner, Peter. 1991. *Social Sciences and Modern States: National Experiences and Theoretical Crossroads*. Cambridge: Cambridge University Press.

Way, Lucan Alan. 2001. "Bureaucracy by Default: Preserving a Public Dimension of the State in Post-Soviet Ukraine." Ph.D. diss., University of California, Berkeley.

Webber, Carolyn and Aaron B. Wildavsky. 1986. *A History of Taxation and Expenditure in the Western World*. New York: Simon and Schuster.

Weber, Max. 1949. *The Methodology of the Social Sciences*. Glencoe, Ill.: Free Press.

———. 1978. *Economy and Society: An Outline of Interpretive Sociology*. Berkeley: University of California Press.

———. 2002. *The Protestant Ethic and The "Spirit" of Capitalism and other Writings*. New York: Penguin Books.

Wedel, Janine R. 1998. *Collision and Collusion: The Strange Case of Western Aid to Eastern Europe, 1989–1998*. New York: St. Martin's Press.

Wengle, Susanne and Michael Rasell. 2008. "The Monetisation of L'goty: Changing Patterns of Welfare Politics and Provision in Russia." *Europe-Asia Studies* 60, no. 5: 739–56.

Whitefield, Stephen. 1993. *Industrial Power and the Soviet State*. Oxford: Clarendon Press.

Williamson, John. 1990. "What Washington Means by Policy Reform." In *Latin American Adjustment: How Much Has Happened?*, edited by John Williamson. Washington, D.C.: Institute for International Economics.

———. 1994. "Comment on 'Russia's Struggle with Stabilization: Conceptual Issues and Evidence,' by Sachs." *Proceedings of the World Bank Annual Conference on Development Economics 1994*: 81–85.

———. 2002. "Did the Washington Consensus Fail?" www.piie.com/publications/papers/paper.cfm?ResearchID=488 (accessed April 24, 2010).

Wines, Michael. 2001. "In Russia's Far East, a Region Freezes in the Dark." *New York Times*, February 12.

Winston, Clifford. 1985. "Conceptual Developments in the Economics of Transportation: An Interpretive Survey." *Journal of Economic Literature* 23, no. 1: 57–94.

Winston, Clifford and Barry Bosworth. 1992. "Public Infrastructure." In *Setting Domestic Priorities: What Can Government Do?*, edited by Henry J. Aaron, Charles L. Schultze and Gordon Berlin. Washington, D.C.: The Brookings Institution.

Woodruff, David. 1999. *Money Unmade: Barter and the Fate of Russian Capitalism*. Ithaca, NY: Cornell University Press.

World Bank. 1988a. *Adjustment Lending: An Evaluation of Ten Years of Experience*. Washington, D.C.: The World Bank.

———. 1988b. *World Development Report 1988: Public Finance in Development*. New York: Oxford University Press.

———. 1994. *World Development Report 1994: Infrastructure for Development*. New York: Oxford University Press.

———. 1996a. *Russian Federation: Enterprise Housing Divestiture Project*. Washington D.C.: The World Bank.

———. 1996b. *Russian Federation: Toward Medium-Term Viability*. Washington, D.C.: The World Bank.

———. 1996c. *World Development Report 1996: From Plan to Market*. New York: Oxford University Press.

———. 2003. *Housing and Communal Services in Russia: Completing the Transition to a Market Economy*. Washington D.C.: Infrastructure and Energy Department, Europe and Central Asia Region.

———. 2005. *From Transition to Development: A Country Economic Memorandum for the Russian Federation*. Washington, D.C.: The World Bank.

———. 2008. *Project Appraisal Document on a Proposed Loan in the Amount of US$200 Million to the Russian Federation for a Housing and Communal Services Project*. Washington D.C.: The World Bank.

———. 2009. Loan Agreement (Housing and Communal Services Project) between Russian Federation and the International Bank for Reconstruction and Development.

Ianitskii, O. 1998. "Sotsiologiia Goroda." In *Sotsiologiia v Rossii*, edited by V. A. Iadov. Moscow: Institut Sotsiologii RAN.

Yergin, Daniel and Joseph Stanislaw. 1998. *The Commanding Heights: The Battle between Government and the Marketplace That Is Remaking the Modern World*. New York: Simon & Schuster.

Yurchak, Alexei. 2003. "Russian Neoliberal: The Entrepreneurial Ethic and the Spirit of 'True Careerism'." *The Russian Review* 62, no. January: 72–90.

———. 2006. *Everything Was Forever, until It Was No More: The Last Soviet Generation*. Princeton, NJ: Princeton University Press.

Zanini, Gianni. 2002. *Assisting Russia's Transition: An Unprecedented Challenge*. Washington, D.C.: World Bank.

Index